IN BROKEN IMAGES

IN
BROKEN IMAGES

Selected Letters of Robert Graves
1914–1946

Edited, with a commentary, by
Paul O'Prey

HUTCHINSON
London Melbourne Sydney Auckland Johannesburg

Hutchinson & Co. (Publishers) Ltd

An imprint of the Hutchinson Publishing Group

17–21 Conway Street, London W1P 6JD

Hutchinson Group (Australia) Pty Ltd
30–32 Cremorne Street, Richmond South, Victoria 3121
PO Box 151, Broadway, New South Wales 2007

Hutchinson Group (NZ) Ltd
32–34 View Road, PO Box 40-086, Glenfield, Auckland 10

Hutchinson Group (SA) Pty Ltd
PO Box 337, Bergvlei 2012, South Africa

First published 1982
Letters written by Robert Graves © Robert Graves 1982
Introduction, commentary and notes © Paul O'Prey 1982

Set in Linotron Sabon by Input Typesetting Ltd

Printed in Great Britain by The Anchor Press Ltd
and bound by Wm Brendon & Son Ltd,
both of Tiptree, Essex

British Library Cataloguing in Publication Data
Graves, Robert
  In broken images: selected letters of
  Robert Graves, 1914–1946
  1. Graves, Robert
  2. Poets, English—20th century—Biography
  I. Title II. O'Prey, Paul
  821'.912   PR6013.R35Z/
      ISBN 0 09 147720 4

CONTENTS

ILLUSTRATIONS

He continues quick and dull in his clear images;
I continue slow and sharp in my broken images.

He in a new confusion of his understanding;
I in a new understanding of my confusion.

Robert Graves

INTRODUCTION

In making this selection of 199 letters I have considered approximately a thousand letters written by Robert Graves to many different people. I have, however, limited the number of correspondents to fifteen so as to avoid giving too diffuse or blurred an impression. Graves has always been an extremely prolific letter writer (in later years letter writing was always the first job of the day and often as many as twenty letters would be written in a morning) until recently, when he stopped writing letters altogether because of bad health; he has always attached great importance to his correspondence as a means of exchanging ideas and 'conversation' between friends. In almost all of the letters he is intimate, frank, confiding and informative, often indiscriminately so: he wrote letters exactly as he talked and, as in conversation, was continually trying out his ideas (whether the other person was interested or not) which he later abandoned or developed in his essays, lectures and prose books. The many sides of his work are discussed in these letters, but I have accepted his own assertion that poetry and poetic criticism are the most important aspects of his work and the emphasis is, accordingly, on these.

As these letters show, Graves is an honest, witty and consistent autobiographer. Parts One and Two are a fascinating supplement to *Goodbye to All That* and fill in a number of gaps of great interest, mostly about things which were too delicate for publication at the time. Part Three deals with the years Graves spent with the American poet Laura Riding[1] whose effect on his private life and on his way of thinking was immense. By his own admission, comparatively little of biographical interest has occurred in his life since 1939, and since then the majority of his adventures have been inside his mind; Part Four, therefore, concentrates more than the others on his thoughts and writings.

Certain 'main currents' in Graves's life are conspicuously absent here: his parents, his first wife Nancy Nicholson, T. E. Lawrence and Laura Riding. The early, wartime letters to his parents have been published in *Goodbye to All That* and in his father's autobiography, *To Return to All That* (1930). No later letters of interest have been discovered and it is thought that many were destroyed in a fire at Harlech after his mother's death. No letters to Nancy Nicholson exist except for businesslike exchanges about finance and the children's schooling. T. E. Lawrence's letters to Graves were published in 1938 in *T. E. Lawrence to his Biographers*; six of Graves's letters to him were published in *Letters to T. E. Lawrence* (Jonathan Cape, 1962, edited by A. W. Lawrence) and although many more exist they were purchased in 1981 by a London investment company and it has not been possible to obtain access to them. Graves's early letters to Laura Riding have been destroyed and it is extremely doubtful that any later letters exist which are publishable in either Graves's or Riding's lifetimes.

Several other correspondences are not included for various reasons. Many interesting letters to Frank Richards, author of *Old Soldiers Never Die* and *Old Soldier Sahib*, were destroyed after his death; all letters to John Crowe Ransom have gone astray; letters to Wilfred Owen (two) and Robert Ross (six), the art critic, writer and literary patron, have already been published;[2] letters to Edith Sitwell, E. M. Forster, W. J. Turner, Alec Waugh and many others are simply not interesting enough, or are concerned more with their 'stories' than with Graves's.

My commentary has been restricted to a minimum, though I hope it is sufficient to allow readers with little knowledge of Graves's life a full appreciation of the letters.

Graves's handwriting, bold and slanting to the right, has remained consistent throughout, hardly altering at all from 1914 to the present day. All except two of the letters (these are indicated by a note) are handwritten, in black ink, usually using a relief nib. Almost all the letters, including business letters, are untidy: mazes of last-minute insertions and additions written vertically up the margins, in corners and in 'balloons', heavy crossings out and substitutions of words.

Graves's spelling is almost always correct and his punctuation is consistent, though in his earlier letters often idiosyncratic. I have silently altered a few slips of the pen and, in very few cases, restored a missing word in a sentence written in haste, where it is obvious what is meant. Where the reading of a word is doubtful, it is given in square brackets.

Addresses are given only where a change is indicated, and dates at the head of letters have been standardized. Some trivial passages of letters have been omitted, also repetitions and any matter which might unnecessarily offend someone still alive. Omissions are marked by a row of four dots on a separate line.

Robert and Beryl Graves and I wish to thank Lady Kathleen Liddell Hart for permission to publish Sir Basil Liddell Hart's letters, also the Liddell Hart Centre for Military Archives at the University of London, King's College, which now owns both sides of the Liddell Hart–Graves correspondence; Sir Rupert Hart-Davis, for permission to publish Siegfried Sassoon's letters and for patiently answering questions and checking my transcripts; Mrs Gweno Lewis, for her help and for permission to publish Alun Lewis's letters; and to the Edward Marsh Estate, for permission to publish Sir Edward Marsh's letter.

We are also very grateful to the following people and institutions for their kind cooperation in supplying copies of those letters of Graves's which are in their possession, and for their help in checking doubtful passages in the copies against the originals: Mr John Aldridge; the Poetry/Rare Books Collection of the University Libraries, the State University of New York at Buffalo, New York (for letters to Alan Hodge and Lynette Roberts); Jonathan Cape Ltd.; Mrs Valerie Eliot; the Lilly Library, Indiana University, Bloomington, Indiana (for letters to Karl Gay); Mr T. S. Matthews; the Berg Collection, New York Public Library, New York (for letters to Siegfried Sassoon and Edward Marsh); the Humanities Research Center, the University of Texas at Austin (for letters to Edmund Blunden and Edward Marsh); and the Beinecke Rare Book and Manuscript Library, Yale University (for letters to Gertrude Stein).

A great many people have generously given their time and advice in helping me produce this book. In particular I wish to personally thank Gretl Aldridge; Claire Blunden; Su Crow; Faber and Faber Ltd; Pilar Garcia; Karl and Rene Gay, for answering a great many questions and for reading my manuscript; Georgina Graves; James McKinley; Lynette Roberts; Martin Seymour-Smith, whose biography of Graves (*Robert Graves: His Life and Work*, Hutchinson, 1982) should be considered as a companion to this volume, for being a continual source of help and advice and for checking my manuscript so carefully; Southern Arts, for a bursary to help with the costs of the book; and my parents. Especially I wish to express my profound gratitude to Robert and Beryl Graves for their infinite kindness and generosity in so many ways.

Paul O'Prey
Deyá, Mallorca, Spain
July 1981

CORRESPONDENTS

John Aldridge (born 1905). English painter, illustrator, occasional designer of textiles and wallpapers, lecturer at the Slade School, member of the Royal Academy. His pictures include many landscapes in oil of Deyá and his portrait of Graves (1968) is on permanent exhibition at the National Portrait Gallery in London. Illustrated Laura Riding's *The Life of the Dead* (1934).

Edmund Blunden (1896–1974). English poet and critic. During the First World War he served with the Royal Sussex Regiment; he studied in Oxford for a year after the war but left in 1920 to join the staff of the *Athenaeum*. In 1924, and again in the late 1940s, he was Professor of English Literature at Tokyo University; in the 1930s he was a fellow and tutor of Merton College, Oxford, and from 1953 to 1964 was Professor of English Literature at Hong Kong University. He was elected Oxford Professor of Poetry in 1966 but had to resign a year later due to ill health. His books of poems include *The Waggoner* (1922), *The Shepherd* (1922), *English Poems* (1925) and *Poems of Many Years* (1957). His war memoir, *Undertones of War* (1928), is, with Graves's *Goodbye to All That* and Sassoon's *Memoirs of an Infantry Officer*, one of the best and most permanent personal accounts of the war. His other works include studies of Leigh Hunt, Charles Lamb, Thomas Hardy and P. B. Shelley and scholarly editions of the poems of John Clare and Christopher Smart.

Jonathan Cape (1879–1960). Founder and chairman of Jonathan Cape Ltd, publishers who published several of Graves's books, including *A Survey of Modernist Poetry*, *A Pamphlet Against Anthologies* (both books written with Laura Riding), *Lawrence and the*

15

Arabs, *Goodbye to All That* and *The Reader Over Your Shoulder* (written with Alan Hodge).

T. S. Eliot (1888–1965). Major American poet, critic and playwright. During the 1920s he edited the influential magazine *Criterion* and later became a director of the publishing firm Faber and Faber Ltd, which published several of Graves's books, including *The White Goddess*, for the publication of which Eliot was directly responsible.

K. C. Gay (born Karl Goldschmidt, 1912). Private secretary to Graves and Laura Riding 1934–39; as a German Jew he was a refugee in England at the outbreak of the Second World War, but later served in the Pioneer Corps and the Royal Navy. After the war he returned with Graves to Mallorca and worked with him as his secretary until 1965, when he became Curator of the Poetry Collection in the Lockwood Memorial Library at the State University of New York at Buffalo. He is now retired and lives in Mallorca.

Captain Sir Basil Liddell Hart (1895–1970). English military historian, writer and lecturer. During the First World War he served with the King's Own Yorkshire Light Infantry. His many books include studies of the theory and strategy of war, several biographies (including *T. E. Lawrence: In Arabia and After*) and several military histories which are now established classics, such as his histories of the two world wars. In 1965 he published his *Memoirs* in two volumes.

Alan Hodge (1915–79). English writer and historian. He collaborated with Graves on three books: *The Long Weekend*, a social history of Great Britain from 1918 to 1939, *The Reader Over Your Shoulder*, 'a handbook for writers of English prose', and *Work in Hand*, a volume of poems (with Norman Cameron). After the Second World War, during which he was assistant private secretary to the Minister of Information, Brendan Bracken, he cofounded and co-edited with Peter Quennell the magazine *History Today*.

Alun Lewis (1915–44). Welsh poet. Before the Second World War he was a school teacher, but in 1939 he joined the Royal Engineers, and in 1941 he took a commission in the South Wales Borderers.

He died in Burma. In 1942 his first book of poems, *Raider's Dawn*, and a volume of his short stories, *The Last Inspector*, were published. His second collection of poems was *Ha! Ha! Among the Trumpets*, published posthumously in 1945 with an introduction by Graves. A miscellany of his letters and hitherto unpublished short stories, *In the Green Tree*, was published in 1949.

Len Lye (1901–80). New Zealand artist, writer, film-maker and kinetic sculptor. Went to England in 1927 and soon became friends with Eric Kennington and, through him, with Graves, Riding and Ben Nicholson, Graves's brother-in-law. Graves helped him sponsor his first film, *Tusulava* (1928). Lye designed the covers for several Seizin Press books, including Graves's *To Whom Else?*, and also designed the cover of *Goodbye to All That* (Jonathan Cape Ltd, 1929). He stayed with Graves and Riding in Deyá in 1930, when a selection of his letters, *No Trouble*, was published by the Seizin Press. During the thirties he worked with John Grierson's GPO film unit, then the most artistically viable documentary film unit in Britain. Lye was a highly original experimental artist; his most important experiments in film were with techniques of animation and with 'direct' techniques of scratching and painting onto film. His films include *Colour Box* (1935), *The Birth of the Robot* (1936), *Trade Tattoo* (1937) and *Rhythm* (1957). After the Second World War he went to New York and in 1947 became a naturalized American. For several years he worked for *The March of Time* documentary film series and, after *Rhythm* and *Free Radicals* (1958), took up kinetic sculpture and gave many lectures on art and film-making. The Len Lye Foundation is in New Plymouth, New Zealand.

Sir Edward Marsh (1872–1953). English patron of the arts, founder and editor of the *Georgian Poetry* anthologies, translator of La Fontaine's *Fables* and Horace's *Odes*, eminent civil servant and, for twenty-three years, private secretary to Sir Winston Churchill. His autobiography, *A Number of People*, was published in 1939.

T. S. Matthews (born 1901). American journalist and autobiographer. In 1929 he began working for *Time* and later became an editor. His book of memoirs about Graves, Riding, Schuyler Jackson and others of his friends, *Jacks or Better* (retitled *Under the Influence* for publication in the United Kingdom) was published in 1977.

Robert Nichols (1893–1944). English poet and playwright. Served with the Royal Artillery in the First World War but was of a nervous disposition and was very quickly sent home as 'shell-shocked', although he had not been involved in any fighting. His poetry was enormously popular in 1917 after the publication of his war poems, *Ardours and Endurances*; other volumes of poems include *Aurelia* (1920), *Fisbo*, a satirical poem (1934), and *Such Was My Singing* (1942). In 1918 he lectured in America on British war poets, and was Professor of English Literature at Tokyo University 1921–24.

Lynette Roberts (born 1909). Welsh poet. Her books include *Poems* (1944), *Gods With Stainless Eyes* and a book about Captain Cook's journey to Australia, called *The Endeavour*.

Siegfried Sassoon (1886–1967). English poet and autobiographer. During the First World War he served with Graves in the Royal Welch Fusiliers, was wounded twice and awarded the MC. In 1917 he protested against the progress of the war by refusing to serve further but was persuaded by Graves not to persist in his protest but to appear instead before a medical board which Graves had arranged for him; consequently Sassoon was sent to Craiglockhart War Hospital where he was treated by Dr W. H. R. Rivers, the psychologist, anthropologist and neurologist, and was a fellow pa-tient of Wilfred Owen's, whom he influenced a great deal. Sassoon wrote some of the most powerful, savagely ironic anti-war poems of the war, describing the horrors of the trenches and attacking the stupidity of the generals and politicians. For some time after the war he involved himself seriously in Labour politics and was, for a while, literary editor of the *Daily Herald*, but later resumed his prewar life of a country gentleman and continued to write rather poor satirical verse and his autobiography in six volumes. Towards the end of his life he became a convert to Roman Catholicism.

Gertrude Stein (1874–1946). American writer. From 1913 until her death she lived in France, mostly in Paris, with her companion–secretary Alice B. Toklas; she conducted friendships with many of the leading painters and writers of the time (e.g. Picasso and Hemingway) from her '*salon*' in the Rue de Fleurus. As a writer she was prolific, experimental and widely influential. She wrote two autobiographical volumes, *The Autobiography of Alice B. Toklas* (1933) and *Everybody's Autobiography* (1937).

BIOGRAPHICAL NOTES
1895–1948, including principal publications

24 July 1895	Born at Wimbledon, London.
1908	Went to Charterhouse School.
July 1914	Left school.
August 1914	Took a commission with the Royal Welch Fusiliers.
April 1915	Went to France with the British Expeditionary Force for the first time.
May 1916	*Over the Brazier* published.
July 1916	Seriously wounded at the battle of the Somme.
Late 1916	*Goliath and David* published.
February 1917	Finished active service and became an instructor of cadets.
November 1917	*Fairies and Fusiliers* published.
January 1918	Married Nancy Nicholson.
February 1919	Demobilized.
October 1919	Went to St John's College, Oxford, to study English Literature.
March 1920	*Country Sentiment* published.
February 1921	*The Pier-Glass* published.
June 1921	Left the university, without taking a degree, and went to live in Islip.
May 1922	*On English Poetry* published.
March 1923	*Whipperginny* published.
May 1924	*Mock Beggar Hall* published.
February 1925	*Poetic Unreason* published.
July 1925	*Contemporary Techniques of Poetry* published.

January 1926 Joined by Laura Riding and with her, Nancy Nicholson and their four children went to Egypt, where Graves was Professor of Literature at the University of Cairo.

June 1926 Left Egypt, returned to London and began his literary partnership with Laura Riding.

September 1926 With Laura Riding to Vienna.

January 1927 Returned to England.

May 1927 Rented a flat in Hammersmith and with Laura Riding founded the Seizin Press there.

November 1927 *Lawrence and the Arabs* and *A Survey of Modernist Poetry* (with Laura Riding) published.

July 1928 *A Pamphlet Against Anthologies* (with Laura Riding) published.

May 1929 Separated from Nancy Nicholson.

October 1929 Graves and Riding left England and went to live in Deyá, Mallorca.

November 1929 *The Shout* and *Goodbye to All That* published.

November 1930 *But It Still Goes On* published.

February 1931 *Poems 1926–1930* published.

July 1931 *To Whom Else?* published.

February 1932 *No Decency Left* published (written with Laura Riding, both using the pseudonym 'Barbara Rich').

March 1933 *The Real David Copperfield* published.

May 1933 *Poems 1930–1933* published.

May 1934 *I, Claudius* published.

November 1934 *Claudius the God* published.

August 1936 Left Mallorca at the outbreak of the Spanish Civil War and with Riding and their secretary Karl Gay when first to London, then to Lugano in Switzerland, then back to London.

April 1938 *Count Belisarius* published.

June 1938 Went to live in Brittany with Riding and Alan and Beryl Hodge and worked on the *Dictionary of Exact Meanings*.

November 1938 *Collected Poems* published.

December 1938 *T. E. Lawrence to his Biographers* (with Basil Liddell Hart) published.

April 1939	To America with Riding.
August 1939	After his partnership with Laura Riding broke down, returned to England and lived with Beryl, his second wife, in Devon.
September 1940	*Sergeant Lamb of the Ninth* published.
November 1940	*The Long Week-End* (with Alan Hodge) published.
February 1941	*Proceed, Sergeant Lamb* published.
March 1942	*Work in Hand* (with Alan Hodge and Norman Cameron) published.
January 1943	*Wife To Mr Milton* published.
May 1943	*The Reader Over Your Shoulder* (with Alan Hodge) published.
October 1944	*The Golden Fleece* published.
November 1945	*Poems 1938–1945* published.
May 1946	Returned to Deyá, Mallorca, with Beryl and their three young children.
September 1946	*King Jesus* published.
May 1948	*The White Goddess* published.

PART ONE

1914–1919

In July 1914 Robert Graves left Charterhouse School and went to spend the summer, before going up to Oxford in October, at Harlech, North Wales, where his parents owned a house and where he had spent his holidays for several years past. He was dreading going to Oxford: at Charterhouse he had been unhappy and unpopular and Oxford promised to be merely a more boisterous repetition of the ordeal. He was vaguely thinking about running away to sea when, on 4 August, Britain declared war on Germany. Graves immediately joined the army and on 11 August began training as a recruit officer with the Royal Welch Fusiliers at their regimental depot in Wrexham. Although the newspapers assured everyone that it would be a brief war, over by Christmas at the latest, Graves hoped it would last long enough to delay him from taking up his classical exhibition at St John's College at the beginning of term.

One of Graves's close friends at Charterhouse was George Mallory, the mountain climber who died on Mount Everest in 1923; Mallory was a young master at the school, recently down from Cambridge, and used to take Graves climbing on Snowdon during the vacations and in term time edited with him and two other friends a new magazine called *Green Chartreuse*. While at Charterhouse Mallory wrote a biography of James Boswell, with which he was helped by Edward Marsh, the eminent civil servant, patron of the arts and editor of the best-selling *Georgian Poetry* anthologies. Graves met Marsh in Mallory's study in 1912, when Marsh was forty-one years old and private secretary to Winston Churchill, then First Lord of the Admiralty.

Both Graves and Marsh were descended from Spencer Perceval, the Prime Minister who, in 1812, was assassinated in the lobby of the House of Commons; after Perceval's death Parliament voted that his widow (who was expecting her twentieth baby) should receive

27

an annual income of £1000 for the rest of her life as compensation, and that a trust of £50,000 should be established for his twelve surviving children and their descendants. Marsh inherited a portion of this money, which he jokingly called the 'murder money', but refused to spend it on his own requirements, instead using it to set up a brilliant private collection of paintings which included the work of many young, modern painters, and to help many young artists and writers who were in need of financial assistance. He was devoted to art, the theatre and, particularly, to poetry. By 1912 he had become the doyen of an elite artistic and literary circle in London.

In 1911 there began a vigorous revival in English poetry, after a serious decline in the late Victorian and Edwardian periods, and Marsh, with his close friend Rupert Brooke, wanted the new poetry to reach and be appreciated by a large audience. With this aim, they decided to compile a popular anthology of the best of the new poetry and at the end of 1912 the first volume of *Georgian Poetry* was published, edited by Marsh. (Four more volumes were to appear, with Graves contributing to volumes III (1917), IV (1919) and V (1922).) In the early twenties 'Georgianism' became a term of reproach, but at its outset it was, more than anything else, simply a reaction against the neglect of poetry and a revolt against post-Victorian dullness and artificiality.

Since the age of fifteen Graves's ruling passion has been poetry and therefore meeting Marsh was of immense importance to him. Marsh had no intention of founding a new school or movement, but he and his circle firmly believed (and time has proved them right) that a new and vital age was beginning in English poetry, and that they were at the centre of it. Graves described his first meeting with Marsh in *Eddie Marsh, Sketches for a Composite Literary Portrait of Sir Edward Marsh:*[1]

Eddie befriended me before the first world war when I was a sixteen-year-old Carthusian, and I felt greatly honoured to be asked what contemporary poets should, in my opinion, be included in the first issue of his *Georgian Poetry*. He politely rejected my suggestion of Frederick Langbridge as a little old-fashioned to include in his new team, and asked to see poems of my own. When he had read them he frowned and told me gently that I was using 'an outworn vocabulary' and must reform it. This criticism I took deeply to heart and have never used a *thee*, *thou*, or *where'er* since that day; or hardly ever.

28

Thus Graves became one of Marsh's protégés and a long friendship began which was to be of great importance to both men.

By December 1914 a state of deadlock had been reached between the opposing armies on the Western Front and optimism about a quick end to the war was fading fast. Graves, a second lieutenant, was eager to get to France and expected his sailing orders at any moment. His first letter to Marsh was written from the regimental depot before what he thought was his final leave.

3rd Royal Welch Fusiliers
Plas Darland
Wrexham

26 December 1914

Dear Eddie

On Sunday I went over to see Ralph Rooper[2] at Gresford where I also met Fishbourne just back from Flanders with many wonderful tales of the War and a wounded head. They began talking about you as a common friend and that reminded me that last time I met you at George Mallory's you asked me to look you up in Town this winter. I am getting a week's leave from January 2nd–9th before I go out to the slaughter – a sort of respite like Jephthah's daughter had in which to bewail her virginity – and would like to look you up sometime then from 18 Bina Gdns W. where I shall be staying.

Will you be in Town then?

Yours sincerely   Robert R.[3] Graves

Contrary to his expectations, however, Graves did not go out to France immediately, but returned to Wrexham and stayed there until April.

22 January 1915

Dear Eddie

After forty-eight hours' leave in London I am suffering crushing boredom here as a reaction to the mental debauch of meeting you and others of my intelligent and humane friends.

If you have lost the verses I lent you, your overworkedness is ample excuse, but should you still have them I would like to have them returned and to know quite briefly how they strike you: be as cruel as you like as I wrote them all here where lack of criticism leaves me in doubt of their worth.

I have bought Rupert Brooke's *Poems* of which I had only seen a very few before: I think he is really good. What a torture his sensitiveness must always be for him, poor fellow!

Yours very sincerely   Robert Graves

Edward Marsh's reply has been lost, as have all of his letters before 1930.

3rd February 1915

Dear Eddie

No, I'm not annoyed, why should I be? I always try to look at myself objectively and dispassionately because this helps me to get the full flavour of romance out of life: so now I can see that it would be most extraordinary if my technique wasn't obsolete. Influences at work – first, in my reading, the immense preponderance of the 'classical' over the modern; second, my old father, a dear old fellow who in young and vinous days used to write with some spirit and very pleasantly; but now his inspiration has entirely petered out. He was hand in glove with Tennyson and Ruskin and that lot and has been trying to mould me in the outworn tradition, and tho' I have struggled hard against this as you must see, the old Adam is always cropping up unnoticed . . . And there is my uncle C. L. Graves of the *Spectator* who exerts a similar influence, which is made stronger by his great avuncular kindness and generosity. A boy like me who has – though George Mallory lectured me on the danger of this assumption – been so forlornly *sui generis* at home, school and now again in the regiment, would have to be a Hercules to struggle successfully against parents, uncles, schoolmasters and the books he reads.

However, I am still in my teens and when this ridiculous war is over, I will write Chapter II at the top of the new sheet and with the help of other young Georgians to whom I trust you will introduce me, will try to root out more effectively the obnoxious survivals of Victorianism.

No, I am *not* annoyed! The obsolete technique was responsible for the 'bugaboo about' which you dislike. It was a laboured effect after the pouting effect that suits the tone of the poem: I won't try it again.

Well, *au revoir*, till after the War, if the Gods are kind: I know I am a prig but three years' misery at Charterhouse drove me into it, and I am as keen as you for the regeneration of poetry.

Yours always   Robert

The 'war poetry boom' began in April 1915, after the death of Rupert Brooke, arch-Georgian and Marsh's closest friend. Brooke, an RNVR sublieutenant, died of blood poisoning on a French hospital ship in the Aegean Sea, before he had had time to be involved in any fighting. He was in many ways typical of his generation, particularly in his sentimental patriotism and naive enthusiasm, and his death had an extraordinarily powerful emotional effect on the British public, who immediately turned him into a legendary romantic hero; his poems suddenly became immensely popular and influential and inspired hundreds of second-rate imitators. Marsh was deeply affected by Brooke's death: he wrote to Brooke's mother (who was later to prove a great source of trouble for him and an obstacle in his attempt to write a memoir of his friend) that Rupert's death had caused him the greatest sorrow he could have, and that 'the loss to the future cannot be guessed'.

In May Graves, who at that time admired Brooke and thought him highly original, wrote to Marsh from billets at a coal-mining village called La Bourse, having just had his first experience of the trenches.

	3rd Royal Welch Fusiliers
	attached 2nd Welsh Regt
22 May 1915	3rd Brigade
	1st Division

Dear Eddie

A three days' spell in billets gives me the chance I have been wanting for some time, of writing to tell you how truly grieved I am about poor Rupert's death, for your sake especially and generally for all of us who know what poetry is: my Father (dear old man!) said that this was a fitting end for Rupert, killed by the arrows of jealous Musagetes in his own Greek islands; but fine words won't help; we can only be glad that he died so cheerfully and in such a good cause. What mightn't he have written had he lived?

I feel here exactly like a man who has watched the 'Movies' for a long evening and then suddenly finds himself thrown on the screen in the middle of scalp-hunting Sioux and runaway motor cars: and rather surprised that I am not at all frightened, and that the noise doesn't disturb me at all yet. You may disbelieve the following but I swear to you, Eddie, it's a true bill, that a violent artillery duel going on above my dug-out two nights ago simply failed to wake me at all though I was conscious of the whole place rocking, but, when this had ceased, I was awoken by a very persistent lark which hung for some minutes over my platoon trench swearing at the Germanoes.

So far I have been let down very lightly but of course no one expects to dodge everything and the best I can hope for is to 'do the Blighty touch', i.e. get a wound serious enough to qualify me for England. There are three touches: the Base Touch, The Blighty Touch and the Six-foot Touch (*absit omen*). It's hard to know if you're alive or dead with Busy Berthas booming overhead. This last sentence recalls a recent improvisation of mine, not brilliant but perhaps suggestive. I'll only give you three verses: they are not very clear I fear.[4]

> . . . You're charging madly at 'em yelling 'Fag!'
> When somehow something gives and your feet drag,
> You fall but feel no sort of pain,
> And find . . . you're scooping tunnels in the hay
> In the big barn ' 'cause it's a nasty day'
> Oh springy hay and lovely beams to climb!
> You're back in sailor suits again.
> Ah, this is a queer time.
>
> Or you'll be dozing safe in your dug-out –
> A great roar, the trench shakes and falls about;
> You're choking, choking – then, hullo!
> Marjorie's walking gaily down the trench
> Hanky to nose (that powder makes a stench!)
> Getting her pinafore all over grime.
> Funny, she died ten years ago.
> Ah, this is a queer time.

. . . . .

The trouble is, things happen much too quick.
Up jump the Bosches:[5] rifles crack and click
And then the whole scene melts away . . .
But fellows do object to passing straight
From Tipperary and the hymn of Hate
To Alleluiahs and the full rich chime
Of golden bells.
                    They swear and say
'By God, it's a queer time.'

I am rather sick at not being with my own regiment, the
Fusiliers. This attachment system can't hope to be a success: I
can't think what good Kitchener imagines that he will get out of
it; it is merely a continual source of annoyance to the men
attached and the men to whom they are attached. But I suppose
the Welsh Regiment, except in point of smartness and discipline, is
not far removed from the Fusiliers: the men are recruited from the
same district and class.

I know it is very rude and inconsiderate of me inflicting my
verses on you, but last January you told me to bring my technique
up to date and try and do a bit better than what I showed you, so
I send a thing I wrote at Wrexham with your advice still ringing in
my ears.[6] I think it really is a bit better – but I don't know – and
that the language is more or less what I used to speak at the age
of nine.

I am aware that I am presuming on our quite short
acquaintance but you haven't snubbed me yet and must be
accustomed to unconventional (which means bad-mannered)
people.

Tomorrow we go, they say, into some trenches where we and
the Bosches are sitting in each other's pockets, the whole place
mined and counter-mined, complete with trench-mortars, gas and
grenade throwing parties, so now for a little sleep.

Yours in the muses   Robert Graves

In September Graves was with the Second Battalion of the Royal
Welch Fusiliers when it took part in the ill-fated Loos offensive;
afterwards, when what was left of the battalion was reorganizing at
Annezin, he wrote to Marsh, who was preparing *The Collected
Poems of Rupert Brooke* for the press, which included his memoir
of Brooke as an introduction.

Please note changed address: this is quite enough to reach me.

2nd RWF
British Expeditionary
Force
France

October 1915

My dear Eddie

Your letter came to cheer a very lonely soldier: this life is enough to send anybody off his head even when he's in the society of people he likes. But I left the good old Welsh Regiment after three months and came here to the only more or less intact regular battalion in the Army, and a crack one at that, and a type of regular officer who lives the sort of life I have always abominated. I have less objection, tho', to the idea of *living* among people whose sole topics of conversation are wine, women, racing, hunting and musical comedy, than I have a sentimental dread of *dying* in such a society.

I don't know how I came through the last show unhurt; when our losses in combatant officers are considered, the odds worked out at three-to-one against my being the lucky survivor. Oh Eddie, there were some awful scenes that morning of the 25th! Our job, tho' fortunately we only knew this afterwards, was to engage the Germans opposite our trenches as hotly as possible but not with the object of breaking through, as this was known to be impossible, but just to relieve pressure at Loos.

I expect leave in November, when I will be able to tell you more, if I may. The men were splendid. I am the only survivor now of five 3rd Battalion officers who came up together five months ago into the very same trenches from which we attacked on the 25th September.

I have only met one single educated person since I've been out here and that was when the 9th RB were sent to our battalion for instruction in the trenches and the platoon officer whose men mixed with mine came into my dug-out and started quite spontaneously to talk of Samuel Butler and Richard Middleton[7] thence to Rupert Brooke and Denis Browne who was one of his intimates at Cambridge. He is a musician, Arthur Parry's his name, and he's the only educated person I have met in this country all these months. Ten new subalterns have come in to make up for our casualties: the two who have come into my company are a classical schoolmaster (Aberystwyth and London!)

and a rather aggressive estate-agent. The schoolmaster has a flair for Virgil and thinks that Keats was 'quite a good poet': thank God I'm not *in statu pupillari* to the man but can actually lord it over him as being a veteran (so far as they go now) and a two-star man, and can put some bounds to the pretensions of the estate-agent too.

The Captain who commands my company is a regular with some considerable service and can't see the use of 'a man like Graves who never goes with a woman or gets tight or shows any interest in hunting or racing or the stage and can't even play Auction.'

However, I am hoping to get a separate job in charge of the battalion sapping platoon which will save me from too close a comradeship with these people. However, I get on very well with the men which is some comfort, and occasionally hear from George and other good friends at home and make shift to cheer myself with vague dreams of a glorious *après-la-guerre* which I don't really expect to see.

But my chief solace, which makes up for everything really, is a fairly regular correspondence with Peter – or so the Gods call him, as Homer would say, though men call him George Johnstone[8] – my best friend, a poet long before I'll ever be, a radiant and unusual creature whose age hovers between seven and seventy, and though now in the first half-dozen of the Sixth Form at Charterhouse he's still wholesome-minded and clean-living. Thank God he's too young to come out and get killed before another year or so. When I go west I want you to write to him and look him out and be as good a friend to him as you have been to me. He'll repay it.

In the last month or so an inspiration seems to have come to me of what the New Poetry is to be and I feel that given a good rest and congenial society to settle my shaken mind I could write something really good. But here thought is quite impossible. My only hope is for a 'cushy wound' or for some high-souled General (if only I kept a pet General) to get me a transfer to a Reserve Battalion in England or a nice base job or indeed any old thing, for tho' still loyal and willing I've ceased to feel aggressive and winter is hard at hand. However – '*c'est la guerre. Et quand finira-t-elle? Oh, encore deux ans.*'

I want very much to see that memoir; how sickening about the mother. Peter has one like that too, the Hon. Mrs Edward Johnstone (née Agar Robartes[9]) by whom fortunately I have never been rebuffed, yet of whom the Charterhouse Headmaster, who makes my friendship with the boy an exception to his usual merciless ban, told me: 'There's no getting out of it: in the case of Peter that woman's quite insane.'

I must confess to you now that I was home on leave early in September and never looked you up. Fact was, my family kept me up in North Wales the whole week except one night I snatched to spend at Charterhouse with George and the next morning taken up in buying clothes for the winter, and I knew you were only to be found at certain weird hours of the evening so made no attempt that day at all.

Now I'm going to inflict some verses on you.[10]

. . . .

In another three days we expect to be back in the line – and as our place will be in the precise spot where all this Kilkenny Cat fighting is in progress I'll want all your best wishes. And now farewell.

Yours affectionately   Robert

When the new National Ministry was formed in May Churchill lost his position at the Admiralty and was instead appointed Chancellor of the Duchy of Lancaster, a sinecure he accepted and retained until November, when he decided to resign and go on active service at the Front with a battalion of the Grenadier Guards. Marsh, who had remained with Churchill as his private secretary until this time, was now given a job by Asquith, the Prime Minister, as secretary in charge of the Civil List pensions.

At the same time, Graves was gazetted a special reserve captain and transferred to the 1st Battalion which was reorganizing in billets at Locon, near Cambrin. There he met Siegfried Sassoon, another of Marsh's friends, who had also taken a commisson with the Royal Welch Fusiliers and had just arrived in France for the first time. They liked each other immediately, though neither was impressed by the other's poems. Sassoon's poetry had, until then, been some-what dilettantish, consisting, as Graves wrote in *Goodbye to All That*, of 'a few pastoral pieces of eighteen-ninetyish flavour, and a satire on Masefield[11] which, half-way through, had forgotten to be a satire and turned into rather good Masefield.'[12] (This was 'The

36

Daffodil Murderer', published in 1913, a satire on 'The Everlasting Mercy'.) Sassoon read Graves's poems, which he was then preparing for publication with Marsh's help, frowned 'and said the war should not be written about in such a realistic way'; Sassoon had not yet been in the trenches and Graves told him that once there he would soon change his style.

Also in November, *Georgian Poetry 1913–1915*, dedicated to the memory of James Elroy Flecker (1884–1915) and Brooke, was published. Marsh sent a copy to Graves at Montagne, where the battalion was ordered to forget the trenches and train for the open warfare that was bound to follow once the Somme defences had been broken through.

10 December 1915   1st RWF
                                                                                                 BEF

My dear Eddie

I have just got *Georgian Poetry* and your last letter: I was waiting for the book to arrive before I answered the letter that promised it. I am tremendously grateful as I have been without fresh books for a long time now and at a very loose end in the evenings in this dull little place, for we're here for two months, we are promised, training in open fighting about thirty miles behind the line in the Somme department: our battalion has been given the compliment of being made the divisional training school. It's great to know that we won't have any trench-work for so long and that we'll have Christmas out and can be sure of living and keeping well till February at least.

Congratulations on getting that job with Asquith: it must be a great relief to know that you're pulling your weight again after rotting about in that stagnant Duchy business.

This battalion, for a change, is full of delightful people: the CO is a brilliant soldier called Minshull Ford whom we all worship, a man of immense technical and practical knowledge, and a very kindly, tactful person who doesn't grouse.

The younger officers are an exceptionally nice lot and I'm very cheered with life. Siegfried Sassoon is here and sends his affectionate remembrances: a very nice chap but his verses, except occasionally, don't please me very much.

That reminds me about the verses Monro[13] forwarded to you. It's very unfair. My father has again played me false: I especially charged and adjured him to do nothing with the copy he'd got

37

until I'd picked out what I wanted to keep and put these few to a thorough examination and revision. It makes me hot with shame to think what crude miscarriages you've got there of mine. I *am* angry. Please forget you've seen them at all until I send you a revised version. Please!

Yes, I wrote to Arthur Parry, a sort of cheero! letter the other week but was not quite sure if his battalion was the 8th or the 9th RB so I expect it's been wandering about the Pas-de-Calais in a vague way for some time.

The country is lovely round here, actually <u>hilly</u>! Around La Basée the nearest approach to a hill was the Canal bank or the sides of a mine crater.

I don't know what this mobile training is leading up to, whether it's the Spring Push, as they say, or whether we'll be sent to some other war theatre like Egypt, Serbia or Mesopotamia. I don't really care so long as we're lucky enough to avoid the trenches in January.

We were up at Festubert the other day. The state of the trenches there made me think a little.

I only hope all these rumours of riots and quarrels in Boscheland are true: we all feel much more optimistic now and have at least a sporting chance of coming safe through the whole lot, we think. Golden *après-la-guerre* seems appreciably nearer now.

I'm glad you liked my old father. He's a man who's never made an enemy in his life and I firmly believe hasn't committed the smallest peccadillo since he was my age, and has worked like a black in beastly surroundings for years and years though hopelessly dreamy and unpractical and absent-minded. I do admire him – even when he's most hopelessly and pathetically wrong-minded.

Well, *au revoir*.   Robert

You are a brick, Eddie

In the following letter, Graves refers to a letter written in January 1916 which never reached Marsh; such losses were rare, as the postal service to and from the front line trenches was remarkably efficient, with letters and parcels taking, on average, only four days to arrive, sometimes only two.

In a letter of 9 February he had written to Marsh:

I have to live up to my part here as I have learned to worship my Regiment: in sheer self-defence I had to find something to idealize in the Service and the amazing sequence of R W Fus. suicides in defence of their 'never-lost-a-trench' boast is really quite irresistible. Result: I am getting horribly Praetorian and drill-bookish and find it impossible to write you a decent letter.

At this same time, however, Graves discovered, and was greatly influenced by, the poems of Charles Hamilton Sorley (1895–1915), who was one of the first to realize the true nature of the war and one of the three important poets to be killed in it (the other two being Isaac Rosenberg and Wilfred Owen).

24 February 1916

My dear Eddie

I am so sorry to hear that you never got my long letter written in January all about how much I loved *Georgian Poetry*, and kindred subjects. An eight sheet letter gone west! And I'll never be able to recapture my first fine, careless rapture after the first reading of that splendid book which is perhaps the most treasured possession I have out here. To quote a boy in England: 'You must have thought me an awful old pig for not writing about it.'

I love nearly every piece in it. 'Nearly', because I thought 'The Wanderer' wasn't good for Masefield who has lately grown very Yeatsian and flabby: he is at his best I think in 'The Old Bold Mate of Harry Morgan' and the more masculine chanties: and occasionally I dislike W. H. Davies,[14] though I thought 'The Bird of Paradise' very good indeed. Of course, 'King Lear' is all poetry and jolly good poetry but I can't love and sympathize with Gordon Bottomley[15] as I can love Hodgson's[16] 'Bull' and most of all Rupert's 'Heaven' and 'The Great Lover' and 'The Soldier' and all the rest. I was especially charmed too with 'Goat Paths' and 'The Three Jolly Farmers'.

I think the reviews I've seen have been ridiculously badly written: so damned patronizing too, most of them. It's splendid that the book's selling so well notwithstanding.

I've just discovered a brilliant young poet called Sorley whose poems have just appeared in the Cambridge Press (*Marlborough and Other Poems*, 3s. 6d.) and who was killed near Loos on

October 13th as a temporary captain in the 7th Suffolk Regiment.
It seems ridiculous to fall in love with a dead man as I have found
myself doing but he seems to have been one so entirely after my
own heart in his loves and hates, besides having been just my own
age and having spent just the same years at Marlboro' as I spent
at Ch'house. He got a classical scholarship at University College,
Oxford, the same year as I was up and I half-remember meeting
him there. Don't you like this:

> All the hills and vales along
> Earth is bursting into song,
> And the singers are the chaps
> Who are going to die perhaps.
>   O sing, marching men,
>   Till the valleys ring again.
>   Give your gladness to earth's keeping,
>   So be glad, when you are sleeping.
>
> Cast away regret and rue,
> Think what you are marching to!
> Little live, great pass –
> Jesus Christ and Barabbas
> [Were found the same day.
> This died, that went his way.
>   So sing with joyful breath,
>   For why, you are going to death.
>   Teeming earth will surely store
>   All the gladness that you pour.][17]
>
> Earth that never doubts nor fears,
> Earth that knows of death, not tears,
> Earth that bore with joyful ease
> Hemlock for Socrates,
> Earth that blossomed and was glad
> 'Neath the cross that Christ had,
> Shall rejoice and blossom too
> When the bullet reaches you.
>   Wherefore men, marching
>   On the road to death, sing!
>   Pour your gladness on earth's head,
>   So be merry, so be dead.

He seems to have been under Rupert's influence rather in his
method. Listen:

... Victor and vanquished are at one in death:
Coward and brave: friend, foe. Ghosts do not say
'Come, what was your record when you drew breath?'
But a big blot has hid each yesterday
So poor, so manifestly incomplete.
And your bright Promise, withered long and sped,
Is touched, stirs, rises, opens and grows sweet
And blossoms and is you, when you are dead.

He wrote that out here in June: he came out, like me, in May.
What waste!

Work here goes on as when I last wrote. I continue to lecture all
day to smaller or larger audiences, more or less appreciative as the
weather varies. I had eleven hundred men and fifty officers this
morning for a forty minutes on one of my favourite subjects: how
to keep happy, though in the trenches. I can't imagine myself
facing an ordeal like that a year ago, but I've altered a bit – '*C'est
la guerre*'. This reminds me: I wrote yesterday to Monro about my
verses suggesting that phrase as the best title I have yet thought of.
'*C'est la guerre*' has been consecrated by countless instances of
French and Belgian fortitude in trouble and is perhaps the best-
known expression in all the allied armies. It has a laugh and an
apology in it and expresses just what I want, an explanation – an
excuse almost – for the tremendous change in tone and method
and standpoint which you must have noticed between the first and
last parts of the verse-cycle, a hardening and coarsening and loss
of music. It gives a clue, then, to the contents of the book and yet
has nothing highfalutin' about it which would make me ridiculous
in the eyes of the Regiment and of Ch'house: which is most
important. Do say you like it.

As for leave, well, when and if I get it on about March 10th I
am looking forward like anything to staying with you for the two
days you promised me. I'll let you know more definitely as soon as
I hear: as a matter of fact on March 10th I am contemplating
trying to get an operation done to my nose, removing some stray
cartilage: which will I hope protract my leave to three weeks. If I
can protract it into the Easter holidays I will do all I can to
arrange a meeting between you and Peter, if I can only catch him
away from his mother, the awful woman I told you about. You
must know him. I sent him a copy of *GP* but haven't yet heard his

verdict. Thank God he's not quite old enough yet to be a soldier and get killed out here.

Erzeroum is a good egg isn't it? It has had a tremendously cheering effect on everyone here who understands anything about the war. Today we hear that the Bosches are pushing at Verdun. We expect with gas because this is the favourable season for winds from the Bosche point of view. In the words of the old song, the war-worn band of instructors feel:

> When the bugle calls we shall march to war
> And not a man will fear it,
> And I don't care how soon the bugle calls,
> So long as I don't hear it.

But fie! That is not our official attitude.

I hope my dear old father hasn't been making a nuisance of himself to you as he is only too apt to do. But he's a nice old man really.

I want to see that *Memoir*[18] of yours, and hope that the *Georgian Picture Book* you were going to do when the war broke out will eventually appear.

Six inches of snow here and very cold – those poor devils in the trenches on a 'brass monkey' day like this!

Yours affectionately

Robert Graves

Graves's leave was postponed, however, and in March he rejoined the 1st Battalion, now back in trenches at Fricourt, on the Somme.

15 March 1916

My dear Eddie

It's rather trying, having to go back into trenches after a three months' holiday, especially trenches like this where the two parties are so exceedingly embittered against each other: I have to get used to all the old noises, from the crack! rockety-ockety-ockety-ockety-ockety of a rifle bullet, to the boom! ... swish ... swish ... Grr ... GRR! ... GRR! ... *ROAR!* of a fifteen-inch shell and there are a lot of new terrors since last December. The *specialité* here is 'canisters', round, tin, barrel-shaped trench-mortars filled with about twenty pounds of the highest explosive. About ten or twelve times as much stuff is handed round now than when I first came out, but I always enjoy trenches in a way, I must confess: I like feeling really frightened and if happiness consists in being miserable in a good cause, why then I'm doubly happy. England's is a good cause enough and the trenches are splendidly miserable: my company firing-line averages 30 yards from the Bosches, the mud is *chronic*, there are few parts of the trench where one can stand upright without exposing oneself, and not a single canister-proof dug-out. If only it was blowing sleet and a gas attack was due tomorrow my cup of happiness would be full. We work all day and night and enjoy ourselves thoroughly, wading knee-deep through our native element, and humming the popular tune:

> *Après la guerre finie*
> *Et les Anglais partis,*
> *Toutes les mademoiselles de Béthune*
> *Auront bébés anglais jolis.*

Thanks ever so much for *Letters from America*[19] most of which I had already read in S.S.'s copy the afternoon I came back here. I haven't yet had time to read H.J.'s preface but I have read the book itself and been absolutely delighted especially with the South Sea Chapter and the one about (I suppose) Denis Browne. I wanted to be told all about the South Sea islanders whom I have always liked since my great spiritual father, Samuel Butler, put them among the three comeliest, healthiest and best-bred peoples of the world. It's astonishing how Butler overshadows and colours all life for me; never a day passes but I think of him in a score of connexions just as Handel overshadowed and coloured life for Butler himself. That's why I was so pleased with Rupert for quoting 'The Discobolus' in connexion with Montreal, because for me, that poem[20] is the only thing which makes the town live.

> Stowed away in a Montreal lumber-room
> The Discobolus standeth and turneth his face to the wall,
> Dusty, cobweb-covered, maimed and set at naught.
> Beauty crieth aloud: an attic and no man regardeth.
> O God! O Montreal!

And the triumphant ending:

> But none the less blasphemed he Beauty saying:
> 'The Discobolus hath no Gospel, but my brother-in-law
> Is haberdasher to Mr Spurgeon!'
> O God! O Montreal!

Do you know his beautiful ballad 'Wednesbury Cocking' which he lays no claim to having written himself but obviously did. It appears in his *Alps and Sanctuaries* and starts . . .

> At Wednesbury there was a cocking,
> A match between Newton and Scroggin;
> The tarriers and nailers left work,
> And all to old Spittle's went jogging.
>
> To see this noble game
> Many gentlemen resorted
> And though little money they had
> That little they freely sported . . .

I would love to think that Rupert knew and loved Butler as much as I do.

I think S.S.'s verses are getting infinitely better than the first crop I saw, much freer and more Georgian. What a pity he didn't start earlier! I suspect Gosse[21] of being his retarding influence – 'keeping me to my moons and nightingales and things,' as S.S. put it himself yesterday – but this is private.

He has written a perfectly ripping one about a mutual friend of ours called Thomas,[22] a subaltern in this battalion whom I believe I told you about before – did you see it? S.S. and I have great difficulty in talking about poetry and that sort of thing together as the other officers of the battalion are terribly curious and suspicious. If I go into his mess and he wants to show me some set of verses, he says: 'Afternoon Graves, have a drink . . . by the way, I want you to see my latest recipe for rum punch.' The trenches are worse than billets for privacy. We are a disgrace to the battalion and we know it: I don't know what the CO would say if he heard us discussing the sort of things we do. He'd probably have a fit. His saying is that 'there should be only one subject for conversation among subalterns off parade.' I leave you to guess it. It's a great standby to have S.S. here in such society, though one or two of our brother officers are exceptionally nice.

Why should the Germans get Verdun? Why this pessimism?

I haven't yet been able to do anything with 'Star Talk'. Excuse writing, etc.

Yours affectionately   Robert

What was that thing that Shakespeare wrote – 'Oh, let the canister clink!'[23]

At this time the troops were issued with a new type of anti-gas respirator, another in a long line of unsatisfactory experiments; this new one differed from previous models in that it forced the wearer to breathe through his nose, which Graves was unable to do due to a boxing injury. The battalion doctor advised him to have a nose operation as soon as possible, so in April he returned to England and had an operation (which was badly botched and has caused him trouble late in life) at the Millbank Hospital in London. Afterwards he went to Harlech to convalesce and was there when, on 1 May, his first book, *Over the Brazier*, was published.

To Siegfried Sassoon

2 May 1916

Erinfa
Harlech
N. Wales

My dear Sassons[24]

This is the first day that I have felt really strong enough to write you the letter you deserve, being now more or less recovered from the amazing lot of blood I lost last month.

Well, old thing, I'm really desolated at having deserted you and the battalion but I couldn't help it. My people forced me before a specialist who ordered an immediate operation which he said would only take three weeks, which would have meant that having got a three weeks' extension to my leave I would have gone straight back to the battalion. As it was, it proved much more serious and I am on a month's back leave after which – bloody Litherland, I suppose. But I swear I'm not skrimming my shanks: though I can't pretend I like Fricourt better than this heavenly place I honestly would go back tonight if I could.

I can't do purple patches well, but Merioneth now is nothing but bright sun and misty mountains and hazy seas and sloe blossoms and wild cherry and grey rocks and young green grass. I am writing in my small, white-walled cottage[25] of which I must have told you – the one that once belonged to a consumptive coachman, then to a drunken carpenter, then became a brothel, then a Sunday school and now serves as pleasaunce for me and my two sisters. There is an especially nice small round beechwood table to write on, most inspiring and helpful if one's writing anything important.

I called on Mr Gosse and we had a long and inspiring conversation: he's an awfully nice old man. I haven't yet seen Mr Festing Jones[26] but I'm going to when I get back to London about the 15th. Eddie came and saw me in hospital which was very noble of him; he told me he had heard from you and that you have been doing silly things in No Man's Land with bombs – I'm glad you've found out what a tonic patrolling is when you're in dull trenches, but for de Lawd's sake honey don't overdo it. Next week is the anniversary of my setting sail for Troy; I'm glad I'm spending it in England: it often proves fatal out in France.

My book was to have come out yesterday but I haven't yet got a copy. The cover is a very weird one by Lovat Fraser:[27] as you might almost guess, he is back in England suffering from shell-shock. I had a wonderful two days down at Charterhouse. Peter was exquisite as usual: I had tea in his study and went for a walk with him after, the longest time I have ever been in his society. It's very extraordinary though that if you add up all the times we've been together they would only total up a few hours, probably not a whole day yet. I seldom get a letter less than fifteen pages from him. He's writing very well now, suddenly. I wonder when you'll meet him.

It's very jolly to think of you safe awhile at the Army School. Is it Flixécourt? If so, how jolly! I've been there.

I had a very painful interview with Richardson's people who came and pressed me for all the minute details of his death.

I asked Monro about your book and I'm sorry to say it's off for want of paper which now costs three or four times as much as it did before the war: it's silly to be thwarted by a little thing like that. He said that but for the agreement he'd signed with me he mightn't have done mine. Perhaps really though, you're luckiest. I'm hoping to get a lot of work done here this coming fortnight: it's much easier now I am in civils again, complete with flannel bags, silk collar and garish tie and my old brown coat. I don't expect that I'll get out again much before September. I only hope that I get back to the First Battalion again instead of the 2nd or 8th or 17th or even some other regiment altogether which is quite possible. When you write let me know as much battalion news as

46

you can scrape up and don't forget to salute A Company, old Cottrell, Greaves and Reeves for me.

There is a peculiar cuckoo in the woods just outside with a bad stammer. It says cu-cuckoo and sometimes even cu-cu-cuckoo. I must tell the *Spectator* about it.[28]

I have all my Samuel Butler books here so I'm in clover in that respect.

Hospital was bloody: there was always a strong light shining in your eyes and the orderlies were most undisciplined and kept on dropping plates and talking in loud voices and pressing loathsome food on you at inopportune moments. Never again, if I can help it!

Yours affectionately   Robert Graves

At this time Sassoon nursed 'a personal grievance against the Germans' because of the death of his close friend David Thomas (Dick Tiltwood in *Memoirs of a Fox-Hunting Man*); he had now 'more or less made up my mind to die because in the circumstances there didn't seem anything else to be done.'[29] However, as he describes at the beginning of *Memoirs of an Infantry Officer*, his personal war against the Germans was interrupted in March by his being sent to the 4th Army School at Flixécourt for a month of 'blank-cartridged skirmishing in a land of field-day make-believe'. He rejoined his battalion, at Mametz, in April, and for his part in a raid on German trenches, during which he rescued a badly wounded lance corporal from a mine crater close to the German line, and for doing 'what I could to tidy up the mess in No Man's Land', he was awarded the Military Cross. Because of his renowned and reckless heroism he was nicknamed 'Mad Jack' in the 7th Division.

No date [early May 1916]

Dear Siegfried

Thanks awfully for your gracious and ornate letter: I had just sent one to you to the battalion which I trust will be forwarded. By this post I am ordering Rupert's two books for you, and am sending herewith an advance copy of a book by the unknown squirt you mention: only, inquiries at the bookshop for *Round the Brazier* proved fruitless. *Over the Brazier* is the nearest I can get to it. Be careful about leaving it about.

I'm so glad about those two patrols: Tommy *will* laugh if he's the cause of you getting a Military Cross.

My *Spectator* and *Punch* uncle, C. L. Graves, is down here and at present is engaged in trying to review thirty volumes of recent verse on one page of the *Spectator*. The batch includes Sorley, Blackall (late of the RWF who writes very roughly but often most effectively), Gibson's[30] *Battle* and the said *Over the Brazier*. I insist on a decent review of Sorley and he meets me more than half-way because he knows and likes the mother very much. There are two emendations I should love to put into Sorley. Perhaps I shall suggest them to his editor. In the 'millions of the mouthless dead' poem the words 'It is a spook' have been changed in the second edition to 'It is a ghost' which is obviously wrong because, well, they all were ghosts. 'Spook' is an attempt, very unsuccessful, to avoid this truism. I'd like to read 'It is a *lie*. None wears the face you knew'. Then in the 'Odyssey poem' at the beginning of the glorious ἀοιδος passage (I quote from memory):

Whose eyes were blind, whose soul had sight,
Who knew the fame of men in fight,
Bard of white hair and trembling foot
Who *sang* whatever God had put
Into his heart . . . And there *he sung*
Those war-worn veterans among.

Impossible, isn't it? But why not: 'And there *he's sung*. . . '? Peter, who is as fond of Sorley as we, and to whom I was bewailing that we'd never meet him to talk to, replied cryptically but not unconsolingly, 'How do you know we won't?'

What did your Marlburian say about Sorley, and was he 'so'? As his book contains no conventional love-lyrics and as he'd reached the age of 20, I conclude he was.

My uncle is an yknarc[31] but pleasant old scarecrow and I would like him very much but for two impossible stumbling blocks between us: his hatred of the Welsh, whom I love, and my love for Samuel Butler, whom he hates too. He complained last night, very significantly, that the two gods of the younger generation are S.B. and Edward Carpenter,[32] but chiefly the former. He is a person who ought to know, and I'm very pleased at the news that Rupert loved Samuel, Eddie tells me. I wonder if Sorley did – anyhow, he seems to have loved Rupert. Who else do you think lies at the root of Georgianism, more or less remotely? I think: Middleton, John Davidson, Havelock Ellis, Shaw, Ibsen, Brieux, Masefield, and perhaps the Irish school of A.E. a little.[33] Rather a mixed community, but don't you agree?

I have decided (WR, DV and all that sort of thing) to go up to Oxford after the war, for a year at least; rather with the view of finding out the nice people and consolidating them. Why can't you come too S.S.? I'm sorry I'm bound to Oxford by my old exhibition, but I can't help thinking that it's Oxford that's going to have the next batch of brilliance. There is also my friend Ralph Rooper, scholar of New College, a most humane, understanding and excellent person just after your heart. I don't think your age matters much: be born again like Nicodemus.

I'm doing some quite decent work here, I think: you will see the results in good time. I saw only one of your things in the old *Gazette*. I was so ill at the time that I couldn't take it in properly: it was the dragon one[34] and I only remember it was very nice in the middle.

I wonder how the returning veterans from France and Mesopotamia, [upper] Salonika, etc., will get on with the raw freshmen who go up with them to the Varsity. There will be a colossal BEF clique, the most select of whom will be, of course, the infantry. I suppose Flixécourt, or wherever you are, is to fit you to command a company when the next vacancy occurs? I hope so.

By the way, wasn't Montagne glorious? Years hence we must *faire* a pilgrimage there and revive memories and I must call on my old landlord bloke, Monsieur Caron Elie.

I am frightfully jealous of my uncle because he met Butler several times. It *is* unfair.

I didn't intend this lengthy letter at all. It forced itself on me. Let me know when you get leave next and I'll run down to London from Liverpool to see you: unless you find time to come up and swank at Litherland.

Goodbye and luck,   Robert

. . . .

When this convalescence was over Graves joined the 3rd Battalion, in huts next to a munition factory at Litherland, near Liverpool, where it had been shifted to from Wrexham as part of the Mersey defence force.

3rd RWF
The Huts
Litherland
Liverpool

27 May 1916

My dear Sassons

Nous voici at Litherland again (not that I've ever been here before but I've heard such a lot about it) and bored with it already. Of course everyone was very affable and I've met a lot of old comrades-in-arms including dear old Watkin who got hit when we were with the 2nd Welch together; but the subalterns are all at present terrified of my three stars and are ridiculously respectful, and I'm tired of playing at being a senior officer. However, I managed to get my Medical Board to give me 'General Service' and don't expect to wait long before getting out again. It's a squalid place, very, and the TNT factory is more than a nuisance: it's positively dangerous: it's not right us getting gassed while still in Blighty. There is only one subaltern who has the vitality and personality to interest me at all, and last night in the Adelphi I saw him dancing with the famous 'Waterloo Elsie' woman, to whom Walwyn had introduced him! The lad is still eighteen, has the vocabulary of a navvy and drinks complicated cocktails every night till about three in the morning. You will have guessed that Sandhurst has been the ruin of this genial young fellow; it's a great grief to me. Walwyn, whom I met here for the first time but who has now gone off on some staff job, is my idea of a 'first class four-letter man'. In front of Mrs Watkin last night he told one of his promising young Sandhurst protégés to go and 'take on that young bitch sitting over there; I'm too old'.

A great, a hardly bearable disaster has overtaken R.G. His Peter has been taken from him by the terrible old mother who has been nosing around and reading all his letters. So terribly has she been shocked at finding quotations from Samuel Butler and Carpenter and people in them and at such signatures as 'ever yours affectionately, Robert' and 'best love, R' that she has extracted a promise from the poor lad that he will have nothing to do with me till he leaves Ch'house. Complications too long to enumerate leave no loopholes of evasion for either of us, so I am now

widowed, laid waste and desolate. However, Peter in his last letter
said that he'd never forget me and after these few years all will be
as before: and perhaps he'll be able to rebel sooner, and it's better
than him being killed anyhow.

Your jingle letter[35] was quite one of the nicest I've ever had: you
are a dear. One of these days I'll try a reply.

I met old Festing Jones whom I like awfully: a queer, Butlerian
frankness about him. 'My father was an illegitimate, y'know,' he
said at dinner quite abruptly.

I gave your love to Eddie: he's in good form these days. As
company commander here, officer in charge of trained men,
captain of the week and a few other odd appointments, I don't
have much spare time now. 'I want to go home' – to France.

Yesterday we played the South Lancashires at cricket (*quel
débâcle!*). My two scores of one and three were quite among our
best. They declared at 250 for 6 and beat us by an innings and
God only knows how much.

Goodbye,

Yours affectionately   Robert

23 June 1916

Bloody Litherland

At any rate in France there
are no flag-days or Rose-days!

Dear Sassons

It is with bitter disappointment that I hear that you've been in
Blighty on leave and dined with Eddie and never let me know.
God! man, I'd have come down from John o' Groats if you'd told
me.

This is indeed an awful place. I'm so restless and enthusiastic
and want-to-get-back-to-the-boys-ish that I have succeeded at one
time or another in offending most of the more considerable people
here, including the Adjutant, Kearsley, Holroyd who is supposed
to supervise the two trained companies one of which I command,
not to mention the CO and the assistant Adjutant Karn. So you
can imagine how jolly life is, with no Peter to illumine the gloom
in an atmosphere clogged with moral and actual smut. Ohé! Roll
on the trenches! I hear you've been risking your precious life again
among them craters: I am pleased, damned pleased, you're doing

so well; wish to hell I was with you – go on risking, and good luck. It's a man's game!

What books would you like? Shall I send you W. H. Davies's two new little ones, *Farewell to Poesie* and *Childlovers* or have you got them?

I haven't yet got them reviews typed but they are very affable, mostly. The *Spectator* gives me over a column starting: 'Mr R. G.'s verses have a quality which renders them memorable' and signed J.St L.S.[36] The *Times Literary Supplement* talks of 'a complete sincerity which allows no hint of the imitative: if its rawness is sometimes repelling yet as the writer has an ear for musical cadence he often lays a spell on the reader and achieves something like true beauty . . . Something new in the world of fancy . . .'

The *Nation* shuffles and refuses 'to predict anything certain . . . from such immaturity . . . If he will develop a broader and deeper temper and perceive that flexibility is a means not an end, he should do excellent work.'

Those are the most important ones. I have been frantically busy lately what with 'Captain of the Week' and the trained men (night ops three days a week) sweating about the country all hours, so of course when the match is burning my fingernails my bloody verses insist on forcing themselves to be written by me: they flock on me in shoals and I can't refuse them: I can't give them a hurried birth and then strangle 'em straight away. They want washing and clothing and suckling and what not in my precious time, and then what happened to my Regimental duties? Regimental duties take precedence over company duties, but poetical duties take precedence even over Guards of Honour and GCMs. I hope you are still writing with the same sudden genius of your last trench-letter. How strange that you have all at once struck what you have been searching for for so long; but I suppose now you want another little cushy Flixécourt tour to give you the time and leisure and quiet.

Best of luck when the Delayed Offensive actually comes, and may I be there with you old man! I have heaps to tell you that I've not the time to write: it is now 1 a.m. Sunday morning ('God save us all and the wind it be howling round the cabin,' as Synge would say). I'm getting my latest things typed to send you. The rules of the 'mutual admiration society' demand a similar step on your part. Or write, at any rate.

Sorley is still selling, and *The Times* has labelled him 'Enrolled among the English Poets' for which God bless that usually bloody paper. By the way, don't you love?:

I tried to follow, but what *do* you think?
The mushrooms here are pink!

You might remind Old Greaves he still has my *Letters from America* and to keep it against I return. Love to the lads.

Ever yours affectionately   Robert

Isn't it splendid that the RWF have now twice been singled out for special mention in a daily *communiqué?*

On 1 July the Somme offensive began, and all available trained officers and men in England were sent out to replace casualties. Graves was ordered to rejoin the 2nd Battalion, then in trenches at Givenchy.

To Edward Marsh

No date [July 1916]

In the train on the way to
2nd Royal Welch Fusiliers
BEF

My Dear Eddie

I told my sister before I went off to give into your charge the last few poems I wrote: I had shown you one or two before and regret not having had time to put them right where you pointed out their obvious weak spots. I hope you'll like this one called 'Babylon', written the day before I left England. I don't intend to make a will: it's bad luck, but remember that if anything happens you're the only person I can trust as literary executor for my poor 'Remains'. I want you to have an absolute free hand to chop change arrange anything I've written exactly as you like. And in this case any money coming from any new edition of *Over the Brazier* or any further publication is yours to use as you like: but it is not likely to incommode you with its quantity.

I hope to God that S.S. is all right: I saw a man in hospital at Rouen who was hit with the First Battalion just as they had gone over the top on the 1st of July, but he seemed to think they met with little opposition at first. Eight lines of doggerel:

'Farewell,' the corporal cried, "La Bassée trenches.
No Cambrins for me now, no more Givenchy's
Cuinchy's nor Loos's neither – God Almighty!
I'm back again at last to good old Blighty.'
But cushy wounds don't last a man too long
And now, poor bloke, he sings this long, bitter song:
'Back to La Bassée, back to the same Hell,
    Givenchy, Cuinchy, Cambrin, Loos, Vermelles.'

Goodbye!
    Yours affectionately   Robert

Graves did not post this letter for some time and added a postscript
just before he sent it off: 'Since I wrote I have been with the battalion
in the La Bassée trenches and out again and moved to where I was
when I left the other battalion, or in that region. *Compris?*' This was
on the Somme front line, near Mametz Wood.

Graves's reception in the officers' mess had been unexpectedly
chilly because of a rumour that he was a spy, started by a regular
second lieutenant jealous of Graves's Special Reserve captaincy, and
based on his German middle name, von Ranke, and the fact that the
most notorious German spy caught in England had been called Carl
Graves. 'My enemy put it out that Carl and I were brothers. I
consoled myself by thinking that a battle was obviously due soon,
and would put an end either to me or to the suspicion – "So long
as no NCO is told off to shoot me on the slightest appearance of
treachery." Such things were known.'[37]

How much Graves was upset by this situation is shown in the
following letter to Sassoon, written on the way from Givenchy to
Mametz.

13 July 1916   Buire

My dear Sassons
    It's heartbreaking how Fates keep us apart. The night I got your
note I couldn't come over to see you, for Regimental reasons; this
morning ditto. This afternoon I got one and a half hours' leave,
rode over to Méaulte, through Méaulte, all round Méaulte –
nobody knew where you were and it nearly broke my heart to
have to come back ἀπεακτōς. The officers here, with very very
few exceptions, are first-class four letter men and nobody loves me

– they won't give me a company though third senior in the battalion – everybody's as damnably cold-shouldered as the lower forms of a Public School. If only you could have come over here with Holmes and cheered me up!

Contrary to my usual principle I'm at last looking out for a cushy wound. This time thirteen months ago I was a much bigger bug in the Second Welch than I am now, and my peace of mind was much greater. I'm homesick for the First Battalion, I am. And nobody to cheer me up.

That messenger you sent disappeared before I could give a written answer: I do hope you weren't hurt and didn't think I was being casual.

I want to go home to a quiet hospital ward with green screens and no cracks in the ceiling to make me think of trenches.

Best love, old man   Robert

Sassoon, it turned out, was back with the transport, having a rest.

But I sent him, by one of our own transport men, a rhymed letter about the times that we were going to have together when the war ended; how, after a rest at Harlech, we were going for a visit to the Caucasus and Persia and China; and what good poetry we would write. This was in answer to a rhymed letter he had written to me from the Army School at Flixécourt a few weeks previously.[38]

Both letters were published in 1917, Sassoon's 'A Letter Home' in *The Old Huntsman* and Graves's 'Letter to S.S. from Mametz Wood' in *Fairies and Fusiliers*.

On 20 July, during an attack on High Wood, Graves was seriously injured in the eye, leg and chest by shell splinters. Unconscious, he was carried down to the dressing station where the doctors examined him and told his colonel, 'Tibs' Crawshay, that there was no possibility of his surviving the wound, and when next morning Crawshay made out the official casualty list ('a long one, because only eighty men were left in the battalion'), he assumed Graves's death, reporting him 'died of wounds', and wrote a letter of condolence to his parents. However, in the dressing station that morning, 'clearing away the dead, they found me still breathing and put me on an ambulance for Heilly, the nearest field hospital.'[39] A few days later he was moved to Rouen.

26 *July 1916*   No. 8 General Hospital
                                                 Rouen

My dear Eddie

As you may have heard, the old Bosche has punctured me with a 5·9 howitzer shell clean through chest and back, but I'm ridiculously well considering and my cheerfulness and good condition go on improving each other like wild-fire. It was on the 20th in an attack on High Wood. I am lucky to have escaped like this with no broken limbs, and everything going well.

I had the luck to meet S.S. on the 16th, his battalion being alongside ours and we had a great talk about poetry and important things like that and sketched out a wild Eastern tour together for *après-la-guerre*.

He improves more and more and has been doing still more fantastic deeds of Derring-do.

This afternoon I had a sort of waking dream about meeting and making friends with Rupert; it was absolutely vivid and I feel now I know him ten times better than before. We talked poetry most of the time and he said, amongst other things, that it wasn't so bad being dead as you got such splendid opportunities of watching what was happening. The thing ended by your Gray's Inn housekeeper appearing, whereupon Rupert went up and had a bath and I saw him no more.

I wonder what suggested it?

They'll move me home in another week or so: I hope I hit a nice hospital. In a month, they tell me, I'll be convalescent again. Good! I got three or four other little wounds but nothing to signify. It is so jolly now to feel that I'm out of it all for months and months, for the whole war with a little luck, and such jolly sickleave prospects before me.

I came of age on the 24th, think of that!

I hope you and your work are going on all right: the general situation seems quite cheerful doesn't it? But the poor old Prime Minister must be having a rotten time with these wretched Irish.

Do send me something new and jolly to read: nothing here but ghastly romances of jealousy, rape and murder: most disturbing to the sick patient!

Goodbye

Yours ever affectionately   Robert

                                          Queen Alexandra's Hospital
                                             for Officers
4 August 1916   Millfield Lane
                                          Highgate N.

My dear Sassons,

   I hope you haven't taken the casualty lists seriously again. They *are* fools. I'm as right as rain and hope before many days to be up in glorious Merioneth again basking in the sun and storing up a large mass of solar energy against our great Caucasus trip *après-la-guerre*. The rumour of my death was started by the regimental doctor and the Field Ambulance one swearing I couldn't possibly live – but it takes a lot to kill Youth and Ugliness however easily Youth and Beauty fade and die. Tibs has written me a ripping letter apologizing about the mistake.

   Eddie tells me you were quite sad about my demise – dear old thing, I hope you didn't avenge me with bombs or do anything rash! Tomorrow my mater and pa will be *flooded* with condolences about me – awful nuisance – and my pay and allowances will be awfully difficult to get now. I have, however, instructed Peter – via my brother – to employ all his literary skill in a letter of pathetic reproach to his mother about my death and the way she's treated me and him. It's an ill wind, etc.

   Please reassure Holmes and Julian and Edmund Dadd and Joe Cottrell that they haven't yet seen the last of me. I'm sending you some kippers: hope they'll not arrive too high.

   Best of luck, and remember the man who cried out to the red-bearded hangman: '*Non, tu ne me pourras [sic] pas tuer.*'[40] Don't succumb, however many and wise doctors give you up. *Memento Caucasorum*!

   Yours very affectionately   Robert

A ripping hospital this. By the way, I died on my 21st birthday. I can never grow up now.

By the time this letter arrived in France, however, Sassoon was also back in England because of lung trouble, and was feeling 'nine parts dead from the horror of the Somme fighting'.

To Edward Marsh

7 August 1916

My dear Eddie,

If I wasn't such a desperately honest chap I'd cover my wickedness by swearing that I'd written to you and that someone had forgotten to post the letter – but what really happened was I started writing then stopped because I was waiting to give you a bit of news which didn't arrive, then forgot and imagined I'd written. Such millions and billions and squadrillions of letters came condoling, inquiring, congratulating – I never knew I had so many friends. Mostly rather tedious. But three lovely ones today, the first from old Siegfried (whom by the way I always call 'Sassons' since Tommy was killed: he invented it) at Oxford and he's coming to see me in a week (Eddie, what *is* a spot on the lung? A wound, or tubercle or what?) and as I'm going to be able to travel in 'a week or ten days', the medico says, I'm going to lug him up to Harlech (I hope you liked the Harlech part of the Caucasus letter: I wrote it within 50 yards of the dead Bosche in Mametz Wood!) and we'll have high old primitive times together.

By the way, Mark Gertler[41] would paint the Bosche so well: do ask him sometime.

To resume, next was your letter which I'm endeavouring to answer in a manner that will show my appreciation. Next, a wonderful composition from dear old Ralph Rooper starting: 'Oh my dear, dear Lazurus'; he has also been mourning me for a week. It's awfully jolly to have such friends: I'd go through it all again for those three letters I got today; straight I would.

I never knew S.S. was in England. I'm so relieved he's out of it.

I've had ridiculously little pain, the worst being when they tear the sticking plaster that holds my leg bandage in position . . . off the hairy part of my leg.

I had an immensely uncomfortable journey down to Rouen because they wouldn't risk tipping me off a stretcher onto a bed and a stretcher is agony after the first few minutes – no support for your back, if you can understand. Also, I sneezed by mistake this afternoon which was most painful. But I've not had a thousandth part of what I suffered when they cut my nose about at Millbank: that made this a beanfeast by contrast.

As a matter of fact, I did die on my way down to the Field Ambulance and found myself just crossing Lethe by ferry. I had only just time to put on my gas-helmet to keep off the fumes of forgetfulness but managed it and on arrival at the other side began to feel much better. To cut short a long story, old Rhadamanthus introduced himself as my judge but I refused to accept his jurisdiction. I wanted a court-martial of British officers: he was only a rotten old Greek. He shouted out: 'Contempt of Court' but I chucked a Mills bomb at him which scattered the millions of the mouthless dead in about two seconds and wounded old R. in the leg and broke his sceptre. Then I strode away, held a revolver to Charon's head, climbed into the boat and so home. I gave him a Rouen note for 50 cm. which I didn't want particularly. Remained Cerberus whose three heads were, I noticed, mastiff, dalmatian and dachshund. He growled furiously and my revolver was empty, and I'd no ammunition. Happy thought: honeyed cakes and poppy seed. But none was handy; however, I had an excellent substitute – Army biscuit smeared with Tickler's 'plum and apple' and my little morphia tablets carefully concealed in the appetizing conserve. He snapped, swallowed, slumbered. I tiptoed past him, a free man and found myself being lowered on the floor of the 99th Field Ambulance. The doctor was saying 'hopeless case' (and this part of the tale is true, truer even than the rest) and I winked at him and said 'dear old doctor' and went off again to sleep.[42]

My sense of humour may have been enfeebled but I laughed till I was nearly ill yesterday over 100 copy lines which a Charterhouse master told my brother[43] to write the other day, to the effect that he mustn't be a baby. I can't reproduce the original exactly, but the result was ludicrous and more so as it was written in the very choicest copper-plate handwriting. It went something like this for eight pages:

I must endeavour to emerge from my present phase of infantility.
The symptoms of babyhood must be eradicated from my composition.
It behoves me to comport myself in a manner less typical of extreme
    juvenility.
I am bound by a moral obligation to rid myself of the characteristics
    of a youthful and childish baby.
I must not be a baby. Oh God, save me from shrinking
    smaller and smaller, from boyhood to babydom and finally from
    vanishing completely away, etc., etc.

Don't you love the 'youthful and childish baby'? It has a wonderful naiveté about it. Is the thing so funny because it was shown up to a master, or what?

I'm longing to see you on Saturday. Try to bring Ivor Novello[44] with you. I'd love to meet him, if he wouldn't be bored and you, busy man, could kill two birds with one stone by coming up and back with him.

Peter has promised thro' my brother to act on my suggestion and write his folk a tragic letter of cold pathos and reproach about my death for my country and the way they've treated him and me. He'll do it well; he's an artist. Charterhouse is at Camp on the Plain now.

I'm afraid, great as is the love I bear you, Jane Austen is too hard a nut to attempt to bite at with these weak jaws. Thanks awfully tho'. I have my Sorley here: he's my chief standby.

I see in the *Mail* today that a damnably nasty German cousin of mine has been killed flying. I remember once my sister in her young enthusiasm told him: 'Oh Wilhelm, what a lovely squirrel.' Up went his rifle and the squirrel fell dead at her feet. He couldn't understand her tears of rage. She'd admired the squirrel: he'd got it for her and was prepared to skin it then and there for her.

The brute used to climb up the only greengage tree in the orchard (this was Bavaria) and throw us down the stones. How I hated him! I was too young to climb trees myself.

I hope to hear from Ruth Mallory soon about George: I wrote to her yesterday. I've not heard a word since he left Havre.

I'm looking forward to Arthur Parry's letter.

Now goodbye till Saturday. I must write to Ralph ere they dout my light.

Ever yours affectionately   Robert

Funny that in 'The Queer Time' I should have talked about 'clutching at my right breast': it's just what I did on the 20th July!

Graves and Sassoon convalesced together at Harlech and spent their time getting their poems in order; Sassoon was working on his *Old Huntsman* collection and Graves on *Goliath and David*. 'We made a number of changes in each other's verses; I proposed amendments, which he accepted, in an obituary poem, "To His Dead Body" – written for me when he thought me dead.'[45]

In November they rejoined the battalion at Litherland, and shared a hut. A month later Graves attended a medical board; he was not yet fully recovered but when the president of the board asked him if he wanted a few months more home service he answered, with what Sassoon in *Memoirs of an Infantry Officer* describes as 'a sudden angry pride', that he should be much obliged if the board would pass him fit for service overseas. So, at the beginning of January, he prepared to go back to France for the third time, 'a glum, twenty-one-year-old veteran'.

At this time he received a letter (which has since been lost) from another young poet, Robert Nichols, who although he had never met Graves asked if he could dedicate to him part of his book of war poems, *Ardours and Endurances*, which was soon to be published. Nichols had been at Trinity College, Oxford, before the war but left in 1914 to take a commission with the Royal Field Artillery. However, after only three weeks in France he had been sent home as a neurasthenic (see page 319) and after five months in hospital was released from the army. Just as suddenly as he had written to Graves, he had sent a copy of his first book, *Invocation*, to Edward Marsh, who had responded encouragingly, and almost instantly he had entered the small circle of Marsh's closest friends.

> *S'addresser à*
> Capt. Robert Graves
> 3rd R W Fus.
> The Huts

7 January 1917
> Litherland
> Liverpool

Dear Robert Nichols,

I had M. Forbes's letter forwarded to me today from old Enrico Festing Jones, and contrary to my usual habits, answer at once.

Of course you may: I'd simply love it. It's hard to say how cheered I am: Orderly Room and battalion drill and company ledgers and the town of Liverpool and the enforced society of young gentlemen whose sole amusements are liqueur shifting and promiscuous fornication, had almost convinced me that there was no God in Heaven nor any bay trees on Parnassus. I feel tremendously honoured.

Funny how things happen. As you may suspect, I'm a very very ardent Sorleian and when I saw your letter in the *Westminster*

Gazette about him (I had missed the article about the Literary Losses) I asked S. Sassoon (a poet of some note who funnily enough has strayed into this battalion and shares a hut with me) who you were because I felt sure you were a fellow of the right stuff. He reminded me of that *Oxford Poetry* book and I remembered that your things were far and away the best in that collection and that Eddie Marsh was very keen on them. I've got a very bad memory, worse since I met an old shell last July, and I somehow didn't connect the two. Did you know Sorley before his death? I met him at Oxford in 1913 when we were both up there for scholarships, but didn't realize who he was – wasted opportunities, horrid to look back on. I suppose you've got the new edition with the prose illustrations? They are good.

This fellow Sassoon, not exactly a prepossessing name for a poet, perhaps, was out in France with me in 1915 and is a most extraordinary good man. He writes in all these old papers: *Nation*, *Westminster Gazette*, *The Times*, the *Spectator*, *Saturday Review* and things, and says what he means very courageously. No Union Jack flapping or sword waving, but just a picture of France from the front trench, and our 'brutal and licentious soldiery'. He's not musical, always, but it's good stuff; original too and not redolent of Masefield as is so common these days and contains no ode either to Kitchener or Rupert Brooke. Look out for his *The Old Foxhunter and Other Poems* [sic] about February or March, with William Heinemann. I was to have brought out a second volume at the same time, but hitches occurred as are usual and it's off now. Heinemann wanted too big a book. I hate huge, lumpy, complete collections. Life's too short for that: we aren't all Keats or Sorleys. In the *Brazier* there are only about ten that I'd have liked to print. Publishers, patrons, and above all literary executors have a most damnable power over the mere writer. Well, cheeroh, and best of luck and don't recover from your shell-shock too soon. I'm rather stupidly going back to France this week with only one lung – having deceived the medical board. Chiefly because I want to hurry into hospital again and do a bit of writing for which soldiering provides no leisure.

Yours   Robert Graves

I hope to see you sometime when I come on leave, in London, say, or *aprés-la-guerre* at any rate. But before you write out the dedication, please consider first if you've got a family or friend or patron who'd be offended. They are most awfully touchy about these things.

Have you seen that book called *Wheels?*[46] I hear our Evan Morgan[47] was to have contributed but failed to provide anything at the last moment. What a pity! I should have loved to see his poems wedded with Iris Tree's – a fitting and loathsome union.

To Siegfried Sassoon

25 January 1917   No. 5 IBD
                                                                 Rouen
                                                                 BEF

My dear old Sassons,

I have been posted to the 2nd Battalion and go up tomorrow: all the other fellows are going to various RWF Battalions – chiefly 38th Divisional. Harper goes to the 16th. It's most damnably cold here, especially in tents. I saw Lawrence Armrod today, also Egerton. On the 48 hours leave I saw Peter and had a long talk with him: he was extraordinarily intelligent and seems now to have read about four times as much poetry as myself – makes me rather afraid of him.

Also I met Robert Nichols: you'll be amused at where I found him – in a private hospital having an injection of 606:[48] his commission has been cancelled on this account. But I liked him in a way: quite enthusiastic about the right things and very well read. So I gave him a hell of a lecture on his ways, and finding he took it well, made friends with him. It was the usual story – shellshock, friends all killed, too much champagne, sex, desperate fornication, syphilis.

I spent today going round the Rouen churches and the Cathedral – by God, they are wonderful, almost persuade one to be a Christian.

About going to the 1st Battalion: I'll tell you how to do it if you are posted to another. Get hold of Egerton, ask his address from the Hôtel de la Poste in the Rue Jeanne d'Arc – he knows all about you. Then suggest to him you'd like to be temporary unfit for a day or two till the First Battalion want an officer. I think he'll arrange it. Use a little suction.

On reporting here to the 5th IBD Adjutant the first thing that I met was the old *Brazier* on the Orderly Room Table; rather amusing.

I'm looking forward like anything to *The Old Huntsman*: it's going to be the hell of a book. My love to Mr Robert Hamner:[49] tell him the composition of a letter absolutely devoid of a single 'whimsicality' is too great a strain on my one remaining lung but that I'll beat him at squash as soon as I next come out of hospital.

I hope the Chiswick stunt[50] is all right. Send me the bill as soon as you get it.

Yours ever affectionately   Robert

PS. I have just arrived at the Second Battalion. James Cuthbert is commanding. Tibs was shot last night through the arm and thigh by a bloody fool of a 20th Royal Fusilier: I don't think he's bad. De Miremont and D'Arcy Fox have gone. We are at 'freeze' in both senses. Young Jagger has flu. Everyone else I know is on leave. Decent dug-outs here, at any rate.

When Graves arrived at headquarters the battalion doctor, Captain Dunn (who in 1938 wrote *The War the Infantry Knew*) asked him what he meant by returning so soon; Graves answered: 'I couldn't stand England any longer.' Dunn then told the acting CO that Graves was unfit for trench service and he was therefore put in command of the headquarter company and went to live with the transport at Frise Bend.

From there he wrote to Robert Nichols who was then writing his poem 'Faun's Holiday' and who had asked Graves to help him 'feed his faun with cherries'.

2 February 1917

My dear Robert

What a ripping letter! I wrote you one a day or two ago and though it's a bad habit I must write another. You're lucky, to be able to be so happy in England: I couldn't while the War lasts. How should I feed your faun with cherries? Would I were able! But the Somme and Hippocrene are both frozen over hard and white with snow above. But I'll try to break a hole in the ice and sing dolorously like a sad bittern or an orphaned pismire.

To Robert who'd have me feed his Faun with Cherries[51]

Like a sad bittern, I
Sing to you mournfully.
Here by a snow bound river
In scrapen holes we shiver,
Why should your poet rhyme
June grass and summer ease,
Sleek fauns and cherry time,
Vague music and green trees,
And Life born young again
For your gay goatish brute
Drunk with warm melodies
Singing on banks of thyme,
Lips dark with juicy stain
Ears hung with bobbing fruit?
No, Robert, there's small reason;
Cherries are out of season.
Ice grips at branch and root
And all the birds are mute.

I love what you say about a lofty spirit. Lofty without being
pompous, hard without being cruel; also soft without
sentimentality. A poet has to be such a hell of a lot of things
besides a mere craftsman. My idea of a poet is a woman suffering
all the hardships of a man; hardening her weak softnesses; healthy
and clean, loving the elements, loving friends more than life itself,
proud, whimsical, wise, simple. But appreciating the refinements of
Life as much as the harshnesses – warm sun on the bare chest,
comfortable armchairs, a good fire, a jolly red Burgundy or claret,
music above all and colour and sleep, and mountains seen from a
distance as well as from the precipice face of Lliwedd.
    Yes, please send me de Vigny, tho' he did read Milton (or was it
Bridges?[52]) Look here, Robert; I'll risk your being annoyed, if you
are you'd be no friend of mine, but nowadays one doesn't 'view
the constellations quietly, quietly burning', at least not after one's
left school. 'Moral austerity'? Sorley talks of the spiky stars that
shine: less luxuriant, sharper, more effective.
    Call me a grandmother: I like being ragged. But oh, Robert,
you've got all the qualities of a poet if you want, and it seems
such a rotten stunt for you to sit in a *kimono* to view
constellations quietly, quietly burning, and read Bridges. You want
to get away from all that into a new method. Yes, Bridges is just
what you claim for him, a nice common little geranium flower

from the nursery gardens – better than the tea roses of the nineties or the passion flowers of these bad fellows like Byron and Co., but brethren, as the parsons say, there are harebells and rowan-trees on your own hills, what need ye more? I don't apologize for this. I mean it and I feel Somme trenches give me the right even to blasphemy of the Holy Spirit if I feel so inclined.

Yours affectionately   Robert

In February 1917, Graves's health broke down again. Dr Dunn diagnosed bronchitis and sent him to the Red Cross Hospital in Rouen, where he had been taken after being wounded in the previous July. At the hospital an RAMC major recognized him and said: 'What on earth are you doing out in France, young man? If I find you and those lungs of yours in my hospital again, I'll have you court-martialled.'[53] From Rouen he was sent to Somerville College, Oxford, which had been converted into a hospital for the duration of the war.

In February Graves's second book of poems, *Goliath and David*, partly edited by Sassoon, was privately printed at the Chiswick Press (200 copies) and distributed to friends and various literary figures by Graves, Sassoon and Robert Ross, who helped and advised Graves a lot at this time.

After a while in hospital Graves went up to Harlech to convalesce, and from there wrote to Sassoon who was now back in France with the 2nd Battalion. By not being there himself Graves felt that he was somehow letting Sassoon down, but Sassoon wrote that he was unspeakably relieved to think of him safely back home.

                                                                                         Erinfa
26 March 1917   Harlech
                                                                                         N. Wales

Dear old Sassons

Please forgive my not writing: it has been one of the worst symptoms of my late collapse that I haven't been able to make up my mind to start or finish the most pressing things, and the correspondence about *Goliath and David* has been most exacting. Thanks awfully for all you did to edit the book. It has been a great success all round. Especially old Gosse wrote a ripping letter, which is most important.

While in Oxford I saw a lot of the Garsington[54] people who were charming to me, and of the young Oxford poets, Aldous Huxley, Wilfred Childe and Thomas Earp – exceptionally nice people but a trifle decayed, as you might say. While there I arranged about a job which seems quite likely to come off and is indeed practically settled: an instructorship in No. 4 Officer Cadet Battalion with its headquarters in my own college. It should also last about eight months.

I have just come up to good old Cymraeg after a very tiring week in town seeing people, especially the Half Moon Street set:[55] great fun.

I don't dare tell you how jolly it is here for fear of making you envious: Good God, the Somme was awful when I left it last month! Here, absolute peace and quiet: soft colours, sheep, stolid peasants, rough old rocks. Heaven!

I sent a copy of *Goliath and David* to old Professor Sorley[56] who retaliated, dear old man, by sending me the sixty-second copy (of a limited edition of sixty-six) of *Letters from Germany and the Army*: C. H. Sorley. They are the full context from which the ones you saw in *Marlborough and Other Poems* are taken.

I'm glad you're with young Orme: he's a good lad: give him my love. A thing few people realize is what a jolly good fellow (though quite unlike 'Young Joe') old Yates is: always grumbling and very much on his dignity but he's got a kind heart and won't be bullied.

I have just discovered a great poet, a chap called Skelton (1460–1525) of whom there's been no edition since 1843[57]: a true Englishman and a man after my heart; wrote beautiful doggerel nonsense and thoroughly irresponsible and delightful jingles, though 'the first scholar in the land' according to Erasmus. Of him more anon.

I am most tremendously looking forward to *The Old Huntsman*: I don't see why it shouldn't be awfully successful, with all the reviewers and literary patrons squared.

But 'syphilitic' and the *Spectator*! Haw! Haw![58]

The pacifists are putting up at the next election not a measly and pathetic conscientious objector but a soldier called Armstrong with only one leg, a D S O and an MC. What a score! Where are you now more or less?

Best love,

yours

Robert Wingle[59]

P S. I was up at Litherland the other day and saw Bobby; just preparing to go out again. Dear boy! I wonder what Beaumaris thinks of its Town Clerk!

In April Graves became an instructor in one of the officer cadet battalions quartered in the men's colleges at Oxford.

'D' Company
No. 4 Officer Cadet Battn
Wadham College
Oxford

21 April 1917

My dear Sassons

At last I am comfortably settled down here, and by Heaven, it's a good game now that I'm cured of the desire to go back to France (I know I'm more use here and would only crock up if I tried a fourth time) and if it wasn't for you being out there again I'd feel this was too good to be true. Get a cushy quick, old thing and I'll work this sort of a job for you here. Anyhow, get sent to Somerville if you get over to Blighty at all: in time to read your reviews with me.

Well, where to start my news? I think with old Gosse with whom I went to tea last week: he was adorably kind and so was Mrs G. They are ripping friends to have. It appears the bloody paper question is holding up *The Old Huntsman*. It's going to be a hell of a success when it does appear: I've seen Uncle Charles about it, breaking it gently to him that it's pretty strong meat and I think he'll review it well notwithstanding, on the strength of your M C and so on.

Old Gosse wrote me a letter of introduction to John Masefield who is coming to live here for the summer, next door to Robert Bridges. What a pair!

The *Life of Swinburne*[60] is fine: a curious cyclone of a man; and do you know, exactly like Robert Nichols with whom I am now on the best terms. Robert is an awfully good chap and you'd like him awfully after you'd read his new stuff. I admit his temperament is not ours but the circumstances I first met him in last January were more the exception than the rule and it seems to have been largely bad luck.

He's written a poem which on reading the other night (I admit I had well drunk of good ripe Burgundy) absolutely knocked me.

It's called 'The Assault'[61] and mostly about 'them there zero' and 'over the top with the best of luck'. I do hope the battalion is still going strong. Lawrence Ormrod is a dear and old Dunn and Yates I really do feel very warmly about. I'm sending old Father Yates some fish. I'd do the same to you if I wasn't pretty sure that you keep well supplied. My salaams to the Worm: he's a good lad.

I've been a lot over to Garsington considering how damned busy I am. Lady Utterly Immoral is such a ripper and Julian[62] and I are most intimate now. How much did you get from the *Nation*? I got 30 shillings this morning, i.e. 3 shillings a line, pretty good going.

Have I told you of my sudden discovery of John Skelton (1460–1525), the court poet of Henry VII; one of the really good men? When he heard of my grand passion for him Robbie embarrassed me rather by buying me the only complete edition of J.S., 1843, very rare and beautifully bound. I still get letters about *David and Goliath* [sic]. Such kind ones from Drinkwater[63] and Gordon Bottomley and Duncan Grant[64] and a nice grubby little postcard from William Davies. I can't write much here but I hope to do a book of studies chiefly about Poetry and Children and France and things.

Best love   Robert

At the Hindenburg Line in April, Sassoon was shot through the right shoulder while leading a bombing party in an attack on trenches recently recaptured by the Germans; though wounded, Sassoon continued bombing until he collapsed; he and his men succeeded in driving the Germans out of the trenches 'and the brigadier sent Siegfried's name in for a Victoria Cross – a recommendation refused, however, on the ground that the operations had been unsuccessful; for the Cameronians were later driven out again by a bombing party under some German Siegfried.'[65] Robbie Ross was the first to hear of Sassoon's wound and told Graves, who immediately wrote to Sassoon at the 4th London Hospital on Denmark Hill. Two pages of the letter have been lost.

22 April 1917

Poor Old Sassons!
    '*Blessé pour la patrie*' and according to Robbie rather too

slightly to serve any useful purpose. I wrote to you in France yesterday; how stupid because it was a decent sort of letter!

My sister Rosaleen is nursing at your hospital: I'll tell her to come and visit you.

I'm so glad you're at home in time for your reviews, as it seems the book is coming out very soon.[66]

. . . .

you've expanded it and made it a little clearer, and 'Noah' looks quite different and very brilliant in print. 'The Last Meeting' looks very well and I expect will sound ripping if decently read. My only regret is 'Stand-to: Good Friday Morning'. A blasphemous poem must be frightfully good to hit it and you hadn't the patience to work this right: I know it was a very obstinate poem but you could have solved it. The best stanza in this book, probably in any book of war poems, is the middle one of 'Died of Wounds'. It knocks me more every time.

But they're all ripping however often I've read them; I have to take the 'lutanies of sin' on trust because I can't understand them but I'm sure they must be good.[67]

And I'm deeply grateful for the 'Letter' put so importantly at the end: it is really most awfully good, sort of slips down your throat without having to be swallowed if only you'll alter the punctuation of the first stanza in the next edition. That is a full-stop after 'send it' and a colon, or semicolon, after 'row'!

Sassons if you can tell me about your sickleave, etc., and when you'll be fit for light duty I could get you a job in a cadet Battalion: possibly here but certainly somewhere nice (Cambridge?), through my colonel.

. . . .   [Unsigned]

The officers at cocktail bars is a splendid touch. I hadn't seen that poem before.[68]

Two years ago today I set sail for France!

Hard work in the damp Oxford climate proved too much for Graves's poor health: 'I kept myself going for two months on a strychnine tonic, then fainted and fell down a staircase one evening in the dark, cutting my head; I was taken back to Somerville.'[69] After a short time there he was sent to Osborne Palace, on the Isle of Wight, which was being used as a convalescent home for officers.

70

Sassoon was also convalescing, at Chapelwood Manor in Sussex, and was in a great state of agitation because of his ambivalent attitude to the war; in *Goodbye to All That* Graves describes a letter he received from him at this time:

In April, Yates had sent him a note saying that four officers were killed and seven wounded in a show at Fontaine-les-Croiselles – a 'perfectly bloody battle'. But the Battalion advanced nearly half a mile which, to Siegfried, seemed some consolation. Yet in the very next sentence he wrote how mad it made him to think of the countless good men being slaughtered that summer, and all for nothing. The bloody politicians and ditto generals with their cursed incompetent blundering and callous ideas would go on until they tired of it or had got as much kudos as they wanted . . . [he] went on to say that if, as a protest, he refused to go out again, they would only accuse him of being afraid of shells. . .[70]

At this time Sassoon began writing his most powerful antiwar poems; at the end of June he sent Graves one which he had just written, on the death of one of their brother officers, called 'To Any Dead Officer'; he later revised it considerably, adopting several of Graves's suggestions, and published it in *Counter-Attack* (1918).

30 June 1917   Osborne
                                                                Isle of Wight

Dear old Sassons

Without doubt a great poem: poor little Orme, he'd have been awfully pleased with it. The simple effect would be strengthened by a more regular sweep in the first half of each verse: as it stands it would worry people who didn't know much about poetry: it breaks the flow of sense.

Trusting to your good nature I've pencilled in some tentative suggestions.

The short seventh line comes in well, though. It has a more definite reason for faltering than the third.

Filthy is not quite right somehow I think.

Thinking – the metre makes it ∪ ∪

Grumbling – the metre makes it — ∪

And anyhow it's not an antithesis, as it seems to be.

With is the word, I'm sure.

Three years is preface to the *two years* in the last verse.

I don't think that the tragedy can quite take the strain of *young feller*. I wish it could, but I'm very doubtful.

What a ripping way to turn the metre at the end to get the smooth excellence of the last line.

I know you'll forgive these remarks, because you've patched up poems for me before now. And without my corrections it is a great poem, so you needn't notice them.

> . . . and Caesar said
> 'Why, it is excellent: I like the thing.'[71]

Robbie has my *Fairies and Fusiliers* manuscript if you happen to be in town and want to see what I've been at.

Best love

Robert

Just after posting this letter another arrived from Sassoon, which again Graves describes: 'Down in Kent he could hear the guns thudding ceaselessly across the Channel, on and on, until he didn't know whether he wanted to rush back and die with the First Battalion, or stay in England and do what he could to prevent the war going on. But both courses were hopeless.'[72]

He told Graves he had other things in his head, not poems, and Graves wrote back:

I have just posted a letter I wrote this morning but your new one has come. Look here, why don't you come and see me down here.

. . . .

Do say you're coming: I want to know what characteristic devilment this is. Are you standing as pacifist M P? That's the most characteristic thing I can think of next to your bombing Lloyd George.

Yours,

R.

I've also written on Sorley. Bob Nichols of course is no Sorley but he's next best, a devout admirer.

I've a copy of my new poems here.

In July Robert Nichols's book of poems, *Ardours and Endurances*, was published (and proved to be one of the best-selling books of the year). He had, however, changed his mind about dedicating it to Graves.

No date

My dear Bob,

. . . .

Here we live among decaying royalty and the mouldered memories of Prince Albert Great and Good, in whose honour I and a journalist called Bartlett[73] have formed a rag society; now very strong and hilarious after two meetings. We affect Albert chains and sidewhiskers and invent monstrous yarns about our hero.

I liked Evan Morgan so much, prepared though I was to dislike him cordially because I had somehow met more of his enemies than his friends.

Congratulations on your reviews in both *The Times'*, *Sunday* and Ordinary. Aren't you sending me a copy of *Ardours*? I haven't seen it.

As you say, S.S. has spoilt his *Huntsman* by one or two quite frigid and meaningless pieces, but then that's Heinemann's fault. I am just finishing my new book of poems, *Fairies and Fusiliers*, and I hope Heinemann will think well of it.

People are talking now of Edward Eastaway,[74] and W. J. Turner.[75] Both, so far as I can judge, are a wash-out. I'm sorry about that dedication. Still, I quite see it can't be helped. We caused great fun down here yesterday, the journalist and I, by fixing up a most picturesque and smelly drowned sailor on the beach which deceived many, including majors and colonels and their kind.

I have with me here my Sorley, my Skelton, my Keats and my ballad book; also my dear Apuleius, so I'm not too badly off. I'll write you a critique of *Ardours* when I get it.

Yours ever

Robert

A few days later he wrote to Edward Marsh.

No date [Summer 1917]

My dear Eddie

I am ashamed not to have written to report progress for so long but I've been ill again; collapse after too much work with my cadet battalion. I hope you're fairly happy in the Colonial Office: it sounds awfully dull. I hope you're properly impressed with

Robert Nichols's book, *Ardours and Endurances*. It is
tremendously new and strong I think, especially the soldier pieces
and 'The Faun' in spite of a conventional theme. The last part of
the book was dedicated to me until the last minute when one of
Bob's lost loves consented to accept it. Rather a disappointment.

I hear you've been converted to Siegfried Sassoon's new poetry:
the later stuff is very curious and vigorous. I don't know if you
realize that you are responsible for giving me advice which I
passed on to him. But the earlier sort he wrote, though I suppose
very perfect technically, means nothing at all to me: a pity, I think,
he included it. I am just getting a book ready for Heinemann if
he'll take it, now that I've got enough written to satisfy the 3
shillings and 6 pence or 5 shillings public. Naturally it shall not
appear without your inspection and approval. It is to be called, I
think I told you, *Fairies and Fusiliers*.

Old Gosse gave me an introduction to Masefield at Oxford but I
missed him; however, he has read my *Goliath and David* and
seems to approve.

Yours affectionately   Robert

To Siegfried Sassoon

3 July 1917

My dear Sassons
Bob Nichols writes:

Dear Robert
Eddie Marsh writes to me telling me that Masefield has just sent him a
note – there is a sentence concerns us. 'Nichols, Graves and Sassoon are
singing together like the morning stars.' So Bravo the three of us! Send on
the news to S.S.
Thine   Robert Nichols

So I hope you're pleased. Father Watkin tells me you're going to a
cadet battalion at Cambridge. Is this approximately the truth?
Poor old Watkin, his wound has healed and broken twice and it
now has healed again, probably only to go back to the start again.

Attwater is in hospital with him, flu, at Fezackerly.

I don't know what to do when I leave here. I don't want to go
back to Litherland and I'm afraid of overdoing it again if I go
back to a Cadet Battalion, even though more healthily situated

than Oxford or Cambridge. They say that Gales is a good place. I may apply to get there.

I am feeling much better than when I came. Oh, I forgot, the Poet Laureate[76] likes Robert Graves's work too (not only S.S.'s) and sent a special congratulatory message to him through the mouth of Masefield. I often show your things to people to see what they say and they seem to love your newer poetry especially 'Young Croesus' and 'The Bishop'.

Yours affectionately   ·R·

Edward Marsh was then preparing *Georgian Poetry III* for the press and wrote to Graves asking permission to use some of his poems in the anthology, which was to contain the work of eight other young poets, as well as Graves, including Sassoon, Turner, Nichols and Rosenberg.

8 July 1917

My dear Eddie

It was very exciting to get your letter about *Georgian Poetry 1916–1917* and I need hardly say how bucked I am. Please take whatever you like out of this lot which I send, and out of the old *Brazier*, except the 'Foxhunter'.[77] I'm awfully sorry but there are personal reasons why it shouldn't be published again: some people in the regiment were very sick about it when it came out first, and only condoned it because the *Brazier* was such an obscure production: now I'm not going to make matters worse if I can. I'm sure you'll understand. Then there's Osborn of the *Morning Post* to consider: Robert Nichols told me he'd like me to be included in Osborn's anthology[78] which includes Nichols and Siegfried and, I think, Turner, besides Rupert and Julian Grenfell[79] and Sorley and the great dead, so of course I was very pleased. But Osborn just happens to want the things of mine you don't, except, I think, 'Goliath and David', so it's not so bad. But I can't remember, because I was ill at the time, exactly what he wrote to ask for: will you mind please asking him what he proposes to print, and arranging accordingly. Oh, and 'Double Red Daisies' and 'Dead Cow Farm' are appearing in *Oxford Poetry 1917* because Earp and Wilfred Childe asked me for something as a souvenir of my stay with them.

But I only wish I'd known about *GP* first so that you could have had first choice. I'm awfully glad you're so impressed with Bob Nichols, he's a great lad. And you've chosen the best of S.S. Turner I don't much believe in.

I don't know yet about this Heinemann book: whether Heinemann will take it, but now I've got a lot of allies in High Places and in the press I expect he will. I sent one of my copies to Ross, who is acting as go-between, to see if Heinemann would consider it: you remember H. wrote through Ross last October saying he'd like to see anything I'd written, but then Monro held me up. Do you think now that Monro would be inclined to let me reprint three poems out of the *Brazier* in the new Heinemann book, it would help such a lot: 'The Poet in the Nursery', 'Cherrytime' and 'The First Funeral'? Only three: I'll not be able to come to London for weeks or months so I'm afraid I can't see these people personally; but I'm much less ill now and can write again.

I am very fond indeed of Nichols but he's rather violent and I was ill when he came to see me: *hinc illae pyramides*.

Yours affectionately
Robert

Sassoon, encouraged mainly by Bertrand Russell, decided to refuse to serve further in the army even though it was clear he could, if he wanted, remain on home service and not go back to the war. He made his intentions and motives public by publishing in the press a statement called 'Finished with the War', in which he wrote:

I am a soldier, convinced that I am acting on behalf of soldiers. I believe that this war, upon which I entered as a war of defence and liberation, has now become a war of aggression and conquest ... I am not protesting against the conduct of the war, but against the political errors and insincerities for which the fighting men are being sacrificed.

Graves, although agreeing with Sassoon's opinions and thinking him 'magnificently courageous', believed Sassoon was in no proper physical condition to endure court martial and imprisonment; he also believed that the gesture was a futile one, as nobody would follow his example either in England or Germany. His initial reaction is shown in the following letter to Edward Marsh, who had been reading the manuscript of *Fairies and Fusiliers*, and had sent Graves a list of notes and a letter about Sassoon (which has been lost).

12 July 1917
(In bed, 12 midnight)

My dear Eddie
   What an excellent and sensible letter!
   About Sassons first. It's an awful thing – completely mad – that he's done. Such rotten luck on you and me and his friends, especially in the Regiment. They all think he's mad: and they'd be prepared to hush it up if the Army Council don't get to hear of the bomb shop incident,[80] but I don't think S.S. will let them hush it up. I don't know what on earth to do now. I'm not going to quarrel with Sassons: I'm so glad you realize that he's not a criminal which was the line I was afraid you'd take. Personally I think he's quite right in his views but absolutely wrong in his action . . . It would be true friendship for me to heap coals of fire on the head of the dog that bit me by turning pacifist myself but you can be quite assured that I'm a sound militarist in action however much of a pacifist in thought. In theory the War ought to stop tomorrow if not sooner. Actually we'll have to go on while a rat or a dog remains to be enlisted and the remains of the famous Kilkenny cats will look nothing remarkably small compared with ours. 'Better no world than a world ruled by Prussia!' (there speaks my old Danish grandmother!) This S.S. business has taken me at a very bad time, nervous breakdown, and again today the worst possible news about my friend Peter who appears to have taken a very wrong turning and to have had a mental breakdown.
   I only wish I'd known about S.S. in time: it would never have happened if I'd been there but I've not seen him since January. Thank you so much for approaching Monro again about the *Brazier*. But I somehow don't expect any luck.
   Now about the poems. I'm awfully glad you like most of the new ones: I haven't been at all sure about them, being alone with nobody to tell me are they good or are they bad, so it's most reassuring.
   The great test is 'Finland' which you have ennobled yourself in my eyes by appreciating. It was made in a poetry game I played with Sassons once on that set subject. He wrote an extremely decorative sonnet which though most admirably tooled and finished had not the true spiritual feeling of my nonsense.
   Everything you say about my notes I thoroughly agree to: I

welcome a friend who tells me that I may strangle my offsprings at birth when they are obviously abortions; I shall go through them very carefully in view of your remarks about strangers' misconstruction of their spirit, and promise to cut out any bramble or stumbling block. Ronald is always occurring for Roderick even when I know what his name is: it's like the way I used to call Mother 'Mrs Kingscote' after the school matron, in the holidays. Yknarc times, as a matter of fact, are a quotation from *Erewhon*:

Lo, with the dews of these most yknarc times
My love looks fresh.

Thank you so much for reading through them. Ross is showing the poems to Heinemann without the prose first: that's more diplomatic, I think.

If you find you happen to have any old poems of mine which might be rewritten I wish you'd let me have them.

Today I heard from George Mallory, 83 Portland Place W., a convalescent home. Do go and see him if you can. Excuse this scrawl, I'm upset thoroughly and very tired.

Yours affectionately   Robert

I enclose an old poem reset.

The 'worst possible news' Graves had received about his friend Peter was that he had been arrested for making 'a certain proposal' to a Canadian corporal stationed near Charterhouse.[81] This news deeply shocked Graves and cured him of the 'pseudo-homosexuality' his experiences at Charterhouse had induced in him. After his arrest Johnstone was sent to be treated by Dr W. H. R. Rivers, the eminent psychologist, neurologist and anthropologist, and later joined the army. Graves did not meet him again until after the war, when they were both up at Oxford; Graves found him then disagreeably pleasant and 'so greatly changed that it seemed absurd to have ever suffered on his account. Yet the caricature likeness to the boy I had loved persisted.'[82] They never met again, though Johnstone left him his books in his will, a bequest refused by Graves on Johnstone's death in 1949.

Graves decided he must personally attend to 'this Siegfried business' and, although not yet fully recovered, attended a medical board and asked the doctors as a favour to pass him fit and discharge him from Osborne. He consulted with Marsh about what to do and also wrote two letters: one to the 3rd Battalion at Litherland asking the colonel to be sympathetic when considering Sassoon's actions, the other to Evan Morgan[83] who was private secretary to W. C. Bridgman, Minister of Labour, asking him to use his influence to prevent republication of, and comment on, Sassoon's statement, and to arrange for a suitable reply to be given if a question was asked about it in the House of Commons.

. . . Evan's Minister persuaded the War Office not to press the matter as a disciplinary case, but to give Siegfried a medical board. I rejoined the Battalion and met him at Liverpool. He looked very ill; he told me that he had just been down to the Formby links and thrown his Military Cross into the sea. We discussed the political situation; I took the line that everyone was mad except ourselves and one or two others, and that no good could come of offering common sense to the insane. Our only possible course would be to keep on going out until we got killed. I expected myself to go back soon, for the fourth time. Besides, what would the First and Second Battalion think of him? . . .

He refused to agree with me, but I made it plain that his letter had not been given, and would not be given, the publicity he intended. At last, unable to deny how ill he was, Siegfried consented to appear before the medical board.[84]

	3rd RWF
19 July 1917	Litherland
	Liverpool

My Dear Eddie
It's all right about Siegfried. After awful struggling with everybody (I arrived at 59 minutes past the eleventh hour) I've smoothed it all down and he's going away cheerfully to a home at Edinboro'. I've written to the pacifists who were to support him telling them that the evidence as to his mental condition given at his Medical Board is quite enough to make them look damned silly if they go on with the game and ask questions in the House about his defiance.[85] I'm quite knocked up. About the poetry I'll write later when I've got some sleep.
Yours affectionately   R.

How splendid about Winston![86]

Graves himself gave evidence at the medical board and was in such a bad state of nerves that he broke into tears three times while giving his statement; he was told he ought to be before the board himself. Sassoon was sent to Craiglockhart War Hospital near Edinburgh, a convalescent home for neurasthenics, with Graves as his escort: 'Siegfried and I both thought this a great joke, especially when I missed the train and he reported to "Dottyville", as he called it, without me.'[87] Graves returned to the 3rd Battalion.

31 July 1917

My dear Sassons

The blushing star came back all right to be met with a strafe from the adjutant for not telling him he was in the middle of a revolver course. Otherwise all well. Yesterday afternoon had a great game of squash with young Freeman who goes back to France tomorrow. Well, you are notorious throughout England now you silly old thing! Everybody here who's been to France agrees with your point of view, but those that don't know you think it was not quite a gentlemanly course to take: the 'quixotic-English-sportsman' class especially. But you have accomplished something I suppose. Now that you have been immortalized in the columns of the *Daily Mail* and *The Times* I suppose strings of newspaper reporters are surging round the doors of Craiglockhart and the inmates seething within? What a ridiculous business! I hope it won't injure your poetry: and that old Gosse won't think better of celebrating his protégé in the *Edinburgh Review*. I'm longing to get my Sorley back. Hurry up with it. Any poetry appeared yet? Don't forget to weight your lines a bit more.

Be good.

Yours affectionately   Robert

I met Castle yesterday, who introduced himself. He's in my company: a good fellow. I have discovered that the adjutant has a soul. He reads poetry and before the war spent two years at Oxford House in the slums, besides playing cricket for Middlesex and hunting. He reads the better sort of poetry too, Robert Nichols and Rupert and that wicked old creature S.S.

Poor devils at Pilkem!

At Craiglockhart Sassoon was also a patient of Dr W. H. R. Rivers, as were Wilfred Owen and Frank Prewett (1893–1962), a

Canadian-born poet whom Graves became friends with at Oxford after the war, referred to in later letters by his nickname Toronto. Rivers was very interested in poetry and on hearing about Graves from Sassoon he went to buy Graves's book, but bought, by mistake, Charles Graves's ('my *Spectator* uncle') *War's Surprises* instead.

On 8 August Sassoon wrote telling Graves that he had been asked to contribute some poems to an anthology being prepared by Bertram Lloyd and that when sending off his poems had written to Lloyd suggesting he ask Graves for a contribution as well. He also wrote: 'What do you think of the latest push? How splendid this attrition is!' And quoted Lord Crewe: 'We are not the least depressed.' Graves matched this with a remark of Lloyd George's.

Army Form C. 348

Memorandum

From: Robert
To: Sassons

9 August 1917

Dear old Sassons

I don't think of sending the Lloyd man anything. It's a bad principle I think to make oneself cheap, and he might (as Bobbie would say) be a Conscious Object and bring discredit on the dear old Regiment and get me court-martialled and sent to Craiglockhart for contributing to his book. But seriously, I don't believe in advertisements of that nature and I don't think you ought to get anthologized without due regard to your position on the slopes of Parnassus.[88] The Second Battalion is at Nieuport. Old Yates was on leave last night and told me all the news. He says that they're not depressed more than usual out there: they still don't think beyond the mail and the rum-issue. They're again in the Army of Pursuit.

I met Tibs in Chester yesterday: they say he won't be given another command in France: he was too outspoken about the 33rd Division, on the Somme. Young Stan sends his love. Heinemann is going to publish my things this autumn. Enclosed his letter. Say you're pleased: I'll not send in the proofs before you've seen them. Mind you lose them in a railway carriage like I did yours. If you find you have any nice poems lying about that you don't want send them here and I'll change them to suit my mood and let them masquerade as my own like a few words of mine in *The Old Huntsman*. It will save me putting in what Heinemann calls 'the less successful ones' of my own.

What a disappointment for Rivers to get *War's Surprises*: it must have justified its title when it arrived. I spend most of my spare time at the Racquet Club hitting about with old John. I am really getting quite fit again now – but not for France. Bobbie wrote that he'll be back here 'in the fold' in about 3 weeks. Yes, this attrition is a peculiarly jolly business. As Lloyd George says: 'Why should we not sing?' and also: 'The Blinds of Britain are not yet drawn.' I'll send Rivers a copy of the *Goliath and David* (my last) as a token of esteem and regard: salute for me that excellent man. Send me Sorley when you can and also if you can the Elizabethan [Song] Book (though I believe I gave it you). There's a man here who can play them well.

Best love

Robert

At this time Graves was preparing his third volume of poems, *Fairies and Fusiliers*, for publication; originally he had intended to dedicate it to Siegfried Sassoon but at the last moment decided instead to dedicate it to the Royal Welch Fusiliers.

13 September 1917

Dearest Sassons

If you'd been anyone else you'd have thought me a first-class four-letter man for changing the dedication like that, but you know it wasn't meant for anything, except that I was afraid at the last moment of a dedication to an individual for fear of jealousy from Gosse, Ross, Marsh, Masefield or anyone like that of my 'friends and lovers' not to mention the family. Also, I thought that to point my devotion to the regiment would strengthen my expression of hatred for the war.

I see your point, and as I want to take your advice wherever I can I have written to cancel this if Heinemann agrees. But a dedication means an extra leaf to a book already so thin that quite recently Heinemann nearly decided to wait to the Spring till it got bigger. Robbie stopped him. If he insists on the dedication, at any rate it shall read simply 'To the Royal Welch Fusiliers'. I'm so sorry for my stupidity. Talking of Heinemann, Viscount French is to inspect us in three weeks: any messages? Pyers Mostyn is back here with three gold stripes from Messpots,[89] Eric Procter with four after a head wound again, both looking very fragile. Hawes is a captain again and sends his love, so also did Tibs I forgot to tell you. Bobby is due back this week, quite well again. Poor Julian[90] was ill since he was discharged, brainfever due to worry about Ginchy where he somehow thinks he didn't do well enough, but he's in a good place I hear from 'Birdy' S. I do my best to cheer up the listless atmosphere of Litherland with wry jokes and my usual grotesques; but I'm the only captain in camp and click for every duty going. I have now sixty officers in my company. There are 190 in mess here, worse people than ever. You are much better off: at least, Sassons, I'd like you to tell me honestly are these shellshock fellow-patients of yours getting on your nerves? I'd be very unhappy if I thought they were: you talk of golf with lunatics, but I hope to God it's not as bad as that. Damn Rivers, why should he go and get ill like that and leave you? Who's there instead? I wish somehow I could work special leave to go and see you: I'm not really entitled to, now I've had my final leave, but perhaps if you wrote and asked me to come I could get it. But one thing good is that you're writing again: actually as much as 3 hours a day! Stick to it and show me something good before New Year. Try, now you've got such good clarity of expression, to cut down the slang as much as possible: personally I don't mind because I know what you're at, but one or two people have not been as overcome by the 'Dead Officer' as it ought to make them, because they've been put in a wrong mood by the telephone metaphor – the ideal is to use common and simple words which everyone can understand and yet not set up a complex by such vulgarities but to make the plain words do the work of the coloured ones – badly put, still –

I'll send you my photo when I get them; they've been due a month now, blast them.

Some unknown friend sent me the *Loom of Youth*:[91] what an amazing book! I'm going to find out if Alec's poetry is as good as his prose: he must be a wonder boy: he is I believe old Gosse's nephew. Gosse, rather alarmed at first, has been enthusiastically converted by the three editions in a month the book went into.

Robert Nichols will write to you for my proofs when you've done. I have been all the week with a travelling medical board, as military representative, and have watched the fat old doctors passing the twisted weedy old syphilitics up from C3 into A: my only duty an occasional signature.

Tired. Goodbye.

Best love   Robert

Not wishing to spend another winter in the unhealthy huts at Litherland, Graves asked at his next medical board to be passed in the category of B2, which meant 'Fit for garrison service at home'. He was then sent to the 3rd Garrison Battalion of the regiment at Kinmel Park camp, near Rhyl. When he felt better, he got himself passed B1, or 'Fit for garrison service abroad', hoping to be sent to Palestine, but when his orders arrived they were for him to proceed to Gibraltar which upset his plans: 'Gibraltar being a dead-end, it would be as difficult to get from there to Palestine as it would from England. A friend in the War Office undertook to cancel the order until a vacancy could be found for me in the battalion stationed at Cairo.' [92]

On 19 October Sassoon wrote, from Craiglockhart, that Rivers had told him he suffered from a very strong 'anti-war complex'; he didn't know what this meant and wanted to consult a 'first-class alienist' to find out whether he was really 'dotty' or not. At Craiglockhart Graves had talked of 'good form' and said that other members of the regiment thought Sassoon wasn't 'acting like a gentleman', just as he had written in his letter of 31 July (see page 80): this attitude, wrote Sassoon, was simply a form of suicidal stupidity and credulity, and, if Graves had real courage, he wouldn't acquiesce as he did.

27 October 1917	attached 3rd Garrison Battalion Royal Welch Fusiliers Kinmel Park Rhyl

My dear Sassons

I don't remember if I told you I've managed to get struck off the Gibraltar draft and am now waiting orders for Egypt which may come in any time, and then I'll be still a fortnight in England before going out – then once in Egypt I get a medical board and so on to the land of Canaan. My book is due this week or next but the binding is very uncertain these days.

I saw Silent Knight[93] yesterday who is expecting to follow my example by getting garrison service abroad: he told me what perhaps you have heard that in September the 1st Battalion RWF and a line battalion of Middlesex were selected to go down to Étaples and quell a mutiny among the base details down there. Jocks (who as a result of a row between a military policeman and a Maori about a girl, in the course of which a Jock got accidentally shot) went off into a great disturbance (you know how badly they are treated at the Bull Ring) and locking up their officers, went on the spree for two days and played Hell. Rather a compliment for the First Battalion being chosen, but rather a rotten job . . .

Don't be so silly about being dotty: of course you're sane. The only trouble is you're too sane which is as great a crime as being dotty and much more difficult to deal with. That's the meaning of an anti-war complex. You see what other folk don't see about the rights and wrongs of the show. Personally I think you see too much. About 'good form' and 'acting like a gentleman'. You are purposely perverse in attributing those things to my lips. What I said was 'The Bobbies and Tommies and so on, who are the exact people whom you wish to influence and save by all your powers, are just the people whose feelings you are going to hurt most by turning round in the middle of the war, after having made a definite contract, and saying "I've changed my mind" '; they'll only think it 'bad form' and that you're 'not acting like a gentleman' which is the worst accusation they can fasten on a friend. You can only command their respect by sharing all their miseries as far as you possibly can, being ready for pride's sake to finish your contract whatever it costs you, yet all the time denouncing the principles you are being compelled to further. God knows you have 'done your bit' as they say, but I believe in giving everything. Thus you'll be able to do more good both now and after the war than anything you are likely to do through your present means.

'If you had real courage you wouldn't acquiesce as you do.' Sorry you think that of me – I should hate to think I'm a coward. I believe though in keeping to agreements when everybody else keeps them and if I find myself party to principles I don't quite like, in biding my time till I have a sporting chance of rearranging things. One must bow in the house of Rimmon[94] occasionally.

Your conscience is too nice in its discernment between conflicting forces. 'Be still my soul: the arms you bear are brittle!'

But as you say, I wish to God our people could state definite peace terms. Young Freeman and young Moody have both been wounded I see: I hope not badly. Reggie hit in the ankle: he commanded the 2nd Battalion in the second day of their Polygon Wood show. The battalion did magnificently and got all objectives, after having a rotten time the first day. The CO (Poore), the adjutant Casson, Colquhoun the signals officer and the orderly room sergeant were all killed by the same shell, in a crater.

Old Gosse has given us a good puff in the *Edinburgh Review*: have you seen it? But he's a bit sick with you evidently. *Georgian Poetry 1916–1917* is being dedicated to him – he's very bucked about that.

I'll let you have back the £20 when I get some money from bridge earnings. You saved my life the other day by that loan – thanks awfully.

This afternoon, after a busy morning with Fusiliers, I am going down to Rhyl for the Fairies, not the fairies with rouged lips and peroxide hair but the real fairies: the colonel's kids have invited me to a special nursery tea and tiddlywinks. It's going to be great fun. They call me Georgy Giraffe and consider that I must be a damn sight finer fellow than their father who is only 5' 6" tall.

Goodbye

God bless you   Robert

In November Sassoon went before a medical board, first demanding an assurance from the War Office that no obstacles would be put up to prevent him from returning to a front-line battalion; in a letter to Graves he said that he no longer cared whether he lived or died.

This was in striking contrast to Graves's situation and mood: he was now very happy that he would not be going back into the trenches, and had also fallen in love with seventeen-year-old Nancy Nicholson, daughter of the painters William and Mabel Nicholson, sister of the painter Ben Nicholson, and herself an artist and an ardent feminist. At this time, when Sassoon was writing his brilliant series of sarcastic antiwar poems and Owen, under Sassoon's influence, was beginning to write the intensely realistic and mature poems for which he is now admired, Graves's poems became, for a while, self-consciously romantic, nostalgic and trivial – many of them being simple nursery rhymes – in an attempt to forget the horrors of the war.

No date

Dear old Sass.

I wrote a letter last week and forgot to post it: now it's stale so I'll write another. Your poems are damned good, but perfectly horrific as they're meant to be. Do cheer up, Sass. If you still want to know the meaning of a strong anti-war complex it's just this: that you're so obsessed with the idea of the perpetual horror of this war that you can no longer, as in 1916, make plans for after the war, and can never conceive, as I still can, of a new world, emptier but wiser and happier than anything that has gone before. This phase is like a nightmare which you find yourself unable to wake up from: if you make the tremendous effort which people make in their sleep knowing all their nightmare to be a lie, and wake up, you'll have as it were sound sleep for the rest of the night and a jolly morning.

Sassons, you are disappointing. There are we three inevitables, two Roberts and a Siegfried, rising side by side on the roll of fame, all still young and more or less undamaged and now just because of a corpse or two, and some shells, you are trying to drop out because your heart has gone. Sassons, what about Tiflis? Tomsk? Thibet? War's a joke for me and you when we know.[95]

Don't send me any more corpse poems, stick to your splendid Thrushes.

I saw off my sister Rosaleen to nurse in France on Thursday. On the way back here I met one of your bombers you had with you when you were hit, 31 Evans of B Company (I think that's right) on leave from the Second Battalion at Passchendaele. We hadn't talked more than a few seconds when he suddenly asked about 'Mr Sarson, him as was with us on the 27th. Is he better of his wounds?' 'Well, yes,' I said, 'he talks of coming back now; they say he's volunteered.' 'The boys, the few that's left, 'll be glad to hear that,' he said. 'I'll tell 'em. Oh, Mr Sarson never got the wind up (like Mr — Sir, you know), we'd follow him anywhere. It's different with an officer like that somehow: we could trust him.'

This was on a small visit to Nancy Nicholson who is working on a farm at St Ives, Huntingdonshire. Robbie doesn't like the idea of her. So you can quiet him down, *if he mentions her.* She's doing a children's book with me.[96] Otherwise leave her out of the conversation. I don't want to have unfriendliness and I'll not even allow dear Robbie to bully Nancy. I'll parade her one day for your approval. She's an unusual person, young, kind, strong, nice-looking and a consummate painter as well as a capable farmer's boy. I know you'd like her.

I had a ripping letter from Masefield thanking me for the book. The reviews have hitherto been inadequate except that in these times of paper shortage all reviews are very much cut down.

Best love   – R.

To Robert Nichols

No date [November 1917]

Dear Robert

I should like news of you: I know you're still alive because of a most thoroughly excellent poem in *The Times*, quoted again in this week's *Bystander*. I am gladder than you can guess that you and I are taking the same line about the war: as usual we're right when the other poets are wrong. We are singing together in *Oxford Poetry 1917* which has come out and in *Chamber's Journal* I see an article by E.B.O. who is styled the author of *The Muse in Arms*, an anthology which looks as if it's got a publisher now – he quotes us both, yours highest of course. *Georgian Poetry* is due today: a good stunt; again we top the roll.

Have you got the copy of *Fairies and Fusiliers* yet? It looks all right, uniform with Masefield but red buckram. Usual misprints. 'Stronn Beer' and, in 'A Child's Nightmare', 'Overpowered me foot and head' instead of 'hand'. On December 12th at that Vandervelde show at Mrs Colefax's house with Gosse in the chair it should be rather fun. I am billed to read but think it's extremely unlikely I'll be there: so you must read mine for me, you're the only one I can trust.

Also the 'Irish Literary Society' have asked me to read a paper to them on the Georgians in January. Again, can you take this on? I'll send you particulars. It's all good propaganda.

That bad man Frankau[97] is boosting himself and I suppose will deceive many. But not all. And none of the people who know anything about Poetry. Fortunately he's adopted Kiplingesque so he's easier to see through. I'm pretty busy here: part of the Battalion have gone over to Ireland and I'm Colonel of the 400 odd men, the 30 NCOs and the 61 officers left.

Robert, I do hope your health is better and your pocket and especially your heart (I know your brain is all right by 'To Those at Home'). It's only fair to tell you that since the cataclysm of my friend Peter, my affections are running in the more normal channels and I correspond regularly and warmly with Nancy Nicholson, who is great fun. I only tell you this so that you should get out of your head any misconceptions about my temperament. I should hate you to think I was a confirmed homosexual even if it were only in my thought and went no farther.

I have written three good poems since the last one I read you; two of them damned good. I am getting a much clearer idea of what we are after. My God, Robert, we have lit such a candle as by God's grace will set the whole barn alight.

I felt this most when reading *Oxford Poetry* and seeing the works of the other people there. And when I read the *Poetry Review*. It's jolly to be able to talk like this to you without the false modesty of usual talk. By the way: I'll tell you the job you want: that is lecturing in America on the war aims of our allies. You have the reputation, the power and the spirit, and as about a hundred people of the literary persuasion are on the stunt, why not you? Masefield is going, I hear. If it pleases you, write to Gosse or call on him *very politely* (17 Hanover Terrace, Regent's Park). He should be able to work it. You'd get a grand time, excellent experience, a big boost and would at the same time be doing more for England than any other way I can think. I'd go like a shot only I am still able to fight again and I feel I must.

I think I have found a new poet as yet unfledged. One Owen, subaltern in the 2nd Manchester Regiment.[98]

You owe me two letters. Write.

Yours affectionately   Robert

No news yet of going to Egypt.

To Edward Marsh

29 December 1917

My dear Eddie

I wonder what you've thought of my silence? I am awfully sorry but there has been a good reason. I've been busy arranging wedlock, with Nancy Nicholson, daughter of William Nicholson the painter, and the date fixed is January 23rd, unless my long delayed move for Egypt intervenes; I think the church is St James's, Piccadilly. Will send you a formal invitation. Have been also very busy with *Fairies and Fusiliers* which has been as favourably reviewed as I hoped, and also for the last two months, nearly, have been in charge of a detachment of 600 fusiliers and 80 officers up here, when the rest of my battalion suddenly moved off to Ireland.

Many thanks for *Georgian Poetry*. It's a great success I think, and the selections, especially from the new arrivals, admirable. The critics, as usual, have exercised their stupid wits on it and made fools of themselves, especially that ass Shanks[99] in the *New Statesman*. Still, I don't suppose you mind: sufficient is it to know yourself as the Father of modern English Poetry with fillets and palm leaves and a grateful flock of poetry lovers at your knees. Eddie, I am just beginning to feel that I know what I'm getting at and in this next year of 1918, if I'm spared, I hope to satisfy the expectations you've had of me since I was a sixteen-year-older at Charterhouse, by doing some work of really lasting value.

George Mallory, as my oldest surviving friend who first introduced me to mountains and, through you, to modern poetry, my two greatest interests next to Nancy and my Regiment, is going to be my best man on the 23rd.

Sassons is amazingly well again and now he's passed for France again, quite happy. I have a new poet for you, just discovered, one Wilfred Owen: this is a real find not a sudden lo here! or lo there! which unearths an Edward Eastaway or a Vernede, but the real thing; when we've educated him a trifle more. R.N., S.S. and myself are doing it.

Best love

Robert

To Siegfried Sassoon, who was with the 3rd Battalion at Limerick

11 January 1918

My dear Sassons

I'm sure if you bit old Flood's ear nicely you could get leave to come to the wedding. Should be rather a rag as all the best sort of people will be there: no relations bar a very few will be allowed to come on after the ceremony to drink champagne at the studio in Appletree Yard,[100] only the elect people of God will be there. I took Nancy to see Robbie and I'm very relieved to say that they liked each other though R. was ill and Nancy shy. The date is fixed for January 23rd: meanwhile I have been to see Sir James Fowler re chests and so on and he says it's no good my going on active service though my lungs are soundish. Says I'll break down. So I stay back I suppose: it seems rather silly after all my sabre rattling: still, I suppose it's good news for Nancy. Shall get a good job somehow, somewhere, possibly another instructional job in a healthier spot.

Did you see that *South Western Gazette* Prize Essay Stunt about 'Poetry, and its development in 1917'? In the general run of essays the five poets most generally quoted were, alphabetically: John Freeman,[101] Roberto Graves, Bob Nichols, Sassons and Squire.[102] ('Good idea,' as Nancy said.) Us three sandwiched between two people who we know don't matter much.

I have just written a poem that Robbie says is a masterpiece. It seemed all right when I casually examined it the morning afterwards. I'd written it on the back of a telegram from Practician and the cover of an old chequebook: and still I think it's rather a hit. Shall send it somewhere and get increment. Called 'The God Poetry'.

Hear Bob Nichols has joined Bach Thomas, Phillip Gibbs and company in France. Send news old croney wingle.

Love   Robert

Sassoon, however, was unable to attend the wedding because he was on a gas course at Cork. After the wedding and a short honeymoon, Graves returned to the 3rd Battalion at Rhyl, and Nancy went back to her farm for a month.

6 February 1918

Dear old Sassons

I have been intending to write for so long but find it difficult: don't know why. Was the wedding a success? ask me! It would have been more so if you had been able to attend. I am for the moment confined to my couch with a cold but in the last three days have written 45 letters, 3 new poems, recast four old ones two of which I sent to *Colour* and got £3·3·0 by return, read two books, pasted in my press cuttings, compiled an address book and played patience, and even washed my face – no, I haven't, but I shaved once.

Bob Nichols is back in London since February 1st; write to him. Did I tell you that Alec Waugh is an enormous admirer of your poems? I have it on the authority of Scott-Moncrieff who gives Waugh's address as: Lt A. Waugh, 233rd M G Coy, BEF, France. I wrote to him yesterday. He is producing a book of poems in the spring, Moncrieff says. I wonder will it be good? I expect not.

I hear you're under orders for Palestine from a subaltern called Roberts whose letter just arrived from Limerick.

I am getting a job in No. 17 Cadet Battalion here as soon as the details leave for Ireland, so that Nancy and I can make up our minds to settle down. The contrast between you and me makes me so ashamed: that's why I find it difficult to write. But Sassons, though I know you wanted to return to a line battalion I know it's much better as it is; the strain in Palestine isn't nearly so great on you and you aren't likely, or so likely, to get killed. I'm most awfully keen on you living on because as soon as the war stops I know your nerves will get absolutely rested again and you'll be your old self (like when you saw me here the other day only more so) again and write miraculous poetry.

Best love always,   – R.

In February Graves transferred to the 16th Officer Cadet Battalion also at Kinmel Park. In May he heard from Sassoon who in March had been posted to the 25th Battalion in Palestine, but who was now back in France again.

Officers' Mess
No. 16 Officer Cadet Battalion
No. 16 Camp
23 May 1918   Kinmel Park
Rhyl

My dear Sassons

Just got your letter from France at the same time as one from your Egyptian base camp, and am very sick to think of you back in France. I had nobody to worry about there till quite lately and didn't read the roll of honour, but now there's you and Silent Knight and Tony Nicholson, my brother-in-law, and several more.

Well, I suppose they'll give you a lot of training before they oppose you to the Hun as I imagine your yeomanry don't know much about crater-fighting and gas and so on. Well, about war, no more: cheer up only. They can't kill you, and anyhow not before you see my child ('our child', sorry, Nancy) which is just signalled and should appear about Christmas. (This is a secret to all but our most intimate friends: hope you're pleased.)

If it's a 'he' we'll call him 'Siggy' – no, we won't but Lorraine[103] might be a pretty girl's name.

I haven't seen Bob Nichols but am writing today and will give him your salaams.

I have written little, but what I have I think well, lately. E.M. says so.

Ivor Novello is setting a series of songs for me, did I tell you? And very well indeed. I do admire a man who can amass thousands by a song like 'Keep the Home Fires Burning' and also write really good music besides.

I hope you'll get leave one of these sort of days: only I'm so tied down to this OCB that unless your leave coincides with mine, I'll not be able to see you in London.

Eric Kennington[104] has done a pastel head of me: his exhibition of war-impression pictures comes off in June and will make Nevinson[105] and Nash[106] and Lavery[107] and Orpen[108] look awful fools. He is a consummate pastel-monger: and such a nice man. He introduced me to your pal Philpots: who is charming.

I wish you wouldn't think of legacy leaving: your generosity is touching but tho' you may not believe it I definitely prefer your present friendship to future grateful recollections and when Nance and I get our home going (and you can be assured old poet that it's going to be a real good place) we want you to make it your HQ for as long as you can bear it. Don't be afraid that we'll play the Watts-Dunton;[109] only I do want you to be properly looked after. You wouldn't recognize me these days, the way Nance has smartened me up. I wash my eyes and neck and ears every morning and evening and brush my teeth inside and out. And my clothes! I'm an awful toff now.

We are hoping to rent a quite ideal place very near Harlech, an old manor house with a ghost and a farm and an orchard and heaps of rooms and everything perfect, which is falling vacant since the presumed death of its owner, a colonel in the Grenadier Guards. Nancy has worked there and knows the running of it and the rent is ridiculously low. But it's still in the air, tho' as soon as we possibly can, we'll take it.

W. J. Turner's new book[110] is amazingly good here and there, in fact nearly all, but occasionally he gets nervous and drops the tray with a beastly crash.

So glad you still keep up your spirits.

Scott-Moncrieff is sending Wilfred Owen here, when he's a bit stronger, to my battalion. I say, when you come back wounded, do come here too. It *would* be jolly. I have no doubt at all that you'll like Nancy: she gets better and better on acquaintance. I didn't know a great deal about her when we got married except what I saw at once by instinct, but, my goodness, instinct is nearly always right.

Give my love to young Stan Harper. Remember our 'day-aht' at Rosslyn, how good the strawberries were and how shocked Stan was at you bathing in the river? Great days.

Have you written anything lately?

Cheerioh. Yours affectionately   Robert

At the end of June Sassoon wrote, feeling 'heavy as lead', and asked Graves angrily why he hadn't written for so long; he said he would 'do you all down yet' and with two wooden legs and a cork arm write a magnificent tragedy or, if he were killed, haunt Graves and Nancy in their 'beastly old house'. A week later (5 July) he wrote more calmly and sent Graves £23 for his twenty-third birthday.

Bryn y Pin
St Asaph
North Wales

9 July 1918

Dear old Sassons

Two letters to hand, a) a most staggering and wholly pleasing birthday present of which more anon and b) a letter pretending anger, jealousy and dottiness all very badly attempted.

Still, the letter I sent you from Maesyneuardd was a bad one, I'm afraid, but I hope you liked the one sent from here, just after, to make up for it. I say I'm awfully sorry I'm such a swine to be happy and I swear to you that if I only had myself to think about I'd change places with you at once despite my hellish fear of the La Bassée country and my waking terror of poison gas, which is my most awful nightmare whenever I feel ill and think about the line. As for my not 'writing deeply' blast you, you old croaking corbie aren't I allowed for the honour of the Regiment to balance your abysmal groanings with my feather top rhymes and songs? And I have written croakingly too lately but I haven't sent you specimens because I think it's bad taste and most ungrateful when God's so nice to me. I've almost got the new book together and I forbid you to get the posthumous VC till it's published. It won't be as striking as yours but it will be damned good in spite of occasional corpses that blunder up among the nursery toys. It shall be called *The Patchwork Quilt* I think, with an explanation perhaps of this kind:

> Here is this patchwork quilt I've made
> Of patterned silks and old brocade,
> Small faded rags in memory rich
> Sewn each to each with feather stitch,
> But if you stare aghast perhaps
> At certain muddied khaki scraps
> Or trophy-fragments of field grey,
> Clotted and torn, a grim display
> That never decked white sheets before,
> Blame my dazed head, blame bloody war.

Or not?

So glad you're still fond of me: and I of you, dear poet, like hell, even as per previously published statement in 'Two Fusiliers'.

Please don't think I am embarrassed by your present. On the

contrary, I immediately cashed it and started turning it to good use, ordered a year's supply of *New Statesman*, *Times Literary Supplement*, *Country Life*, *Farmer and Stock Breeder* and *Mirror* (£8 odd) with the double purpose of obtaining literature where none grows otherwise and of giving Nancy something every morning by the hand of the postman who is usually unkind to her.

Then I further enjoyed myself by tipping my young brother John Wingle at Charterhouse, and my niece Janie whom you also know I think (£1 10s).

On Saturday Nance and I are going on the bus to Chester to buy comforts and comfits with the balance and to have for once in our married life a good square meal (we live on bad buns and buttermilk most of the time because they can't cook here: joys of married life again). Nancy, like David Townsend whom you used to rag, is so fond of eating that she herewith sends her loving thanks for the present: she would sell her soul for 'a nice light luncheon' complete with roly-poly pudding and the good rich turbot and the large field.

I say, do come over in August if only just to see and approve of Nancy: it won't affect the leave of the battalion as much as all that.

This won't 'stir up your antagonism' will it? You've never succeeded in quarrelling with me yet and you'll like me much better now that Nancy has taught me to wash properly. Nancy says she is glad you tried to reform me in that respect but that you should have been firmer. Also, that she wants (i.e. we want) you to be Godfather next January: your duties are to stop the child becoming dirty or too religious, and to send it a copy of your collected works at its confirmation which should prevent it taking the ceremony seriously. How the poor Nancy-bird hated the marriage service!

I haven't seen *Motley*[111] yet but shall buy it as soon as possible. Dearmer[112] gets worse and worse on reading unlike your work and mine which improves. There is one couplet absolutely typical of all that is worst in the soldier poet: I forget the second line but the first is:

Even the poppy on the parapet.

The stresses fall absurdly, the sentiment is mawkish: it is very bad.

May we never write so! Robbie hasn't answered my last three letters: what's he up to?

Yours affectionately,   Robert

Thanks most awfully for the present.

On 13 July Sassoon was shot in the head while making a daylight patrol through No Man's Land, but was not killed.

16 July 1918
Two years ago today I wrote that thing from Mametz Wood.

Dear Sassons

Another long letter thanking you among other things for your birthday present is with your battalion, just missed you. But I must write again. How clever of you to get a bullet thro' your napper and write me a saner letter than you have sent me for some time past. I hope you are having a good time at Boulogne: my sister Rosaleen is at 54 Gen. at Wimereux, Boulogne, and you might see each other if you are there for long.

I do hope you're all right: can't you give the Line a rest, or are you so bent on getting killed? I had already started a letter:

> Poor Fusilier, vexed with the Fate
> That keeps you there in France so late,
> When all our friends of three years past
> Are freed from trench and road at last;
> Dear lads, one way or t'other done
> With bloody France and homeward gone
> Crippled with wounds or mad or blind
> Or leaving their poor clay behind
> Where still you lag, forlorn and drear,
> Last of the flock, poor Fusilier!

but it will have to be rewritten . . .

I say I've had a rotten time in the last few days: Nancy's mother died suddenly of pneumonia; she tried to conceal flu because my brother-in-law was on leave from the 2nd Division and she wanted to give him a good time. Poor old Nancy's awfully upset, but being very brave about it.

Well, I really do think this time that the War's tottering to an end, and I am sure that the American peace-ideals are worth something: it's not all grab and bluff like our politicians' ideas: and they won't allow us to grab more than our due at the Peace Conference where they'll have a most important say. Well, I am counting on it ending within about 9 months from now and I'm in the position of having to decide where we're going to live. Nancy insists on a Sussex farm and what could be nicer? We'll have to hurry up or your godchild won't have a decent house to live in. The idea is to take the house over in September and the land next spring: my sister Ros is coming across to help Nancy who reckons she could carry on a small dairy farm of about 100 acres quite well. The only drawback to this scheme is one concerned with the dibs, though to rent a farm, as we're going to do, costs little once we've got the stock. The drawback I mean is the fear of getting into debt at the end of the first year if it's a bad one because we'll have no capital and I hate cadging on our penurious relations. I think you'll have to promise to help us out if we get into a hole, with some of your Persian gold: I don't suppose there'll be any need to ask you, but if you'll say you'll support us over a bad time it will be a great relief in times of drought, plague, storms and pestilence.

I wrote a trench poem the other day to show you I could write just like you, about two men I knew killed by the same shell, one a sodden Anglo-Argentine and t'other a boy of 18, very young looking; the first called out 'mother mother' and the other cursed God and died. The last verse is pure Sassons, as your parody was once pure Masefield.

> Then Sergeant Smith, kindest of men,
> Wrote out two copies there and then
> Of his accustomed funeral speech
> To cheer the womenfolk of each.[113]

Bless you,   Robert

On 24 July Sassoon wrote a verse letter from the American Red Cross Hospital for Officers at Lancaster Gate, which Graves quoted in the first edition of *Goodbye to All That*, but which was removed at Sassoon's insistence before it was released (see pages 197 and 207); Graves wrote instead ' . . . he wrote me a verse letter from a London hospital (which I cannot quote, though I should like to do so) beginning:

I'd timed my death in action to the minute . . .

It is the most terrible of his war poems.'[114] Another line of the letter, referring to Graves's request for a loan if necessary, was: 'Why keep a Jewish friend, unless you bleed him?'

27 July 1918

Dear old Sassons

God preserve you from your friends the Rottalines and the Bolshevists and the syphilitic young poets! But Sassons, don't try and break my heart. It's quite unnecessary. Of course the query 'Why keep a Jewish friend unless you bleed him?' is answered by:

Why keep a German friend unless you grieve him!

But if you aren't good I'll send you back your blasted cheque for £23 and make it up to £31 or whatever represents your age, to spite you. And send it direct to your bleeding bankers about which you swank so.

Seriously, Sassons, do be good and let Rivers decide what's good for you: to pretend to be dotty when you're far saner than all that strange *galère*[115] of visitors is a rotten game to play on an old friend.

Gratters on your cuff: didn't realize you'd made good at last. Got any VCs this time? Then why the hell not? Will you go over my ms. for me if I send it you in, let us say, a fortnight? I like this ceremony of friendship and you generally know where my work is bad. I say, old *Ardours* is an absolute looney now (don't tell him I said so) from his letters: you sound positively, painfully sane compared with him. Write a nice letter or I'll send you my £150 of war loan put by against a rainy day as well as the £23 or £31. Did you see Scatter Ford's photo in today's *Mirror* as promoted brigadier?

Bless you   Robert

Where is Bobbie by the way? I'll be up in London first week in September.

On 24 July, *The Collected Poems of Rupert Brooke, with a Memoir* was published. Marsh had begun this memoir soon after Brooke's death, but Brooke's mother had continually raised objections and delayed publication.

28 July 1918

My dear Eddie

Excuse pencil, but Sunday morning is always spent in bed and Nancy won't allow ink in bed (don't blame her either). Today I got your *Memoir* and have been reading it this morning: it is awfully well done and more and more do I regret that the meeting you promised me in 1914 with Rupert never came off. How impossibly these days such enjoyment of life and feather-heartedness reads: I'm much more of an optimist than any of my friends (indeed I expect the war to finish within a few months) but my capacity for such prehistoric happiness as Rupert had is nothing.

I have a philosophic happiness of a sort by comparing my state, say, with that of *Ardours and Endurances* or poor old *Counter-Attack* with this new hole in his funny old head; and here I have flowers and good friends and poetry and fair health and work and my fusiliers and above all Nancy, but times are very bad aren't they? Poor Nancy's mother died the other day of pneumonia and it's been rotten since then: the mother was quite one of the best painters going, in the front rank, tho' she painted very little.

Little poetry worth anything being written (by the way, my friend Peter is publishing a little book privately but it won't be good except for an occasional line; curiously twentieth-century and un-Georgian). I read Davies's *Poet's Pilgrimage* to Nancy with great pleasure: a delicious book, we both loved it. Davies is a great man, one of the few. How he knows the Welsh!

I don't suppose Ivor has done much more with them there songs?: meanwhile, Eddie, I am just finishing my new poems (lots of new ones you've not seen, and I think very good) to send to Heinemann.

Would you be awfully nice then and either send me the originals, or kinder still, typescripts, because I want to get the thing ready in a week or so.

We are also well on into a children's book of rhymes which Nancy is illustrating.

You'll see the ms. of both of course. But there's not much that will want changing, I hope.

Thanks awfully for the *Memoir*.

Yours affectionately   Robert Graves

Graves continued mechanically at his cadet battalion work and tried to forget the war by writing a book of romantic poems and ballads called *Country Sentiment*, the manuscript of which he sent to Sassoon. Sassoon's reply and list of criticisms have been lost, but it is clear that he did not like the book.

26 August 1918

Dear old Sassons

I have adopted most of your suggestions for which thanks awfully: especially 'bloody' for 'merry'.

I'm sorry about the letter but look here why not send an answer reproaching me in your own melodious quatrains for my shortcomings, which I'll print alongside: gives you a chance of propaganda and gives me an extra poem, some of the 'guts' you say I need, and an advertisement.

I can't think what to substitute for 'Dear Welshmen from the coaly South' and can't cut it out without leaving a gap. You might let me be sentimental where sentiment is true: good God, *didn't* they sing those chaps anyhow? Like hell they did; 'chapel burglary or rape, hymns all the time indeed'. *And* in tune.

I'm glad though that you like at any rate an isolated poem here and there: 'The Leveller' is as good a skit on Sassoon as 'Daffodil Murderers' [*sic*] was on Masefield and equally deserved.

Old boy do you want me to stop writing altogether? I can't write otherwise than I am now except with hypocrisy for I am bloody happy and bloody young (with only very occasional lapses) and passionate anger is most ungrateful. And I can't afford to stop in these penurious days and anyhow my 'antique silk and flower brocade' continue to please the seventeen-year-old girls and other romantics for whom they are intended: and why not? Worrying about the war is no longer a sacred duty with me: on the contrary, neither my position as a cadet instructor nor my family duties permit it. I am no longer fit to fight and I am out to get as healthy as possible for the good I can do in England. Curse me to hell: I shall hate it: but I must be honest according to my lights however dim they have grown. As Squire said in his last review of you, you seem to think that there are more people who love War than there really are in this fifth year of war with our 3½ million casualty list. And poetry shouldn't be all propaganda because a war is on.

My occasional reminders are quite enough I should have said.
Please be kind to me Sassons, for the sake of Fricourt now again
overrun by Welch troops, and the woods beyond.

Yours affectionately   Robert

                                        No. 16 Officer Cadet Battalion
11 September 1918   Kinmel Park
                                        Rhyl

My dear Siegfried

Robbie, possibly in collusion with you, advises me to postpone
my book and make it more homogenous, either Fairies or
Fusiliers, preferably the latter.

Don't worry about me: I am going to write you a heavy epic
soon; I am not entirely swamped by the approaching family. I
have just been woken up from my summer sleep by the first rugger
practices: and shall start life again.

Remember Tommy when roused at rugger, how he suddenly
hardened and flashed and cursed and shouted and did gigantic
things?

Charming man Drinkwater, thank him from me. I have put
'Sospan Fach' as right as I can where you found it wrong and sent
it to *Reveillé*: it's the most likely thing to please them.

'Ancient History' is wonderful: but don't use 'some' in the 2nd
line, use 'his', and put 'huddling sharp/rough chin' or something:
the little extra strength is needed and 'blossoms twisted in smooth/
sleek hair'.

Very well, shall not go to America unless I have to leave here.
Hope Bob Nichols won't lose his head. Have written to him.
'Comrade Why Do You Weep?'[116] is good: the other also: but
'Comrade' is first class.

Convalescent poems seem to breed poets: any news of Owen?

Nancy is away at present, her brother is just back from
California.

Bless you,   Robert

E.M.: Victoria 8700 Extn 639

In September Graves and his father-in-law, William Nicholson, decided to produce a new, bi-annual 'miscellany' of poems, stories and
pictures, to be called *The Owl*.

At the beginning of October Robert Ross died and Tony

Nicholson, Graves's brother-in-law, was killed in France. Graves wrote to Sassoon, who was still convalescing.

12 October 1918

Dear old Sassons

These are rotten days aren't they, everybody being killed or gratuitously dying. Tony Nicholson was a charming person, very much of the David Thomas type though not quite so simple-minded: I had to break the news to Nancy again. However, she took it all right and our baby is going to be all right, the doctor promised: I'm a selfish devil, but that's all that seems to matter much.

Poor little Robbie! I'm glad he died so easily though; and really I expected him to go suddenly, with those precarious kidneys and heart, any day. But there'll never be another Robbie, cynical, kindhearted, witty, champion of lost causes, feeder of the fatherless and widowed and oppressed. I felt his loss more than people could suppose: I thought that it was no good doing anything about it and so sent no wreath or wrote to anyone: an irony that it would just have been on a question of this sort that I would have gone to consult Robbie himself.

I was in town the next day where I stayed a week and saw a lot of people, and got *The Owl* started, the miscellany of which I told you. At present we have promises from Max Beerbohm, Masefield, J. C. Squire, James Pryde,[117] S. Sassoon, W. J. Turner, Kennington, W. Nicholson and we are getting also I think with not much difficulty, Augustus John, Lytton Strachey, de la Mare, Arnold Bennett and all the rest of them who are any good in art or letters. Heinemann will publish: W.N. is looking after the illustrations and Turner and myself after the letter press. So you see you'll have to give us something really worth while: but it's all more or less unofficial still. The idea is quality, no especial line but anything good, and nothing controversial.

Nancy and I have taken a new house at Rhuddlan, quite close to here though it means I'll have to use a bloody bicycle. Could you come and spend a week-end, i.e. Saturday afternoon to Monday morning, for I want to see you about all sorts of things and especially to meet Nancy.

Bless you   Robert

In November came the Armistice. Graves wrote to Robert Nichols, who was in America lecturing on British war poets for the Ministry of Information, from his father-in-law's studio in St James's.

permanent address
11 Appletree Yard
St James's
London

No date

Dear Bob

Have just had your charming letter forwarded from New York: I really think it's extraordinarily good of you to give me all this help on the other side of the world and hope some day I'll be able to pay you out.

In three or four days I hope to send you the typescript of a dozen poems or so with the necessary information attached.

Meanwhile, now I've got your address, I want at once (underlined heavily) your contribution to *The Owl* which is assuming very definite shape now.

. . . .

I know I can trust you to send something really good, and not something written in an unlucky moment years ago and consigned since to the very back of the washstand drawer: or perhaps you never write bad stuff now: I wish I couldn't.

Business part over: oh Bob isn't it extraordinary to feel that the War's won at last: I keep a small silk Union Jack at the stairhead to remind me of it so that I shan't grouse at the petty annoyances of peace.

Things were very quiet up here on the 11th: London was full of buck of course but in North Wales a foreign war or a victory more or less are not considered much. Little boys banged biscuit tins and a Verey light or two went up at the camp but for the rest not much. A perfunctory thanksgiving service with nothing more cheerful in it than a Last Post for the dead; and then grouses about demobilization. Funny people *les anglais*. As soon as I can get demobilized I propose to go up for a month or two to Oxford to learn a bit about agriculture and shall then retreat to my lovely Wales and grow cabbages like old thingummy the Roman Emperor – Galba wasn't it?

Our baby comes at New Year: anxious times but Nancy is very well and full of cheerfulness.

Poor Robbie's death was a great shock: it was also the same day that Nancy's brother was killed in France: ay 'tis a true word 'Until the Death goes all estates, princes, prelates and potentates, both rich and poor of all degree.'

Thank God that there are still living four or five poets (and you will bring back from America some more) to do something with the language of the conquering races of the world.

Bless you,
           Robert

Nance sends her love.

In January Nancy's first baby, Jenny, was born. Now the war was over Graves's idea was to leave the army and go up to Oxford and study agriculture. Sassoon was also going there, on Dr Rivers's advice, to mix with college life and study 'historical and political subjects' (before the war he had gone to Cambridge University but had left without a degree); Lady Ottoline Morrell had engaged rooms for him from a Mr Garlick in Merton Street, and he wrote to Graves that they would have to found a debating society and dining club, with Frank Prewett, Masefield, Marsh, Lytton Strachey, Liebknecht[118] and Trotsky as honorary members.

No date   11 Seaside Villas
                  Hove

My dear Sassons
I find I can't get demobilized till I rejoin at Limerick so propose to go there on Wednesday. I wonder if you'll come too so that we can spend our last days of 'soldiering' together.

I have been engaged in an invigorating game of correspondence with the cadet battalion. I am a master at this and always take care to have the right on my side even if I have to apologize for it afterwards: have just had the shrapnel fragment removed from my eye: it proves to be a chip of flint from the cemetery where I was wounded. What splendid news that you're coming to Oxford: I will have to live on the hills outside and am consequently writing to Ottoline to see if she can find a house at Garsington.

We'll certainly be able to found *some* club! I expect you'll find me spending all my leisure in your rooms at Garlick's, between lectures, and we expect you to spend your evenings up

with us pretty often. Thomas Hardy is sending us a poem,
bless him.

Yours affectionately   Robert

Godchild sends love.

Sassoon's reply to this letter has been lost, but he was obviously not
amused by Graves's suggestion they should go to Limerick together.
Both men were now socialists, though Sassoon was, for a while,
more extreme in his opinions than Graves.

13 January 1918

All right, old Sniffle-and-cuff!

Though you *do* write bloody good poems I'm sorry you're such
an ass. I wanted you to come to Limerick only to have our last
joke together at the expense of the same military system which
you really, I believe, secretly love: at any rate I am holding up
your old sentimental letters from Fricourt and Arras to blackmail
you with if you get narsty. Did you ever find heroics in my
handwriting? Answer, devil a one. So put *that* where the parson
put the pornographic pamphlet.

As for your Lenin and Trotsky, I respect them for their
thorough-going idealism: it seems that they are simply trying to
get down to the bedrock of solid security by reducing everybody
to the original state of proletarian veg, everyone to dig, reap, hoe
and beget children: and to hell with intelligence and capitalism. It
is the only answer to the dark question at the end of every story
by Dostoievsky, Kuprin,[119] Tchecov [*sic*] and all the other-skies:
knowledge is a sham, wealth is a sham, both only bring misery on
others. So let's either kill everyone with either of these two
accessories, or rob them of their wealth and make them resign
their knowledge. I hope we'll leave them to it: despotism and
cruelty had gone too far in Russia: they are solving the question in
their only way. But I think that despite Lloyd George, Clemenceau
and the Capitalists, we can save Western Europe from so deep an
operation and at any rate leave the bourgeoisie alive: being a
bourgeois myself, I feel I want to remain alive. But of course I am
already a proletariat and am qualifying for a manual worker so
I'm safe enough. You're not even a proletariat.

I wonder, will we perhaps be able to study social questions

106

together? I suppose you'll not help me learn about how to grow veg and the kindly apple tree?

Poems are brilliant. Don't like 'ugly work' so much; the touch is in places obvious. I have just written a masterpiece, though you'll sneer at it I know. My God, we'll have fun at Oxford, old frump!

Mr Louis Untermeyer,[120] who reviewed us in the *New York* I forget what, sent us a sentimental message:

'Hail! Hail! etc! (sic)

Your works bring the sparkle of youth to my senile and semitic eye . . . ' etc! as he would say. Didn't even mention Bob Nichols, Louis didn't, but seemed bucked enough about us.

I think one of the tests for worthiness to enter our dining club premises must be an appreciation of Sorley: Masefield gets in easily as he said the other day that to him twice as severe a loss as the ravishing of Belgium and the sack of cities and cathedral burnings, and the loss of the cargo of the *Lusitania* and so on was the death of Sorley – or words to that effect. *The* great loss of war.

Eddie not quite so sound, because Sorley spoke evil of Brooke in one of his letters, but almost so.

Lenin and Trotsky . . . I wonder . . . Though perhaps Liebknecht.

Anyway, Jenny and Nancy send their love.

Yours,   ·R·

Despite Robbie Ross's calumnies about Nancy's negro blood, the baby is pink and white all over.

To Edward Marsh

                                         3rd RWF
January 1919   New Barracks
                                         Limerick

My dear Eddie,

Am now garrisoning the town of my ancestors and have mud and stones thrown at my back in O'Connell Street by my fellow countrymen who mistake me for the brutal invader. You said in your letter of January 13th you would see about me at the War House – if you wish to earn Nancy's undying gratitude as you have already earned her husband's, tell someone to expedite

Captain Graves, 3rd RWF, Limerick's demobilization, dispersal centre London, Group 43, application made December 17th by St John's College, Oxon: release signed by Colonel Webb 16 OCBn, same date.

Hope you liked the poems I sent you.

Usual apologies for my presumption on your time, and affectionately as usual,

Robert

You know Sassons is coming up to Oxford: what fun we'll have.

To Siegfried Sassoon   11 Seaside Villas
                                                               Hove
Taffy Day[121]
(How drunk they'll all be.)

Dear old Sassons

Got demobilized on Valentine's Day and caught the flu[122] immediately after. Have been busy dying with no prospect of a military funeral at the end: better now. Going to Harlech on Friday next to get really well.

In spite of flu have written some perfect poetry, nearly all of which you'll hate. Oxford next term, I hope: shall invite you up to Harlech if I find there's any food or lodging available: but don't expect you'll come. I had a lovely time (all considered) at Limerick, no work of any sort and everybody entirely charming to me and only, so far as I can make out, on your account. Write a brief letter please.

My daughter Jenny is charming.

Ever: Robert

PART TWO

1919–1929

As soon as Graves was well enough to travel, he, Nancy and Jenny went to Harlech, where William Nicholson had lent them his house to live in. Graves was still mentally and nervously organized for war and found it hard to readjust to civilian life:

Shells used to come bursting on my bed at midnight, even though Nancy shared it with me; strangers in daytime would assume the faces of friends who had been killed. When strong enough to climb the hill behind Harlech and revisit my favourite country, I could not help seeing it as a prospective battlefield . . .

Very thin, very nervous and with about four years' loss of sleep to make up, I was waiting until I got well enough to go to Oxford on the Government educational grant. I knew that it would be years before I could face anything but a quiet country life . . . I felt ashamed of myself as a drag on Nancy, but had sworn on the very day of demobilization never to be under anyone's orders for the rest of my life. Somehow I must live by writing.[1]

Following Dr Rivers's advice Siegfried Sassoon had gone to live in Oxford soon after he was demobilized (expecting Graves to do the same), but he stayed for only two terms, and left to become the first literary editor of the new and then not very respectable socialist newspaper, the *Daily Herald*. Through Sassoon, Graves became a regular book reviewer for the *Herald* which, he wrote in *Goodbye to All That*, spoiled his and Nancy's breakfast every morning:

We read in it of unemployment all over the country due to the closing of the munition factories; of ex-service men refused reinstatement in the jobs they had left when war broke out, of market rigging, lock-outs and abortive strikes. I began to hear news, too, of the penury to which my mother's relatives in Germany had been reduced . . . Nancy and I took all this to heart and called ourselves socialists.[2]

After the war Graves remained studiously independent of the many

111

literary coteries and movements which were such a leading feature of the postwar literary scene in England, and was part neither of the modernist avant-garde nor of the conservative phalanx. In May 1919 the first number of *The Owl* was published and was one of the few of the many little magazines then circulating to remain successfully neutral in literary politics and to make merit the sole criterion for selection of material, as Graves wrote in the foreword:

It must be understood that *The Owl* has no politics, leads no new movement and is not even the organ of any particular generation – for that matter sixty-seven years separate the oldest and the youngest contributors. But we find in common a love of honest work well done, and a distaste for shortcuts to popular success.

For the second number (November 1919) Graves wanted some poems of Edmund Blunden, a young poet whom Sassoon, in the *Daily Herald*, had been one of the first to recognize; Blunden, who had privately published his poems before the war, went to France in 1915 as an eighteen-year-old second lieutenant in the Royal Sussex Regiment, spent two years at the front, was awarded the Military Cross and, badly gassed and shellshocked, was invalided home to a training camp. He was married in 1918 and demobilized in 1919; when Graves first wrote to him he was at Plymouth, with his wife, waiting to take up the classics scholarship at Queen's College, Oxford, which he had won before the war when a student at Christ's Hospital.

8 July 1919   Slip Back
                                                               Harlech
Dear Mr Blunden
    Siegfried Sassoon lent me a copy of '3 Poems' and one of 'The Barn'. And I think them the real stuff. Can you send me something for my *Owl*, a 10/6 quarterly of Pictures Prose and Poetry of which the last number had contributions from S.S., Robert Nichols, W. J. Turner, W. H. Davies, Masefield, Hardy, Galsworthy, Max Beerbohm, Orpen, William Nicholson, Bianco,[3] Kennington and so on. Could you send a few for me to choose from? I'll be very careful with them. We pay contributors well, but how well depends on the sales rather.
    Have you anything else in the 'brishing-hook–bine-head' vein?
    Yours fraternally   Robert Graves

Robert Graves at Islip, *c.* 1923

Siegfried Sassoon in costume. 'Portrait of an old fashioned Poet' at the
Wilton House Pageant, 1933

A Study in Dubiety   Max Beerbohm
  Mr. Edward Marsh wondering whether he dare ask his Chief's
leave to include in his anthology of " Georgian Poetry " Mr.
George Wyndham's famous and lovely poem : " We want eight
            and we won't wait."

Edward Marsh, 'A Study in Dubiety'
(cartoon by Max Beerbohm)

Edmund Blunden, 1924

Portrait of Robert Nichols by
Augustus John, 1921 (*National
Portrait Gallery*)

Cartoon of Blunden by the poet
Ralph Hodgson (*National
Portrait Gallery*)

Portrait of T. S. Eliot by E. O. Hoppé (*Mansell Collection*)

Ap 5
1946

My dear Eliot:—

I am in an unfortunate position about the Pound affair. I agree that poets should stick together in the most masonic way, and recall that Milton though he had a low opinion of Davenant did rescue him from the gallows because he was a poet: a compliment that Davenant afterwards redrew.

But since 1911 when I first read Pound in Harriet Monro's Poetry magazine; and since 1922 when I met him for the first & last time at All Souls in T. E. Lawrence's rooms, I could never regard him as a poet and have consistently denied him the title.

Now if it had been you, that would have been a very different thing. I would have appealed in person to the Supreme Court, because after all though naturally I prefer some of your poems to others, you are obviously & unquestionably a poet. But, you would never have

gone mad, as Pound did from vanity, and aligned yourself with the worst of the bad wops.

I am shocked but not surprised at the treatment given him by the guards: your ex-compatriots have always been more savage and ruthless to traitors than you proud ones — and that is just too bad. But the real poets have supported our sufferings with dignity & courage.

If there were a single line or stanza of Pound's that recurred to my mind as true and beautiful, or merely as true I should join in your plea — but to do so just because he is a 'name' would be unprincipled.

Forgive me. May I myself be judged with equal severity in the Last Day. Yours v. sincerely
Robert Graves

I expect to return to Mejorca on May 15 for good. Could I have The White Goddess typescript back for some last minute emendations?

Letter to T. S. Eliot, 5 April 1946

12 July 1919

Dear Blunden

Thanks awfully. 'I love your loathsome poems.' I have taken out two or three poems to send my *Owl* co-editor, Turner, to look at. 'Pan Grown Old' is my favourite. May I presume for a moment? Titles aren't your strong suit. All this Pan business is played out anyway. Why not call it 'A Country God'⁴ and remove that rather Unenglish 'complex' from the reader's eye?

And do you mind us (if we print it) putting Capital letters at the beginning of the lines? It doesn't make any difference really and you don't mind doing it yourself one time in three.

War-poetry is played out I'm afraid, commercially, for another five or ten years. Rotten thing for us, but it's no good blinking at it.

Country Sentiment is the most acceptable dope now, and this is the name I've given my new poems.

Let's see any prose you have too.

Fraternally   Robert Graves

Did you know 150 wounded Coldstreamers were drowned in that evil boyau⁵ in late 1914?

Blunden replied accepting Graves's change of title and told him he had been invited to call on Graves's uncle, C. L. Graves, at the Athenaeum Club to discuss his career prospects. That summer Blunden's first child, Joy, was born (but died a few weeks later, at the end of August).

~~July~~ *no!* *August 14th, 1919*

Dear Blunden

We are printing the 'Country God' in the next number of *The Owl* (only November I fear) but Turner thinks he'd better send the Prose back to you – liking it very much all the same – as *The Owl* after that will be March 1920 and it's a long way off. Shall write to you again before then and (BDV) probably see you and family.

Love to Joy; good name. 'Sweet Joy befall her!' Which of you feeds on 'Songs of Innocence'? I expect your way of writing poetry is entirely altered by getting married: or that's what's happened to me. One gets a surer touch and doesn't kick one's heels quite so high: even, I should think, in Plymouth. I feel so happy this week doing things in poetry that I have tried at unsuccessfully for weeks: hope you are able to write yourself, and good luck on holiday.

Yours fraternally   Robert Graves

Oh dear! when shall I learn to write as tidy as E. C. Blunden.

But, good my sir, it will do you no *earthly* good to meet C.L.G. It's like shaking hands with a marble Roman emperor at the British Museum.

Cast yourself at Hardy's feet or kiss the shadow of Masefield if you like: that is an act of worship.

Entertain editors to expensive meals: that is policy.

But call on C.L.G. at the Athenaeum and you will profit nothing in any way: morally, mentally, financially. He will talk like an encyclopaedia with insomnia and give you damn little to eat.

Go and pull old Sassoon's bell instead and you will be far happier at the end of the day.

Smoke is also rising at Slip Back at B34 C70.94 straight into the air. Oh so hot!

In October Graves and Blunden went up to Oxford; the town was so overcrowded that it was impossible to find unfurnished houses to rent, a problem which they both solved by pleading ill-health and obtaining permission to live outside the statutory three mile radius, on Boars Hill. Several other poets lived on the hill at that time, including Robert Bridges, Robert Nichols, and John Masefield, who liked Graves's poetry and offered to rent him and Nancy a cottage at the bottom of his garden.

Soon after settling in there Graves received a letter from Edward Marsh, correcting the punctuation in several of Graves's poems which he was including in *Georgian Poetry 1918–1919* and which were also to appear in *Country Sentiment*; however, Graves had already passed the final proof of that book, although it was not published until March 1920, and so the changes came too late.

Dingle Cottage
Boars Hill
Oxford

No date

My dear Eddie

We are now here among Masefield's cabbages settling down
nicely.

. . . .

You know what house-moving is so you'll understand the delay.
I came across England on top of a lorry full of furniture – Wales,
Shropshire, Worcestershire and Oxford in October – that's the
way to see things. I find things funny in Oxford, my intellectual
and moral guardians have an amiable if shifty way that contrasts
humorously with the fierce and direct methods of my chutney-
eating Colonels in the Army.

Thanks most awfully for all the trouble you've taken about my
stops; the dreadful thing is that I'd just sent back the revised
proofs and 'It comes too late' as the man of 80 said once when he
drew the winner in the Calcutta Sweep, so it'll have to wait for a
second edition. You are right every time. I'm so sorry.

Please punctuate as you think best for the *Georgian Poetry*
proofs.

About the other corrections: please omit the 'and' before 'the
jangling jay', but I do feel I'm right about cutting out the last
stanza in that poem.[6] I feel that this is one of the many occasions
on which I've finished a poem decently and then moralized on
for another verse unnecessarily. I am so terrified of being
didactic.

What did Siegfried Sassoon the poet say to the intelligentsia of
Balliol when he lectured there last term? He said: 'Gentlemen, the
golden rule of writing poetry can be summed up in six words' (the
men of Belial [*sic*] pricked up their ears for something terribly
earnest and brilliant and Sassons went on):

When in doubt
Cut it out.

And it was S.S. who insisted in this case: I'm sure he's right. That
was where the original version ended. And you see, after all, the
horrid birds *did* have the last word.

115

Please cut it out Eddie and forgive my insistence: I am so sorry, and so sure I'm right.

Yours affectionately,   Robert

In November, *Georgian Poetry 1918–1919* was published and although it again proved popular with the public, critical reaction was extremely hostile. The anthology had outlived its purpose and, now that the horrors of war had ended, its particular form of simple bucolic joy had lost its previous poignancy and topicality; the new volume was dominated even more than the previous one by the insidiously 'pleasant' Neo Georgians.

30 November, or so, 1919

My dear Eddie,

I have signed please and when the storm outside subsides a little shall go and get the great man's signature at the top of the garden.

About *GP* (orange wrapper). I agree with Robert Nichols that it's one of these books that somehow don't reach you with a first glance but then continue to improve almost indefinitely.

The best individual poems I think are 'Everybody Sang' [*sic*],[7] 'The Lime Tree' [*sic*][8] and Lascelles Abercrombie's show.[9]

Of the new admissions Shanks is far the best I think and Brett Young's[10] the least compelling. Lady Fredegond Astor[11] is nice but not very exciting.

'It's a very arboreal book,' said Bob Nichols to me, and I remarked on the apparent instability of all the elms as contrasted with the enormous vitality of the nightingales. But that was only a joke and against ourselves really too.

I think it's probably the best volume yet. But I wish the older blokes wouldn't borrow Turner's moonwashed apples and parroty jungle and fishy-conservatory. It upsets one so; I know Turner's scenario is fearfully good as written by himself and tempting for idea-less people to copy but I really think that when they do that it's a signal for someone with a more personal style to take over the torch. This craving for exotic colour is the sign of anaemic old-age: University dons always love red robes and their wives purple hats. And in the vacation they revel in foul red sunsets on Brighton esplanade. *Compris*? If the tendency increases you'll have to go and publish in British North-Borneo or Brett Young's E.

116

Africa on bamboo paper using ape-blood for printer's ink and crocodile for the binding.

Edmund Blunden is getting into his stride finely here, and is, don't you think? just the sort of chap for next time: after all, he does write Blunden. At present I admit he's a bit of a gamble (and even a year younger than Robert Graves, the Georgian infant). I'll get him to send you some new stuff.

I am hoping by New Year to have a tiny book of new poems to send you, privately printed by the Chiswick Press with a Nancy illustration.[12] Have you seen the new *Owl*?

Congratulations on the book and forgive my bad jokes. Love from the family.

Yours affectionately   Robert

In March *Country Sentiment* was published by Martin Secker, and Nancy gave birth to their second child, David. Blunden, meanwhile, was in Peterborough with his wife Mary hand-copying over 700 unpublished poems by John Clare (1793–1864), the Northampton-shire poet who had been hitherto neglected except for brief recognition by Lamb, Keats and the poetry-reading public of the 1820s; Blunden's selection of his poems[13] was the first scholarly edition of Clare to be published.

Blunden now began writing the best and most original of his own poems, portraying the evil of the war against a contrasting background of quiet, though sometimes sinister pastoralism; his first important book of poems was *The Waggoner*, also published in 1920, which Graves helped him put into shape.

5 April 1920

Dear Mary and Edmund

Curse you to Hell for not having written. Why not remember your living friends instead of grubbing in Museums after the Dead? All well here; Nancy has been up some time now and swaggers about in her breeches and smocks as of old. John David is a great little lad and treats us well. We are alone here in the house, Jenny is still away; a cold keeps her at 𝄞 with Margaret and Auntie Fanny. But thank God we have a maid in here every day who is very capable and trustworthy and has a Scottish Mother, so we're well away. Nichols is gloomily enthusiastic about his new religious play. There is £5 waiting for you from *The Owl* but W.N. asked me for your address and I couldn't give it: he's now at Maesyneuardd, Talsarnam, N. Wales if you want to raise the wind.

Nancy's Mother's exhibition is on Wednesday and I am going up to see about it tomorrow. What's the news of Clare? And his disciple Porter?[14]

The hill is lovely now and we've actually got our garden planted. I have written a large number of beautiful poems including three about old Angel, thus making a complete cycle on the subject: I must give her some more tea when they get printed. One about her hope of Salvation, another about her parrot and a last about old Becker appearing to William Henry. What about the *Waggoner*? I hear Aldous Huxley was v. much impressed by 'Almswomen'.[15]

Love   R and N

My *Country Sentiment* is selling like anything and the reviews are good.

                                                        X John David
                                                        ·Λ· Smuts
                                                        Λ· Bingo

'Angel' was Mrs Delilah Becker, from whom the Blundens rented two rooms of a cottage on Boars Hill; she was locally known as the Jubilee Murderess because she was said to have murdered her husband in Jubilee year ('calmly with his cobbling knife/She stabbed him through'). Graves liked her very much and published two poems about her: 'Delilah's Parrot' and 'The Coronation Murder' and sent her a pound of tea every year until her death.

Blunden now left the University and joined the *Athenaeum*, a weekly magazine of literature and the arts edited by Middleton Murry, as an assistant editor and writer of essays and reviews, and thus began a long and prolific career of writing.

After the birth of the second child money began to be a serious problem in the Graves household; Graves decided to write to Marsh and ask him for assistance from the 'Rupert Brooke Fund' (see page 194). 'Put this on record as my first appeal to charity,' he wrote, 'and I hope to God it will be my last.' Marsh sent him a cheque immediately.

15 June 1920

My dear Eddie

Ever so many thanks. We are now firmly established for some time, and can breathe again. If I was a Catholic I would now be offering up a 1,000,000 Paternosters for the repose of R.B.'s soul; but anyway they wouldn't be necessary I suppose. So sorry you are actually in a nursing home! Cheer up!

May I pass the Blundens on to you as a sacred charge to keep an eye on them? They are a most diabolically proud couple, Edmund especially, and will rather starve than ask for help if they need it. Mary Blunden is expecting another baby; the last one died because they couldn't afford proper care, and Mary is very much dreading her confinement. Edmund works much too hard and does too much for charity. He is, on the whole, the 'intrinsically' (whatever that means) best fellow I've met since I left school (Siegfried only excluded) and is going to beat the lot of us as a poet if he goes on at the present rate; and if he learns to let himself go 'all out' a bit more. They go to London this week; c/o the *Athenaeum* will be their address till they settle into rooms permanently.

Will send you my new poems the moment they are typewritten: I hope it won't be too much of a shock. I seem to have travelled a long way in the past three years. Love from all here.

Affectionately   Robert

In October Nancy started a general shop on Boars Hill in partnership with a neighbour, the Hon. Mrs Michael Howard (Mrs Howard looked after the accounts and Nancy looked after the shop). The *Daily Mirror* advertised the opening on its front page with the headline 'SHOP-KEEPING ON PARNASSUS' and crowds came up from Oxford to see it.

Soon after the opening of the shop Edward Marsh sent Graves his share of *Georgian Poetry* royalties.

7 October 1920

My dear Eddie

Many thanks for the large and timely cheque which was greeted with great joy. I have been in Town once only since last May; that was just the other day and Siegfried told me you were away on a week-end which was disappointing: I never seem to see anybody these days and when I do they excite my shell-shock so that I am useless for days after. I showed the last few months' crop of poems to Secker and he wants to publish at once, there is enough for 5/-, so being fed-up with things at the time, I consented. The book will be called *The Pier-Glass* and include the *Treasure Box* poems, the other lot I sent you and one or two fresh ones. But the *pièce de résistance* is the set of four dramatic pieces of which 'The Gnat' and 'The Pier-Glass' which you have seen but which are reorganized and improved to a tremendous extent, form part; people may dislike them, but, as coming from R.G. who has a reputation principally based on nursery rhymes, they will insist on notice of some sort. I'll send you the proofs, if I may, for minor corrections.

I am worn-out from much work, chiefly in the last few weeks, helping Nancy with her shop she has sportingly started up here. Looking forward to seeing the effect of Vachel Lindsay[16] on an Oxford Audience in the Schools next Friday. It is, of course, a unique event. Old Raleigh[17] is a sportsman, and a man of his word: he promised me to get Lindsay a hearing when he came over, and the Schools are only inferior to the Sheldonian in prestige.

The children are well.

Awfully glad Blunden has had such a success: thanks awfully for looking after him. You'll have a lot of interceders for your halidom (right word?) at the Final Trump, chiefly from the Poets' Corner. Am engaged at the moment in trying to write a poem on Ham. The person not the food.

Yours affectionately   Robert

Although Graves was dissatisfied with Martin Secker as a publisher, he preferred to let him publish his poems rather than William Heinemann, who had published *Fairies and Fusiliers* and was a friend of William Nicholson's, because Heinemann had recently tried to give Graves advice about how poetry should be written, which Graves resented. However, in October Heinemann died.

Graves took no part in undergraduate life, but spent his time looking after the shop, the children, writing essays for his tutors (he found the course tedious and the dons uninspiring) and writing poems. His closest friend at this time was T. E. Lawrence, whom he had met early in 1920. Lawrence was then a fellow of All Souls'

College and rewriting his history of the Arab Revolt, *Seven Pillars of Wisdom*. Graves visited him frequently in the mornings between lectures and Lawrence often asked him for advice about small points of style in his writings, and for many years Lawrence was the only person Graves trusted for practical criticism of his poems. Lawrence was not a poet himself and, according to Graves, frankly envied poets; his chief hero was the poet Charles Doughty (1843–1926) and in 1921 he wrote a preface and an introduction to a new edition of Doughty's *Arabia Deserta*.[18] Before it was published Graves wrote to Blunden (whose second child, Mary Clare, had just been born) asking him to get the job of reviewing it for the *Athenaeum*.

27 October 1920

Dearest Edmund

Tremendously pleased about the new baby: give it my love and our love and everyone's love. By the way, Lawrence's edition of Doughty's *Arabia Deserta* is shortly out at £9 9/- a copy of which will be yours (for keeps) (only four review copies issued) if you arrange with Murry to review it yourself. Otherwise the *Athenaeum* will not get a copy: this is unofficial but from Lawrence's own lips. It wants to be reviewed as *literature* not as *Near Eastern Politics*, etc.; that's why Lawrence has hit on you for the job: Heinemann's death has eased the old *Penny Fiddle* a lot; it ought to come out now for certain.[19] We miss you two awfully up on the Hill. Best love to Mary and we are so awfully relieved: it's been a burden on our minds for months. Wish you could see Jenny and David.

Yours ever   R.G.

After six months however, the Boars Hill Shop was such a failure that Graves and Nancy closed it down and found themselves £300 in debt, which they were unable to pay. William Nicholson sent a £100 note in a matchbox as his contribution and T. E. Lawrence, who had become special adviser to Winston Churchill, then Colonial Minister, to help him sort out the Middle East crisis, sent them £50 in cash and four draft chapters of *Seven Pillars of Wisdom* to sell.

Despite his recurrent domestic problems during this 'reconstruction' period, Graves was writing prolifically. As well as a novel about his war experiences, which he abandoned, he wrote a great number of poems, publishing a new volume every year between 1920 and 1925, and alternated them with four short prose books on poetry – in particular, on its psychological aspects and its therapeutic use as 'the physician of mental disorders'.

In 1949, when considering these early books on poetic theory in the introduction of *The Common Asphodel*, Graves wrote:

As a neurasthenic, I was interested in the newly expounded Freudian theory: when presented with English reserve and common sense by W. H. R. Rivers, who did not regard sex as the sole impulse in dream-making or assume that dream symbols are constant, it appealed to me as reasonable. I applied his case history method of accounting for emotional dreams to the understanding of romantic poems, my own and others', and found it apt enough; though poems were obviously complicated, I wrote, by 'the secondary elaboration that the poet gives them when no longer in a self-hypnotized condition.'

The first of these books was *On English Poetry* (1922) which was described in its foreword as an 'irregular approach to the problem of the nature of the poetic art: workshop notes' and was dedicated to 'T. E. Lawrence of Arabia and All Souls' College, Oxford, and to W. H. R. Rivers of the Solomon Islands and St John's College, Cambridge'.

In March *The Pier-Glass* was published and Blunden wrote to Graves saying he was delighted by it and would review it well in the *Nation and Athenaeum*. Graves's reply is on printed notepaper.

HOWARD & NICHOLSON
THE BOARS HILL SHOP
OXFORD

10 March 1921

Dear old sock

Thanks awfully. Let me see about news. We have all been ill. We are all somewhat recovered. The shop is flourishing, *quâ* shop; *quâ* anything else, for instance a harmony of Howard and Nicholson, it is in a bad way. Mrs Howard, Nancy thinks a fool; I know her for a knave, crooked as Angel's little brick path or the windings of the Isis. Anyhow, knave or fool, she is intent on ruining us. T. E. Lawrence went off to arrange the destiny of the East and before he went gave me a present of four articles to publish in America; worth about £800, less agent's fees.[20] He said that poetry was underpaid; so I am not as cross about Secker's paralytic methods as I ought to be, with this small present in my pocket. The only trouble is that he doesn't want any publicity in England and it's almost impossible to secure the copyright from piracy even by printing the articles in a special edition of *The Owl* (as I intend) none of which (except the British Museum copy) shall be available for public scrutiny; so if I can't find any way out I shall honourably forfeit cash by not publishing at all. They are marvellous stories; by a great man. I esteem it not the least of your honours that Lawrence believes in you.

Well, if the *Athenasian* [*sic*] gives me a good chit it will weigh against the defection of the *Spectator*, hitherto my only staunch supporter. They liked Dame Jane and Sharkie, but thought Watkin's 'Pensioner' was not the Gnat but Prinny! and explained my obscurity at length. Heavens! Shall write to *Serendipity*, many thanks.

Tired of Boars Hill, too many B B's (chiefly female) about. Show me a nice healthy hill in Suffolk and a cottage, and we'll come like a shot.

Judith Masefield illustrates J. M.'s new poem (out May 1st).[21] Heavens again! How does he keep on at it? By the way I have given up sticking up for Mrs M.; she is . . . (just that or worse). I am enjoying a recurrence of shell-shock, have written two goodish poems in the last six months and destroyed two failures. And six times rewritten my book on poetry which is now being taken to Cambridge to be vetted with its author by Dr Rivers of St John's – the greatest living psychologist. Or so people say. Pawling is going to publish it; now to be called *An Anatomy of Poetry*. Pawling I have also urged to publish Rosenberg before anyone else hears about him. Think I'll be able to get a job as poetry reader to Pawling. Jenny talks and swears; David crawls and chuckles. We had to sack Margaret,[22] she got unbearable and was dishonest (not financially but was spoiling Jenny's health without our knowledge).

Siegfried in the Pink as you say; but so lazy! I'm awfully pleased to see him his old self again all withstanding. Nancy sends love to Clary and Maire.

Affectionately   Robert

Much touched by your appreciation of the *Pier-Glass*. You can see it better if you think of it as half a reaction against shell-shock by indulging in a sort of *dementia praecox*[23] (the medical name for John Clare's ailment) of fantastic daydreams, cf. 'Trolls Nosegay', 'Hills of May', etc., half as an attempt to stand up to the damned disease and write an account of it (hence, 'Incubus', 'Gnat', 'Down', 'Pier-Glass', 'Reproach' and so on), the obscurity of which is not half so obscure as the original. I wrote each not less than eight times before I understood what they were to be about ... I read your weekly comments on life with much pleasure. I ordered a copy of *Pier-Glass* to be sent you. Didn't Secker send one? Please answer.

Graves explained the problem of the shop and his intention of leaving the university more fully to Edward Marsh, in a letter thanking him for another payment of *Georgian Poetry* royalties.

13 April 1921

My dear Eddie,

Ever so many thanks for the cheque which is peculiarly opportune, as I must explain. This news is mostly *private*, please remember, but I want a sympathetic ear to pour it into so here goes.

In October Nancy started the Boars Hill Shop of newspaper fame with one Hon. Mrs Michael Howard, a near neighbour. The arrangement was that I should keep things going by my Govt Grant at the University and that by the time I finished (June) the shop ought to be a pretty brisk business. Mrs Howard did the shop accounts and Nancy the actual dirty work, serving and going round for orders and keeping the place straight. Mrs Howard made a ghastly mess of her side and couldn't keep the necessary capital in the business so cleared out and Nance and I took it on together, I doing the accounts on top of my University work. Then we lost our nurse so Nancy had to do children, housekeeping, and half the shop, and I the other half shop, accounts, my University work, etc. Then it appeared that the shop was even worse off than Mrs Howard made out in her accounts, and there is no prospect of pulling straight. We put a manageress in but once the personal touch was removed, trade slumped to very low water. We couldn't get anyone else to take on the shop because the landlord will only let us have the ground-site if we run it ourselves. So the long and short is that we have to quit and sell up almost at once. I forgot to tell you that I went and saw a nerve-man in Wimpole Street who told me that I must do no work at all (underlined) for several months, so I have had to leave the University. We can't afford to live on the hill, our cottage is unhealthy and our neighbours are not neighbourly so we are hoping to move to WORLD'S END, ISLIP, with the money from Lawrence's articles he gave me before he went off, if we can get the lawyer to raise the remaining purchase money on mortgage; and there live in true country sentiment, not this suburban squalor. But it's a baddish lookout at the moment, especially as Nancy's feeling the strain even more than I.

I suppose Oxford will one day give me an honorary degree so I'll have M A on my tombstone eventually; but there is still a sneer for me in Churchyard's lines:

Ay, *Skelton* wore the laurell-wreath
And passed in schoole's, you knowe!

and my father is upset at my chucking it like this.

What I propose doing is to recoup some of our losses by writing a set of articles in the *Weekly Dispatch* on our adventures in trade. It ought to be a good stunt. Since the end of term I have written nine poems, most of them sparkling and some of them I hope important. They have all gone off to the Press to make their living, one is appearing in the *Spectator*, one in *Today*, one has appeared already in *New Republic*, two certainly and probably four are to appear in the *London Mercury*, one has gone to the *Nation* (who never acknowledge) and one to the *South-Western Gazette*. I'll send you copies when I can do so. I haven't had a *sou* from Secker, who hasn't advertised the book in a single paper: he is quite hopelessly unbusiness-like and has the distinction of being the only publisher in London not on the telephone. I think he's going bust pretty soon: I'll move back to Heinemann's as soon as possible.

Excuse the tale of woe, and understand my gratitude at being able to pay the milk bill and the charwoman's wages from your cheque.

Yours affectionately   Robert

Graves sent the eighth draft of *On English Poetry* to Siegfried Sassoon, whom he now rarely saw more than once a year and rarely corresponded with; Sassoon had left the *Daily Herald* and ceased to involve himself in Labour politics, and had instead resumed his prewar life of a country gentleman.

29 May 1921

Dearest S.S.

I want to send you my book about poetry which is now after 8 rewrites more or less complete. Rivers is very encouraging (I will send you his letter) and I feel that Rivers is really all that matters if you give your approval to the literary parts which he does not pretend to understand. If there is anything too radically wrong to discuss in a letter, do be a good friend and see me here, for I can't get away to see you. It is more like a manifesto now, ain't it? and less like a jumble. But I am so afraid of being dull and pompous, that I would rather be thought flighty and casual.

Tell me if you think I could get anything from the serial rights in the *Mercury* (say) (the *Fable of Mr Poeta and Lector* is already sent to W. H. Davies's *Form*), if so, what parts should I try on them?

I am terrified of Squire and Middleton Murry and company. The scientific part of this book will probably sting them to great rage and as for old Gosse . . .

Anyhow, I won't publish till I have heard what you say. You kept me from publishing a very bad book once (*Country Sentiment* in a rudimentary form) and your tone when I last showed you this one was enough to alter it very considerably; for the better I hope.

I wish you would make a point always of returning the compliment with your stuff. *Picture Show* is just spoilt by lapses which I could easily have shown you, and one or two of which you might have admitted. Are you in London or at Porlock? Eddie met you in London on Friday, he says, so I am confused.

I am feeling very conceited and want taking down; I dare say when domestic troubles vanish and I no longer feel the necessity of cheering myself up with self-praise about my writing I will be all right again. But at present, as you may gather, I am insufferable.

Love,
                                                                              Robert

In June Graves, Nancy, David and Jenny left Boars Hill and moved to the World's End cottage in Islip, a village a few miles the other side of Oxford.

Islip was a name of good omen to me: it was associated with Abbot Islip, a poor boy of the village who had become Abbot of Westminster and befriended John Skelton when he took sanctuary in the Abbey from the anger of Wolsey. I had come more and more to associate myself with Skelton, discovering a curious affinity. Whenever I wanted a motto for a new book I always found exactly the right one somewhere or other in Skelton's poems. We moved into the Islip cottage and a new chapter started. I did not sit for my finals.[24]

Blunden, similarly, had a 'curious affinity' with John Clare and in a letter of 9 July told Graves he *was* John Clare. With the letter he sent six poems for Graves to consider for use in *Oxford Poetry 1921*, which Graves was editing with Alan Porter and Richard Hughes the novelist, a close friend of Graves's; Blunden also wrote that the new poems which Graves had sent for him to read had never arrived.

12 July ? 1921   The World's End
                                                             Islip

Mr Clare,
Dear Sir,
    or shall we say

                    Mr Shakespere [*sic*]

                            Most honoured sir,
For indeed if Clare confidently thought he was Shakespere and you are Clare as I have no reason to doubt, therefore, etc., QED. It is quite possible on the other hand that I am Skelton, and your senior by a good many years. Let us only hope that Shakespere was not Skelton, or we get a 'which is absurd, therefore'.
    Anyhow, as I have also no doubt that we are goodish poets without any necessary preincarnation let's start all over again.
    With
        'Robert Graves
            to Edmund Blunden greeting.'
And O Edmund it grieves my heart that such a good long sweaty newsy letter as I sent you and so neat a typescript of perfectly excellent poems has gone West or in some other direction. I had

only one other copy and that has sailed East this week among the treaty terms that Lawrence is trying to force on two unwilling old mediaeval gentlemen in Arabia. (Ah, the Red Sea in August! Gawd!) Let's hope the poems may get mixed up with the treaty provisions and secure a spurious immortality in a Blue Book.

What else? Oh.

Your very excellent and already (bar one) previously noted poems to hand. I am printing 5 of them (but not the gipsy one, I prefer the other one in the same *Mercury* about basking in the sun) and will undertake you get your share of cash if anyone does. Mark E.B. 'priority', Mr Blackwell![25]

Islip is Heaven. Stone houses. Cricket. An old stone bridge where was a Civil War skirmish. Flowers. River. 4 Publics. A famous molecatcher. A square church. Gossips. The Rectory where Dr South the Divine used to powder his nose or was it his wig, I quite forget. Edward Confessor's birthplace. Not Edward Carpenter oh dear no! The quarry from which Westminster Abbey came. Cows and other rustic birds including the whirry-dor and the piffle with the rusty-breasted cornemute, now unhappily as mute as its last syllable. A retired serjeant major and a postman who was butler to My Lord the fifteenth Lord Valentia. A village schoolmaster with ambitions. Nip-cats playing at tip-cat but I have patented that rhyme and if you pinch it you shan't play on my lawn. What else? Immmemmorial elmms as the bees say when they're not too hot.

Oh yes, and my morning quip with old Tompkins, the friendly despotic farmer who wears the grey bowler and when he rides, rests the handle of his crop in the hollow of his thigh in a manner reminiscent of I don't quite know who but someone very important like Tarquin or Jorrocks or old Dowdall on Boars Hill.

This is a jolly house we've got.

And we really intend you all to come definitely and stay with us. Note that we are on the London N. Western Railway and that we will even stand the yawling of Mary Clare if you bring her.

The people here are much the nicest-mannered lot I've ever struck in England; they think I'm dotty of course but have taken me for a village mascot already.

Nancy's message to you besides the invitation is (This is what N.N. didn't say but might have if she hadn't been too busy painting the stairs – all colours, in semi darkness) that your hair is

128

too blonde for her taste and that she don't like your conk and prefers the poetry you were writing when the *London Magazine* was still running, to your present output. I addressed that letter to you care of that hopeless rag the *Nation* who have <u>not yet</u> replied about that poem I sent them. In your hebdomadal, do stir 'em up.

I have written an (untenderly) humorous article for the SPE tracts:[26] however, it is more glorious to be written about like you, than merely to write. However, they pay a pound a page, and are in want of contributors. Why not in your leisure time, which I imagine is small, write an article on Christ's Hospital local words, and draw the moral in your own way. Then let me do a similar one on Charterhouse and combine the two into a joint essay on institutional dialect. Especially find out what words are coming in or dying out, since you first went there. What is the 'correct' word for 'Father', 'Food', 'Work', etc.

My new poems are good poems they tell me. I am half way to a new collection. But what will you think of my prose book on how to write Poetry (now with Heinemann's)?

Diccon Hughes did go to America, disguised as a bottle of scotch.

Love to Mary and the Suffolk dumpling.

Oh, no more paper.

Ever   R.G.

Partly because of the decline in popularity of *Georgian Poetry* and the association of Graves's name with it, Graves's books no longer attracted the public or critical attention his first two books had received; *Country Sentiment* was hardly noticed and *The Pier-Glass* was also a commercial failure. The result of this neglect was beneficial to his poetry: he no longer tried to write for the ordinary reading public but wrote only when a poem 'pressed' him to be written, and then he wrote with a greater discipline. 'As a result of this greater strictness of writing I was soon accused of trying to get publicity and increase my sales by a wilful clowning modernism. Of these books, *Whipperginny*, published in 1923, showed the first signs of my new psychological studies.'[27] Graves wanted to dedicate this, his seventh volume of poetry, to Edward Marsh, and sent him the manuscript in December, after he had received the next payment of *Georgian Poetry* royalties from him.

8 December 1921

My dear Eddie

Thanks awfully for the cheque, welcome beyond usual. When you have read the book please make up your mind if you think it good enough for the dedication; please take great care of the manuscript as I haven't duplicates in many cases; and return as soon as possible. I particularly want to know your general opinion on the last two longish blank verse things and on 'In Procession'. The lyrics are mostly sure of themselves. And the jokes.

My prose book will be out fairly soon; it is dedicated to Lawrence (T. E.) and Dr Rivers the psychologist who are responsible for it being written in the way it is. An important book Eddie, I honestly believe. Are you ever in Oxford? Nancy has her new baby in January, at Brighton; I stay on guard with the other children.

Yours affectionately   Robert

Marsh's taste in poetry was notoriously conservative and his greatest dislike was the modern tendency towards obscurity; his reply to Graves's offer of the dedication has been lost, but he obviously did not appreciate the poems which were being dedicated to him.

There are few people to whom I would dare send this letter without fear of offending them; but you I can be sure of.

17 December 1921

My dear E. M.

Thanks very much for the letter and suggestions; look here, about the dedication, the *Egregius Maecenas* is not for the public eye until you leave public life and settle down as a GOM (does not stand for gugga old Marsh, don't worry!). I am only very sorry that you can't swallow the book whole, in fact I'd like really to wait until I produce a book you really did like; at present I feel as if I had given an inappropriate wedding gift, and you see the trouble is there are people who 'get' both those long poems straight off and like them or say they do. You acknowledge that there is passion and spirit in my new writing; but you can't catch the drift – it isn't, be assured, that your brain is ossifying but that mine is liquefying and *Feather Bed* represents a particular variety

130

of liquefaction suited to the problem proposed. Rachel's real reasons for leaving him don't matter a *damn*; the point is that she does leave him and that he is unhappy and angry and jealous; the reasons, if it were a prose story, would appear; she found herself between two forces, love of him and fear for her immortal soul if she loved a free thinker; so she ran away into the funk-hole of a convent, not being able to trust herself outside.

The technical interest of the construction is the way he thinks in extravagant and apparently irrelevant pictures, but always they have a reference and a bearing force on the trouble at hand – the question, what shall he do about her. Eventually he decides to chuck it all up. The violence of his passions sends 'projections' in the form of spirits into the room around him; the rabble of theologians, spikes, etc. ('spikes' = high churchmen) represents the *legacy library* which is to be such an influence on her in the convent; the Mother Superior and Sister Agatha are similarly synthetic spooks of his own fancy having no real relation to actuality. He has been reading the *Awful Disclosures of Maria Monk* I doubt not.

This is only one thousandth part of the sense of the poem; and it is written on the whole for ten years hence when knowledge of morbid psychology will be commoner than now.

You know, Eddie, that one can only write a poem *one way* if it worries to be written and I have done this as conscientiously as I could.

You say my style is a wonderful instrument but that I am not, you think, putting it to its best use. The best use is *surely* to write the necessary poems, and I assure you I haven't a moment to waste on the unnecessary. I am not a leisured scribbler; I do my fourteen hours a day seven days of the week and hardly have time to touch pen and ink.

The 'False Report' stands good for any case of this sort; a big man or a great Nation supposed to have gone soft, smothered in pillows of sloth, uxoriousness or too much money or too much praise. There are always those to sing his dirge, but:

Philistines and dullards
Turn, look with amaze
At my foxes running in your cornfield
With their tails ablaze.

A trick which Samson served on the Philistines, but you don't know your Samson evidently.

Thank you for correcting a few slips which had eluded me. But your diagnosis about freaks of fancy is wrong; or at any rate there is no harm in freaks of fancy if they are subtly related to a constructive purpose and I will be ready to give you a reason for every word in the book, and not a mere personal reason but a universal reason for its necessity. The scansion of ideal you will understand when you've read my prose book; you have the Anglo-French heresy of only two standardized kinds of syllables, long or short.

Quite seriously and without any breach of friendship, indeed just the reverse, shall I keep the dedication for another book, especially the collection which I am contemplating in another year's time of the best of my early work from *Over the Brazier* to *The Pier-Glass* the dedication of which you earned really more than the *Whipperginny* volume, that is, you were more responsible for them? As I say, I don't want to associate your name with work which does not altogether appeal to you, especially as it won't altogether appeal to the Press; the important pieces being in an altogether unaccustomed form. But Eddie, they *are* honest and some few who have seen them, like them.

With very best protestations of affection and I am not in the slightest hurt by your attitude if you are not hurt by this; because I am trying to be honest to myself and to you.

Affectionately   Robert

Marsh, however, good-naturedly accepted the dedication.

On 29 April Graves went to London to have lunch with T. E. Lawrence and to read his poetry at a meeting of the Anglo-French Poetry Society, whose secretary was Edith Sitwell; he also called on Siegfried Sassoon, who had avoided seeing Graves for the past four months because he did not like Nancy and was resentful of her 'monopolizing' Graves; he was in a state of 'nervous exhaustion' when Graves called, and was the 'opposite of cordial', and when they met shortly afterwards by chance, in Piccadilly, Sassoon, 'self-conscious and nasty-tempered', quarrelled with Graves and was rude to T. E. Lawrence, who was with Graves.[28] A subsequent letter from Sassoon admits that the responsibility for the quarrel was his, having at last said things he had been repressing for a long time; the point was, he wrote, that he had always been passionately attached to Graves and in return was continually treated with half-pitying disapproval. His feelings had been hurt so much that he had finally been stung to hurt Graves in return.

29 May 1922

Dear Siegfried,

If I have hurt your feelings I am very sorry; but it is no insult to friendship on my part. Because you quarrel with those two monstrous young men Osbert and Sachie[29] I don't see why I shouldn't go and see Edith (for the first time) when her brothers are in Italy. I find her very interesting as an extreme case of the romantic poet writing by free association and at any rate on the surface pleasant. I told you the truth about it; I had decided four days previously not to turn up and to send a wire instead as Nancy was ill. She recovered the day before, and I went. I came to see you but got hung up in an argument with W. J. Turner and if you're cross with me still, well, be cross but remember that I am the mountain and you are Mohamed in point of mobility and that if you maintain a stony aloofness from my company for about two years (except for the day you came over from Ottoline's with the odours of Garsington about you and the day Toronto and you stopped off at the Golden Cross), why, you can't expect to know what I'm talking about or what I am, much less what my poetry is driving at and you might as well be dead and I too for all the friendship that is likely to remain over from 1919 or so.

I work a 14 hour day and am enjoying it. I can't possibly get away and if you are as anxious as I am to be friends again, which I doubt, you'll come along here and find out something about myself, my work, my friends, Nancy and the children. I want to ask you about a lot of things and I wish you wouldn't rhyme Bach with Hark instead of coming to see us.

Yours ever,   Robert

Sassoon replied that it was discreet of Graves to wait twenty-eight days 'epicritic dissociation' after their meeting on 29 April before writing; he examined the problems between them, but with several sarcastic references to Graves's understanding of psychoanalysis. He said Graves's objection to the 'Hark and Bark' [*sic*] rhyme was pedantic and it wouldn't be changed because the bad rhyme was intentional. The poem referred to was 'Sheldonian Soliloquy (During Bach's B Minor Mass)' which was published in the *Nation and Athenaeum* on 27 May.

. . . Skins perspire . . . But hark! . . .
Begins the great B Minor Mass of Bach.

31 May 1922

Dear Siegfried

It boils down to this: When I married I identified myself and do identify myself more and more with Nancy. If only you had accepted or if only you will still accept us as that physical monstrosity the Phoenix-and-Turtle (see William Shakespeare) the whole conflict finds its solution. You identify me in your mind with a certain Robert Graves now dead whose bones and detritus may be found in *Over the Brazier, Fairies and Fusiliers* and the land of memory. Don't. I am using his name, rank and initials and his old clothes but I am no more than his son and heir and so it is as an old friend of my father that I want to meet you; my father had a sort of hero-worship of you and I have heard him talk of you with great awe even. That's exactly how I feel at present, that I only know about you by legend.

About Ottoline. She has always been very good to me personally, but very bad to my friends. Nancy has very real reasons* for wanting to have nothing more to do with her; and while being quite free to go over to Ottoline and be nice to her I feel it is only at the price of hurting Nancy. So I met her yesterday and kindly but rudely refused to go over there. She boasted that you had been over there several times lately and I was not hurt or surprised. By the *odours of Garsington* I mean an atmosphere which is consciously or unconsciously aware of a hostility between my present life and the life that Garsington plots out for me.

Your joke about my didacticism is an old friend: 'Dear Robert is getting so pompous.' But remember my Scotch and German ancestry.

I do not 'pity' you on account of your life or your ceasing to write lyrically; on the contrary you are a lucky dog to have got the moon under such control. But your letter came as a great shock to me that you are in such a state about my (to you) wrong

134

development and that you feel so badly about it. The shock tells me that my attitude to you must be wrong or I wouldn't get the shock. So I implore your cooperation to put things right – and at once.

Come here from June 7th to June 10th when the room will be spare and we'll start a new show. But this running away and repression is worse than anything.

As for your sneers at my analysmus – who was it said I must go and see Rivers about my book on poetry, eh? Besides, you have been through it yourself or you wouldn't be able to write so pointedly.

My objection to Hark and Bark was not that I felt the tradition of poetry insulted but that it summarized your epicritic attitude to B Minor and the forces of healing in general.

Now Sassons buck up and make an effort.

Yours affectionately,   Robert
*On reading this Nancy tells me: 'I was brought up in this tradition and find it confirmed by experience' is a better way of putting it.

I didn't write before because I didn't somehow think of it. April 29th was on a long time-fuse.

Sassoon's reply to this letter (if he wrote one) has been lost.

Despite the hostile criticisms of *Georgian Poetry IV* Marsh decided to produce a fifth volume; Graves wrote to him in June suggesting changes in the arrangement of the book which might avoid further hostile criticism.

No date [June 1922]

Dear Eddie
Re *G P*
May I impudently make recommendations as follows.
First about new arrivals:
E. Blunden; of course.
F. Prewett; certainly – I hear you have some good new stuff of his.
E. Rickword;[30] when he is not playing at being Turner.

Herbert Palmer;[31] at any rate his sonnet 'Ishmael', do you know it?

Peter Quennell;[32] it will do him no harm personally; I can answer for that and it is magnificent stuff much of it, especially 'Procne Vision' and the others at the top of the wad which Lawrence passed on to you.

Next, if you consider this appreciatively, why not muzzle the critics' sweeping jibes by dividing the book historically into two parts: I The old hands, II The ones who are now not more than 32 or 33 – i.e. those who at the outbreak of war eight years ago had not settled down seriously to write or formed their style for good; in other words those whose characters are entirely moulded by war-experience and after-the-war experience.

This grouping will make the book look more sensible and will account for the breaking of the excellent Abercrombie–Hodgson–de la Mare–Davies–Brooke tradition of early Georgianism.

It will be kinder both to old and young to put 'em in separate cages if the murmurings I hear are to be trusted.

At present you are ploughing with a Bull and a young Camel.

By that token the Bull has begotten a rather ineffective Ox, which disgraces its very excellent sire and annoys the Camel. Its name is not Georgianism but Georgianismatism and it is against the inclusion of this occasional Ox that the real hostility to recent volumes lies.

Tortures wouldn't drag from me the names of this sham-Georgian school but it is recognizable by its infernal cleverness and damnable dullness. Remember the end of the Yellow Books and forgive my impertinence, and don't trouble to answer but take this view (about the Ox) as expressing the secret opinions of that group of writers Turner, (Blunden), Nichols, Sassoon, Graves, etc., the Camel which thrust its nose into the Arab's tent in 1916 (see the Fable).

Ever   R.G.

So sorry I'm hopeless about seeing you at convenient times and seasons; but the effect of London is to send me a bit dotty, I lose direction and concentration.

For 'Bull' read the original Georgians of volumes I and II, Masefield, Abercrombie, de la Mare, etc., and for 'Ox' read 'the NeoGeorgian moonlight school which had perverted the genuine Georgian tradition'[33] (Sir John Squire, John Freeman and Edward Shanks).

Several poets declined Marsh's invitation to be included in this fifth volume: Masefield (who had refused to be in volume IV), Nichols, Turner (because Marsh was not appreciative of his recent work) and Sassoon ('out of cussedness,' he told Graves); Walter de la Mare also had doubts about contributing but did, probably out of loyalty to Marsh, and the same is perhaps true of Graves.

No date [June 1922]

Dear Eddie

We are grand fellows for mislaying each other's letters and manuscripts, now I have mislaid your last to me but I think I can remember the points of importance.

About *Georgian Poetry* and Robert Graves. He is very proud to serve again in the old ship in spite of storms, squalls and barnacles; I hear that S.S., R.N. and W.J.T. are for various reasons absentees; I am sorry about Turner but the others know their own business best.

About the list from *Pier-Glass*. You can print as many as you please; it won't injure the sales, which are non-existent. But – if you could see your way to equalize the representative poems of 1920 and 1921 with 1922 I would be much happier.

If you really want as many as ten may I suggest:

'Lost Love'
'The Pier-Glass' } common ground
'Patchwork Bonnet' } between us

'Fox's Dingle' and 'The Kiss' – I do not like: particularly 'The Kiss' was a left-over from 1918 and does not belong in the series.

'The Stake' and 'Troll's Nosegay' – are alternative suggestions from you which I would accept.

Of later work I would not think of pressing on you stuff you don't like or find obscure; but there is certainly common ground here again. In my prose book, 'The General Elliot' is a good anthology piece, and I like it. 'A Lover Since Childhood' and

'Sullen Moods', the same. They occur in Number 23 of *The Mercury*. The latter has a misprint, 'hold it there' for 'hold it *here*' and in the last verse but one, 'No, stir my memory to disjoin' is now changed to:

> Rather, remind me to disjoin
> Your emanation from my own.

To complete the ten, if you feel like that, I would be very pleased if you could see your way to putting in the 'Children of Darkness' poem which you told Lawrence you liked; an obscurity in the last stanza which you jibbed at I think I have cleared up.

In the list you suggested you put in 'Distant Smoke'. Could you possibly manage 'The Lord Chamberlain' instead? It is the best poem I have yet written according to several people whose judgement you respect. I think you expect it to be more obscure than it is; the theme is really a very straightforward account of the inter-recognition of two people each of whom (see my book, on 'Multiple personality in poets') is accustomed to adapt himself so much to circumstances that his life is the life of a chameleon. The important line is:

> When Proteus meets with Proteus each
> annuls, the variability of the other mind.

The piece is a comment on the inadequacy of the present tradition of history and literature to cope with the psychology of poets – I suppose that's what it amounts to – in this particular point.

Excuse me sending you these again to look at, but I think in anthologies there should be cooperation between editor and author: and I am trying to make my contribution representative.

Your choice of Blunden pleases me; but 'The Canal' and 'Eclogue' in a recent *Nation* are most important.

On July 1st I hope to see you at the Bridges' and Nancy and the children will be there too if my plot goes well.

All affection,   Robert

PS. Peter Quennell has a poem for your inspection which Diccon Hughes will convey next Saturday. But also 'The Man and the Sunflower' is to me a very good poem indeed, also 'Invocation'.

To Edmund Blunden

No date [June 1922]

Dear Edmund
  I think your 'Eclogue' is first class.
  Yours ever   Robert Graves

In the postscript I wish to record a strange feeling of conflict
between us not only based on mutual overwork or unenterprise in
seeing each other. I'd like to have that business out with you when
possible, but I don't know on what it's based except on the
discordance between your home life and mine: I think of you with
great friendship and having lost most of my literary friends lately I
would not like to lose you without an attempt at reconciliation. I
am certainly as much to blame as you are in this case.
  With love to Mary from us all. Our new child is a perfectly
charming nature [*sic*] and called Catherine.

Blunden replied that the feeling of conflict between them was because
he had felt pained and isolated after being told of a conversation at
Islip, in which Graves had referred to him as morally feeble and by
heredity liable to lapses with the bottle, and that he felt an ethical
guidance in Graves's general attitude to him which he resented as
an infringement of his own personal liberty. As to the discordance
between their home lives, he replied that he was happy with his wife
and with his home and had no wish to steal Graves's thunder or to
'have it installed'. At the same time he admitted that he owed a
tremendous lot to Graves, and that his example and influence had
been of great assistance to him in many and various ways.

No date [after 20 June 1922]

My dear Edmund
  Good for you, a very frank and temperate statement and so far
as I am concerned the conflict is at an end between us. The
reported conversation which showed us at Islip as regarding you
'as morally feeble – by heredity liable to lapses with the bottle' is
simply false and I wouldn't believe it if I heard it of you. All I
have ever said is that you have an 'inferiority complex' (excuse
technicality) concerned with your father's shortcomings as I have

with my mother's and the conflict between your father and that sort of context on the one hand, and your Christ's Hospital tradition on the other is a very important motive in your poetry.

You identify yourself with Clare because he represents to you the victim of village life, unsuccessful in his attempts to win recognition in spite of the help given him by old Blues on the *London*. Where Clare failed you are out to succeed and thus avenge him. You have avenged him most miraculously and restored him to popular recognition. His ghost ought to have burned out its discontent. Now I hope you will lose a little of your sense of identity with Clare so that you won't think of madhouses or Mary Joyces or of Clare's pastoralism as an end in itself. I am fighting down a similar sense of identity with Skelton. These ideas have a cramping effect on work, don't you think?

The news that you and Mary are happy together makes my heart leap for joy; that was the conflict between us when you were here. I was deliberately imposing a counter-irritant to the people who were trying to make you think of poetry as more important than Mary and Claire. In emphasizing this with too heavy a hand I was wrong and I am sorry. This is the explanation as far as I can feel it and Nancy was adding fuel to the fire, you know her very decided views. We were trying to force things against the natural development in you and our punishment was your sense of pain and isolation resulting in silence and avoidance of us.

Well, Edmund I am feeling very happy. Send all our tribal affection to Mary whom I for one love most brotherly. About your owings to me. Understand this as my own view of a psychological necessity that if I have assisted you in any given way your assistance to me though it may have taken a very different form must have been no greater and no less. I find my debt to you immense and conclude that the *vice versa* holds good, that's why I didn't want a break-up.

My prose book has appeared in America and I have sent E.M. and S.S. a copy each because they are historically earlier friends. When the book comes out over here in a week or two you can expect a copy suitably inscribed to you and Mary. I am getting at a lot of very important new stuff about poetry now which puts the said book out of date a good bit.

Best of luck. I like the *Old Homes*[34] and feel it marks the end of the purely pastoral chapter. All very well here: we propose caravanning this July in a baker's van.

The Shepherd[35] contained some lovely poems and I want your oughtograph [*sic*] when I can.

I have had a severe misunderstanding with Siegfried but I think that it's about ending. I feel a similar one with de la Mare. But the S.S. and the E.B. ones I felt acutely.

Bless you all,
Affectionately   Robert

Although Graves had left the University before taking his BA degree, his friend Professor Sir Walter Raleigh, as head of the English School at Oxford, arranged for him to apply for the higher Bachelor of Letters degree with himself as Graves's tutor (on condition that he didn't have to give him any tutorials); for this Graves had to submit a written thesis on any subject he chose:

I found it difficult to write my thesis, *The Illogical Element in English Poetry*, in the required academic style, and decided to make it an ordinary book. I rewrote it some nine times; and did not like the final result. I was trying to show the nature of the supra-logical element in poetry, which could only be fully understood, I wrote, by studying the latent associations of the words used – the obvious prose sense being often in direct opposition to the latent content. The book's weakness lay in its not clearly distinguishing between a poet's supra-logical thought processes and the sub-logical process of the common psychopath.[36]

To Edward Marsh

No date [early July 1922]

My dear Eddie

How goes it? The occasion of this letter but not the motive is to ask you to yield up Peter Quennell's poems.

In another couple of days I'll send you some new poems of my own; hope you'll like 'em, they will go into the *Whipperginny* volume. My prose book ought to be out very soon now; I played the fool with it when it was already in proof and ran myself into a fine expense which I'm afraid won't be covered by the sales – a year's work gone west. I am now getting at a very exciting part of the study of poetry, in a second book called *The Illogical Element in Poetry*, meaning of course the Supra-Logical – Illogical is a leg-pull. What do you make of the ballad of John Barleycorn for instance? Can you see in it an undercurrent of allusion to something else?

My idea is, Eddie, that though there may be an outcry against this analysis habit of mine, I can't stop it in myself, and actually it has no dangerous effect on poetry because one can't analyse beyond a certain point, and below that point is the unconscious which after all is the starting point of poetry. Surface analysis will only prevent writing by formula and the experience gained will enable the unconscious to create work with greater depth and sincerity than before.

A hostile attitude to the analytic method and a contentment with what is labelled Georgianism stultifies my present poetry for the reader. I don't say my present stuff is better than its past or better than other people's; I only say this is what's happening, and promise that my thought has not run ahead of emotion.

Blunden has amazing reviews: and the book which is far too long deserves them on the strength of the four or five real poems included. The two great faults of the book are self-pity and selfishness, and this Clare reincarnation delusion.

I have found a very good poet indeed, John Ransom,[37] an American, and intend to get him published over here as he fell completely flat in America (*Poems about God*, Holt, New York).

I wish I could see you on a set occasion here. Don't you come to Oxford ever? My trouble here is that Nancy isn't very strong and we have no servants, so I am largely nurse to the children, gardener, allotment tiller, housemaid and cook. I get about an hour a day of writing, including letters, and can only escape in the evening to see anyone after the children are in bed. When I come up to London about four times a year it is a hopeless struggle to get away and when I do arrive I'm not in a state for intelligent talk owing to my nerves. I am not complaining for I am completely happy in spite of debts and all; but that's how it is.

[Unsigned]

Graves had started a correspondence with John Crowe Ransom probably in June 1922; Ransom was then teaching English at Vanderbilt University in Nashville and editing the famous poetry magazine, *The Fugitive*, whose contributors included Robert Penn

Warren, Allen Tate and the critic Cleanth Brooks. Ransom wrote in his first letter to Graves that he wished to dedicate his next volume of poems to him: 'because you represent as I see it the best tendency extant in modern poetry.' Ransom was one of the few contemporary American poets Graves admired and he undertook to find an English publisher for Ransom's second book, *Grace After Meat*, and to write an introduction to it.

Soon after becoming Graves's tutor, Sir Walter Raleigh died; he had been writing the official history of the war in the air and, needing practical experience for the task, had made many flights with the RAF but caught typhoid fever on a flight out East and died, with only one volume of the history completed (published 1922).

His death was followed shortly after by the death of Dr W. H. R. Rivers.

No date [July 1922]

My dear Siegfried
    Rivers!
        But there it is.
    Do you know if his new book on Dreams was finished; in a state to be published? It is about his most important work. You ought to see about it, in case it just gets forgotten.
    You are luckier than me about this, because Rivers followed Raleigh and they were both in the inner circle of my friends, and my book, the one I'm on now, was an offering to both and the only test of its truth was Raleigh on the literary part and Rivers on the psychological. But that's unimportant; the bad part is that both R. and R. were killed by complete fedupness with being Dons; they undertook too much outside work for their age, sixty-two and fifty-seven, and it broke them. I think both had done their spade work and left successors to carry on.
    Rivers incomparably the better brain, I should say certainly the first scientist in England. Raleigh the only human force in Oxford and death on the Old Clothes Merchants of literature.
    Bless you Sassons and if you don't buck up a bit I'll die really this time just to spite you. 1916 was a threat only.
    Yours affectionately   Robert

To Edmund Blunden

No date [August 1922]

Dear Edmund

Many thanks for your merry note. We are just back from our outing in the caravan – caravan by courtesy only, a very ancient baker's cart drawn by a horse (born (actually!) before the invention of motorcars). And once the shafts dropt off and always it was raining but the children grew fat and strong on it and we elders blessed with all the gift of years are none too bad neither.

If you have no employers to give you a copy of my indiscretions let me know by return and I'll send you one with a very good will. But it's always worth dunning the employer first.

Nichols never sent me so much as a piece of his cake or a slice of his father-in-law's prime bacon.[38] We were all against him marrying and producing offspring after his kind and I give him credit for sensing this.

Football is in the air here already. I'll be captaining the village I expect and it's the first year we have entered for my Lord of Jersey's League competition so there is a general thrill in the air.

I am full of bounce intellectually – do you find this trying or do you like my Graveyard wart-removing type of work better? I have my teeth into Shakespeare's secret sorrows at present, *The Tempest* is yielding up its dead to me.

Have just sent my new poems *Whipperginny* to be typed. I see no chance of a cessation of the flow of poetry I fear, there being no two alike in the last batch it looks as if it was my natural medium. Prose I enjoy writing at last, but it takes me so long, every word being rewritten about eight times and then not pleasing.

Can Mary let Nance have the playground[39] back as Catherine has started rolling and does no longer stay put?

. . . And with thy spirit. Have you any very lively or exciting prose of any sort but (say) of the 'Lost Leader' quality for a new *Owl*? We pay. It's going to be rather fun, new people discovered and I am getting some unpublished Herman Melville and lots of go other-wise. But don't mention the *Owl* to anyone else for special reasons.

Ever

R.G.

Blunden replied that he probably could write something for *The Owl* but asked what he had done wrong as a poet, that he should be asked for prose. He also asked what Graves's theory on *The Tempest* was, and did he agree with a new theory identifying Caliban with Shakespeare. Graves's ingenious insight into such problems should be 'heartily supported', he wrote. He too was captain of his village football team (Stansfield in Suffolk) and much of their correspondence (particularly Blunden's side) is concerned with the appalling losses of their respective teams. At the top of his letter Blunden drew a caricature of Graves and Nancy surrounded by eight children with the caption: 'Premonitory design for your Brass in Islip Church'. Graves's comment on this ('h' in the following letter) reads rather ironically now. Enclosed with Blunden's letter was a circular letter (signed by Blunden) from the *Nation and Athenaeum* requesting poetry submissions.

No date [August 1922]

Dear Edmund

a) I asked for prose because you said you had finished with verse and because prose writers are fewer than poets and in this age more excellent. T. E. Lawrence is contributing a part of his Arabian story, Lady Jekyll is giving a recipe for plum pudding, Max[40] is writing on Hall Caine and an Indian philosopher[41] is presenting a new philosophic system in brief which is (by the way) going to have a shattering effect on the philosophic dove cotes. So you are in a merry company.

b) Give our love to Mary and say we think of her with warmth.

c) *The Owl* ought to be ready fairly soon; can you do aught in a fortnight?

d) Middleton Murry May Make Mince-Meat of Me. He is a Croce-ite[42] and his brain is (to quote Clutton Brock) like a sleepy pear. He won't understand and he has already been indirectly rude to me.

e) *The Tempest* is a long tale.
   Principally this:
   1 *Die Schöne Sidea*[43] and its Spanish original.
   2 The voyage of the *Sea Venture*.[44]
   3 *Isaiah* 29.
   4 *The Sonnets*.

5 *Eastward Ho!*[45]
6 *Bartholomew Fair*[46]
7 Shakespeare's will.
etc.

The whole structure rests on the similarity of emotional disturbance between 1, 2, 3 and 4 and the historic setting as deduced from 4, 5, 6, 7, etc. *Answer*: Caliban is W.H., not Shakespeare. Sounds dotty, but ain't.[47]

f) I will send you some verses. May I tell you why I don't send to the *Nation*? And others like me? Because Massingham or his minion *never lets a contributor know in less than 3 months* whether he accepts or rejects. Except sometimes, if he gets excited, by return of post. The market being insecure nobody offers.
Put this tactfully to 'em and believe me yours sincerely.

g) Fun to arrange an inter-village match (hire charabancs) some time next year. At some intermediate point.

h) Re. church brasses. No, not at all. And I hope you won't either.

i) Am going to publish an 'indecent and blasphemous' poem for private circulation soon. You shall have a copy if you review it with some attention. About 700 lines of the poem and an introduction and a signature are to be offered for 5 bob or so. Called *The Feather Bed*, have finished it in about 12 months since the 1st draft.

j) Don't mention these things, that is, the *Owl* and *Feather Bed* and *The Tempest* in your discourse till you hear from me. I am getting some unpublished verses by Herman Melville for the *Owl*, too. I am writing to have you sent an *On English Poetry*. I will sign it when you sign your *Shepherd* for me.

[Unsigned]

In December *Georgian Poetry 1920–1922*, the last volume in the series, was published and Graves again 'dipped' into the 'Rupert Brook Fund'; he wrote to Marsh:

No date

Dear Eddie
Very many thanks indeed for that merry evening; and for the

Rupert cheque: it remarkably approximated to the sum needed to restore my local credit, and I will say ten thousand (quite unnecessary) Ave's for Rupert's soul and if you like for yours.

I'm very pleased with *GP* indeed. I was afraid it was going to be a quite different sort of book. It contains at least half a dozen memorable poems; which is greatly in excess of the complement of usual anthologies.

Bless your heart.   Robert

In February 1923 Sassoon sent Graves a copy of Rivers's *Conflict and Dream* and a book of poems by Martin Tupper, the Victorian poet, which Sassoon had bought in Weymouth for a penny and found 'unreadable'.

No date

Dearest Siegfried

Very many thanks for *Conflict and Dream*: I find nothing in it that contradicts and much that confirms the work I'm doing now on *Conflict and Poetry*.

Also I am very glad to meet Tupper in the spirit of friendliness which I never allowed him before: and really he's a good bird at times. Future literary historians will compare your anti-major complex:

When I am old and bald and short of breath,

and elsewhere, with Tupper's sonnet on Army Caste.

Hard Routine
Sets caste and class each by itself aside.
You fierce-lipped major, rich and well allied,
To these poor privates hardly deigns to speak.

And the idea of comparing the Great Exhibition of 1851, the material side of it that is, with the emotional aspect you will be accused of having stolen straight from his:

Great Exhibition
Yet was it an unsatisfying meal
A poor dry pittance to the souls of men.

Other points of contact between you and him there are but not many, you having a direct opposition to his religious complacency, a necessary reaction in the 50ies when the country was recovering from a terrific shaking in the early century and the lean times after the peace; an objection to the family system, which suited him but failed you; an objection to Royalty-toadying (owing to your collateral family history) while with him it was a form of life inseparable from religion, from the position of the Queen (the first religious sovereign since George III before his madness) as head of the Church. And so on.

Tupper wasn't good or bad; he was inevitable and contributed to poetry what at any rate was a jumping off ground for your poetic violence and cynicism. *Requiescat in pace.*

I enclose a poem retaining the original: unless you demand it.

I also enclose proofs of *Whipperginny.* They are uncorrected. Have been sorting all my letters and papers including yours and Rivers's and reading them. I feel ashamed of myself for my recent bloodiness to you, but you have been bloody too, haven't you?

Love from   Robert

PS. On Sunday we go to camp, for a week, in two Army tents at Toronto's farm at Tutney. Come and visit us there. 'Swallow your pride, let us be as we used to be.'[48]

R.G.

The poem Graves sent a copy of was the verse letter Sassoon had written from the American Red Cross Hospital at Lancaster Gate after being wounded in July 1918 (see page 208).

In 1922 Graves met Basanta Mallik, the Bengali philosopher, who was to be of great though ephemeral influence on him. Mallik had been adviser on International Law to the Maharajah of Nepal and assistant tutor to his children, and in return for his excellent services the Maharajah had sent him to Oxford to study British political psychology, a knowledge of which, the Maharajah thought, might prove useful to the Nepalese government. Mallik, however, stayed longer than expected, turned to philosophy and, overcoming a long-standing grudge against the British, made many friends.

Under Mallik's influence Graves became extremely interested in metaphysics, as he wrote in the first edition of *Goodbye to All That* (he omitted the whole passage in the 1957 revised edition):

Metaphysics soon made psychology of secondary interest for me: it threatened almost to displace poetry. Basanta's philosophy was a development of formal metaphysics, but with characteristically Indian insistence on ethics. He believed in no hierarchy of ultimate values or the possibility of any unifying religion or ideology. But at the same time he insisted on the necessity of strict self-discipline in the individual in meeting every possible demand made upon him from whatever quarter, and he recommended constant self-watchfulness against either dominating or being dominated by any other individual. This view of strict personal morality consistent with scepticism of social morality agreed very well with my practice.[49]

Mallik went back to Nepal in 1923 and invited Graves, Nancy, the children, and T. E. Lawrence to visit him there at the Nepalese government's expense; Graves decided that if Lawrence went, so would he; but Lawrence had recently entered the ranks of the Air Force and he declined, though he wanted to go 'too much for it to be a wholesome wish'.[50] Mallik remained an influence on Graves for several years but by 1936, at least, when Mallik returned briefly to England, this influence had been dispelled.

Graves's poems now became heavily philosophical (*Mock Beggar Hall* totally so), a development which he later realized was 'misguided'. The first of these philosophical works was *The Feather Bed*, a long poem published in July 1923 by Leonard and Virginia Woolf at the Hogarth Press.

To Edward Marsh

No date

My dear Eddie

Many thanks for your long letter: I'm glad you like *The Feather Bed*: it was over-subscribed and can't be printed again because Hogarth Press are limited for type, which is a pity. As a matter of fact I'm having a copy specially bound for you but the girl who is doing it is so damned sluggish that it will not arrive for weeks I fear.

I don't know when I'll be able to get up to London to see you, the trouble at present is that I have been working all this year on more or less unprofitable writing. My cursed treatise on poetry goes on plaguing me: time after time when I think I've finished, I have to rewrite three or four chapters. I wrote an opera[51] for my father-in-law to press on the Polly people; rather good fun but I don't see any hope in it; it was done on request and I spent weeks on it and then I have been editing a new *Owl* which is admirable in contents but if we sell all the 1000 copies at 10s. 6d. we will hardly be able to get the typing back. Now I have finished a book of philosophical poems[52] (with a few ones you'll like very much perhaps interspersed but the bulk dull to people who are not interested in thought along these lines).

Heinemann are thinking of doing a *Collected R.G.* but can't make up their minds that unless they get help from America such a book would pay; and I don't think America is keen either. Personally I should have thought a book containing all my so-to-speak Georgian poetry and stopping short in the middle of the *Whipperginny* obscurities ought to be able to whip-a-guinea from 500 pockets without much delay? Don't you?

Of Peter Johnstone I can't think sanely: Dr Rivers (my friend and Siegfried's) once told Dr Head[53] that in his opinion Peter was the most dangerous young man in England to have about a house. I don't quite know what he meant, and please don't tell this to Peter (possibly it has already come to him), but anyway it will be a long while before I can meet him again without being extremely upset because I was once very fond of him and am not so any longer. I hear privately that Romer Wilson[54] has married and sailed to America with a man I know well called Edward O'Brien; I understand that two prominent Georgians, also my friends, will be much upset at this intelligence but God forbid that I should talk scandal, I'm only extremely unhappy at the tangle.[55] I shall send you my new stuff when it's typed.

. . . .

I suppose we'll see a lot of the other Peter[56] for the next three years, he comes up in October.

I occasionally hear from Lawrence (T.E.) who has made friends with Hardy who is near him.

If the Brooke fund is still functioning as widow's cruse for us poetic Elijahs in this Samarian famine, a half-pint of oil and a cracknel or two will not come amiss. I can no longer meet the eye of the bank cashier any more than he can meet my cheques; Nancy is not in a condition to do as much of the work as usual and I have to be cook-housemaid-nurse-washerwoman all the time (no help from outside) and enjoy it very much and it's good for work but I find it hard to make ends meet. The three children are extremely well, so am I, and so on the whole Nancy and I count ourselves the happiest of God's creatures when there is no deficit and no returned cheques. The house is spotless and all my poems scan and I have been re-elected local football captain.

Yours affectionately   Robert

In February 1924 Sassoon sent Graves a copy of his poem 'Primitive Ritual', written after reading Frazer's *The Golden Bough*; Graves sent back a criticism of the poem and suggestions for improving it. Sassoon wrote saying he liked his comments and offering to lend him £30. He also sent several more poems for Graves to comment on.

No date

My dear Siegfried
    Your letter demands answer in detail; I am glad you think I talked sense about 'Primitive Ritual'. I wouldn't if I were you cut out 'hear the moan of pluvial dirge subsiding'. It is good for what follows. The *breeze* phrase I found too heavy, but the *subsidence* is all right. Your alterations in the *envision* phrase are admirable.
    The 'Banbury Road' poem goes into *Mock Beggar Hall*; of which I sent off proofs four days ago. Please return this poem; it was too long for the *Nation* but Woolf was nice about it. I am more hopeful about you and *Mock Beggar Hall* after what you report of Hodgson and Turner and their arguments. I *loathed* philosophy until I met Mallik (as he *loathed* poetry till he met me) and as Head will have possibly reported to you after his conversation with the two of us, he (Head) told Mallik that he had no use for metaphysics because its assumptions were all out of date, having been put out of date by new discoveries of physics and psychology; which pleased Mallik and me because from Head's point of view there can be no possible exception taken to *Mock Beggar Hall* and Mallik's metaphysical book; at the places where traditional metaphysics break down we have fundamental suggestions to make. So I am hoping that, like Head, your objection is not to abstract ideas, but to scholastic philosophy which gets you nowhere mentally or morally; so please read *Mock Beggar Hall* in the hope of finding some sense in abstract ideas.
    Possibly your 'devildoms' are due to a form of absolutism in

151

your loyalties. As for falling in love, I heard about that, as it were from the horse's mouth, and was sorry but rather relieved in the sequel! I am referring to events since we last met.

As for T.E.L., your devildoms are possibly to be compared with his, but on the whole I would less like to be him than you so far as peace of mind is concerned. When you saw him that day he was working all day and also all night and eating practically nothing and trying to escape from everyone. He wanted to see me for advice about his book.

I haven't seen him since and have had two letters, the last nine months ago; I understand he's still in the same state mentally, but better physically.

As for my drudging domestic duties I have none; my domestic duties would kill you very quickly, but keep me happy and vigorous. As for money. We are absolutely broke at the moment and I am awfully grateful for your offer and indeed perfectly ready to take money from you as a friend and to feel no obligation, but friendship at World's End implies friendship towards the whole damn lot of us, and until you realize that I am completely satisfied with this life, debts and all, and am not so far as I know Nancy's drudge or 'the Hen-Pecked Husband or Hammond's Depressed Villager or the Impoverished Genius with the Awful Wife and the Squalling Brats' (for these parts am I starred among literary gossipers), until then I say you and I are at too great cross-purposes to be really friends again for a while, and the question of obligation must not be allowed to rise (what rot, Robert, you owe him £10 already). I can imagine nothing better than that we two should be back in friendship, but it seems clear to me that while there is all this secrecy and avoidance on your part there can at the best be merely a sort of superior literary acquaintance between you and me. I admit there must be faults on my side but am not aware exactly where they lie: you must tell me.

. . . .

Your poetry on the whole I like very much indeed. By all means print 'Westminster Abbey'. How, by the way, do you scan the *decorous* line? It sounds as if you sounded it deckerous and not decoarus. It's a really good piece.

The 'Freeze of four Seasons' is probably all right but looks like something enthusiastically written up in a bathroom.

'Any Poet' – something written neatly and gravely in an album with different coloured sheets.

'Invocation' I like extremely as also 'Life's Looking Glass'; 'Song' is all right in the 1902 (Coronation year) mood. I don't understand who The Druid is and what he is prosephying [*sic*], but *scarfed* is good.

'Elegies' I and IV are excellent but I have not sufficient sympathy with Vaughan, Crashaw and Chatterton (the last a hopeless fraud, to my reading) to appreciate II and III, but I can see that II is all right really. Also I greatly like the Marlborough poem in the *Nation*. My regards to Noah and Polidore, also to Delphine and W.J.T.

Robert

PS. I want you to come and stay a night or two nights with us; you needn't work and can go away when the baby cries too loudly. Then I can talk in detail about this whole poetry business. Any day will do; but I propose to make your coming here fairly soon a test case of your goodwill.

Affectionately   Robert

You will find Nancy perfectly reasonable if you treat her as a fellow human being not altogether lacking in wits or kindness. This letter is an awful muddle but I am really trying to put things right in my clumsy way.

Sassoon replied that talk of a 'superior literary acquaintance' between them was nonsense, that he would visit World's End as soon as the weather improved and that he thought Graves was Hardy's 'poetical grandson'. He also sent a cheque which, he wrote, 'will not cause you to think you owe me £100'.

19 February 1924

My dear Siegfried

Ever so many thanks for the cheque which has just restored our self-respect: we can face coalmerchant, grocer and butcher now with more than 7d. in coppers to which net personality we were reduced. I enclose two poems, or at any rate one, just written: 'From the Farm Yard', and 'At the Games' if I can find a copy. The latter has been taken by *English Life* and I have entered it also for the Olympic Games Prize.[57]

May I send you my choice of early poems for a First Collected Edition, which William Nicholson wants to decorate and place somewhere? I am on using only the fairly simple ones to understand, therefore stopping short half-way through *Whipperginny*, and cutting out all poems I wrote in too idle a mood (I have had my 'star-warbled madrigals' too – only they take a different form from yours).

I admit the weather is bad. And so long as there is no ill-will floating about (which I take your word for) I hope that your methods of reintegration will succeed by whatever means, and we will hold you excused from a visit.

Exceptionally in haste.

Later. I am glad you like and admire Lawrence. You have much in common and he has great hopes of your future work.

Nancy is much easier to get on with now, everybody seems to agree, especially if no particular effort is made to smooth her down.

I very much want to meet the Woolfs.

Affectionately   Robert

PS. Can't find 'At the Games': sending you the first drafts of 'The Farm Yard' if you are interested in constructive problems.

In August Graves stayed with William Nicholson at his new house at Sutton Veny, Warminster; Sassoon was another summer visitor there, but they just missed meeting. Back at Islip again Graves wrote:

No date

Dearest Siegfried

I hear we were unlucky at Sutton Veny by two days: I wanted to see you too about this collected poems business. Secker wants to do them and it is only a matter of getting copyrights from Heinemann and Harold Monro. I am suppressing about half the *Brazier* and *Country Sentiment*, about one third of *Fairies and Fusiliers* and *Whipperginny* and the two long prose ones in *Mock Beggar Hall*; only the prologue and epilogue of *Feather Bed* go in and a number of recent poems which are being printed in *Mercury*, *Adelphi* and elsewhere. I have arranged the collection not according to the books which make it up but into:

1. Early poems 1914–1917 on miscellaneous subjects.

2. War poems 1915–1919.
3. *Country Sentiment*; out of various volumes 1918–1920.
4. The restless unhappy *Pier-Glass* phase 1920–1921.
5. Gradual recovery in first part of *Whipperginny* 1921–1922.
6. Later philosophical pieces 1922–1924.

It becomes intelligible that way: but I want your approval.

My *Meaning of Dreams* comes out next month. My book about poetry has at last found a publisher, Cecil Palmer, and is called *Poetic Unreason and Other Studies*. At Sutton Veny I wrote a 30,000 word Biblical romance called *My Head, My Head*. I am tidying it up a bit now but it's all right. In it I make my peace with Moses whom I used to loathe.

Good bathing here and some empty beds and admirable cuisine. We expect you when we see you: to do more would be flying in the face of providence.

Squire begs me to urge you to publish your poems: I will not be so impudent but *Recreations* was a good piece of work and there are several poems since I have liked under various titles.

. . . .

I saw Lawrence the other day for the first time for two years: he and the Hardies are inseparable now it appears. It was to Lawrence that T.H. made his magnificently Hardyish remark. Lawrence had said something a trifle disrespectful of Homer and T.H. replied rather warmly: 'Really, I have a far higher opinion than that of the *Iliad*. It reminds me at times of *Marmion*.'[58]

Affectionately   Robert

In August Marsh began 'the biggest literary operation of his life': the translation of La Fontaine's *Fables*. In November there was a general election, Churchill was returned as MP and appointed Chancellor of the Exchequer, under Baldwin, and although Marsh knew nothing of economics Churchill retained him as his private secretary. A few weeks after the election *Forty-Two Fables of La Fontaine* was published.

No date

My dear Eddie

Thanks ever so much for La Fontaine. I am reading it alternately with that nihilist Gertrude Stein's *Geography and Plays* in order to bring out the rival flavours of each.

Your work is admirably neat and lively: and I could not have imagined a more suitable translator of La Fontaine than yourself: humour, colloquial knowledge, scholarship, administrative ability; particularly the last. There should be, I agree, that sort of real-unreal atmosphere which makes reference to Dan Leno and beano on the one hand and cit. and mumchance on the other, right. La Fontaine was a Liberal: I know you have no politics but your long association with that party has made it suitable for you to undertake his Private Secretaryship. And he is a poet of Cabinet Rank.

The only detailed criticism I have yet to make is did La Fontaine write vulture in his fable of the Braggart Cock? If not, *do* vultures eat live animals? I thought they only picked up offal (offal but offaly nice). So one of your former associates fell down on a point of zoology: do pheasants eat mangold wurzels? They don't. Dear Eddie, it has been very well worth doing. Congratulations.

I am writing a treatise on the various rival techniques of modern poetry;[59] showing their historical necessity and meaning. Defending where defence is needed. About 8000 words, awful sweat. It was nice of you to walk over the other day and see the four reasons for my never coming to town; it is the life I have chosen and it suits me. In fact to have no leisure time on my hands at all has been the only possible cure for my neurasthenia from which I still officially suffer and actually, if I start at all a different life from this. Travelling is the one thing sure to upset me; a train journey to Oxford even leaves me utterly unstrung for the rest of the day. Can't quite explain it, but there it is.

I say, if you have those *GP* royalties yet which you hoped in the Spring would appear in the Summer, or if you can extract them from Monro, do let us have some. We are, as is usual at this season of the year, juggling one overdraft against another; a good time is coming perhaps but we want to live to see it. Sorry to bother.

Yours affectionately   Robert

Marsh immediately set to work on a sequel of the La Fontaine book. He wrote to Edmund Blunden, who in March 1924 had succeeded Robert Nichols (now in America) as Professor of English Literature at Tokyo University, and told him of his recent visit to World's End: 'I had a Sunday at Oxford lately, and went to see Robert Graves whom I found radiantly happy at a teatable with five or six bread-and-buttery children and the village postmaster and wife. His combined jobs as Poet and maid-of-all-work suit him curiously well – and I was greatly struck with his beauty.'[60] He also wrote to Nichols saying he still found it impossible to sympathize with Graves's psychoanalytic method of literary criticism but, after receiving the following letter, he could not afford to dismiss his critical apparatus altogether.

No date

Dearest Eddie

Ever so many thanks for the cheque which came in the nick of time: (they always do).

So glad you are doing La Fontaine again. I have come to the conclusion that technically you are a good deal the best of the poets you have anthologized (excuse the Latin idiom).

Hope *Poetic Unreason* doesn't bore you and that you'll not take as offensive my remarks about Rupert: he has been overpraised for what is to me least important in his work and not enough praised for his real contribution. I should have made this clearer perhaps.

Enclose uncorrected proofs of my play.[61] Stupid play, but the songs are nice and so is the play within the play.

If funds permit we visit London on the 20th for a week when I hope to see more of you than I have for years which alas isn't saying much.

Yours affectionately   Robert

Poetic Unreason was published in February; Graves sent a copy to Sassoon, who replied that, though he hadn't yet had time to read it, he had spoken with Sir Edmund Gosse who was enthusiastic about the book and who intended to make Graves the subject of his next *Sunday Times* article; Sassoon sent Graves a copy of his new book of poems, *Lingual Exercises for Advanced Vocabularians* and urged him to write Gosse a charming letter.

2 April 1925

Dearest Siegfried

You make us very happy by the double inscription: really to have you as a friend again is the best thing that has happened here for years. While there was a conflict on, it spoilt my relationship with Nancy as well as my relationship with you. Congratulate the author of *Recreations* on his second slim volume.

'Prelude' particularly is a lovely thing: of the others I like 'Marlborough' and 'Grandeur of Ghosts' best. 'Conclusion' with two or three slight alterations would please me as well as 'Prelude': these are the two definitely *Shropshire Lad* phrases in the second stanza; the rest is typically yourself. 'Primitive Ritual' is infinitely better in the present version.

Of course it is a great thing for me if Gosse treats about me: I do like him genuinely, but circumstances forbid me from thronging his threshold. I am afraid he can't sincerely praise the book in any wholehearted way. Observe the *Times Literary Supplement* today, on this question. It is a deliberate misrepresentation of my main points, because to concede them involves too much. *Manchester Guardian* did the same but more bitterly. I only hope that Henry Head gets the drift: he will at any rate treat it seriously, which the literary critics say they can't.

Do come over here when the weather mends: we have also been given a car (valued at seven pounds, ten shillings) but have no garage to put it in and the other night a wheel flew off on Boars Hill, for which we owe mechanics a good deal. Otherwise it's as good as your Gwynne.

. . . .

Love from

Robert

Graves submitted *Poetic Unreason* as his thesis and he was awarded the B Litt degree which he now needed, having decided to violate his oath never to be under anyone's orders again and take a job. Cottage life with four children under six years of age and with Nancy ill had become impossible.

Then the doctor told us that if Nancy wished to regain her health she must spend the winter in Egypt. Thus, the only appointment that could possibly meet the case would be an independent teaching job in Egypt, at a very high salary, and with little work to do. A week or two later (this is how things have always happened in emergencies) I was invited to offer myself for the post of Professor of English Literature at the newly founded Royal Egyptian University, Cairo.[62]

158

No date [October 1925]

Dearest Siegfried

I have (on nicer notepaper than this) applied for that Cairo appointment. There were three letters of invitation from independent sources – Sir Sidney Lee, Sir Izzy Gollancz and my brother Philip who has secured George Lloyd's backing (isn't he High Commissioner of Egypt or something?). And apparently the 'little ray of sunshine' as I once heard T.E.L. queerly but accurately called, has been stirring in the matter. I have also forwarded heavy introductions from the Pontine Bob;[63] Colonel Sevenpenny Buchan;[64] the Vice-Chancellor of this University; and Old Old Squishy Oxford.[65] So it should come off. I am begging Bennett not at any rate to crab my chances. I <u>can</u> behave respectably at times now can't I, Siegfried? This letter suggests that I have been seeing Thompson lately as is indeed the case. But it is also due to a hopeful lightheartedness about Cairo: and by the same post I was asked to stand for Liverpool, the same job.

'Meanwhile' (as your poems so often finish) I haven't ten bob in pocket or prospect: and may have to dart up to London suddenly so for God's sake send me the ha'porth of tar to save the ship, and I'll pay it back in enamel of the purest white.

Love from
                                                                        Robert

Arnold Bennett, in fact, had been one of the people who recommended Graves for the job.

No date

Dearest Siegfried

Thanks so much for the cheque which should tide us over the present discommodity. I had a reassuring chit from Arnold Bennett: I have a very poor opinion of other people's opinion of me – though I am fairly happy in my own conceit – and always surprised to find that anyone likes my work or character.

I have a lot of work on hand: and apparently Eliot will collaborate with me in a survey of the untraditional elements in modern poetry.

In spite of mixed weather we are well enough but rather unhinged by this Cairo project. I suppose it would be hopeless to suggest you coming to Cairo with us? It would make it so much more attractive for both of us. I suppose you wouldn't consent as my assistant, and pool the salaries? T.E.L. gives an encouraging view of the job: apparently it is whatever one cares to make it and one is not encouraged to be energetic.

Yours affectionately   Robert

In December the Hogarth Press published a long verse satire by Graves, *The Marmosite's Miscellany*. While waiting to hear if he had the Cairo job or not, Graves arranged his poems for a collected edition; he sent the list of poems he had selected to Sassoon, also a preface or 'summary' he had written for the book, and asked his opinion. Sassoon disliked the preface and objected to the omission of some of his favourite poems such as 'The Picture Book', 'Faun' and 'The Next War'.

No date [December 1925]

So sorry, Siegfried, that you have this chill. It seems a popular trouble, particularly on the liver. I quite agree about the summary: it is scaffolding to the rearrangement of the books which can now be removed after having done its work.

Of those omitted which you question particularly: 'The Picture Book', I don't like it at all: partly because of its anti-German sentiment, partly because it's not very strong in the first three verses. 'Faun' I'll put in: I wrote it when I was sixteen and so long as it's dated I don't mind putting it first.

'Careers' is too Nursery Rhymes from *Punch*.

'The Next War' – not, to my mind, amusing enough to carry off the propaganda. But I'll put it in if you think.

My *Marmosite* comes out this week: I'll send you a copy. Here is my 6d. worth meanwhile.

We did enjoy you last week.

Will you add enclosed poem to the others after perusing it: it is clean enough work and though not in your line, all right. I have two poems recast of the *Country Sentiment* period coming out shortly in the *Spectator*: you'll like those.

No more news about Cairo. But re-reading Lawrence's letter it is plain that Lloyd is under the impression that he has the giving of the job: Hogarth seems certain that I'll get it.

Bless your old wits.

Love from Nancy and the children   Robert

The idea to collaborate on a book about modern poetry with T. S. Eliot had been Graves's. He had first met Eliot in 1916, and in the fifth of his Clark lectures at Cambridge in 1955 he described the impression Eliot made on him then:

a startingly good-looking, Italianate young man, with a shy, hunted look, and a reluctance (which I found charming) to accept the most obvious phenomenon of the day – a world war now entering its bloodiest stage, and showing every sign of going on until it had killed off every man in London but the aged and neutrals. I was due to return to the Somme any day, and delighted to forget the war too in Eliot's gently neutral company.[66]

Graves, however, later resented Eliot's 'neutral' poetry of despair and boredom of that time ('Who forced him, during the Battle of the Somme, to attend London tea-parties presided over by boring hostesses?'[67]) and the fact that Eliot had no war neurosis to recover from after the war and could step forward as the prophet of a new age:

The new key-word was Disillusion – not the Byronic melancholy and the Sorrows of Werther which had been in fashion after the Napoleonic Wars, but a hard, cynical, gay disillusion. It needed a poet for its expression, and there was T. S. Eliot waiting. His 'Love Song of J. Alfred Prufrock' and 'Preludes' struck just the right note.[68]

However, for a short time in the early twenties and again in the forties, Graves and Eliot were friends, though not close friends. To Graves's proposal Eliot replied that he would be 'honoured' to collaborate with him on such a book, though warned that he might find himself with very little time for doing his share of the work. Eliot was then editor of the *Criterion*, a small, highbrow, extremely influential literary magazine.

Graves's letter suggesting the book, as well as a subsequent letter to Eliot, have gone astray; this is therefore the third in the series about *Untraditional Elements in Modern Poetry* (there was a brief, earlier correspondence, in 1923, when Graves submitted some poems to Eliot for the *Criterion*, which Eliot did not accept).

No date [November/December 1925]

Dear Eliot

I have got this English Chair at Cairo and sail on January 8th on a three-year contract. I shall get on with my share of our projected volume and if I find that it's getting on too fast I shall possibly finish it myself. But not without giving you fair warning and a chance to collaborate.

I enclose some criticism sent me by Laura Gottschalk. If you would like it for the *Criterion* please let me know at what date it would be likely to appear. It hasn't yet appeared in America but possibly will.

Please return the typescript if you don't want to use it.

Yours   Robert Graves

In 1924 the Fugitives awarded a prize to Laura Gottschalk [Riding] for her 'teasing' poem 'The Quids'; Graves saw and was very impressed by the poem and asked Ransom if he could see more of her work. Through Ransom, Gottschalk sent Graves a manuscript which she was having difficulty finding a publisher for; Graves liked it and replied that he could probably get it published in England. In September, Ransom wrote:

She is a brilliant young woman, much more so in her prose and conversation even than in her verse. She was recently divorced from her husband, a Louisville College Professor. She has had a remarkable career – up from the slums, I think, much battered about as a kid, and foreign (perhaps Polish Jew?) by birth. English is not native to her, nor is the English tradition, greatly to her mortification. As a fact, she cannot to save her life, as a general thing, achieve her customary distinction in the regular verse forms. And she tries perhaps to put more into poetry than it will bear. With these misgivings I will go as far as you or anybody in her praise. She is now in New York trying to make a living doing hack literary work. She is very fine personally, but very intense for company.

So much for her – and I'm awfully glad she has picked up such a good friend in you.[69]

Graves wrote to her inviting her to come to England: 'Wiping her slate clean of literary and domestic affiliations with America, she became for the next twelve years the best of "Good Europeans",' Graves wrote in *The Long Weekend* shortly after their separation in 1939:

the Americans only knew her as 'the highest apple on the British intellectual tree'. In England she was assailed as a 'leg-puller', 'crossword puzzle setter', 'Futurist', 'tiresome intellectualist', and so on: none of her books sold more than a few dozen copies, nor did she ever . . . consent to give the larger public what it really wanted. She was the one poet of the time who spun, like Arachne, from her own vitals without any discoverable philosophical or literary derivations: and the only one who achieved an unshakable synthesis. Unshakable, that is, if the premiss of her unique personal authority were granted, and another more startling one – that historic Time had effectively come to an end.[70]

She joined the Graves household on 2 January 1926, just in time to accompany Graves and his family to Egypt.

The following postcard to Siegfried Sassoon shows a picture of *'Le Caire – Intérieur de la Mosquée Sultan Hassan'* and is postmarked 3 February 1926.

We in no way regret our coming yet and are in process of settling down agreeably: I have yet to present myself at the University but nobody is ever in a hurry here: and indeed expedition is the height of vulgarity. We are getting a very decent little flat with a garden and everything as it should be in three weeks' time. We all send our love. You need have no qualms about Laura G. who in every way confirms our happiest suspicions about her. My *Future of Poetry* comes out in the *Fortnightly* in two parts in March and April

    Yours   R.G.

To T. S. Eliot

16 February 1926   6 Rue Sabbagh
                                      Heliopolis
                                        Cairo

Dear Eliot
    Egypt is not to be despised as a resort, but the University is a beautifully constructed farce in the best French style and dangerous if taken in the slightest degree seriously. My rather serious nature has to be closely guarded against a conscientious explosion: the heavy pay and impossibility of getting any work done with students makes me rather ashamed of myself. Anyhow there's opportunity for my own work here. Laura Gottschalk is with us, as I think I wrote and I have a message for you from her: that a clean and revised copy of 'The H.D.[71] Legend' I sent you is

163

to be forwarded to you from our agent Pinker.[72] He also has two critical essays of hers, 'Criticism and the Poet' and 'Genius and Disaster'. One of these, I can't remember which, I sent you a rather messy copy of: Pinker now has copies of both in proper shape and will send you them.

I am going on with the proposed *Untraditional Elements in Poetry*. Have you any objection to her collaborating in this business after what you have seen of her work? She is far more in touch with the American side than I am and is anxious to get ahead with it. She suggests that at the end of a year – until which time you could promise nothing – you might come in as arbiter between our contributions. Please tell me how you feel about this. Her list of poets corresponded exactly with yours: and her critical detachment is certainly greater than mine.

I think the University will soon have to be reconstituted with English-speaking professors instead of Frenchmen as it is at present in the Faculty of Letters. The students speak no French and very little English. If this happens and you are in want of a holiday, it would be fun for you.

Yours ever   Robert Graves

PS. I am/we are, much enjoying your *Collected Poems*: and admire your ruthlessness in suppressions.

. . . .

No date [postmarked 31 March 1926]

Dearest Siegfried

I need not old-soldier you about Egypt and after all its main features are exactly as one imagines them from Europe. I did not share Jenny's disappointment over the Nile: 'The book at school is all wrong; it says the Nile's waters are even bluer than the sky and they're just a dirty green,' but I had discounted the camels and donkeys as much exaggerated but find them only too true. I had expected trams in Cairo but not such nice ones. The Sphinx has really a beautiful face and a tail newly unearthed, coiled round its haunches like a kitten's and a copybook between its paws. The food is very nice and so is the sun.

The University is a comic-opera: I have never been so useless in my life before or with such pomp and circumstance. I had a lecture a week ago and have my next a week hence. 'Shakespeare was a great poet. He lived in London and wrote plays. London is in England. Plays are what you get at the theatre. A poet is a person who . . . Oh, yes, I'll spell the word on the blackboard. POET. No, Shakespeare is not another word for Byron.'

Anyhow, Nancy is getting well: main thing, and the children who all got measles are now recovered. I am writing: I think readably. Laura is even more Laureate than ever. We intend to return at the end of May if there's any money to return on: which will be seen in due course.

. . . .

I had a nice Lamb-esque letter from Edmund. I would welcome a letter from you but know it's unlikely that you'll have any small-talk fresh enough to keep for the voyage here. Laura and I are writing a book together about poetry and so on. It is extremely unlikely that Nancy, Laura and I will ever disband, now we've survived this odd meeting and continue to take everything for granted as before.

The cinemas here are pretty bad but ice-creams are obtainable.

. . . .

I miss football very much and don't take enough exercise.

An Englishwoman in the next street was strangled last week by a camel driver and we had an earthquake on Monday.

Love from us all   Robert

No date [May 1926]

Dearest Siegfried

We shall be at Appletree Yard about the middle of June. Egypt has done its duty in several ways: chiefly, Nancy is very much better. Last autumn it looked as if she'd be a confirmed invalid: now really she's capable of doing a day's work without collapsing. I don't think the climate has had all that to do with it: in some ways it's been actually bad – it's a rheumatic place and bad for the nerves – but we have had a nurse in charge of the children, and Nance has been able to rest, and we found a doctor here who really diagnosed her case correctly. Then, I've had an interesting time and done more reading in four months than in the last four years. Not much writing, but enough.

Laura is just a hundred times more to us than we ever hoped

(these instinctive decisions are for the best) and we can't remember the time she wasn't with us.

I think it's most unlikely that I shall return to this job; I may have to for a short time: but it is quite impossible to do any good with the students and my colleagues are bloody. So I am trying to arrange a lecture tour in America for the autumn and hope to hook a job at some university while I'm there.

What did you do in Egypt Robert? Oh, I won twenty piastres off the High Commissioner at bridge and shook hands with the King whom I mistook for his chamberlain and lunched with the National Poet of Egypt very much like Old Tom, and took tea with the Chief of Police and dined three places off from Mr Howard Carter, and saw the Holy Carpet (two days later at a local cinema) and orally examined seventy candidates for teaching diplomas and lost my hat in the desert and drank a lot of glasses of iced coffee and had a bad stomach for four successive months.

Love   R.G.

After a brief stay with William Nicholson at Appletree Yard, Graves, Nancy Nicholson, the four children and Laura Riding (L.R.G.) returned to the cottage at Islip.

24 June 1926   World's End

Dear Eliot

Laura Gottschalk and I tried to see you in town last week but were told you were in the country.

About the prospective *Untraditional Element*, etc.: I have done a little work on Isaac Rosenberg and L.R.G. on John Ransom and Marianne Moore; principally a preliminary essay on Regionalism as a critical clue in American poetry (i.e. a false clue).

In rejecting 'The H.D. Legend' among the three notes of L.R.G. which were sent you for the *Criterion* didn't you feel it might do for a part of this prospective book devoted to 'Legends', e.g. the other Imagists, Sandburg, D. H. Lawrence?

About L.R.G.'s poems. The ones sent you from Egypt will be out shortly in a book so are not available. Likewise 'John and I' which Pinker sent you, so she is sending you others.

I have left Egypt: because the climate didn't suit the children and the University was just comic opera. If you want a sinecure at

£1170 free of Income Tax between October 1st and June 1st (passage paid) I daresay I could get it you. The students are noisy: the other professors are mostly Belgians. You do about two hours a week. Nothing but elementary school, say 6th, standard. Cairo is about the only possible sequel to 'The Hollow Men'. The officials are very decent. I don't recommend the job at all: but there it is.[73]

Have you any book reviews for L.R.G. and myself?

Yours ever   R.G.

13 July 1926

Dearest Siegfried

. . . .

We are at last sort of settled in to our satisfaction. The children, plump-faced, giggling little wretches (I quote from memory) are at school again: all but Sam.[74] I am starting to write again. I send you this book because you thought it dull in the *Fortnightly*: it looks even duller now. The *Fortnightly* are printing another similar essay on the English Language: and the Hogarth Press afterwards: Hogarth Press are also printing a long poem of Laura's called *Voltaire*.

Nancy is making a valiant effort to draw again. I know no other chit chat. I saw Toronto's Madeleine who is deaf and beautiful as always and says Toronto has stopped writing poems completely.

. . . .

I am busy getting my *Collected Poems* arranged according to the rule that only real poems are admitted: confections barred even if they have a wide anthology circulation. I have pared down the introduction to almost nothing at all. Laura agrees with you about that. I am so glad that she liked you as a person: and she now likes your poems more and more. They may be clumsy at times she says but they are real: which is the only thing that counts in the end.

Bless you   Robert

July 13th today. 'I'd timed my death in action to the minute . . .'

No date [early August 1926]   9 Ladbroke Square
London W11

Dearest Siegfried

Re. my last note scribbled on one of your envelopes. What has happened is this and it must on no account be misunderstood.

We began feeling the financial pressure rather acutely and found that it was difficult for Laura and me to do any serious work at Islip together owing to the noises and interruptions and responsibilities. Nance was at a loose end as there's the nurse looking after the children and I was doing the cooking and housekeeping: so she asked L. and me to leave her the job of running the house all by herself: and come up to Town to write seriously.

We expect my sister Ros will share this basement flat with us. At any rate I have taken it for a month. We chose it because it is so near you. We have plenty of writing commissions to get on with.

We do so much want you to see us when you return. By then we'll all be together, at present only one room is inhabitable and Laura's taken a room with the landlady.

Love from   Robert

After leaving Egypt Graves never took another job; he and Laura Riding now began their remarkable literary partnership which was to continue for the next thirteen years, during which Graves was led by her to a more ruthless self-examination than he had hitherto attempted and to a rigorous revision of his thoughts on poetry. Their first work together was *A Survey of Modernist Poetry*, the book Graves had originally planned to write with Eliot.

18 September 1926

Dear Eliot

I have just written to Faber to apologize about that suggested critical book of modern poetry. What happened was that Laura Gottschalk and I undertook a commission for Heinemann to write a book on a similar but not identical subject. Now we are nearly done we find that it has covered too much of the other ground, so much as to make it impossible to write the other book. The only satisfaction we have with regard to you is that we are now permitted to discuss your poems: and without your work a discussion of modernist poetry is *Hamlet* without . . . well . . . at least . . . the Gravediggers and the Ghost. There is no Prince of Denmark obviously discoverable. We hope you'll forgive us in this.

The book for Heinemann is supposed to be 'Modernist Poetry Explained to the Plain Man' but it's rather more elaborate than that we fear.

Yours sincerely   Robert Graves

18 September 1926

Dearest Siegfried

It was a disappointment to miss you but Enoch shall have his Arden if he Wills.[75] Ever so many thanks for Phineas Fletcher.[76] I *do* like a book as beautifully edited as that.

What we came to tell you was quite casually that we are going off together to Austria for a bit: unconventional but necessary and Nancy's idea. She finds that now she's well she can't bring herself to resume the responsibility of the house unless we aren't there to force it on her: and that she can't begin to draw again unless she's alone, and she is longing to draw. We find in our turn that we can't get on with our work unless we have her equally busy. So we are going to Vienna or somewhere near and be damned to scandal. At Christmas we'll try to come back for a visit. And in the Summer, Nance and the children will come to us there.

We are all very happy about it, though we'll miss each other very much of course, and especially we'll miss the children. Funny life, ain't it?

A further necessity is to avoid paying Income Tax on my Egyptian salary which is due unless I am out of England six months of the financial year: and would be heavy.

We all send you our love   Robert

PS. We go off on Tuesday afternoon from Victoria at 2 o'clock.
Please: this is important. What is the exact text of:

Because the Duke of York, etc.?[77]

We want to quote it in one of our books (appreciatively).

9 Mühlgassen
Tür II
Wien IV

No date

Dearest Siegfried

This address for the next few months.

Vienna is a lovely town and promises a good atmosphere for work.

Nancy sounds happy enough, and much busied in trying to assure well-meaning half-friends that she is *not* the deserted wife of the usual romance: but that on the contrary she has 'shipped us off for a holiday' and is too fond of us not to be able to stand any amount of scandal resulting. She has longed for this privacy for years to start her drawing again and regain some sort of independent completeness, and now there's a nurse for the children and Laura to look after me, it is too good a chance to miss.

But I see you shaking your head and sighing!

Any new poems? What about 'The Duke of York'?

Love
                                                                    Robert

In October Sassoon wrote, explaining that although he thought Graves's actions sensible and quite understandable, he nevertheless found it difficult to write to him. He himself was leading his usual monotonous life of writing poems he never expected to publish. Robert Nichols was back from America and Sassoon said he felt totally out of sympathy with him. He also told Graves that he had persuaded Chatto's to publish a new edition of Wilfred Owen's poems and asked Graves if he still considered Owen to be a poet, or was he 'too deficient in subtlety'? Graves and Riding were working on their second book together, *A Pamphlet Against Anthologies*.

No date

Dearest Siegfried

A good letter from you. As we never see a soul in Vienna to talk to, except people in shops and then in German, our mail is a great excitement.

We work hard and occasionally go to a cinema or a concert. We heard Roland Hayes sing spirituals: magnificent.

NB. Please don't omit to answer by return how your Duke of York poem goes: we are mentioning it in our book about anthologies as an example of the 'true anthology epigram'; that is, having a sort of fugitive quality which makes it incongruous among your serious works, yet certainly not a thing to be lost. Anthologies of fugitive verse are about the only kind which don't do actual harm to poetry: that is the point. The false anthology pieces like Yeats's absurdly sloppy 'Innisfree' is quite a different matter . . .

Nance is happy as anything now that she is drawing again and apparently about to make a lot of money. How nice when I can lay down my pen for a bit and let her support me with her little paintbrush!

I am so glad I am not thrown into Bob Nichols's society again: he must be awful. Laura's sister[78] in California invited him to dinner under the impression he was a dear friend of mine and ended with the conviction I must be a damned queer person myself.

I have been reading Wilfred Owen again. It's all real enough. The poetry is not of course in the propaganda but in spite of the propaganda. I still get absolutely dithery thinking about the War so I can't judge Owen fairly: but I say he's all right and risk it.

'Deficiency in subtlety' I do regard as a failing in poetry but not in the loose sense of subtle as meaning just 'tricky' but in the original latin sense of '*subtiles*' which means 'close-woven', as opposed to the raggedness of 'Innisfree' and so on.

Heinemann's are sending me the Sackville-West.[79] I am sorry she's likely to get the Hawthornden Prize because of my nice *Collected Poems*: and I am being so rude in my new critical work to all the Old Stagers that this is my last chance. Still, what is £100? I shall turn to politics and go into training for the Nobel Prize.

Laura is sweet to me and is gradually teaching me how to ratiocinate clearly.

Love   Robert

Only one of Graves's few letters to Blunden while Blunden was at Tokyo has survived.

171

No date

Dearest Edmund

I occasionally feel a warm gush remembering you – sufficient to overcome my dislike of writing letters that take months to answer. This is an occasion. One of our greatest bonds I discover suddenly is our hatred of the French: never so strong in me as it was in you when we were on Boars Hill: but increasing daily. Through a study of contemporary and ancient English Lit: through living here for three months and seeing how infinitely more human and sensible and decent the Germans and Austrians are. I left Egypt at the end of the academic year. I refused to be made a fool of. Particularly by the French who ran the Letters side of the University. Cut my losses – about £1500 one way and another and came home.

Am here dodging income tax: also writing hard. Chiefly literary criticism in collaboration with Laura Gottschalk an American poet who now lives with us. We return in January to Islip. I don't know what the financial solution is for us, Edmund. It's all the fault of the Romantic reaction to the Patronage system.

I have *Collected Poems* out at New Year. Also several critical books including an obscene and ill-tempered Kegan Paul volume, *Lars Porsena, or the Future of Swearing and Improper Language*. Which I'll send you to make you laugh and blush.

Dear Siegfried is still my dear Siegfried. Lawrence is on the sea on his way to India (as an air-mechanic) to spend three years on the North West Frontier: his book is just coming out.[80] Our children are fine: Nancy is drawing again.

Yours ever

Robert

Blunden returned from Tokyo in June 1927 and he and Graves saw each other again. While in Japan Blunden had written a prose account of his experiences in the war, called *Undertones of War*, the first of the great English memoirs of the First World War. In the first edition of *Goodbye to All That* Graves wrote about his time with Blunden on Boars Hill: 'Edmund had war-shock as badly as myself, and we would talk each other into an almost hysterical state about the trenches. We agreed that we would not be right until we got all that talk on paper . . .'[81] When Graves published his war memoir two years later, however, their friendship ended. Blunden

172

regarded *Goodbye to All That* as in some way a betrayal of the experience of the war and of those who had died in it; he was, perhaps, more deeply affected by the war than Graves; towards the end of his life he wrote: 'My experiences in the First World War have haunted me all my life and for many days I have, it seemed, lived in that world rather than this.'[82] He himself could not say goodbye, and perhaps felt that nobody should. The inaccuracies in Graves's book annoyed him a great deal, as they annoyed Sassoon (see page 197 forward) and when Blunden reviewed it disparagingly all friendship between him and Graves was cut. They were reconciled in Oxford in 1966 (as Graves was 'reconciled' with Sassoon in Cambridge in 1954 – in other words they met briefly and saw their past differences in the more tolerant light of old age), when Blunden succeeded Graves as Professor of Poetry at Oxford. Before meeting, Graves supported Blunden's candidacy for the Chair in the press and wrote to him; Blunden replied (20 February 1966):

I returned from Edinburgh last night and was, I need scarcely tell you, moved and gladdened by a letter from you. That I was so 'editorial' ages ago about your war chronicle has not pleased me much in later days; but I must beg for one thing – do not finally condemn your war poems of the 1915–16 vintage. I think I have said this in print. They do not seem to me to coalesce into a 'Protest', but they are most original. (I was round Cuinchy and the rest not many months ago, and Coldstream Lane – ain't there.)

To Siegfried Sassoon

No date [December 1926]

Dearest Siegfried

The *Lyrical Ballads* gave me such pleasure and Laura too. That's what I call a well-chosen Christmas gift. I do think it so important to have facsimile reproductions of important books of poems. Laura and I were writing about E. E. Cummings and his 'perverse spelling and punctuation', which is, however, very accurate and consistent, in the course of our book about Modernist poetry and decided that at any rate he was making his facsimile reproduction sure for the future: we then took Shakespeare's 129th sonnet, 'the expence of spirit in a waste of grief' [*sic*], and showed how repunctuation, respelling and textual emendations had entirely ruined the sense.

We have done a hell of a lot of work and are coming home at New Year. The *Anthologies Against Poetry* (60,000) is all but done, so is the *Modernist Poetry* book (60,000) in which we discuss just who is real as a poet of Eliot, the Sitwells, the Imagists and all the advanced gang and why – very clearly and decisively I think. Laura has also written *Contemporaries and Snobs*, about 40,000 words, a bombshell for the *Criterion*, *Dial*, *Calendar* and similar coteries. And *Why Poe?*, about 20,000, showing up the whole unwholesome Poe cult. Also, we have done lots of other work. I wrote an article for the *Criterion* about Malinowski's[83] attacks on Rivers in his new anthropology books: he must be a cad. And another on my Wordsworth letter (trying to be funny): but Wordsworth makes all the jokes for me. A few nice poems. Laura a lot.

Nance and I and Laura expect to be at Appletree Yard on January 2nd for a day or two. Nance is getting on finely with her drawing. She is doing a child's gardening book, chintzes and book covers.

In the course of our modernist book Laura and I got more and more to appreciate work like yours and our own which isn't always breathless to keep up with the last-minute Paris fashions – and more and more to hate the influence the French have had on English poetry.

Merry Christmas and Happy New Year. My Christmas gift will be my *Collected Poems*:[84] but it's delayed till January by those slovens at Heinemann's.

Yours affectionately   Robert

30 May 1927   35A St Peter's Square
                                                        London W6

Dearest Siegfried

Laura and I are sharing a flat here and would like you to come and see us when you can face it. We have rather sore heads at the moment because of the breakdown of a number of friends who have not been able to stand the embarrassment of this move; and we are apt to anticipate insults never intended. But I know that your nerves are as bad as ours and that your heart is true; so shall draw no wrong inferences whatever you do about us.

Nancy will stay here when she comes up to London but is, like us, trying to settle herself more composedly. How are you?

Affectionately   Robert

That summer Graves wrote his biography of T. E. Lawrence, *Lawrence and the Arabs*.

5 *June 1927*

Dearest Siegfried

You are a good friend. I am doing a popular six shillings worth for Cape and Doran[85] about T. E. If I don't, someone else will and I'm going to make it good. I have T. E.'s consent.[86]

I am getting information from Hogarth, Buxton, Lloyd, Arnie Lawrence, etc., and have even written to Allenby. Also to Mrs Hardy, E. M. Forster; and Kennington is going to illustrate.

I have to work against time to get it out before anyone else can, and to make it authoritative to discourage imitations. Please get your wits together and put down on paper what you remember of T.E.'s reminiscences or accounts you've had from others of his doings. Then bring them here. I want you to help me with the writing; with blue pencil and red.

I have sent you a copy of my poems. Very soon I am going to give you a limited edition copy which is the same plus nine additional poems with a better paper, longer page and plain white (jap) vellum binding and plain lettering.[87] It won't be out for a few weeks though.

Cape is publishing other stuff of Laura's and mine as part of the contract.

Bless you   Robert

No date [September 1927]

Dearest Siegfried

We look forward to seeing you next month. I have been nearly destroyed by the Lawrence book which was only worth writing in parts, but I suppose Cape knows best: T.E. has behaved beautifully in giving me stuff.

I have written no poems for three months, or anything else.

Nancy and the two boys were here for three weeks in July.

Everything now is far less hectic than it was, in fact very good really.

Laura and I are getting a printing press (Crown Albion, i.e. prints eight octavo pages at a time; Vyvyan Richards[88] is helping us with it) which will be working by next week.

Don't be alarmed at 41. 32 sounds just as bad if you think of it, and 23 rather worse. As for 14! Or 5!

I have had a grand row with Humbert Wolfe[89] over two sixpenny editions I did for Benn's. He printed the first without sending me proofs, and repunctuated and retitled the second without asking my permission; fortunately I got the proofs before they were printed off. The drama is still unfolding. I am getting a public apology.

Laura's *Contemporaries and Snobs*, a very severe show-up of modernist criticism and snob-poets, comes out in a few weeks. So does our joint *Survey of Modernist Poetry*. The former is the better book, the latter the more courteous. We now have a telephone. Riverside 4524. I have accustomed myself to it, after an abstention of twelve years.

Glad to get your cards.

Love from   Robert

Laura says she doesn't know how to greet people 'genially' but she greets you ——lly (anything pleasant you like).

In the August issue of the *Criterion* John Gould Fletcher reviewed Graves's *Poems 1914–1926*, John Crowe Ransom's *Two Gentlemen in Bonds* and Laura Riding's *The Close Chaplet*. Graves took exception to the 'absurd' review of *The Close Chaplet* and Fletcher's assertion that one could 'readily distinguish the derivations' of Riding's style (from Marianne Moore, John Crowe Ransom, Graves and Gertrude Stein); he wrote an angry letter to Eliot, as editor of the *Criterion*, and asked him to print it as a reply to the review. Eliot wrote back to Graves saying that in his opinion the letter was rather too 'warm' for an impersonal matter of criticism and that it seemed to him unwise to publish it, though he would do so if Graves insisted.

No date

Dear Eliot

I'm glad you'll print the letter. My 'indiscretion' is my own funeral. My 'warmth' is both personal and critical; Fletcher's attack was personal and uncritical.

Thank you for information about Fletcher's trip to the States. A pity it wasn't indefinitely prolonged. Thank you also for inviting verse contributions but in the circumstances I do not feel able to offer any for your consideration. It would seem to be approving a popularistic policy in regard to contemporary poetry observable in the last two or three numbers of the *Criterion* with which, frankly, I do not find myself in sympathy. Commercially necessary, I grant, for a monthly: critically indefensible from my point of view.

I am glad of the opportunity of rewriting the letter to make my point clearer. Please understand that I am 'furthering no cause' except that of critical accuracy.

Forgive these remarks. I have recently come to the point of always saying exactly what I mean in matters concerning poetry: and expect reciprocal activity on the part of those to whom my views are distasteful. When, as will shortly happen, I have no literary friends left, this will provide a natural and graceful end to my literary career. Miss Riding is as little interested in her literary career as I am in mine, so you need have no misgivings on her behalf any more than on mine.

Yours sincerely   Robert Graves

Naturally, Eliot took exception to Graves's criticisms of the *Criterion*, but said he did not quite understand them and would Graves please make himself clearer. As for Graves predicting he would soon have no literary friends left, surely, Eliot wrote, all who cared for literature looked forward to 'the same consummation' for themselves.

No date

Dear Eliot

Please treat the following as a matter not at all for anyone else but ourselves. I have had great respect for you in the past as a man who has really cared for poetry on its own account and conducted himself with dignity in the bad atmosphere of literary

177

politics. Your last sentence about desiring the same consummation for yourself as I expressed for myself reassures me that your principles are the same as in, say, 1914. But then I can only read your editorial consent to reviews by literary politicians such as Wolfe, Flint[90] and Fletcher as a gesture of complete hopelessness and bankruptcy; and your editorials and book-notes as a humorous ventriloqual entertainment with a journalistic dummy on your knee. All this isn't my business. But you asked me what I meant and there it is. I don't suggest that it would be possible to edit a monthly and sell it except in this way. Nor do I claim that my literary conduct has been above reproach. It hasn't. (It is, however, only recently that I have realized the extent of my shortcomings and their bad effect on my poetry – but that is by the way.)

Well, that's enough.

Yours   Robert Graves

Eliot replied, briefly and indignantly, that of course he wanted to sell the magazine but Graves's suggestion that he vulgarized it for commerical reasons was unjust. He said he threw up his hands in despair.

No date

PRIVATE

Dear Eliot

No insult intended. Only; once a monthly is launched one has to go on with it and if it is not run in a certain way nobody buys it. I would not suggest that you vulgarize the *Criterion* to increase the sales and fill your pockets: obviously you are not that sort of person but I do think that you have compromised about it just as far as was necessary to keep it afloat and I think poetry has been compromised just to that extent. I am saying nothing against Flint, Fletcher and Wolfe whom I do not know well enough to speak against except to say that they are literary politicians as is manifest in their writings; and you are not responsible for this however long you have known them. Wolfe is of course a politician of the more obvious kind. Flint and Fletcher are more missionary politicians; less personally ambitious, less easy in their flattering judgements of successful contemporaries, but certainly not detached in the sense that I believe you fundamentally are. Let's stop this correspondence, which perhaps shouldn't have been

178

allowed to get as far as this. I am not talking at random about your editorial and other notices, but have no wish to exaggerate the importance either of your editorial activities or my opinion of them. Let's nod and walk on.

Yours   R.G.

Eliot published the letter and all correspondence between him and Graves thereupon ceased until 1946. As predicted, Graves argued with most of his literary friends and acquaintances during the next two years, including Edith Sitwell, Edmund Blunden and Siegfried Sassoon. Edward Marsh later used to boast that he was the only one of Graves's old friends with whom he hadn't quarrelled.

Walton Wood Cottage
Brampton
Cumberland

No date [late October 1927]

Dear Eddie

I am having you sent a copy of my book about T.E. I meant to submit proofs too for Winston's approval – T.E. suggested it – but I was so hard pressed that I never got to the point. T.E. has seen practically the whole of the book, and as you will see his references to Winston at the end are nothing if not complimentary. I wrote 130,000 words in two months besides getting information so you must realize how things have been with me. It's a damned personal book; but T.E. has not made any difficulties. Prefers an attempt at truth to an eye-wash.

I am up here with Nancy and the children now, in a cottage in a wood on the Roman Wall where Nancy finds the true sense of absolute rural quiescence. At the moment Nancy is in London with Laura Riding whose name you have probably heard in one way or another. We share a flat when I am in town or when we are not both here and have written two books together (and are going to start a press this next month). One of these will be sent you, also one of L.R.'s own called *Contemporaries and Snobs* which you may find rather violent. Peter Quennell I believe dislikes her; Siegfried I know likes her. Other expressions are both less and more decided. But she can write like hell and is a member of our household so think of her kindly.

Yours affectionately   Robert

The argument with Sassoon was caused by a letter Graves wrote to Sir Edmund Gosse suggesting he might like to review *Lawrence and the Arabs*. Sassoon, to whom Graves had also suggested he might review it, thought such behaviour a severe breach of literary good manners and told Graves so.

31 October 1927

Dearest Siegfried

I'm not of the Charles Beverly Humbert gang as you suggest but it's very difficult to explain how I am not. It's something like this: I have never in my life tried to arrange a review of one of my own books and have even made a practice of antagonizing reviewers. To arrange a review would be to say that I cared for the opinion of reviewers which of course I don't or that I expected to make money from my books which, again, I don't. I even have a snobbish feeling against selling more than a thousand copies.

If you can imagine me in the case of the Lawrence book being so ingenuously unauthorial that I don't regard it as my book at all, but merely a collation of Lawrence material supplied from various sources and commissioned by Cape and (accidentally) edited by myself as a sort of joke; so unauthorial indeed that I can even act as a tout for it, you'll be at the truth. You can even go further and say that I am anxious not for the money on my account but for Cape not to fall down on the book after having made such big arrangements, particularly as G.B.S. has prophesied that he'll crash on it.[91] I would neither have expected nor wished Sir Edmund to review the book favourably *as a piece of writing by me* – I shall never include it in my collected works – but I would have said that it's a very rich collation of Lawrenciana and likely to interest him, and good to write about. If he is offended I am very sorry – it was, as you say, 'crass stupidity' on my part not to realize that you and he would not understand my perversely impersonal feelings about the book – and if you will write this to him in explanation it would be good – add my sincerest apologies. He'll get his copy anyhow. Let him add it to his library where it has a place in the biographical section, shut the glass case after it and forget that I wrote to him.

As for you Siegfried and the *Herald*; I know you too well to apologize. Forget it. I won't write to E.M.F.[92] after this. Now let's stop!

    Yours as always   Robert

Graves added a postscript to this letter, referring to Sassoon's editing of R. S. Surtees's hunting books about Mr Jorrocks.

Do get on with your Jorrocks book and I'll review it in the *Waste World Journal*, a very good paper, all about what happens to entirely useless things like old sausage skins, discarded felt slippers, etc., after they reach the dust cart. This is *not* intended nastily. But that Colonel Whatever his name's hunting books should be put to (literary) use delights me. *Nothing* is wasted. (My Scotch grandmother!) Seriously, I do think it's going to be a very good book indeed.

Sassoon also wrote to Laura Riding about Graves's behaviour, in reply to a note from her suggesting she and Sassoon meet to discuss the situation in Graves's absence.

4 November 1927

Dearest Siegfried

    If you can't follow your note to Laura about me with a reconsideration of my conduct in the light of my letter, things are very bad between you and me. It *was* a very stupid letter of mine to Gosse; as stupid as your note to Laura who immediately jumped to the conclusion that I had been attempting to force her work on Gosse and was properly ashamed on my account. You needn't mention this last part, if you write to her; but if you can honestly say that you regard Robert as thoughtless but no longer blame him for suggesting to Gosse that he might like to notice the Lawrence book, it will put things fairly right again. Siegfried, we're all fools and blockheads. And you and I have forgiven each other a lot in the last eleven years or so.

    Affectionately   Robert

Sassoon sent the necessary letter of appeasement and in reply received a sharp reprimand for his behaviour in the affair from Laura

Riding. Nevertheless, he and Graves were tentatively reconciled, for the time being.

On 11 January 1928 Thomas Hardy died at the age of eighty-seven. Both Sassoon and Graves had known Hardy, though Graves's acquaintance with him was very slight compared with Sassoon's, who was a close friend of both Hardy and his wife Florence. The 'Abbey business' referred to in the following letter was the extraordinary arrangement made for the disposal of his body, made due to a dispute between his co-executors: Hardy's ashes were interred in Westminster Abbey, but his heart was first removed and buried separately in the country churchyard at Stinsford where his parents, sister and first wife were buried and where Hardy himself had wished to be buried.

20 January 1928
PO, sub specie aeternitatis!

Dearest Siegfried

Yes, a good man and a poet. I learned to expect people to die, in France, and haven't forgotten how to dull my mind to it. But the Abbey business left a bad taste in my mouth; too anatomical in arrangement.

I had a letter from T.E. yesterday written December 27th enlarging on Hardy's greatness: poor T.E. All his friends are dying in his absence.

Two publishers have asked me to 'repeat my success', with Hardy. I refused of course because a) I don't want to be a popular biographer; b) I am not competent to treat of Hardy. Cape was one: he made a point, though, that there would be a sarcophagus biography (two volumes, thirty shillings, Macmillan) in two years' time in which Hardy would be buried completely in dullness. And that a shorter and more living biography by a younger hand would do him more justice. I said only two people could write one: 1) T.E., but he wouldn't have the opportunity, 2) S.S. who might possibly undertake the job from loyalty. So Cape asked me to put it to you for him; adding that he didn't want to pinch Heinemann's authors but if you ever wanted to publish anything with him he'd be glad to do it. He is certainly the most competent and decent publisher in London.

My ? postcard was a note to myself rather than to you. I can't understand your complicated views *de amicitia*, which seem to sacrifice the stupidity of $\boxed{a}$ to the permanent falsity of $\boxed{b}$. After which I lay down my pen and leave you to make all future advances.

Love   R.G.

Sassoon did not reply to this letter and it was more than two years before he and Graves corresponded again.

PART THREE

1929–1939

In 1928 Graves and Riding founded the Seizin Press and began publishing over the next few years several small books, mostly poetry, in high-quality limited editions, starting with Riding's *Love as Love, Death as Death* (1928).

At this time a fourth person entered the unconventional Graves–Nicholson–Riding circle who was soon to be the cause of its collapse: Geoffrey Phibbs, a young Irish poet who became emotionally involved with Riding and who, after he had begun to collaborate with her on a book, grew tired of the tense atmosphere at 35A St Peter's Square and 'ran away' with his wife to Dieppe, to be followed almost immediately by Graves and Riding who persuaded him to return to them. Some time later, on 27 April 1929, there was a fierce argument between Riding and Phibbs, who had 'deceived' Riding and in some way flouted her 'authority'; during the course of the argument she first drank some Lysol, which was ineffective, and then, with Graves, Nicholson and Phibbs watching, stood on the window sill, said, 'Goodbye, chaps', and jumped out of the fourth-storey window; the result of the jump was a broken pelvis, four broken vertebrae and a serious eye wound. She spent the next few months in hospital, all of which time Graves was either devotedly at her bedside or busy writing his autobiography, *Goodbye to All That*. On 6 May he and Nicholson separated; she kept the children and lived with Phibbs until 1935, first in London and then in Wiltshire.

In June Graves arranged a meeting with Edward Marsh and asked him to use his influence in Whitehall to prevent a police inquiry into the affair and thus spare Riding from prosecution or deportation for attempted suicide. After seeing Marsh he wrote to him, on the same day, giving further details of the case. The letter is on Seizin notepaper, as are many of the letters until 1936.

THE SEIZIN PRESS
35A St Peter's Square

Laura Riding
Robert Graves

Hammersmith
London

Telephone
Riverside 4524

16 June 1929

My dear Eddie

You are, if I may tritely return the compliment, a saint. About all this. A few data for you.

1/ Accident happened April 27th at Hammersmith. Hammersmith police took up matter. . . .

2/ Laura is American citizen. She is in formal business partnership with me and, when working, is self-supporting. E.g. income tax half-year demand note to her for £20·13·0 came today.

3/ Police court case inadvisable because
   a) Laura was desperately badly treated, before and after her fall.
   b) She had been under doctors for general run-down-ness before the Geoffrey Phibbs thing started and G.P.'s action was enough to send anyone out of any window.
   c) It would create a general stink involving lots of respectable relations.
   d) No sequel of violence is possible now.
   e) It would interfere with her income, and mine as her partner in business.

4/ The police do not know that Geoffrey and Nancy are living together or of his deception of Laura <u>after</u> her accident, when she was in great pain.

5/ Geoffrey told the police a lot of lies in the first place because he thought it wouldn't matter. He thought that Laura must have died. He had walked away when she was dying, saying that he couldn't stand it.

   He told them particularly that he, as a student of psychology, considered Laura had been mad and enumerated her delusions. Quite falsely.

6/ We will probably leave the country when Laura can travel, i.e. about November, but don't want to insist on that. We

188

don't want to have our return barred. We might want to come over to see publishers or pictures or people or something.

7/ Laura is perfectly calm and content just to be rid of G. and N. in one blow. To her G. is like a monster that she read of in a book.

8/ The police think Geoffrey 'a sound young man'. They told Laura's sister this. L.'s sister is here for a month or two from California. The police will want to put L. in her charge. But her sister has a family in California. Laura doesn't want to be sent to California, not in the least. Nor do I intend to go there. So L. should only be put into her sister's charge until, say, September when her liner ticket expires and she must go back.

Laura is now as sane and far from violence as you or me. Just tired, in pain, and only anxious not to have this police business hanging over her head, to drop on her as soon as she is discharged as convalescent.

9/ There is a mis-statement in the evidence. Nancy gave evidence first and said that she was alone in the room and Laura did the jump when her back was turned. I had to bear this out by saying that I went down for an emetic for the Lysol and returned just as L. made the jump. Otherwise everything is true (as I told it you today) that N. and I said. Though naturally we gave a very bare account. Geoffrey P.'s account I never saw. The police told us bits. God knows what he didn't say. He dragged in the whole sex-complication quite gratuitously and vulgarly. I had merely emphasized L.'s distress at his going off and leaving their joint work in the air. Made it literary, merely. (And the sex side *was* unimportant – to L. and me at least.) The police thought L. a sort of vampire, as G.P. put it.

10/ T. E. Lawrence is in Town. He went to visit Laura while I was at lunch with you. He knows the story, knows all the people in it. He would make any testimonial necessary to Laura as a person to be treated with every possible consideration. Perhaps the Home Office would consider him a good enough surety? Please mention this when you see Secretary. T. E. is legendary for his honour; and really does appreciate Laura as a person of fanatic integrity like himself.

Well. Sort out of this what is useful and put the rest in discard. And if you can get the case dismissed (the papers sent to the Home Office to be dealt with there. Evidence of Nancy, me and Geoffrey in writing) it will be a good bit of work. The police take an old-fashioned moral view and are behaving in the usual bullying way. They blame it all on Laura and think that G. was the innocent hero decoyed into a den of perverts. So they would like to make things as ugly for Laura as they could. Only action from above, from somewhere high out of reach, can make them realize that they are not capable of judging the case. They are all right as traffic-cops. Or in tugs-of-war.

Poems 1929. I shall send no. 18. About 10 days.
Poems 1914–1927. Those too.
Brings my work up to date.
Bless you; affectionately   Robert

Marsh willingly did what was asked of him and all police involvement in the matter ended.

Graves and Riding decided that as soon as she had recovered sufficiently to travel they would go abroad and live together. They planned to make their first stop with Gertrude Stein and her companion-secretary Alice B. Toklas at Paris. It is possible that Graves had met Stein briefly at Oxford in the early twenties, but the main link was with Riding who had corresponded with Stein about language and linguistic techniques, and about her book, *An Acquaintance with Description* (written 1926), which Graves and Riding published in 1929 as the second in the Seizin series; Riding had also visited her in Paris some time during the previous year. Both Graves and Riding liked Stein and respected her work (see *A Survey of Modernist Poetry*) which was of considerable influence on Riding. When Stein heard, by telegram, of Riding's fall, she wrote to Graves.

No date   27 Rue de Fleurus
                                               Paris

My dear Robert
    It was about that that I feared, Laura is so poignant and so

upright and she gets into your tenderness as well as your interest and I am altogether heart-broken about her, I cannot come now because of family complications but tell her and keep telling her that we want her with us, we are to be at Belley right near Aix les Bains and as soon as she can be about and strangely one thinks of her as coming together alright, you and Nancy are wonderfully good, I had an unhappy feeling that Laura would have sooner or later a great disillusionment and it would of course have to come through a certain vulgarity in another ('vulgarities' is her word. I told her that there was a dualism in Geoffrey, that he could not make it. That he was incredibly good, or just ordinary.) and it will make Laura a very wonderful person, in a strange way a destruction and recreation of her purification but all this does not help pain and I am very closely fond of you all. Tell her all and everything from me and tell her above all that she will come to us and reasonably soon and all my love.

Gtrde

18 June 1929

Dearest Gertrude

Laura's address is now Private Wards, London Homeopathic Hospital, Great Ormonde St, London WC1. She has a room to herself and better nursing and food decently served and so on. All much better. She is quickly recovering the movements in the legs that she was afraid she would never have.

I am busy when not in hospital in writing my autobiography. It is a sort of goodbye to everyone but the very very few people to whom one never says goodbye or has ever said a formal how do you do. Quite ruthless; yet without indignation.

Laura says that she is going to write a book about Suicide. But not able to begin for some time of course. And by the time she starts it may be something different.[1]

She is still on her back until her pelvis strengthens. Probably another fortnight.

I think that (by using influence in Whitehall) we have succeeded in quashing any police nastiness or prosecution for attempted suicide.

Good luck

Robert

Bilignin
par Belley
Aix

No date

My very dear Laura and Robert,

I am rather selfishly glad that the result of it all means you both more completely together, you do mean that to me the two of you with Len firmly in the background because after all it is hysteria that is vulgar and the complete absence of hysteria is very rare, there is very little absence of hysteria and you two are it and therefore if not for other reasons very dear to me.

We are here and wanting to see you here both of you with us a quiet and yet sufficiently enlivening spot and all of it. As soon as the pain is over Laura has such real vitality that she will go on and nowadays so fortunately they can get the better of pain and it must be soon done. Do please let me hear from you as I have been doing, and all my love to you both always.

Gtrde

'Len's shape', referred to in the following letter, is an abstract design by Len Lye, the New Zealand artist and film-maker, which appeared for the first time in *An Acquaintance with Description*. Lye had gone to England in 1927, working his way as a stoker on a ship, and had soon become friends with Eric Kennington and, through Kennington, with Graves, Laura Riding and Ben Nicholson.

Graves wrote again to Stein.

No date

Dear Gertrude

Your letter made Laura very happy. Life is easier now though sad. Laura will write soon about seeing you. We all want to see you.

Did you get the shawl safely?

We are so pleased you liked the book. Some copies were badly bound, that is, folded wrong so that the tops of the print did not lie even on opposite pages. So good that you liked Len's shape. He is upstairs doing a thing on Laura's bedroom wall in coloured distemper and chalk.

Laura wants as much of your writing as you yourself consider necessary. What do you suggest and how best can we get them?

About review copies of *Acquaintance*: We have set aside six and
have sent one to the *Times Literary Supplement*. What do you say
to sending the other five to:

Observer ⎱
Nation ⎰ England

Saturday Review ⎱
Dial ⎰ America
New Republic ⎰

Any alternatives? We don't know.
Love   Robert

A copy of 'Seizin Three', Graves's *Poems 1929*, was sent to Stein at
Belley in June. She replied:

No date

My dear Robert
Your[e] a poet alright and it is a pleasure to me I like you to be
a real poet and your head is good and it holds what it has and
that is a pleasure for me because I like a head that holds what it
has and has something to hold. Its a little book and its a lot of
poems pretty much each one there. It goes with a rush. And I have
read it over and I like each one in turn. And it is a biography. A
little and a lot. Thanks and more than thanks for you and for
Laura,   Gtrde

I liked Laura's letter and the finished [scarf] [   ], will be writing
her very soon.

To Edward Marsh

29 July 1929

My dear Eddie
Laura, who is going on very well now, though walking is still
some weeks ahead, wants to know whether you ever had a copy
of her *Love as Love, Death as Death* published in our Seizin
series. If not she wants to send you one as a thank-offering.
By the way the person in the story whom you called an
unparalleled example of duplicity[2] is now sending Laura a lawyer's
letter demanding the return of a few books that he gave her! He's
better than a novel!

I am nearly finished with my autobiography – about 130,000 words. It will have taken eleven weeks from the first to last.

It is an interesting book and contains just about everything.

You can have no objection to your own appearance in it, so I shall leave that as a surprise; because, Eddie, you have been very good to me these last thirteen years, and I could not even tease you in print.

Robert

In October Graves went abroad, resolving never to make England his home again. He and Riding visited Stein at Belley and, on her recommendation, went on to Mallorca. They went first to Palma then, on the advice of a German café portrait-artist whom they nicknamed 'suffering Jesus', went to the village of Deyá, a small fishing and agricultural village on the mountainous north-west coast of the island, which suited them well; they decided to stay – and they rented a house.

Although they could live there on a quarter of the income they had needed in London, money was suddenly plentiful when, on 18 November, *Goodbye to All That* was published; it was immediately successful, and immediately controversial. Few people mentioned in the book liked what was said about them: many of his ex-comrades in the Royal Welch Fusiliers were furious, Marsh was certainly surprised, but not pleasantly, and Sassoon was outraged; both he and Marsh received advance copies and demanded that the publisher, Jonathan Cape, alter the references to them before publication.

The following is one of the very few letters from Marsh to have survived.

6 November 1929

5 Raymond Buildings
Gray's Inn
London

My dear Robert,

Cape has just very kindly sent me a copy of your Autobiography, and on looking through it for a first glance I find a paragraph which fills me with consternation – the one on p. 398 about what you are pleased to call the 'Rupert Brooke Fund'. It is wrong from beginning to end, and may get me into great trouble. There is no such thing as a R.B. Fund. Rupert left his royalties

194

(not in a will, but in a letter to his mother) not to miscellaneous 'needy poets with families', but to three named poets, Abercrombie, de la Mare and Gibson. When I published my *Memoir* with the *Collected Poems*, I made a friendly arrangement with those three and Mrs Brooke that I should take the proportion of the profits which might be credited to the *Memoir*, and lay them out on any object which I thought might from time to time have commended itself to Rupert. (As a matter of fact, for the last five years or so I have used the money principally for buying pictures by young painters which I have given to the Contemporary Art Society.) There is no Fund with a big F, and I am not an 'administrator'.

You knew all this perfectly well at the time, and if, as I suppose you did, you read my *Memoir*, you will have found the facts about the three heirs set out in it.

The whole thing has hitherto been absolutely private. I tremble to think what will happen if 'needy poets with families' see it in print that there is a 'Fund' for their relief. I may be bombarded with applications which it will be distressing to refuse.

Further I *may* get into trouble with the Inland Revenue. Soon after the thing started, I did consult a high official there, who told me that I was entitled to regard the money as a 'casual profit' – but since then they have tightened things up a good deal. I don't think they can possibly come on me for arrears, as I have never spent a penny on myself – but if they see what you have said, they may raise tiresome questions and if they *did* insist on arrears, I should be broke.

I am writing to Cape and asking if there is any possibility of expunging the paragraph, or failing that of sticking in some form of *erratum* slip. It would be hard to devise an effective one, and the best would probably be merely a statement that the paragraph had arisen from a misunderstanding and that the facts are not as stated.

I am not angry with you Robert dear, because I never could be, and because of course you didn't mean to make trouble for me – but I do think you might have taken more pains to be accurate. I'm looking forward eagerly to reading the rest of the book. I hope Laura is well.

Yours affectionately   Eddie

Graves, having heard of the error from Cape, did not wait for Marsh's letter to arrive but wrote to him immediately.

Casa Salerosa
Deyá
12 November 1929   Mallorca des Baleares
Spain

Dearest Eddie

I hear there's a letter on the way for me: but it will take about a week to arrive. Cape wrote me direct. I am *awfully* sorry about my stupidity. It is many years since I read the *Memoir* and I recollected your blue cheques marked in the corner 'R.B. a/c' and I've read many accounts (in the sense that I wrote) in the press of your vicarious benefactions to poets and painters (one in the *Evening Standard* very recently) so that's how it happened. Cape is putting an *erratum* slip in and since it took six days for his letter to reach me and my reply will take a day and then the beastly things will have to be printed and inserted the chances are that the book will not be able to appear until New Year and miss the heavy Christmas sales that we have been counting on. So that will be my punishment.

I do hope that, apart from all that, you liked the book. Laura and I have a house here on a hill overlooking the sea towards Spain. It is very good to be here and we intend to stay a long time. Sun. Olives, figs, oranges, fish, quiet. She is much better and can limp two or three miles at a go now.

If you felt upset by the paragraph so naturally did I when I heard that I had upset you, for I wouldn't have upset you for anything. The book was written in a great hurry and I didn't have time to check references. The phrase 'needy poets with families' I remembered from a letter of yours quoting something Rupert once said.

Ever affectionately   Robert

In 1926 Sassoon, at the age of forty, began writing his autobiography, the six volumes of which (the first three were the fictionalized *Memoirs of George Sherston*) were to obsess him for the next twenty years of his life. The first volume, published anonymously, was *Memoirs of a Fox-Hunting Man* (1928) which was unfavourably reviewed by Graves, though no correspondence passed between them on the subject; the second volume, *Memoirs of an Infantry Officer* (1930), is an account of his war experiences and contains an embittered portrait of Graves, characterized as 'David Cromlech', a 'fad-ridden crank', who is always referred to with a strong undertone of sarcasm (though Sassoon does admit he once felt affection and even admiration for him).

A great deal of *Goodbye to All That* is about Sassoon, and on the whole the picture given of him is fair (during the war he 'alternated between happy warrior and bitter pacifist') and affectionate; Sassoon, however, was furious and made Cape omit two passages from the book before it was published: one was the verse letter ('I'd timed my death in action to the minute') he had written to Graves in July 1918 (see page 98), which Graves had quoted in full; the other was part of the account of a visit to the home of a 'recently wounded First Battalion friend' (Sassoon) in Kent whose mother had disturbed Graves by her nocturnal attempts to contact her dead son by spiritualist means. Although Graves did not name the friend, Sassoon nevertheless insisted on the omission of a few lines on page 290 containing a remark of his, to Graves, that he thought his mother's behaviour pathetic, the dead boy, Siegfried's younger brother, not having been the person she thought he was, and that he feared for her sanity.

It was not until February 1930 however, that Sassoon wrote direct to Graves about the book; at the top of his letter he wrote:

If this letter contains anything unkind, you must remember that *you* have not shown overmuch consideration for other people's feelings.

Grand Hotel
Villa Politi al Cappuccini
Siracusa
Sicilia

7 February 1930

Dear R.G.

Since I left England I have been so persistently reminded of you and your book that I am obliged to try and analyse the exasperation which it has caused me. If I had met you a couple of months ago I should probably have tried to knock you down; but I am no boxer, and even if I had recovered consciousness in time to discuss the matter with you, my powers of arguing would have been unequal to yours, and your theories about how people ought to live and write are still incomprehensible to my jog-trot mind.

But I think it best that I should now let you know what is in my mind, as I find it difficult to believe that you really wish to knock your entire past life on the head by writing a book about it. To begin with it is only fair to you that I should attempt to explain my reasons for avoiding you since November 1927. My reasons may appear trivial but they epitomized strong feelings. My resentment about your behaviour to Gosse (which, to me, meant much more than a 'failure to observe literary punctilios' – when you are 79 and some young spark is rude to you, you will understand what I mean, perhaps) would have disappeared; but you offended me badly when you wrote to me two days after Hardy's funeral. I cannot explain briefly what I went through at that time, but I will ask you to believe that it was a very strange and painful experience. Your letter was very crudely worded and it made me feel that you were part of the vulgar uproar which attended his death. I could not trust myself to answer it temperately, and I foresaw that I could not 'have it out with you' without some intervention by L.R. (who had previously (and pardonably) failed to understand my loyalty to poor old E.G.). Your article on Max Gate[3] made things worse. As you ought to know, T.H. was an essentially *private* character. And the spectacle of the self-advertising antics of literary men exploiting their acquaintance with T.H. maddened me; and your article made me feel that you were making fun of him. There was too much about yourself and too little about his greatness. (The picture of him in your book is misleading, because it shows his simplicity without his impressiveness. Also you have got the *Marmion* anecdote wrong. I was there when it happened. And Mrs Hardy tells me that it was she, and not T.H. who repeated the story about Gosse imitating Henry James. 'T.H. would never have criticized Gosse before a young man, almost a stranger . . . I very much dislike that way of describing T.H. as a rather comic old gentleman.' But perhaps you were unconscious of T.H.'s impressiveness, and of his hatred of 'copy' being made out of people's private lives.)

Anyhow I felt antagonistic towards you for the next eight months, (and had many other things to distract and complicate my life). Your review of my book was not helpful. It seemed to me needlessly ungracious and egotistical. I had attempted to construct something delicate and restrained, and I felt that you had missed the point altogether. Also I objected to being informed that I 'had side-stepped the moral question' – the purpose of the book being to avoid showing prejudice of any kind and to write affectionately about people and events which I had long outgrown. So I assumed that your review was intended to be unfriendly, and wished that you hadn't written it (and reprinted it in America some time afterwards). Last April I went abroad for 4 months, to be with S. Tennant during his pneumothorax treatment. While doing that I heard about your troubles, but felt that I could have been no use, even if required. In the autumn I began an effort to continue my unfinished sequel to *Memoirs*. The extreme difficulty (and discomfort) of trying to recover the essentials of my war experience made me over-sensitive on the subject. From my point of view your Autobiography couldn't have appeared at a worse moment. In fact it landed on my little edifice like a Zeppelin bomb. It was not that you anticipated anything that I wanted to write down, but that you blurted out your hasty version as though you were writing for the *Daily Mail*. Your method, in fact, was the antithesis of mine (though I gather from certain reviews that your style is considered vigorous and flexible). Also I wished that your anecdotal method had been more accurate. Writing about a person, without his knowledge, is a serious matter (especially when that person dislikes being written about as much as I do), and your treatment of me was journalistic and, I think, perfunctory. For instance your account of July 1917 was surely an opportunity for impartial exactitude. If such a story was to be divulged by you, nothing should have been omitted. Yet you omitted the crucial fact, that I only consented to take the Medical Board (after refusing the first one) because you swore on the Bible that nothing would induce the authorities to court-martial me. (What might or might not have happened if I'd held out doesn't matter. But *my reason for giving way* was surely part of the story.) And, by the way, your cutting from the *Bradford Pioneer* appeared after I got to Craiglockhart. I sent you on July 10 a *type-written* copy of my statement. No *printed* copy appeared until Lees-Smith had read it in the House of Commons (on July 24 or thereabouts). This may remind you that you neglected to verify many details – such as your '300 casualties in the last month', on

p. 247, and your 'three out of five officers killed in the Somme fighting' – p. 252. ('300' should be, at the most, 100; if I were at home I could give you the exact figures of officer casualties in July–September 1916, but I know that of those with the 1st Battalion in March not more than six, if as many, were afterwards killed at all, though all except five had faded away somehow by August.)

Such inaccuracies (I could send you a long list of them) are not noticeable to 'the general public', but they are significant to those who shared your experiences. I am testing your book as a private matter between you and me, which is perhaps more important than the momentary curiosity of 50,000 strangers. If such chapters are any good as evidence about the war, they should be valid against the criticisms of your 'former comrades'. Dr Dunn wrote to me, 'I'm very sorry Graves wrote such a book and found a publisher for it.' You may say that Dr Dunn is middle-aged and conventional, but his opinion must be worth something to you, though it is a still small voice among the noise of enthusiastic reviewers. As I am sticking pins into you, I may as well query your account of the cancelled raid – p. 301. I have heard every detail of the story twice over from Dr Dunn (who has dined with me twice in the past 18 months). According to him, the raid was cancelled *because of a thaw*, and the only 'authoritative representative' of the 2nd Battalion at the General's conference was Mann. The main point was that until the final conference, no representative of the Artillery had been asked to attend, and when (at Dunn's suggestion) he did, it was found that the German position could not be shelled owing to the formation of the ground! As evidence against Brigade and Divisional incompetence, Dunn's story, as he tells it, is a masterpiece. Yours is merely evidence of your own self-importance (and your defective memory). At the end of your book you assert that no incident has been embellished. This might be true if you had written it in less of a hurry and taken the proper precautions afterwards.

In the meantime you are making a lot of money, for which I am extremely glad. I have sometimes felt, in the last year or two, that I can be of no use to my friends except by writing cheques (which is an easy way of obtaining a quiet life, which is what I want nowadays). So it may interest, and even please you to know that, although I made a new will last year, you will still be consoled for my death – should you witness that event – to the extent of £300 a year tax paid; which will come in very handy, unless you become a highly paid journalist, which is, I trust, improbable. I have written this letter to relieve my mind, and no reply is necessary. We must agree to differ, especially on questions of 'good taste'. But I do implore you not to write anything more about me. Opportunities are bound to occur, and your silence will be much appreciated by

S.S.

No officer rode into Amiens from Montagne. (It is just possible that the CO did so.) It was 16 miles. So they must have visited your 'Blue Lamp' by train and got home early. I challenge you to produce three names of officers who, to your certain knowledge, visited the Blue Lamp from Montagne. Joe Cottrill may have done. Who else?

Graves replied:

20 February 1930   Casa Salerosa
                                                      Deyá

Dear Siegfried,

   You ask me questions and also ask me not to answer them; you say you are relieving feelings of exasperation. I have also had strong feelings.

   I was polite to Gosse for too long; when in the end I found him back-biting me, to strangers, in his usual grotesque way I considered that I owed him no further consideration and that he was no more than a vain snobbish old man.

   I admired Hardy as a good, consistent, truthful man; I do not believe in *great* men. I treat everyone as an equal unless they prove themselves inferior. *Marmion*: T.E.'s account, which he verified for me. Gosse imitating James: Florence Hardy was wrong; I took a précis of the conversation at the time. Private life: what else are Hardy's novels (the better ones) but private lives?

   My egotistical nature: you misunderstand me. I deny any further interest in great occasions, great men, great emotions, so I can write detachedly. My review of your book: by that time you had faded out completely and I felt at liberty (especially as you hadn't

201

sent me a copy) to write an honest review for your information rather than for the press.

My theories about how people should write. I have none. But I can only read with pleasure books written to be read not written to show how they were written. And about how people should live. I have none. But I choose for friends those who do not sacrifice friendship to loyalty. My troubles: when you heard of them you did not even return the courtesy of the note I sent you saying I was sorry to hear that you were ill. I had given you every chance to come to the scratch after the Gosse business; you failed me badly.

I thought only bees had thoraces and I have never met S. Tennant and you have never mentioned him to me.

About the court-martial and July 1917. If you want me to make the necessary correction I will: I don't think it makes much difference to the story. I think you come out of it better than I do.

Casualties: when I think of A Company in March 1917 Richardson, Dadd, Davies all killed, Morgan and me badly wounded, I find it difficult to accept your revised estimate.

Dr Dunn corrected a few errors for me and said that I only went wrong on hearsay not on events at which I was present. I cannot reconcile this with his letter to you. Particularly about the conference, at which I was present as representative of the Battalion. Dunn wasn't. Mann wasn't. They were both in trenches at the time. I said in my book that the raid was cancelled because of a thaw and so it was. If there was another conference it was after I went back sick.

Your will: is this in good taste or must we disagree? In the circumstances, it would be better if you did not predecease me.

My riches: don't believe the *Daily Mail* reports of sales and winnings. Exactly 400% overestimated.

Blue Lamp. Richardson and Davies, not to mention Stevens. 1, 2, 3, and the day before Christmas. Sensational disclosures followed. Want any more?

16 miles. I once rode fifty in a day the following winter.

It doesn't take long to fuck; but perhaps you don't know about that. T.E. is similarly ignorant, I find.

My vigorous and flexible style. See my answer to Blunden's mean little remarks in *Time and Tide*.

My vulgarity. I am not vulgar. You have an inverted vulgarity which is as bad as the *Daily Mail* sort, and is no more than a reaction against *DM* vulgarity.[4]

I am serious about cutting off my trailing clouds of glory and stuffing them up the public bung.

In your *Fox-Hunting Man*, doing the same thing, you were not always quite serious; that's what I said in the review. While you were serious it was a good book.

The publicity of *Goodbye* is not to be helped; at least it won't earn the Hawthornden prize.[5]

The friendship that was between us was always disturbed by several cross-currents; your homosexual leanings and I believe your jealousy of Nancy in some way or other; later Nancy being in love with you (which no doubt you noticed and were afraid of) for several years (until 1923 or so); then your literary friendships which I could not share; finally your difficulty with the idea of Laura. But it never seemed impossible to me until you broke down over the Gosse business. I can't remember about Hardy: I remember forwarding a request to you from a publisher about his life. When a man dies, I regard him as dead and never go into mourning; a necessary hardness that I have cultivated in the last five years. Your delicate and restrained writing: be yourself, Siegfried.

This is as truthful a statement as I can make; I don't think my memory is defective on essentials.

And so   Robert

Signing fat cheques for your friends: the indelicate irony of it is that had you thought of signing one when you heard of 'my troubles' – which left us all without money – I would not have been forced to write *Goodbye* to contribute to the work of restoration, and you would not have had the Zeppelin-bomb.

Your *Heart's Journey* which I have not seen yet but only read in reviews and in already published fragments, appears to . . .
. . . .
no . . . no . . .

The dots are not omission marks, but Graves's 'comment' on *The Heart's Journey* book of poems.

Sassoon replied immediately.

2 March 1930 Grand Hotel Villa Impoliti
Souraccuser

Dear Robert,

Your letter is, on the whole, a satisfactory counter-irritant, so (as I don't mind being treated contemptuously) I will send another dose of 'The Mixture' as I want to get rid of the mental inflammation which *Goodbye* has caused. You may say 'What boots the inquiry?' But I must ask you to regard me as 'The symbol of a snow white beard'. (I quote Wordsworth.)

Apart from certain things in your book, there are several points in your letter which I can reply to. (Not very important, perhaps, but worth following up.) '*Marmion*'. 'It rather reminded me of *Marmion*' were the actual words used, I think. I wish you'd broken your rule, for once, and regarded T.H. as your superior until you found that you were his equal.

'*What else are Hardy's novels (the better ones) but private lives?*' Is using life as material for novels the same as using private hospitality for journalism?

'*My troubles. When you heard of them you did not even return the courtesy of the note I sent you.*' I heard of your troubles at the end of June. The account I received was sensational and unauthenticated. I did not acknowledge your olive branch at the end of January because I wasn't feeling at all kind about you and didn't want to be involved in reconciliation. My own situation was such that I couldn't cope with much else. Stephen T. (who had been my everything for 16 months – and still is, here and now) was very ill. To be exact, it was in January 1929 that the doctors discovered that he would probably be dead of consumption within a year. He went to Garmisch, had the pneumothorax operation in March, and his life was saved by it. In February and March I saw no one and struggled with my war book. On April 4 I went to Garmisch and was there till the end of July. Once a week his lung had to be reinjected with air so as to keep it out of action. During those three months I was never away from the house for more than a couple of hours at a time, and it was a very difficult time to get through. His old nurse, whom he adored, was also there – always on the edge of a stroke. She was taken back to London early in July, and I took S. home 4 weeks later to find her almost dead. She died in the middle of August. I am not telling you this to get sympathy, but only to explain that I was being put through it rather severely. (As you were.) (And what use would *reconciliation* have been when I read your book?)

'*Your will. Is this good taste?*' My reference to posthumous benefactions was put in with immense deliberation, and full awareness of its indelicacy. I wished you to know that I am fundamentally friendly to your future (if not your present). You see I have an 'Enoch Arden' complex. Also it amused me to think what a grand chance it gave you, of scoring off me. I am not such a simpleton as all that, Robert.

'*Riding into Amiens.*' When you rode fifty miles, did you have a look at your horse next day? (In your book you say that the dentist was '*twenty miles away*'.) My point is that 2½ hours each way would fill up a Saturday afternoon (or was it a Sunday?), that I lived in a billet with the transport officer, and heard the fuss about borrowing horses to go for little rides, and knew the capacities of the 1st RWF crocks; and think that your remarks on p. 231 are misleading and give a disproportionate impression of that aspect of Army life (at that time and place).

'*It doesn't take long to ★.*' Not a pretty remark, Robert. Yes, I know a little about the chronology, etc., of the act. Isn't it sometimes dependent on the taste, capacity, etc., of the participants? I am also aware that two minutes per man was about the time-limit for 'other ranks' (though I should hesitate before I put it into a 'powerful war-book'). Anyhow I accept your trio of 'Blue Lampers'. (C Company remained puritanical.)

'*My vulgarity. I am not vulgar. You have an inverted vulgarity which is as bad as the* Daily Mail *sort.*' My words were: 'made me feel that you were part of the vulgar uproar,' etc. (Your words in your letter were 'Cape says he doesn't want to pinch Heinemann authors, but would like you to write a lively sort of book about T.H.') Does it make one vulgar because one dislikes such writers as your brother Charles? In that case you also are an 'inverted vulgarian', I imagine! Shall we wash out our mutual vulgarity? ('stuffing them up the public bung' isn't a pretty expression, but may be an example of 'detached writing'.)

'*The friendship between us was always disturbed by cross-currents; your homosexual leanings; and I believe your jealousy of Nancy in some way or other.*' I was never jealous of Nancy. But I would have liked to have seen you independently sometimes. In her presence I was nervous and uneasy. She didn't give one much assistance, did she? For *you* I felt affection; but physical attraction never existed.[6] I always felt that Nancy merely tolerated me – except once or twice when she softened a bit.

'*Court martial. 1917.*' You cannot correct your story – except by making it less one-sided (and less imbued with the omniscience of 12 years afterwards). By the way, neither of us had ever heard of Rivers until the Medical Board. How could we have 'already known of him as a neurologist, ethnologist, and psychologist'? '*He died shortly after the war.*' (July 1922 – 3½ pretty useful years?) Couldn't you have written a little more than that? (and have omitted some of the anecdotes).

'*Dr Dunn corrected a few errors for me . . . I cannot reconcile this with his letter to you.*' You would, if you saw his letter (and reminded yourself that he is a shrewd and forbearing Scotchman). Attwater's letter might also interest you.

The cancelled raid in February 1917. I accept your explanation. You must have missed a lot of the story (which lasted two or three weeks, I think). Dunn did not say that he attended any conferences. Mann did – finally primed up by Dunn, who suggested that the gunners ought to be consulted about the 'Artillery programme' which had been formulated without verification by them. I mentioned this as an example of your occasional lapses into 'writing up' your own experiences, where they needed to be made more formidable.

(By the way – nothing to do with the above – on p. 264, your 'In-out-on-guard' story, is an anecdote from Campbell – (awarded a DSO for lecturing, but totally undecorated when I heard him in April 1916). I heard his lecture again, in May 1918, and the anecdote was still there.)

Page 326. Your paragraph about Owen. What is your authority for laying so much stress (by saying nothing else!) on the 'cowardice' story? Two days ago, Mrs Owen has written to me (in connection with the new edition of his poems which is in preparation) and she complains bitterly about your reference to Wilfred. As far as I know, you only saw O. twice (at Craiglockhart, in October 1917, when he conducted you to a golf course to find me – it was a wet afternoon, I remember – and at your wedding!). I saw him every day for about 3 months and can assure you that he was not 'in a very shaky condition', and said so little about being accused of 'cold feet' that I always regarded it as a negligible affair, and had no recollection of it until it was clumsily revived by Scott-Moncrieff in an article on O.'s poems (in 1921). Was it fair on O. to put that in and say nothing else? In the same way – couldn't you have said something pleasanter about Robbie Ross than to perpetuate that awful indiscretion about negro-blood? You say he had 'been good to you', however, which is high praise in *Goodbye*! But couldn't your mind recover any of R.R.'s gracious and delightful doings and sayings? You must have known that he was unreasonable at times (and made unreasonable by what he'd endured from his enemies). But you just chuck your lighted matches down and walk away without worrying about the conflagration caused (putting poison in wells would be a better metaphor, perhaps – for the effects of such reckless reportings take a long time to vanish).

Did you consider, for instance, the possible effects of the 'deleted passage' on p. 290? This is a matter which concerns you and me (and my mother). Your alterations of younger brother to 'elder brother', etc., were unnecessary. Anyone who took the trouble to identify the brother officer could do so; but that doesn't matter. Nor will I raise the question of the exactitude of your story. Nor is it a question of 'good taste'. It is a question of the words you put into my mouth for my mother to read (which she might have done if I'd left England a day or two before I did, in November). It is a question of a personal outrage – (and to me, a *printed* outrage is the worst sort). You might have written that you stayed with me in Kent and I behaved with very little courtesy or consideration to my mother. That would have pained her (and me), but would have been just, and honest. What you did do was to exploit (and betray) something private in order to add a sensational page to your book. You cannot *explain* it away and it is obviously no use your offering excuses to me. All I ask is, did you ever consider the possible effect? (You could not have known that my mother has a weak heart, but you knew that she is well over 70, and has had, on the whole, more suffering and worry than most people.) I did not refer to this passage in my first letter because I didn't want to attack you too violently. I mention it now because it is not an easy thing to forget or forgive.

Your printing of my verse letter without my permission was excusable. You could not have known that I should be shamed by its emotional exhibitionism (though you may have remembered

that I tried to get it back from you some years ago, and you
evaded me by sending a copy of it). It may interest you to know
that it was this particular passage (p. 290) which caused Blunden
to lose his temper with your book. (He afterwards wrote to me 'R.
Cobden-Sanderson,[7] immediately on reading it, and without any
other knowledge, immediately perceived who was meant; and he
possesses no supernatural insight.')

Well, I have more or less aired all my discontents now, I think.
There are many corrections of small errors in your book which I
could offer – in a friendly way. But it is too late for that, and the
public doesn't notice such things. I could also write at some length
on your suggestion that I should 'be myself' (in my published
works). Everyone wants to be himself, if he is any good, I imagine.
Is it so easy, when one is in my quandary – for the duration of my
life – as regards 'temperament'? But if you had read my diaries for
the past nine years I think you would retract your remark. No one
is more aware than I am that the *Fox-Hunting Man* is mere make-
believe compared with the reality of my experience. But it isn't (as
your review implied) a piece of facile autobiographic writing.
Sherston is only 1/5 of myself, but his narrative is carefully
thought out and constructed. I don't see how it could have been
done differently. If I'd been trying to write my own 'serious'
autobiography the whole thing would have been different in tone
and texture. Don't blame me for having won prizes. You can't
accuse me of 'writing for reputation', can you?

After I wrote to you I was able – until your reply arrived – to
go on with my book. In fact I felt positively amiable toward you
(while forgetting everything since 1919). I mention this because I
was being obliged to write about you, as you were in 1916–17,
and before I wrote to you I couldn't do so – for obvious reasons.
But of course my account of our friendship is only a Sherstonized
one, and full of the inevitable touches of 'delightful humour', etc.,
which people enjoy so much.

Your reference to *The Heart's Journey*. I did not send it to you
(apart from feeling estranged) because I thought I was a back-
number (poetically) in your estimation, and didn't want to be told
how I ought to have done it. You had told me that there are 'only
5 good writers in England and America', and I wasn't optimistic
about being among them! May I conclude by hoping that you are
both in good health, as this leaves me (and Stephen, who is always

telling me that I am too hard on you; – poor soul, he has been
bored almost out of his wits by my eternal recurrences to the well
worn theme of your autobiography!).

Yours – I don't really know what –   S.S.

Your exaggeration of the RWF officer casualties can be proved. I
have a detailed list at home. There are no *under*statements in your
book. Nearly all war books fall into that trap (pitching the story
too strong and forgetting the decent elements).

Graves wrote fewer letters during the next five years; there was no
further correspondence with Sassoon until 1933, and he had argued
with almost all the others of his old friends; any new correspondences, such as with James Reeves (see page 245), were carried on
by Riding, even if they had been initiated by Graves. Riding argued
with Gertrude Stein (whom she portrayed as Amelia in *14A*) and all
correspondence with her ceased in 1930 (but was renewed by Graves
in 1946, see page 336). Another reason for fewer letters being written
was eye strain, which affected Graves from 1933 onwards.

Graves and Riding imported all their books and belongings to
Deyá, including the press which they installed in Casa Salerosa;
they began printing again with 'Seizin Four': *No Trouble*, a selection
of letters and experimental prose by Len Lye, who had gone to Deyá
with his South African wife Jane early in 1930. (In 1932, however,
they stopped hand-printing books and the Seizin Press became an
'ordinary publishing concern', controlled by Riding and Graves; the
books were then printed by commercial firms in England and
America and distributed by Messrs Constable and Co. in England
and by Random House in America.) Len and Jane Lye did not stay
long in Mallorca but returned to England where Len worked with
the Post Office Film Unit. He and Graves remained close friends for
many years, and although they wrote many letters to each other,
only the following two of Graves's letters, written to Lye and his
wife shortly after they had left Deyá, have survived.

1 June 1930

Dearest Chaps,

Thank you for the *Sunday* and *Daily Expresses*. So you

quarrelled with Eric,[8] did you? Funny business: his technique was rather like Celandine's when she broke with us. I should have thought he would have been more careful about breaking with you, Len, than that; because you're a Great Man.

What's new here? Thunder this morning, hot sun this afternoon, heavy rain two days ago, yesterday a very breezy lovely shiny day and we went into Palma; this morning, June 1st, drifts of snow on the hills. I went up the other day behind the *Molino* past that Moorish keep and there's a path through the live-oak forest to the top. It took me one hour and twenty minutes to get where I could look down at Valdemossa and across to Palma where I saw the six German cruisers anchored that are visiting. It was a good walk, through cloud part of the way, and it was so sticky by the time I had finished with the olive-tree level and got into the oak level that I took off all my clothes except my shoes and stuffed them into my knapsack. But met no one. I am gradually, in streaks, getting the brown egg colour on my skin so highly prized by collectors. But I have toothache, curse it. Must get it fixed tomorrow.

And the shoemaker and his wife sent you their *recuerdos* and asked for your news. And we have just discovered that your bedroom light is on every night since you went! Gelat[9] says it's *nada! nada!* He took us in yesterday in the auto, with the *modista* who is making me night-shirts instead of pyjamas for the hot weather, and Maria who had lunch with us at the Repla and ate various things for the first time and pretended politely to be bored. And we saw the traffic cop by the Credito Balear directing traffic with one white glove and gently scratching his balls with the other for quite a long time. Green *pimientos* are in season again. Today I got pebbles by the sea: it was a good beach; I found one pebble with that rich emerald colour that means copper; I hadn't met one before. And an extra delicate bit of gob. The flowers in season are lots of poppies and pale-blue chicory.

We get proofs of Laura's Seizin[10] from Palma tomorrow. It's been a long delay but possibly once we start it'll get quicker.

Jane, what sort of job this time? Dull, or even worse? The young, shy, fish-faced half-Spanish son of the acting British Consul is doing typing for us. Just to pass the time. He's really an official in the Spanish branch of the Kia-Ora Lemon and Orange squash business, at Valencia: but the season is over now for the year.

. . . .

We bought a 30 peseta table in Palma – live-oak not olive, but a nice wide one. Our steps have taken three men, if you count Pepe, four days to fix. They aren't yet properly done and the garden's full of litter and stone-chips. A lot of Germans went by in a succession of cars and one stopped and just too late I realized that they were picking our (filthy) Madonna lilies. For the principle of the thing I bawled out things in German and scared them but it was difficult to be really sorry. The flies are a pest now otherwise all nature is lovely. Don't say I don't give you all the irrelevant news.

Love   Robert

That summer Graves's father, Alfred Perceval Graves, who was a leader of the Celtic revival in Ireland, president of the Irish Literary Society, an inspector of schools and a poet, published his autobiography, *To Return to All That*, which included a chapter on Robert Graves and several of his early poems and war letters. Graves, meanwhile, had just finished a play called *But It Still Goes On*.

To Len and Jane Lye

8 June 1930

Dearest Chaps,

What's the time? Nine o'clock Sunday morning. Weather: raining hard so that I can pretend that I'm busy watering the garden. Situation: me writing in the little room, Laura next door just had breakfast in bed, now trying her luck with the door locked. Atmosphere: calm and easy. News: the seedy but honest old waiter at the Repla found my wallet when sweeping out the room and was so pleased that he gave me the account three times of how he thought at first it was a cigarette-case and then *Caramba!* it was *Dinero!!* There is a first-class dentist in Palma I have found. He is Spanish but very gentle and careful: the other chap was a brute.

Yesterday on my way to the sea I passed Mrs Broadwood[11] talking to herself: 'tiresome oh tiresome oh how tiresome,' so I said: 'Tut tut, what's tiresome?' And she startled (like a man caught pissing on the flowerbed) and blushed and said: 'These wallflowers they are so old and rank and I really must get Sebastiaaan to pull them out for me. But Sebastiaan is such a nuisance. You can never find him.'

So I passed on. Down at the sea – near that tower in the pinewoods there's a crack in the cliff where you can climb down right to the water's edge. There was a heavy sea slapping against the cliff, and an underground cave which the waves filled up every time they hit the rock and (through a small air hole about fifty feet up in the cliff) the air, displaced in the cave each time by the water, came whiffling out in terrific wet blasts like a steam whistle. Oh and I found a very good place where there is a big ledge half way down the cliff where one can sit naked out of view of the beach and, close by, a cave that goes right into the rock; and a way down to the *cala* to bathe. The electric light has just gone on. Now why? Probably the church was dark and the Pastor sent Juan out to start the works going for the glory of God.

Laura's operations are successful. After a blank day yesterday.

John Bull, did I tell you?, fucking-well rewrote that story of mine. I told the editor that his office-boy deserved a hard six with the office ruler for the practical joke. He replied that he had himself merely rewritten a few 'crude phrases' and I ought to be grateful. As all legal action is impossible at this distance I wrote to the office-boy apologizing for my mistake and suggesting that as a fraternal gesture he should spit in the editor's inkpot. I promised him a box of cigarettes if he did.

What else? My Mother writes: 'What I call white you call black and vice-versa. But it is a comfort to me, as no doubt to you, that truth is absolute and the most we can do is, as your father says in one of his poems, "to wipe the cobwebs from the sphere of truth."' My father's book is out. It looks pretty dreary by the prospectus.

Oh yes, now this will interest you: Maurice Brown[12] returns the play saying that it would: 'do definite harm to your reputation and prejudice your public against your future work' if produced. Doesn't say 'it's rotten' or that 'we can't risk it' but just this hypocritical tenderness on behalf of my reputation. Anyhow it doesn't matter. I shall tidy it a bit more and then publish it along with 'Papa Johnson', 'The Shout', 'Advocado Pears', that journal, parts of 'Baal', etc., this autumn in a book called by the name of the play. This autumn, too, I'll publish *Poems 1926–1930*. I have written a lot of poems lately.

. . . .

Bless you each and all and I am glad it was a girl, not a boy, a miscarriage, twins, triplets or a phart.

Robert

To Return to All That and *But It Still Goes On* were both published by Jonathan Cape, who also published many other books by Graves, including *Lawrence and the Arabs*, the critical works with Laura Riding, *Goodbye to All That* and *The Reader Over Your Shoulder*. In the early summer of 1930 Cape wrote to Graves saying that he had received offers from German and French publishers who wished to buy *Goodbye to All That*.

No date

Dear Jonathan

Accept the French offer but stipulate that I must be allowed to prepare my own text for French publication; and if there is a chance of getting a Spanish publication they can use the same version. This is because France is nearer here than Germany is; many of the local people can read French, but none German. I want a version which does not give too informative a slant on my private affairs for the people here. Tell Monsieur de Traz merely that I want to shorten the book somewhat and make it more suitable for French reading, there being sentiments in it that could be construed as anti-French.

But It Still Goes On. I sent you the final batch two days ago and I sincerely hope that now you have the whole lot – you acknowledged the first lot, the second was 'The Postscript to *Goodbye*', the third was 'Journal of Curiosities' and 'Alpha and Omega of the Autobiography of Baal'. Now that Laura has been through it and suggested cuts, additions, etc., I feel quite satisfied with the book as a selling proposition. It is 'fine confused reading', but is a statement of a general attitude to events which probably readers and reviewers will find 'stimulating', 'definitely thought-provoking', 'challenging', 'impudent' and so on.

Keep your blue pencil as much away as humanly possible; my popular reputation is that I say what I mean (and though I sail close to the wind I always leave a margin of safety) and I want to say as much of what I mean as possible.

. . . .

Yours ever   Robert Graves

Graves and Riding decided to have their own house built and chose a site just outside of Deyá, on the road to Sóller, about four hundred metres above the sea which it overlooks. Their closest Mallorquín friend was Joan Gelat: one of the most intelligent and ambitious of the village men, who owned land, many of the local water rights, ran a taxi service and a bus service from Deyá to Palma, and supplied the village's first electricity by means of an old-fashioned generator.[13] He was closely involved in all the local business dealings of Graves and Riding and supervised the building of their house (which he and Riding named Canelluñ, a mis-spelling of the Mallorquín – few people could then write the language – Ca Na Lluny, meaning 'the far house'). Graves later portrayed Gelat as 'Master Toni' ('squat, bald, dark-eyed, muscular, smiling . . .') in his short story 'The Viscountess and the Short-Haired Girl' (1958).

Over the next few years a small, close group of artistic friends grew up who used Canelluñ as a sort of 'central base'; none, except Graves and Riding, lived in Deyá permanently, but they came frequently on extended visits. In 1931 the group included, apart from the Lyes, Norman Cameron, the Scottish poet and translator of Rimbaud (who had a house built next to Canelluñ called Ca'n Torrent), and John Aldridge, the painter. Aldridge painted portraits of both Riding and Graves, and designed the covers of several of Graves's books, including the *Claudius* and *Sergeant Lamb* novels and an anonymous novel written by Graves and Riding soon after they arrived in Deyá, called *No Decency Left*. Cape suggested the title to Graves in October 1930, telling him it would sell a million copies, and urged him to write the book. Graves undertook to write the novel and wrote it twice, but the result was not good; then Riding corrected and rewrote it and though it was still bad it was published, in February 1932, and was not a success. They used the pseudonym 'Barbara Rich' and their true identity was never officially revealed.

Graves wrote to John Aldridge, who was back in England.

No date

Dearest John,

No Decency Left at last finished and sent off. Laura had to do more and more rewriting of it until at the end hardly anything of my original remained. Too heavy a touch, too cock-a-hoop a style, too altogether-too-not-good-enough. Now it's all right. Now it's what it should have been. You can look forward to reading it. Take the cover along to Cape when you can. Or send. Please, in talking about the cover don't accidentally mention it as my and L.'s book. But where also made the mistake about its being mine, correct this. Dearest John.

We are not coming to England in September. Not until January 1932. Would you be a good chap and bring David[14] out when you come in the autumn, *if* he comes. He is stupid but obedient and stays put so if you lose him he won't be far from where he last was. Please say you will. October isn't it?

By October the roof will be on our new house. Not of course the inside guts – only walls and roof but protection against the rain for men working inside. It's going to be a beaut.

Norman's bungalow is starting eighty yards off. Will finish much the same time. Please tell anyone who knows about *No Decency Left* and shouldn't really have been told, that it's not mine but mine rewritten by Laura, and absolutely anonymous anyhow.

You will meet Elfriede here and you'll like her. She is living at Salerosa with us.

Best love

                                                                    Robert

Cape, however, did not like Aldridge's cover design but thought it a 'gratuitous handicap'. Graves replied:

No date [August 1931]

Dear Jonathan

Heaven isn't the only person in the secret of Aldridge's design. For instance, there is Miss Barbara Rich <u>who sent him the exact specifications.</u> If you had got the typescript all in a lump at once and in less of a mess I think that you too would have seen at once what it meant. The fish are exact delineations of *macropodus opercularis* and *Badis Badis* (in the aquarium in Miss Rich's reconstituted bathroom). The mixed bathing is in reference to that of Pringle Park in Chapter VII. The female with the crown is Barbara and the other mounted figure behind her is Max. Sea horses, reference to Chapter X, to suit the aquatic scene. The whole underwater allegory is the sunken kingdom of Lyonesse, and the conventionalized heraldry of the seven 'frets' (consult your heraldic dictionary for 'fret') is a very happy touch suiting the formality of the writing. It is all very carefully and beautifully worked out, is a decoration that immediately arrests the curious not to say lecherous eye, and is exactly what is wanted; as the few people who have seen it and are average members of the intelligent public agree.

Dear Jonathan, I know your artistic antecedents – weren't you once a boss in the Medici Society? But on the several occasions on which you and I have got on the subject of illustrations, covers, etc., we have always absolutely been at cross-purposes. You think that my taste is much too modernistic and I think yours disgracefully on the safe side. Perhaps you think my taste is worse than modernistic and (to be frank) I think yours is worse than on the safe side. Well, art isn't an important subject compared with literature, in the relations you and I have been having; and it is unlikely that we'll ever have a serious quarrel about a wrapper. I remember a stiff letter you wrote about Len Lye's wrapper to *Goodbye*; but I can't think that it lost us many thousands of copies, as you expected. And as the photographed head was his, and was the best photograph ever taken of me, I think you were very lucky. In the case of *Lawrence and the Arabs* it was I who decided on having photographs instead of illustrations and who chose every one of them. What I am saying now is that my decision with regard to illustrations has not yet been at fault; I know what the people's eye catches at and this wrapper is not only that but a very beautiful picture. The difficulty about discussions like this is that we can't print two editions, one with a plain wrapper and one with the Aldridge design, to see which sells best. And you can say that if you had provided a cover for *Goodbye* or line illustrations for *Lawrence* you would have sold more than you did.

But being a person of infinite patience I will present you the arguments briefly in favour of the design, having already explained the meaning of it.

1) It is ODD and the title is ODD and the two circumstances will make nine people out of ten who see it in a bookshop open it to see what it is about. Ditto any nine out of ten reviewers.

2) It is slightly indecent and yet formally artistic enough not to offend.

3) It is in very bright colours, and the drawing has that indefinable charm, etc., etc., which characterized Miss Rich, the artist.

4) People like pictures of fish. Ask any kerb-stone artist.

The fifth (and to me final) argument is Laura's admiration of the design. She says that if you don't use it you don't deserve to thrive and oughtn't to have the book. Well, Jonathan, the best thing is, I think, for you to use the cover and then when you have sold your however-many-thousandth copy you will still have a pleasant grievance that with another cover you would have sold another couple of dozen more. A plain cover is no good for a book like that.

Remember that I didn't want to write the beastly book – you bullied me into it – and Laura certainly didn't want to rewrite it for me. It has been an awful bore for us both and we have made a good job of it and you shouldn't grudge us the pleasure of having a cover in keeping with the writing. Laying aside all questions of artistic merit – we put it to your sense of DECENCY. We cannot believe that you, like Scandals the Communists and all the rest, have no decency left.

Yours ever   Robert

Cape admitted that the instances of *Goodbye to All That* and *Lawrence and the Arabs* were 'good debating points' but he remained unconvinced on the present issue and refused to accept Aldridge's design.

At this time the owner of the estate on which Canelluñ was built announced his intention of selling a large part of the land between Canelluñ and the sea to a local German resident who had plans for building a hotel there. At first Graves and Riding were horrified at the prospect of their privacy being invaded by German tourists, but after consultation with the wily Gelat and the proprietor, a friend of Gelat's, they decided 'that the best thing to do was boldly to get the land ourselves and as Deyá has no hotel and is bound to have one, put one up ourselves in a corner of the land far enough removed from our house not to matter.'[15] There were also plans for selling off small plots of land for building chalets on. Four thousand pounds were invested in the scheme by Norman Cameron and, in the autumn of 1932, the first step was taken: the building of a road to join the *cala* Deyá (the cove) with the main Deyá–Sóller road.

Two close friends of Graves and Riding were T. S. Matthews and his wife Julie. Tom Matthews was a young journalist working for *Time* (later becoming an editor) who, at the beginning of 1932, took six months leave from *Time* to write his first novel. He went with his wife and two young sons to Mallorca where he intended to spend his sabbatical leave; soon after arriving there they called on Graves, whom Matthews had met briefly at Islip many years previously, and decided to stay in Deyá, moving into Casa Salerosa when Graves and Riding moved out. Six months later they returned to Princeton, Matthews having written his novel *The Moon's No Fool* (heavily corrected and altered by Riding).

Many letters passed between Deyá and Princeton, and in one Julie Matthews must have (the letter has gone astray) expressed misgivings about the 'Luna-land' project spoiling Deyá. Graves replied:

24 November 1932   Canelluñ
                                                                 Deyá

Dearest Julie

Stung by your sarcasm I write to you. What do you want to know? Deyá is still Deyá only more so. The road has made seven or eight turns and has now crossed by a bridge over the Luna territory into the next property and has two or three more turns before it reaches the stream which it follows to the sea, getting there in January. It is the olive-picking season and there are heaps of olives. Two women are employed by us and will continue for two months till the season's over: they get three pesetas a day and their board and some of the resultant oil to take back home. Now that Laura and Gelat have decided what building plots to sell they are trying to sell them. This afternoon the first one will probably be sold and once one starts the rest all follow in a rush. Well, what else? There's nobody in Deyá of our friends now, except for Gelat of course, and we get a good deal of writing done. Apart from the *Vulgate*,[16] lately I've been getting a book of poems[17] off – not published till early summer – and writing with the help of

218

three large volumes of a Classical Dictionary, an encyclopedia, a Latin Dictionary, four Latin historians, one Greek, and a lot of other books, the story of the Emperor Claudius who was a poor old man who was made an emperor late in life against his inclination and moral convictions; and I think it will be a nice story. (He came between Caligula and Nero.) Laura's not at all well what with her poisoned appendix and things; if only she could get all that better.

The figs are now over, and the oranges and tangerines starting. We have heaps and heaps of olive wood for firing from trees cut down to make the road. The next thing is chickens: the chicken house is being built from a natural cave in Luna territory. Greta Garbo nearly came to Valdemossa going so far as to take a house there. We stopped playing 7½[18] because we lost too much: however, Gelat did all the winning so it wasn't so bad. The spring lettuce is coming along nicely, also spinach, carrots, potatoes, etc.

I am afraid it's too late now about Dickens which is being printed; but I think Tom will think it's all right since Laura went over it, page by page. Salerosa is temporarily empty, but Ca'n Pabo is let. Canelluñ is a very nice house with fires in the brick fireplaces.

Best love and to Tom and Tommy and Johnny

Robert

Before writing *I, Claudius* Graves had 'rewritten' Dickens's *David Copperfield*, removing all the superfluous 'padding' which its original, serialized form had made necessary (according to Graves). *The Real David Copperfield* was published in March, 1933, and received the most hostile reviews of any of Graves's books.

On Easter Sunday 1933 the road to the *cala* was opened by Graves, Riding, George and Mary Ellidge (two English friends), Arthur Barker (the English publisher) and Joan Gelat all driving down it in Gelat's car. However, the road had cost more than expected and Norman Cameron had argued with Riding and left Deyá, taking his money with him; no plots had been sold, Canelluñ had to be mortgaged and now no more money was available for the last payment to the builders. Graves decided to write to Siegfried Sassoon, who some years previously had promised that if ever Graves was in serious financial trouble he would help him if he could.

219

May 1933

My dear Siegfried,

I am writing this to you care of Faber and Faber with whom I have been in correspondence lately over a very fine book[19] by a 2nd Battalion signaller Frank Richards DCM of Blaina, Monmouthshire, in which you come in for a lot of mention: I don't know your address and have heard nothing of you since our last most rotten correspondence three years ago, so am asking them to forward this to you.

I want to know whether you still have money in any quantity, and accessible and if so whether you can lend me some. I need about a thousand pounds, because I have got into a hole, being let down in something by someone[20] – the details are unimportant – and have nothing left in the bank or mortgageable and have exhausted all possible book advances. The last three books I have written have fallen flat and as I am determined to write no more books of which to be ashamed (like *Goodbye*) and which alone sell I don't know what to do. As I don't consider that our quarrel was in any way final or fundamental and found both of us in a bad state, I naturally turn to you. If you can't do anything about it, at any rate please let me know that you get this letter because (posts are bad here) and I want to know at once how I stand.

Robert

I don't say anything about repayment, but I expect that this is not impossible.

Sassoon's reply to this letter, and to the following two letters, has not survived; it is obvious from Graves's letters, however, that Sassoon was not willing to help.

8 June 1933

My dear Siegfried,

Three years and three months seem to have been necessary before the question of our relationship could come up again for review. But if during that time you had ever been in great trouble and I was the obvious person to turn to, you would I believe have sent for me and I would I am sure have come at once: and there would have been a wash-out of all unpleasant memories.

Yes, the thing is serious enough in its way. If the money does not turn up before the end of the summer it means spectacular financial ruin: if it does turn up it means financial security for a number of years.

There is this to say: our friendship began on a basis of common danger and emotions and ideals, and money did not enter into it as a complicating factor. And this, that I am extremely scrupulous about asking people for money: so scrupulous that if I thought that there was any question in your mind beyond the two obvious ones – a) Is this cynical, as if the only link between us were a bad joke about Wills, or is it a real gesture of affection, a sign that there is a willingness to forget the injuries we did each other and return to the original unquestioning basis of friendship? and b) Have I the money accessible without doing injustice to my other friends? – I should be ashamed for both of us. If your answer to a) is favourable and has a responsive echo in the uncynical recesses of your own heart it shouldn't matter so much to either of us whether the answer to b) is equally favourable: because spectacular financial ruin is not really a serious thing except to professional financiers.

I can't write more, out of respect to the phrase you use 'I do feel that you are asking a good deal of me,' until I get some sort of answer to this: but it would be a nice thing if, for a change, money could be the excuse for writing by which a broken friendship gets repaired, instead of a signal that a friendship is wearing out. I am assuming that your life is now permanently settled as mine is, and that the hysterias of 1918–1929 which affected us both have now less than historical interest: and that any new thing that happens between us will have reference to this feeling of permanence and not to any memories of the experimental and painful and cross-purposed moods of the bad years.

Yours   Robert

26 June 1933

Dear Siegfried,

No I didn't think your letter unkind, but I did think it a curious result of such a long deliberation. If in answer to my rather startling first letter you had written: please send particulars of precise date before which money is needed, state what property of yours has been mortgaged, with details, who is the person you refer to who has let you down, with name and all relevant circumstances, and to what extent am I to take literally the statement that if you don't have this precise sum you will lose everything you have – I should have felt that this was businesslike and slightly ironical but would have sent you the information with a number of Spanish documents which you probably wouldn't have learned much from. You said nothing of the sort, merely asking whether it was serious. I replied, yes indeed, and concentrated on your point 'I think you are asking a good deal of me,' which, I assumed, referred to friendship not to sterling.

By now writing that you cannot do anything for me *because* I tell you 'nothing definite' you make it impossible for me to write to you again either on the subject of finance or on the subject of friendship. You expect this friendship to lapse automatically because of your failure to oblige me: for which failure however I must take the blame because I did not give you information for which you never asked.

If you care to answer, do, but it seems rather hopeless, because to make things right between us after such an exchange would mean that you were willing to do more work than your two letters suggest that you have any intention of doing. I only write this letter in the interest of frankness.

Robert

7 July 1933[21]

My dear Siegfried,

Ask yourself whether at any time during the last three years you wouldn't have had a direct and generous answer to any appeal for help of *any* sort you made to me, not merely financial. Ask yourself also whether because of a self-confessed 'Enoch Arden complex' you didn't for years try to keep friendship going solely by means of letters at a time when we were supposed to be bosom friends and when you were as a matter of fact my best friend. Ask yourself also whether after the first row we had, about Gosse, I didn't do my best to re-open friendly relations by writing to you when I heard you were ill – but you didn't answer. Ask yourself further whether my statement of regret for *Goodbye* in my first letter didn't demand a statement of regret for *Infantry Officer*: because you in *Goodbye* were written about with unmistakeable admiration, I in *Infantry Officer* was written about with unmistakeable malice. 'Pecksniffian' means hypocritical: in all these three letters of mine there has not been a single word that was not entirely direct. 'Elaborate argufyings' are merely my attempt to make sense of your purposely obscure statements. I seem to you to be dealing with you as a 'diagram of ratiocinations' rather than as a human being: but this is because you deal with me so un-simply through so many veiled insinuations that to examine them as I have done is the only alternative to accepting them.

My lack of 'gumption' is, I suppose, my not realizing that your constant assurances of help in money if ever I got into real difficulty, which finally became consolidated into an unsolicited promise of so many thousands of pounds as soon as Aunt Rachel died, were merely tests of my mercenariness. No, I have no gumption, then. Your very last letter to me contained a reference to my benefiting under your will. You wanted from me the credit of being above any immediate trouble between us; and yet when I put you to the test you collapsed into bank-manager nervousness. I was 'proposing the impossible'.

All this is rather dirty and I am sorry you didn't immediately answer my first letter by saying straight out: 'No, I can't spare it,' or 'No, I don't want to,' to which you would have got a simple answer, 'Thanks for letting me know so promptly.' What were you doing? Stringing me on to see to what degree I would humble myself for the sake of cash? I don't understand about 'if you are ever in England'. What am I supposed to do? It looks very much as though you felt that having money made you sole arbiter of the difficulties between us. If you are ever in Mallorca and by that time are ashamed of yourself for having played with me like this come and see me. I prefer even an Enoch Arden complex to an Otto Kahn[22] complex.

Yours ever   Robert

In July Graves received a respite from his financial obligations, as he explained in a letter to Julie Matthews.

223

22 July 1933
Isn't that Tommy's birthday?

Dearest Julie,

If I don't write now I never will. I never seem to have time for anything now (damn the light has just dipped three times and will go out at eleven) not even for having my hair cut in the village or going to bathe, and as for the garden I never go there at all nowadays except to get a green pepper or tomato or bit of mint or something. It's just working very hard trying to get my Claudius book finished and it's twice as long (lot of it's) as I intended and I have to read so many classical authorities to get it anything like historical that it's been a beastly job. It makes a nice story but isn't important otherwise. Then John and Lucie[23] have been here and that was very nice but we had nobody to cook the meals but ourselves; and then great anxiety about this road business trying to get money to pay the year's instalment – in the end we got Bernardo, the proprietor, to let it go for another year, just paying interest – and then Mary[24] had her baby and not knowing Spanish and having the village midwife and rather too big a baby for comfort – Laura had to help – and it's been very hot and now that the baby's born and there's a money respite and Laura and I are alone and can have fried onions when we like (Lucie couldn't stand onions or oil in her food) though we miss John who was very nice and did rather a good painting of Laura which he'll have photographed – I forget how this sentence started but anyhow I'm writing you this letter and I've only got from AD 39 to 41 in my *Claudius* to do before I wind up and go over the story tightening it up. Claudius is just being thrown by Caligula into the River Rhone at Lyons because he hasn't brought the bakers' vans from Rome on time. However, he'll swim to land all right, because he's fated to be emperor. The light has gone out and that has woken up the mosquitoes. The candles are flickering with the sea breeze: shut the window. The mosquitoes are burning themselves at the candles.

. . . .

Laura is working upstairs, revising her *Story Pig* book, and smoking cigarettes at the rate of thirty-five a day which is better than sixty. Did you hear about her comic accident – sat on a Ca's Pintat chamber pot which split neatly in two and cut her bottom right across like the sign of the cross – scars she will wear to her dying day.

Best love to Tom and Tommy and Johnny and you. I do hope your baby behaves well.

Robert

To Siegfried Sassoon

17 September 1933

My dear Siegfried.

I have not written before in answer because I have had trouble with my sight, not because I considered the correspondence at an end. Yes, it has not been a pleasant correspondence because there was Robert on one side saying exactly what he meant and there was Siegfried on the other not saying at all what he meant but 'trying to let Robert down easily'. The last letter was a bit better: nastier but plainer. There are still a few points to be cleared up, though. (I noticed the fifteenth anniversary, July 13, on which you wrote.)

I had said that if during the last three years, i.e. from June 1930–June 1933, *after* our breach, you had asked me for help of any sort I would have instantly given it. You answered that in February 1930 you 'indirectly' asked me for an *apology* and I did not give it. Yes, you wrote me a most brutally worded letter. You had already cut yourself off from me brutally: if you had not I should have shown you the manuscript of *Goodbye*, and been a little surprised at your objections to anything in it connected with you. I did not *apologize* to you recently for *Goodbye*. I said that I regretted it. If I had written your two *Memoirs* I should have equally regretted them. This is not in particular reference to what I wrote about you, or what you wrote about me, but merely that they were books better unwritten. I would say just the same about my *Mock Beggar Hall* poems; or your *Heart's Journey* if I had written that. (I wouldn't ask or expect an apology for Cromlech: but I have heard it said – I think T.E.L. said it most clearly – that S.S. was the obvious hero of *Goodbye* and that Cromlech had his face rubbed unnecessarily hard in the dirt.) Anyhow I repeat that if at any time in the last three years you had needed my help in any way I would have given it. You say that a broken friendship

225

cannot be mended by post. Even if it was originally broken by post?

You say that your friends have never regarded you as ungenerous. Who *are* your friends, Siegfried? I know nothing about your relations with Stephen, but I do know that while I was your friend you were never really open with me, or with any other of your then friends and tried to avoid their knowing each other: the best figure that I can think of in comparison is the Catholic nun who isn't allowed to wash more than one part of her body at a time for fear she gets too intimate thoughts about herself as a whole. I have always liked my friends to know each other and if there was anything wrong with any of the less-trusted friends it soon appeared when I saw them in company with the more trusted. My opinion is that you played tricks with each of your friends in turn, never telling any one of them the whole truth about yourself.

I have been assuming in these recent letters that you have succeeded in somehow centralizing yourself in the years you have been in Stephen's company and that you could therefore be addressed in a straightforward way: I have not yet any assurance that I was right in assuming this. About Stephen's illness: I am very sorry indeed to hear that it has been such a long and bad business. I don't say that on *his* account because I don't know him and know nobody who does and you have never said a word to me about him personally or indicated what sort of a person he is. But that you can refer to his illness in the terms that you do in such an otherwise unpleasant letter shows that you have felt very unhappy indeed about it, and makes me sorry that you misunderstood me so completely as to think that I would not have instantly forgotten all differences between us if you had written to me because you were in trouble. I can't say any more than this. Except that I have succeeded in getting a year's respite from my obligations and hope that a book I have just finished will help me out. No, I shall not 'use all this against' you, or tell you that you ought to be ashamed of yourself. Oh, about bank-managers and Otto Kahn. As a class they are a most generous lot. And Otto Kahn is a most generous man. I was not referring to your generosity or lack of it, but to your ill-at-ease-ness with the notion of money: to which you must agree.

Robert

From Siegfried Sassoon

22 September 1933	Fitz House Teffont Magna Wiltshire

Dear Robert

I will try and answer a few of your 'points'. You say I was 'never really open' with you and 'tried to avoid my friends knowing one another'. Let me remind you that I made persistent and misguided attempts to get my friends to know and like one another from 1919 onwards. I quarrelled with the Sitwells because they were unable to like you and W. J. Turner, for example. (Some years ago you wrote me a letter in which you attributed my perplexities to 'loyalty'.)

As regards being 'open' with you, I could never see you – after 1919 – on my own ground. You were never allowed to so much as dine with me at the Club (until one evening (in 1926?) when you were broadcasting about the aircraftman). I had to adapt myself to *your* ground intellectually, also, which meant swallowing a series of theories about poetry, etc., which you have since discarded and which were never compatible with mine.

In 1927 you said to me, in the presence of Glen Shaw (one of the 'friends' of mine about whose existence you are so sceptical) that there were only 5 writers in England and America who were any good. You were talking through your hat (or someone else's bonnet). You now say that practically everything I have published since the war would have been 'better unwritten'.

My answer to that is that the *Fox-Hunting Man* is one of the best-written and most enjoyable books published since 1900, and that the *Heart's Journey* contains some of my best poetry. You prefer deliberate incomprehensibility and sterile obscurity. How can I adapt myself to that? It never seems to have struck you that my 'cutting myself off' from you was merely giving up the ghost. The fact that you dislike and disapprove of almost all of my writings apparently justifies me, since our original bond was a literary one. I myself would prefer you not to select 'dung-worms' as a subject for poetry. And I don't believe that Dickens can be improved on by you.

I do *not* agree with you about what you call my 'ill-at-easeness' with the notion of money. No one knows better than I do what to do with money, and no one has ever been less altered in habits by inheriting money. When I said that I was not regarded as ungenerous by my friends, I was merely referring, indirectly, to the fact that I gave away almost all that I made by my prose books (about £7000). (This is 'plain-speaking' – not vulgar boasting.)

I kept a copy of the first letter I sent you in 1930; it was *not* brutally worded. I merely stated the causes of my 'feeling bad' about you, hoping that you would respond generously and relieve my mind of its [nimbus] of ill feeling. Your response was not at all what I needed, and contained at least two outrageous indiscretions – one about Nancy, and one about T.E.L.

That is about enough for today.

S.S.

No date

My dear Siegfried

In saying goodbye, in what I hope will prove a final letter, I shall not go particularly into the points you have raised but make a general summing up. In reopening this correspondence I was being sentimental, imagining back to the time when I knew and liked you – loved you was more like it. I thought that by now you would probably have settled down into a serenity of mind which would make the revival of our friendship possible. You have ever since then been demonstrating its impossibility from your side, but the real reasons are only now allowed to appear. Your real feeling about me is that I am a disturbing influence, a challenge to your literary self-complacence as the author of some of the best books published since 1900. If thinking that to have written the *Heart's Journey* is to have fulfilled the whole duty of a poet, or that it is anything but a monument to your emotional shortcomings makes you happy I have no more to say. Our friendship never rested for me on a basis of contrasted literary accomplishment: I am not proud of any book I have written or jealous of any of yours. Be a Sir Edmund Gosse if you must; you'll be a good one. That literary chat about selecting dung-worms as a subject for poetry, and the impossibility of Dickens being improved by me, and my deliberate incomprehensibility and sterile obscurity would delight *Sunday Times* readers. I shall let your seventieth birthday pass without so much as a silver scent-bottle in homage. (But I am getting involved in 'points' again, I find.)

'I was merely referring, indirectly, to the fact . . .' Your unwillingness to refer to anything directly wastes a lot of time. I suppose my 'talking through someone else's bonnet' is a reference to Laura. If you had said straight out that Laura was an obscurantist influence on my way of writing that could have passed as an ordinary ignorant remark, or if you had said that Laura herself wrote nonsense that could have been set against the testimony of other people that she is the most accurate writer there is. But you come out with a comic-postcard piece of vulgarity which is the counterpart of the lace-Valentine vulgarity of your *Heart's Journey*: and that ends it.

So, for the last time,
Yours   Robert

I forgot whether I told you that I have got a year's respite for my indebtedness and that you therefore need have no immediate conscience-gnawings about letting me starve.

From Siegfried Sassoon

3 October 1933   Fitz House

Dear Robert.

You are having a fine time, scoring off my loose bowling. You can now say that I am not only a vulgar mentioner of my Will, but also a self-complacent literary man who thinks that he has written the best books of the Century. You can also pride yourself on having solved the great problem of my inaccessibility and all that. You imagine me sitting here and saying I will not correspond with anyone who does not think I am a good poet. How comfortable for you – to feel so sure about someone else's state of mind! – Omniscient and infallible, not the least proud of anything you have written, and dismissing 90% of the world's best literature because it doesn't fit in with your own recipes for writing. (Is there not a *soupçon* of complacency in your attitude?)

As regards 'the lace-Valentine vulgarity' of the *Heart's Journey*, that 'monument to my emotional shortcomings' – I think, if you ever look at the despised volume again, you will find that your phrase can only (if at all, ha! ha!) be applied to a few of the poems, and those were deliberately inserted to represent my 'emotional shortcomings' in 1918–22. At least half the poems have been liked by you at one time or another, and I felt bound to put in a mild defence of them. I am forwarding you a few further specimens of my lace-Valentine complacency, so that you can pat yourself on the back and say what a rotten old writer I am.

My reference to your sterile obscurity, etc., was perhaps a little hasty and unguarded. No one respects your 1930–3 poems more than I do – clean in workmanship, and interestingly puzzling. I am also willing to accept your testimony that Laura is 'the most accurate writer there is'. (But I think you will admit that – for mere mugs like myself – her work needs a good deal of explanatory annotation.) I dislike apparent incomprehensibility, especially when it is done with deliberate virtuosity. But in that matter you must regard me as an '[impassioned] ass in gilded trappings'. Good-bye for now, if it must be so. I shall be glad to become a Gosse, if it means preserving vitality and enthusiasm and hatred of humbug until I am seventy-nine (with a little pardonable vanity – self-defensive – added). But I often feel that I should be glad to walk out and leave it all behind. One feels weary.

S.S.

Now that the road to the *cala* was finished and a respite granted on the payment, all seemed well for the Luna project; but on the night of 29 September, fate interrupted the plan when a cloudburst swept away the new road. Graves made no mention of the catastrophe to Sassoon, however.

No date

My dear Siegfried

One big photograph in exchange for two small ones. No, it's not my job to be omniscient and infallible: you've got me misplaced. And I'm not interested in scoring off you, only in trying to get at the bottom of things. The point of difference between us seems to lie in the reverence that we are each prepared to pay to literary feudalism: you pay a lot, I pay none. I admit about the *Heart's Journey* that I spoke from a four-year memory of the book, but the effect was in general when I read it as though the heart had journeyed up and down the *Oxford Book of English Poetry* and finally arteried itself in A. E. Housman.

I remember when we were in Harlech, in 1916 wasn't it? going over the *Old Foxhunter [sic]* collection. There was a lot of early Nature and Valentine stuff there (Valentines, laced, are the acknowledged world's best examples of amatory perfectionism) and I remember saying 'You ought to cut these out, Siegfried,' and I remember you saying, 'No, they're all right, Robert. You don't understand that sort of writing!'

You appeal to Dickens in one letter. I don't know how you fit that in with your hatred of humbug. I am perfectly certain that you never read Dickens carefully. I challenge you to read *David Copperfield* carefully all through without feeling either sick, disgusted or patronizing [*sic*]: or you're in a worse state than I think, if you can. Dickens wrote against humbug in the same sense as Thackeray wrote against snobbery and James Douglas writes against obscenity. You have probably been misled by reading reviews of my *Real David Copperfield* by people who had not read either the original or my version. I suggest that if you have the time to spare you should read, first my version right through and see if there is anything you miss, and then Dickens's again and see if there is anything that you prefer. So far as I know only three reviewers took the trouble to do this – *New Republic*, *Listener* and *Nottingham Gazette* – and their report was reassuring. All the others argued: 'Dickens is our greatest novelist, *David Copperfield* is his best book – what the hell!' If '90% of the world's best literature' is not quite up to the standard of *Copperfield* it's not even worth rewriting. I don't dislike plain muggery at all. Mugs make good ploughmen, soldiers and mothers. But I do dislike deliberate muggery by people with fine feelings, shrewd brains and a proper independence of mind. Plain mugs or serfs pay literary vassalage to Dickens because 'he's our acknowledged greatest novelist' and because they read him, in abridgement, at the same time as they read Henty, and the Gospel Story and the Brothers Grimm. That's all very well for plain mugs or serfs but people with any clerkly or critical sense oughtn't to allow themselves to fall into this vassal-mindedness. Dickens is not a baron; he's just a journalist who sometimes had a good story to spoil. By making him a baron one is deliberately blunting one's critical sense and falling back on good old fallible feeble human nature as one's sole measure of truth. Which produces absurdities: such as the charge of deliberate obscurity, and virtuosity, against someone who is not naturally a mug and refuses to cultivate muggery because of the comfort it may afford and who writes with deliberate accuracy. No, Laura's work needs no explanation or annotation unless it is the simple foreword 'please read literally, giving every word its full sense value': the *difficulty* of Laura's work is that people won't believe at first that she can possibly mean what she says. And that they don't feel her a companion-spirit in good old f.f. human nature; which makes them uncomfortable and deliberately stupid when faced with perfectly clear statements. I note your preoccupation with the next war, but the next war will be the same sort of thing as the Dickens you consider unimprovable – long, wasteful, emotional and very, very human and oh so boring and forced on many millions of the childish-hearted *Daily Mail*-reading public. But thanks for the poems.

Laura says that it's a pity that you shouldn't be able to know her writing at first hand but get it merely as an influence on me; and that you aren't capable of measuring its influence on me because, while you admit that you really like my last poems, all the other feelings you have about me you get from letters of mine where you have forced me to write with deliberate virtuosity by writing to me in a deliberately muggish way. Quite apart from the fact, she says, that your social grounding in a synthetic world of literature prevents you from understanding her writing like a poet – intrinsically. She recommends you her next book of poems (Arthur Barker. November. Title *Poet – A Lying Word*) to be read intrinsically. She noticed in one of the poems you sent the word 'mindsight', which also occurs in a poem in her book: perhaps that may be a tie that binds.

Yours ever
Robert

I enclose a picture of Laura since photographs seem the order of the day. It is a portrait by a *real* academician, one Arnold Mason[25] who happened to stay here and she looks as damfool in it as you do in those Samuel Daniel togs on Wilton House lawn.

About your poems. I won't criticize them but just say that I don't think it's any use appealing for 'mercy from long ago' or regretting childish 'simplicities unlearned' any more than it's any use looking to the future of perfect physical evolution for the answer to problems. The tiny present crushed between them loses all self-respect and capacity for thinking and doing. As you end your letter, 'one feels weary'. The weariness is, I think, of literature, the mill with two millstones, *The Classics* and *Posterity*.

After a brief correspondence later in October about an unemployed ex-fellow-officer, 'Hyphazuka' Hill (see page 241), Graves and Sassoon ceased to write to each other. It was not until 1954 that they met again and were reconciled, 'clicking' in Cambridge, when Graves was Clark Lecturer there; Sassoon later wrote to Graves that all the years and 'misunderstandings' had melted away when he saw him, and when *Goodbye to All That* was republished in a revised form, in 1957, Sassoon did not object (see Appendix A).

In December Graves wrote to Tom and Julie Matthews. The only friends visiting Deyá then were George and Mary Ellidge, Eirlys Roberts (later to become deputy director of the Consumers' Association magazine *Which?*) and Jacob Bronowski, the mathematician and scientist, who for a time was collaborating with Graves and Riding on *Epilogue* (then still the *Vulgate*); before long, however, he argued with them and left Deyá (Graves later satirized him in his poem 'Dream of a Climber').

No date

Dearest Julie and Tom

1933 has been a rotten year in almost every way: hardly remember a worse, but we are still alive at the end of it and 1934 ought to be something good. In September I strained my eyes and have had to economize so much in their use that I don't write letters except necessary ones or read papers, or books except where work is concerned and even then I usually get someone to read them for me. And I dictate most of my work to Mary. But of course I must write to you after so long and send you what news there is.

I have at last got revised proofs of *I, Claudius* off, and John has done a lovely wrapper, and everyone seems pleased with the story especially Arthur Barker, and Harrison Smith.[26] You shall of course get the most advanced copy available perhaps in three weeks or so (H. Smith brings it out in the late spring). The story only goes as far as Claudius's accession, and I am now writing the sequel *Claudius the God* which is going very well. St Peter and St James will come into it, besides Messalina, Nero, and Herod Agrippa whom I find to be one of the nicest characters in ancient History – the perfect counterpart to Claudius and a prototype of *14A* Joho. I have done 33,000 words since starting in November and that is about a quarter: *I, Claudius* runs to about 170,000 words too. Other work I have not done, except proof-reading for *14A* and my 'Likes'[27] for *Of Others*, and housework. I do all the cooking now and am getting quite good at it. It seems funny that you don't know Mary and George and Jacob and Eirlys who are so much part of our story here. They are all very, very nice in their own ways and extremely different but each is a large subject in her or himself and so I won't say more than that they don't infringe in any way on the region of my heart occupied by you two.

. . . .

Laura is looking very tired but her appendix seems to be quieter lately. Not many foreigners about. Nobody has come to rent (Norman's house) Ca'n Torrent so Jacob and Eirlys are still living there (rent free) which is nice for us because there is a lot of work going on in collaboration and exchange of meals and so on.

Best love to you both and the 3 boys   Robert

In 1934 Arthur Barker published *14A*, a dull and artificial novel written by Laura Riding, nominally assisted by George Ellidge, based on the events at 35A St Peter's Square, which was withdrawn from circulation after Geoffrey Phibbs threatened Arthur Barker with a libel suit. Tom Matthews wrote saying he didn't like it, and in reply received the expected rebuke.

No date

Dear Tom,

Your letter about *14A* surprised Laura and surprised me. Laura did not want to write to say how she felt about it, for fear of making the occasion seem too important, so if I write saying how I felt about it the required indirectness will be achieved, and no harm done. What struck me first was that your letter was a second or perhaps third version of what you originally decided to write: I may be wrong about this but it seemed to me that this was a sort of defiant answer to the inconclusiveness of a first draft, as if to say 'damn it all, I shall say just what I mean without hedging', and the result was that any polite turns of phrase in the first draft were cut out and so-called frankness substituted: with the result that it reads like a very *rude* letter.

I mean there's nothing *gracious* said about the book. Granted that you think that it has technical errors from the point of view of the book market (e.g. a great many characters to remember, or an unusually detailed dwelling on people's positions in a crowded scene), it is most surprising to me that you fail to mention any particular scene which amused or interested you. Leaving out of the question for the moment all irrelevant points such as the identification of the characters with people in real life or all such general questions as the meaning of dramatic unity I am astonished that you don't get any kick from the wittiness and graciousness (I use the same word gracious again, advisedly) of such scenes as the nigger-in-the-train scene, the children-in-bed scene, the Billy-and-Janey scenes, the Joho scenes, or that if you did you did not say. You say in so many words that Laura has no dramatic sense, that she can't write, and that she has failed to convey any clear impression of characters or events. When you reached this conclusion I wonder you didn't reach the secondary conclusion that school-children do when in an arithmetic problem they get the answer '5½ sheep and 4¾ cows grazing in the field' – namely that something is wrong with their reasoning.

I should further guess that the wrongness of the reasoning is due to a curious misconception of the *meaning* of *14A*: as if you read it as a crude sensational revealing, for the sake of money, of a certain hidden chapter of Laura's life – as if you then stood up manfully as a champion of the better Laura whom you knew later to say 'no, it cannot be: this is never the Laura that I keep locked away in my sacred cupboard', like a Churchman indignantly denying that the Virgin Mary may have been Christ's mother by someone other than the Holy Ghost, or that Christ's partiality for John was not a tribute to his superior spirituality.

The Golden Falcon[28] parallel is a cock-eyed one. If only for the fact that the publishers made capital out of the supposed resemblances between Manfred and me to sell the anonymity of the book. My life happens to be familiar to enough American readers through *Goodbye* to have made this publicity trick worthwhile. (And obviously if it had been a book by me the publishers would not have played it.) Whereas Laura is only known in America by her poems, etc. They know nothing about any incidents in her 'life story'. Critics are as little likely to say 'This is Miss Riding's own story' as to say what is the truth but has apparently missed you, 'This is Miss Riding's caricature of herself as she might be if she wasn't.'

If you had had the book sent you without knowing who Laura Riding was except the author of some poems you perhaps hadn't read carefully (obviously I don't mean that you haven't done so) you wouldn't have made the parallel (Catherine is not, for instance, a poet) and wouldn't have had to do so much unnecessary struggling with yourself. You might even have got quite excited in the story (after perhaps an initial difficulty with names such as one gets in a lot of books which one afterwards likes) as apparently some simple-minded secretaries and such in Arthur Barker's office have become in the course of handling the proofs. And it's not flattering you too much to say that you would have appreciated the liveliness of the dialogue and the cinematographic way of telling the story by a succession of shots, better than most people.

But I won't go on too long about this, because it gets a bore. But certainly you're miles out, and it comes from a misapplied loyalty and so no hard thoughts, only surprise.

Love to you and Julie   Robert

1 May 1934

Dearest Julie and Tom

I send you *Claudius* under as they say separate cover. Isn't it a lovely cover? It will be used in America too. This is an advance copy so I don't yet know how it is going to go in England. In case, Tom, you want to review it, I attach some time-saving historical notes to indicate what twists I have put in the story as it came to me from Suetonius, Tacitus, Dio Cassius, Josephus (the main authorities) and the forty or fifty lesser ones. I did not use any History of Rome by any English or foreign modern author, because I didn't want my sense of the originals obscured. But of course I had general Classical reference books to make sure what sort of fancy clothes people wore on different occasions and whether onions were invented and who was second-cousin to whom. If I had used an ordinary history I don't think I would have been able to get any of the sort of excitement into the book which makes books sell.

. . . .

There are so many long local stories to tell you. You remember that huge house, the Molí, with the evil history. It went bankrupt at last and Gelat managed to become the official bailiff and make the inventory. He has left a lot of things out, many of which are at Canelluñ, including some lovely painted chairs.

Tom, you did me a great good turn with your *Copperfield* publicity. Not only is it to be serially syndicated in US (I don't know details yet) but Metro-Goldwyn-Mayer will probably, or else probably not – not clear which yet – use the version in their new film. The position is roughly that they find a lot of work usefully done for them in the book, but don't want to pay, especially as they know that the book has not been copyrighted in America: but then it *is* copyrighted in England where it has sold 306 copies! Thank you, indeed, if anything comes of it.

Mary's baby's very nice and as little trouble as it is possible for a baby to be, but he's a great tie and nuisance when we want to arrange things where babies aren't helpful presences. Jacob and Eirlys are great walkers and go out on thirty-mile pioneering expeditions, bringing back rare plants in as jaded a condition as themselves.

I am ploughing through the second part of *Claudius* which is better than the first in a way, at any rate less gloomy, because he's his own master and any mistakes he makes are his own. The story of King Herod Agrippa which is closely bound up with Claudius's from the point where *I, Claudius* ends is quite fun doing: he was a real wonder, if you read between the lines of Josephus.

. . . .

Laura isn't too well, but keeps up. The bay is lovely since the road was washed away; at last there is a smooth beach, made by the road material washed down, improved with sea sand. About ten yards added to the beach.

Now I must really stop, with much love to you all five from us both,

Robert

Book Society isn't a big thing in England – only 6770 subscribers
– but a good advertisement, insuring the sale of three or four
thousand more.

Later that month *I, Claudius* was published by Arthur Barker in
England (and in June by Harrison Smith in America); it was an
immediate success and Graves was solvent again. For the historical
notes he sent Matthews in this letter, see Appendix B.

In August Graves finished *Claudius the God* and wrote to John
Aldridge with some suggestions for the cover.

No date

Dearest John

Thank you so much for undertaking the cover. I rowed
Arthurby for not sending you a copy of *I, Claudius* and asked him
how he expected you to work for him again if he treated you like
that. The other cover has been frequently praised.

. . . .

About the present problem: it's entirely your show. I gave as
much detail as possible for you to use or not as you choose. A
red-figured vase would be easily possible in Claudius's day as a
fake antique and they might easily gild it, I should say, just to
improve it: I had that rather degenerate idea on purpose. (The
Portland Vase is about that date isn't it? That was done by layers
of different coloured glass, wasn't it, one over the other, and then
cutting away what wasn't wanted. Those cameos of Augustus and
the royal family are the same sort of thing, I think, but done in
chalcedony, or something, which is also in different coloured
layers, but of natural origin.)

The chap with the *patera* is just a grateful citizen – probably a
Gaul from Autun who has just been given the citizenship. Or he
might be shown as a boy of about 12, an acolyte.

The thing I showed you wasn't a *biga* but a *quadriga* (I tried to
indicate four horses): and the special correct triumphal sort, I
warrant you. If you have Smith's *Antiquities* it is there under
Triumphus not *Currus*.

Arthurby is keen on having that blue again to remind people of
the other book.

I have now finished *Claudius the God*, except to go over the typescript, I do hope you'll like it.

Do you see the *Daily Mail*? There was a nice thing last week. TRUNK MURDER LATEST. LORD TRENCHARD TAKES A HAND. But they still haven't found the head. And Margaret Lane marries Edgar Wallace's son. What was that joke of Lucie's about Edgar?

It is very hot and on Sunday we witnessed the most epic bull fight ever seen in Palma. Belmonte's reappearance, really fine, El Gallo at his best and most awful and shameful worst, and a young fellow La Serna, who lost his temper with the President for making him fight a bull with one blind eye, and bought an extra bull (for 2900 pesetas) to show his stuff on, and shoved everyone away and gave a sort of firework display in the middle of the arena which ended him up on the shoulders of the entire audience, who ovated him as far as the Grand Hotel and then again all the way to the boat. We have the coloured advertisement pinned up in the Press room. The best news is that the control of Mallorca will in 3 months' time go from Madrid to Palma, where Gelat knows everyone worth knowing; he expects to be able to sell the road to the general public at cost price which will still leave us with the land improved in value by the existence of the road.

Best love   Robert

In October Graves sent an advance copy of *Claudius the God* to Edward Marsh, who wrote to his friend Francis Brett Young, the novelist:

I'm snowed under with presentation copies. The best are R. Graves's second *Claudius* book which I delight in – I think the two together are an indubitable masterpiece – and Bob Nichols's *Fisbo*. It's a really magnificent piece of satiric writing, full of poetry and wit, tho' I can't be sure that poor Osbert [Sitwell] has really deserved all that vitriol.[29]

Marsh was then helping Winston Churchill on the third volume of *Marlborough*; he had been suffering from ill health for several years and was soon to retire, and begin his translations of the *Odes of Horace*. He wrote to Graves saying how much he liked the book, and Graves replied:

5 November 1934

My dear Eddie,

I am so glad that you liked *Claudius the God*: it meant a lot of work for me because I was never a Classical scholar of any accuracy or distinction and stopped dead off when the war broke out; and you know how careful one has to be even in fiction.

I got the Horace translation from Francis, of whom Dr Johnson said 'Francis has done it the best: I'll take his, five out of six, against them all.' He puts *Dianam tenerae* as the second movement of the Carmen with a note that it is also the 29th ode of the first book. I don't know on what authority, but it looks all right. As for Phaemon's dog. I remembered it in that attribution in a school text-book (a French one, not a Classical one). I looked up Phaemon in the *Dictionary of Classical Biography* and found he was a Cynic and that a mediaeval forgery was fathered on him, a book on the proper care of dogs. That seemed to make the thing likely. Naturally I had no clear notion who wrote that French text-book or where he got Phaemon from. But it sounded a very Greek story to me. Possibly, I argued, the mediaeval forgery was attributed to Phaemon not only because he was a κυνικος but because of a well-known tale of his dog. It was quite late mediaeval – let me find it, wait a moment – Yes, 1545 at Wittenberg in Latin and Greek κυνοσόφιον, but the Latin title was *De Re Accipitraria et Venatica*. Your date 1522, suggests some other work than this as the source.

Baba and Angurinus. I played a trick here. I worked *back* from Seneca's satire, where many of the jokes are obscure, building up references for them in the text. 'Baba' is mentioned by Pliny as a fool. Angurinus is unknown. I had to give them some importance to justify Seneca. I identified Baba with the fool at Alexandria, mentioned in Josephus.

About Brentwood. I wrote the account from a rather small-scale map and then checked it from the ordnance. Of course Brentwood was only a guess, but it seemed the obvious place to hold between London and Colchester. To my delight I found not only the Roman road and the appropriate contours but my British fort on their right wing just where I had placed it! My central fort is built over by the Brentwood High Street and the left fort is where the

Basket II foreground, Gertrude Stein and Alice B. Toklas, photographed
by Cecil Beaton (*Sotheby's*, *Belgravia*)

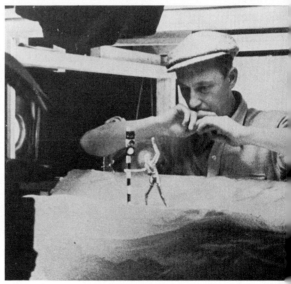

Above Len Lye at work on his puppet film
'The Birth of the Robot', 1936
(The Len Lye Foundation)

Left Jonathan Cape, *c.* 1931

Below left Tom Matthews, New York, 1939

Below John Aldridge at work in his studio at
Great Bardfield, 1949

Above Graves with Basil Liddell Hart, May 1940
Right Karl Gay in army uniform
Below right Alan Hodge
Below Alun Lewis

Top left Lynette Roberts, 1953
Top right Laura Riding in Deyá
Above Deyá (*photo Josip Ciganovic*)

lunatic asylum is now, so one can excuse their absence from the map.

I haven't read *Fishboo*. Bob was always sitting about with a long black coat and a melancholy hat 'deep in a dump' like the description of John Ford by Meres, wasn't it? Death was always at his elbow. But when I last heard from him four years ago he was hinting at approaching extinction with more than usual force. His mother went mad and he is none too secure in his wits, it always struck me.

As for Siegfried, I did my best with him last year. The occasion was that I was in urgent need of a quite large sum of money and I recalled an ancient promise he had made me, about if ever I was in desperate need, etc. I was. Anyhow, all that happened was that he wrote a ratty letter and I had to find that large sum of money elsewhere as best I could: I thought he would be pleased to help me out and touched and so on. The joke is that I would have been able to pay him back, as it turned out, long before I promised. So a charming story was spoiled. The only good that came out of it was that an old fellow-officer wrote to me that he was about to go to prison for debt – a damned good fellow and genuine hard luck and his wife was about to have a baby and so on – and could I lend him a fiver. I had no such thing. So I referred him to Siegfried and Siegfried, to show that he wasn't mean and merely disliked *me*, did a lot for him. The wife had twins of course.

I am still here, have not moved from the island since 1930, hope I won't have to next year, hate going away. I am glad to say there is no news to record except that the financial crisis I was in has now passed. Laura is well, working, and sends her greetings. Perhaps you had heard the absurd rumour going about London that she had taken the veil? The only effect here of the Catalan revolt was that all the tourist trade ceased, because people think of Majorca as Spain, which it isn't, and that it is difficult to get smuggled tobacco because the coastguards are on the alert for smugglers of arms. Our stay here covers the period of British trade-recovery and really it looks a very fine performance: the English do keep their heads. If things ever right themselves again internationally it will be thanks to England.

Ever yours affectionately,   Robert

The film rights of *I, Claudius* were bought by Alexander Korda, the

Hungarian film director and head of London Films Ltd; Graves was engaged to write the scenario in collaboration with Korda himself.

To Julie and Tom Matthews

10 February 1935

Dearest Julie and Tom,

I was so distressed, Julie, that you have been run-down, and suppose that it was largely due to having to give up your home and move down-town, so to speak: must have been beastly. I do hope you are better. You two really must come in the autumn to Deyá. By then we hope to have ready for you a really worthy house: one of the oldest in Deyá, and the best built. It is built on the back of the church (appropriate for you, Tom. In the shadow of the Church – on hot afternoons), facing Canelluñ. And if the children come too there is plenty of room. Laura and I are buying it very cheap – it is part of the Molí estate – and doing some repair work and furnishing it, to act as a permanent guest-house for Canelluñ. It has a small garden and is quite private.[30]

It will be good if you can write your quotas for *Focus*.[31] It is good as a continuous record of the very special friends who centre at Deyá. We already have most of the January records and they are very nice to read, as news-letters.

Thank you, Tom, for liking *Claudius the God*. It is a better book than *I, Claudius*. Neither of them is of any real worth: how can the revivifying of anyone as dead as Claudius be justified except as a literary conjuring trick? (But certainly Claudius has been very helpful in the money way. I am now able to support my children.) I am writing poems again. Soon I shall be working on the film-scenario with Korda. He will supply the proposed skeleton and I will fatten it out and he will then slim it. (Charles Laughton will be Claudius.) It will start under Caligula and go on to the adoption of Nero and Claudius's death. A bore, but necessary. It will be kept as historical as possible. There is also a good chance of a film of Herod Agrippa: Veidt wants to play Herod. This is not public property yet, and the thing depends on the success of the Claudius film.

About the historicity of the Claudian end. *Something* happened. He apparently went to pieces after his censorship. And then he married Agrippina, his niece, which he would have thought most φορτικός (shameful, in bad taste) – the word he uses in his letter to the Alexandrians – so why? One can't believe that she won him by sexual wiles. And had he not, see Tacitus, told the Guards that they might chop him in pieces if he ever married again? He is known to have loved Britannicus and the story of his saying 'Who wounded thee will make thee whole' is a genuine one. He knew that Nero would behave with Britannicus as Caligula had behaved with Tiberius Gemellus. The story of Pallas's honour in the Senate, which is post-censorship, shows great cynicism on Claudius's part. His behaviour at the Fucine Lake (also genuine, compiled from four sources) is more foolery. That he knew he was about to die is true. Something happened to make him play King Log as he did; something more than old age and weariness. It was a deliberate resolution, and a cynical one, and I really believe that this is the only solution to the problem that makes sense. But enough of Claudius.

Our maid Isabel is such a success that we are fetching her younger sister from the mainland to help her, and do the washing. They will have a room in the basement ('cellar' sounds damp and cold, which it isn't). The sister is called Josepha.

Laura is cutting down on her smoking: from forty a day to twenty is the first step, and has bought a smaller coffee cup to halve the coffee. It was getting her down. She is having a jacket made, at the moment, from a sky-blue, hand-woven silk, very ancient, that was the dust-cover for the Madonna in the Molí chapel. The jacket will have silver buttons and will be piped with changing-colour grey-golden velvet.

I never thanked you for the lovely handkerchiefs. I will use them, strictly, for showing a corner from the breast pocket of my gala-suit. Changing the corner often, they will last for years without washing.

Love to Tommy, Johnny and Paul: and to you two, from us both.

Robert

I, Claudius won both the James Tait Black Memorial Prize and the Hawthornden Prize, one of the judges for which was Edward Marsh, who invited Graves to London for the award ceremony.

243

12 May 1935

Dearest Eddie,

I sent you a telegram saying that I couldn't come even if not coming meant forfeiting the prize. I will explain. You can put it, if you like, that I am ill: but apart from recent flu that is not true. The truth is that I have not so much as left this island for four years and every year the idea of going to England seems more and more of a nightmare: I always get ill from travelling in any case (a relic of a journey in a French hospital train in 1916, I think) and urban civilization seems to have grown so much more complex since 1930 that I couldn't possibly face London. To show the sincerity of this feeling, I must tell you that I refused to come to England to talk over the *Claudius* film with Korda even at the risk of his not doing it: so he came here instead. And I have stipulated in my contract that though I am to cooperate with him in the scenario, I am not obliged to change my present domicile. So I shall probably never see the film. Here I am well and happy and able to work, and these next three months are exceptionally busy because I must write the scenario of the film and at the same time a shortened version of the story to sell in England and abroad wherever the film is shown. To come to England would mean that I couldn't possibly get this work done. And so, if you could possibly get the ceremony cancelled, that would be the kindest thing you could do. I see perhaps half a dozen of my fellow-countrymen in a year; of residents I know only the British Vice-Consul and a business man who cashes cheques for me when the banks are closed. The idea of a ceremony with lots of people about all talking English is most horrible to me. What happens is that our real friends always come here sooner or later and when they are here one gets a far more intimate and pleasant experience of them than ever in London. It would make Laura and me very happy to hear that you were coming to Mallorca for a holiday: if Corsica, why not Mallorca? Neither of us will ever forget what you did for Laura in 1929, in preventing the Director of Public Prosecutions from making her any iller than she was.

About the prize: I can't think of it as a public award, somehow. The weighing of this book against that is such a queer business, especially when poetry is in the running against fiction, that I find it easier to think of it as a personal expression on your part (I don't

244

know who the other judges are) that you enjoyed the book; and as you are my friend that gives me real pleasure. The other prize was the James Tait Black Memorial Award, given by the defunct relict of a Scottish publisher named Black, the judges being the Rector of Edinburgh University and the Professor of Rhetoric at Glasgow (I think). It is worth £116 5s. 3½d. and no ceremony is involved.

Claudius has been an extraordinary relief to me: I had been let down by a friend in a business affair and was about four thousand pounds in the red. I wrote the book to clear off part of this; but by midsummer I shall be absolutely clear. This means that I can take over from my mother the expense of my children's education which she has been meanwhile undertaking, and not have to think of any new money-making book for some time. I have written some poems lately, which I think you will find easy. Some of them will appear in a critical twice-yearly[32] that Laura is editing: Constable are going to act as the distributors, but this is not yet official. By the way, Laura has found a young poet who is really good; you would certainly agree about this, because he is not one of the communist-homosexuals, nor in the Eliot tradition. His name is James Reeves, he is about twenty-eight, Cambridge, schoolmastering somewhere, and the poems will appear as a Seizin Press book this autumn and you shall have a copy. It is so many years that there has been a good new poet, that it is worth a jubilee.

One thing living out of England does is to make one feel particularly fond of the King. Other national feast days may be a farce, but the jubilee was really a genuine thing, like the Diamond Jubilee. Coronations are more pompous, but have a sort of uncomfortable experimentalism about them. And what was very nice was his very gentlemanly reply to Hitler's most ungentlemanly telegram of congratulations: from anyone but the King it would have sounded as though Hitler had succeeded in his bullying. But the King treated Hitler as though he really had meant to be particularly nice.

This letter is getting too long. Laura sends her best wishes. I have not told her and will not tell her that you forgot her in your letter, so she takes it for granted that she was named; and the obvious haste with which you finished the letter is excuse enough so far as I am concerned. You never failed to greet her before.

Yours always affectionately,   Robert

We celebrate the Jubilee of our first meeting next summer, don't we? It was 1911 – or was it 1912?

27 *June 1935*

Dearest Eddie,

I sympathize very much with you over the heat, I hope it hasn't got you down. Here it has been bad, but several degrees cooler than Brighton's 88 degrees at midnight, and there is liberty to dress cool as one cannot in London. Nevertheless, could you please let me know whether the Hawthornden cheque has been sent me and miscarried, or whether I have to take any steps about it. The announcement of the prize was about a fortnight ago. I am not greedy, only it may be that there is some confusion. If the cheque is not on its way, could it be sent to my a/c at the Chiswick branch of the Westminster Bank.

In exchange for this nuisance, here's a bit of news you perhaps haven't heard. Geoffrey Phibbs, the Devil as we familiarly call him, who was the cause of my leaving England, and who changed his name to Taylor to hide his shame, has today got married (I don't know to whom) to some unfortunate woman and will go on living in the same village in Wiltshire as Nancy with whom he has been cohabiting (with vows of perpetual love) ever since I left England. She is being self-sacrificing and pretending that it is all to the good and that they are still the best of friends ('he can now have a home and children of his own', as she wrote to my Mother) but obviously the situation will end violently, for Nancy has her homicidal moments. This business to me is only important in the effect it will have on the children. When Nancy revises her opinion of the Devil, they will revise their opinion of me, perhaps: it is due to him that I haven't seen them for five years and that they have been prevented from coming here even under my Mother's protection.

Laura's best wishes, and mine.

Yours ever affectionately,   Robert

In January Graves had received a letter from the editor of *The Times* asking him to write an obituary of T. E. Lawrence, to be filed away in the newspaper's 'morgue'; the editor wrote: 'We have no reason to suppose that Colonel Lawrence is in failing health, but the present biographical details are many years out of date.' Graves wrote to Lawrence asking him whether he would like to do the job himself and 'like the Aztecs, leave nothing to chance. Once, when I had officially died of wounds during the War, my biographical details had duly appeared in the same newspaper, supplied by my father: I did not much like his view of my life.'[33]

At the beginning of February 1935, on the eve of his retirement as 338171 Aircraftman T. E. Shaw, of the Royal Air Force, Lawrence sent Graves a long letter which amounted to a self-written obituary. Less than four months later, Lawrence had a serious motorcycle accident; when Graves heard of the accident, which was believed to be fatal, he immediately wrote an obituary, quoting Lawrence's letter (with some omissions), and sent it to his literary agent telling him to sell it only if Lawrence succumbed to his wounds. On the night of 18 May Lawrence died and Pinker, the agent, sold the article to the *Evening Standard*. Its publication, on 20 May, annoyed A. W. Lawrence ('Arnie'), T.E.L.'s brother and literary executor, and certain of his friends.

Another biographer of Lawrence in his lifetime was Basil Liddell Hart, one of the most acclaimed military historians and strategists of his generation. His book on Lawrence (*T. E. Lawrence: In Arabia and After*) had been published fourteen months before Lawrence's death. He was not outraged by the publication of the letter, but was concerned about a particular sentence, which read (as it appeared in the *Evening Standard*): 'The morgue-men are right in wanting to overhaul their stocks. I believe that the sketch that they have of me is fifteen years out of date. They were right in applying to you rather than ——, who seems to have no critical sense in my regard.'

Liddell Hart wrote to Graves (whom he had never met).

	60 Gloucester Place
24 May 1935	Portman Square
	London W1

Dear Graves

I read with great interest the long letter from T.E. that you published in the *Evening Standard*. As an incidental point, I should be interested to know whose was the name deleted and replaced by a dash – my own or another's? All good wishes.

Yours sincerely,   B. H. Liddell Hart

No date

Dear Liddell Hart,

I saw your account of T.E. in the *Times*: it was a very decent one and I am sure it would have satisfied T.E. I would have deleted that whole passage, not merely the name, if I had thought that people would ask 'Lord, is it I?', because I only put it in to prove my *bona-fides* if anyone thought that I should not have published the letter. Please forgive me for not divulging who it was – unless you have some particular reason for asking the question which would justify my answering it. Have you? Nobody but myself has seen the original letter and so nobody knows what the name was.

Yours very sincerely,   Robert Graves

PS. I expect that you have, like myself, long statements by T.E. in answer to points raised by you in writing your book about him: I imagine that he told you more about the tactical part of the campaign than he told me. He made so many mysteries: told one person one set of facts; another, another. If everyone compared notes most would be known, but not all. What he did in Damascus for example. Major Beck, an old friend of mine (from 1916 when we both lectured to Officer Cadets at Oxford), wrote to me a few years ago for an introduction to Lawrence because of an official account of the Tafileh fighting he was writing: and it appears T.E. gave him what he wanted to know in good measure. Did you see Beck's account?

3 June 1935

Dear Graves,

I much appreciated your letter. The 'justification' for my inquiry was that some people, rather naturally, read my name into the blank. Hence if it was not my name, it would be helpful to know. If it *was*, the fact would have a somewhat interesting bearing on a question of L.'s psychology which I should like to determine. Naturally, I shouldn't expect you to divulge the name if it was someone else's but I should appreciate a private word as to whether it was my own or not. From personal experience I can echo much that you say in your postscript – although he was certainly less mystery-making in the last year or two than when he first came back from India in 1928–9. The most remarkable thing was the way he stood up to the pretty severe cross-examination which I put him through, with the aid of my knowledge of the records (which he hadn't seen for years). A number of times I thought I had caught him out, over things which I doubted, but he justified himself so amazingly well that one had to give him the benefit of the doubt over other things that one couldn't check. I'll tell you more of this later.

Yours very sincerely,   B.H.L.H.

PS. Are you likely to be in England this summer?

Graves replied, writing at the top of the letter:

Private, Secret, Confidential, not to be Divulged, etc.

No date

Dear Liddell Hart,

Let's get it clear. It was foolish of me to have printed the sentence at all, and indeed foolish of me to have printed the letter. I did it as an antidote to the sort of stuff I knew would appear immediately on his death and also because I thought that it would be T.E.'s wish – I hurried it to England by air, to be placed by my literary agent, so as not to miss the day of national mourning for him; and though it was ill-mannered of the *Standard* to head it 'Myself, by Lawrence' I could not foresee that. I then wrote to Eliot[34] as T.E.'s executor (and also my lawyer) apologizing for not asking executor's permission, but pleading justification-by-the-occasion and offering to send the fee to the estate, if needed, when it came through.

. . . .

Graves goes on to complain about the difficulties he experienced with A. W. Lawrence, the Lawrence trustees and their agent. These continued for some time, although later his relations with them improved considerably. A. W. Lawrence was indeed to become a friend. Living in remote Mallorca, Graves was unable fully to appreciate the enormous publicity occasioned by Lawrence's sensational death, the trustees' own difficulties in dealing with impostors, charlatans and those who falsely claimed to have known Lawrence. He still tended to think of him less in terms of his fame than in terms of his own past relationship with him. Also, he explains in the letter, he was upset by what he felt to be A. W. Lawrence's hostility to him over the matter of his part in the film Alexander Korda was planning to make about T.E.L. (it was never made). Korda wanted Graves to write the scenario, and as Graves needed the money he understandably felt nervous about anyone who seemed to threaten the deal. Essentially, however, he explains to Liddell Hart how he stands in relation to A. W. Lawrence, who was T.E.L.'s executor, and who was therefore to play a crucial role in the collaboration they were planning.

Confidence thus established between you and me and further confidence by my admission that I only read reviews of your book, not the book itself, including an ill-mannered one by David Garnett (personal quarrel background)[35] to which I answered – you probably got a newspaper cutting – let me tell you that, yes, it *was* your name, but nobody but yourself shall know that; and in return may I ask for a confidence – did he make a remark to you at any time, saying that I had no critical sense in his regard; and did he congratulate you on your book about him, as giving a very clear portrait of him – as he did in the case of mine – which would probably be the one which would 'stand'? The way that you put it – 'a question of L.'s psychology' – suggests some such history. If this was so, I would not call it a dishonesty in him, but partly pleasure in sitting for his portrait and seeing the result as immediately plausible, followed by dissatisfaction; partly his actor-quality in being several Lawrences at once, contradictory only when related – I mean like George Arliss playing Wellington in one film and Beaconsfield in another – only ridiculous when you see the two films on the same programme the same evening. Perhaps the explanation of his sudden value of my critical sense was that I had lately become quite angry with him for 'foxing', i.e. pretending to be unable to understand simple points of educated experience because he was now a 'simple fitter' who 'only read *Titbits* and the *Happy Magazine*'.

The Spanish paper here quotes the French *L'Oeuvre* as saying that T.E. wasn't really killed – it was all a hocus-pocus drama – and that he is probably off to Abyssinia to protect British Nile-head water interests there. One day they will say that he was really a woman and Feisal's mistress, and that it was the discovery of his sex that made him leave the RAF first and then the Tank Corps – getting back into the RAF by seducing the Air Chief of

Staff. In the papers that are on the way here to me from England I have a statement by him as to his purposeful lying about some points in the campaign – especially the Damascus affair.

But this letter is getting too long.

Yours very sincerely,   Robert Graves

No, I don't come to England much, and won't be there this year. I was there last in 1930 in fact.

14 June 1935

Dear Graves,

Many thanks for your long and interesting letter.

You have my sympathy over the *Evening Standard* letter; although I can quite understand how, accentuated by the headlines, it might jar on sensitive friends, from an historical and more impersonal point of view I can see advantages in letting him be seen in his own words – even though it was only one of the T.E.'s who wrote. Although I feel you could have written a better balanced memoir in your own words, in general, it was certainly preferable to read his than to read what others said about him – to realize the advantage one had only to read a good many of the memoirs that did appear. I argued along this line on the day of the funeral when denunciation of the letter-publishers was pretty heated!

Yes, I read the Garnett–Graves interchange, and wondered whether I ought to chip in with a protest against the unfairness of coupling your book with that of Lowell Thomas. I drew T.E.'s attention to it, however, and got back the reply, 'I haven't seen the *New Statesman* for a long time, so missed Graves's letter . . . but it is rather amusing that, apropos of yourself, I told you how he was never able to let a reviewer alone. I like R.G.: but he is not wise.' After that I thought it better to let it alone!

You guessed correctly about the reason for my question to you – and reference to T.E.'s psychology. I am sure you are also correct, and just, in your explanation of this inconsistent attitude.

As a matter of fact, he told my wife just before the book was published that, after reading it, he wished that it was the only one and that none of the previous ones had appeared. So also had he been rather emphatic in contradicting some of the things in your book. And I remember a talk with him last June – I was praising

251

your *I, Claudius* and T.E., while admitting its skill, said that he did not like the book – all the characters being painted blackly. That you were over-critical in the sense of being too ready to take the worst explanation. We had quite a hot argument, I accusing him of Plutarchian tendencies and contending that your attitude was much closer to the truth of history. Even this was an example of his inconsistency, for no one, at other times, had been more ready to question the 'great man' myth.

But there was more than that behind my reason for inquiring what T.E. had written. For it has a rather delicious reflection on the efforts he made to get me to modify certain criticisms of his actions in the War, in the original draft. It was an aspect quite different from the normal appearance – this care for his historical reputation. Whenever he could produce good enough evidence, I modified them, but in a few cases his explanation or evidence did not satisfy me, so the criticisms stayed.

When it came to the summing up, I did perhaps skip too lightly over his questionable aspects – first, because he had stood up so well to the severe cross-examination to which I had subjected him; second, because I had now found out what I believed to be the explanation of things in him which had caused me perplexity or doubt. I had come to feel that his faults and inconsistencies all lay on or near the surface, and that what lay below was marvellously solid. Having got through the surface strata myself, I was perhaps inclined to forget it might be worth enlarging upon it for others who might read the book.

The book was surprisingly well received in reviews by those who knew him, and the criticisms came mainly from the 'outer circle'. Very naturally, they missed its undertones and caught only the eulogy. I think this may have shaken T.E. who kept a remarkably close watch on all the reviews. Anyhow, I noticed that a characteristic reaction set in from the interest he had shown, and from his zeal to get the military meaning of the Arab show properly brought out.

But these reactions usually did not last, or, at any rate, were fluctuating. Last year, he was curiously uneven in his attitude. Talking in letter after letter of his desire to settle down and do nothing, yet every now and then suggesting that he might be coming back to do something bigger than ever before. Not so long ago when I was arguing that the publicity he had been getting was his own fault, he retorted that he might want all he had and more, as an aid to his future efforts.

I should be interested to know the date of that letter to you.

He was much more complex than his simple-minded worshipping friends realized. This makes it very difficult in some ways now. Some of them are so sure that they knew him – usually those who knew him least. This has its amusing side, since he summed up most of them for my information. But it makes things difficult as anything one may do or say is liable to upset someone. I have got to speak on him next Tuesday, having reluctantly yielded to pressure from a number of his friends, and I fully expect to be torn in pieces afterwards. You are lucky to be out of the way.

There is one further thing in your letter which came as rather a surprise to me. I am interested to hear that Korda has arranged with you to write a scenario of the *Revolt* film, for I had been given to understand that I was to do it.

When the idea came up last summer, Korda asked me if I would do it, to which I first replied that it was contingent on T.E.'s decision. I went down to see him about it and he told me that the Trustees were correct in approving the arrangement, and that he was agreeable to my doing it – but also said that he intended to step in himself at a later stage and try to stop the thing. This he did in the autumn when the contract had actually been settled, and successfully persuaded Korda, in his own inimitable way, to hold it up.

Then I had an inquiry whether my own book could be filmed. I gave the same answer as before, that I would do nothing without T.E.'s agreement. I mentioned it to him casually when he was next at the flat, not imagining that he would think of such a thing; to my surprise his attitude was quite different; he told me in detail of certain Film Companies who had been discussing the idea of my book, a thing quite unknown to me, and settled with me that we would wait for a firm offer and then consider it.

Now, since his death, the Korda film has come up again as well as other approaches. When I got these I asked Arnie about it, to which he replied that he understood that I was going to do the scenario of the *Revolt* film and hoped that I would keep myself for that.

So that's how matters stand, as far as I'm concerned. From your letter Korda's moves and intentions would seem to be somewhat perplexing. Of course, should his idea be that we are both to do it and collaborate in some way, I should not be inclined to make difficulties – as I feel that we both knew him well enough and have sufficient similarity of view, to work in together without friction. Tangles seem a characteristic and inevitable part of anything connected with our subject!

Yours sincerely,   B. H. Liddell Hart

PS. You do honour to the Hawthornden. I congratulate the selectors.

In a long letter of 18 June, Graves wrote to Liddell Hart:

Let us be Plutarchean for once and make a comparison between T.E. and Jesus Christ. 'There is something singular in this parallel and what has not occurred to us in any other of the lives we have written, that T.E. should exemplify the maxims of J.C., and that J.C. should proclaim beforehand the happiness of T.E.' (Publicola and Solon). No room for the whole thing here, but anyhow the Devil was (you agree) constantly leading T.E. up to an exceeding high place and showing him all the kingdoms of the earth, etc., and they had the same proud humility, and logical-witty mastery of evasion, and *both had mothers*, and both tried to manage without women (with as little offence to women as possible) and both had fanatic disciples, and both were profoundly mistrustful of themselves, and both believed in being all things to all men, and after both their deaths it is impossible to rise at a dinner to mention them in any but hushed awed tones, for fear of blaspheming.

Yes, T.E. told me (what he told you) about the gloom of *I, Claudius*. He professed to like the sequel better. Anyhow *Claudius* wasn't written as a work of art – T.E. could never understand that the word artist made me sick, particularly when 'great man' went with it – but as a money-maker. It was fun to write, in parts, and it is (faintly) critical, in parts, of the failure of historians to make the most of their stuff, and is very pointedly, in style, *under*written, as a criticism of the failure of novelists to hold their readers' attention with rhetorical *overwriting*. But it claims no more than readability. My only real work is now, and has always been, poems.

I want to get clear about your book. I understand that you originally felt that T.E. was a legend-bubble and needed pricking. The view of him, for instance, encouraged by me, annoyed you. So you proposed to use your military knowledge and technical wide-awakeness to change all this; if necessary to be harsh. So he encouraged you by giving you material he had, on one pretext or the other, withheld from me and by being 'rather emphatic in contradicting' certain things in my book. Bless his little heart! There was nothing in the book he did not see and pass! Four-fifths is his own material transcribed, the rest is the most authentic material I could collect from the most reliable witnesses. Did you find that my view was as far out as all that? I must get your book: it will be interesting. I did not get it at the time because I was so bored by the whole Arab revolt by then.

That letter was written to me on the fifteenth of March. (In the course of it he coupled my name with Augustus John's (artists) apparently in compliment, but perhaps also to infuriate. I suppressed the passage.)

I understand that what you have written is in confidence, and please understand the same about what I have written. I was very grateful for your letter. We agree, I think, about T.E.'s fundament of decency and good honest qualities; and his Athanasian three-in-one incomprehensibility (J.C. and T.E. again) is no more than a joke which we can share at his expense. If he were alive he'd, of course, be able to find a logical evasion of the charge of duplicity, or triplicity.

Yours very sincerely   Robert Graves

In the same letter Graves also told Liddell Hart that he thought A. W. Lawrence might take some kind of action against him over the *Evening Standard* letter publication. Liddell Hart replied that this was regrettable and would have been against T.E.L.'s wishes, though it might have amused him; he wisely advised Graves not to be too worried and not to be too hard on A.W.L., who was rather distraught after recent events and oppressed by a multitude of counsellors, notably Lady Astor, the Conservative MP: 'I should not be surprised if she excited him over the publication of the letter in the *Evening Standard*, for at the funeral she was the one most vociferous in her denunciation of your "shameful" behaviour.' No, he went on to say, *Lawrence and the Arabs* was by no means far out, and Graves's deductions about his own book were correct. In the same letter he wrote:

I understand your rejection of the 'artistic' attitude and assertion that you write merely for money. It's a very natural reaction from the popular expectation that writers, etc., can live on air. But I suspect it is also, in a measure, a pose. You have done it successfully enough, however, to take in quite a lot of people. But you really ought to be more consistent – your action in writing, as you told me, to offer to hand over the fee was hardly consistent!

This was written on 24 June; on the 27th Graves replied, again heading the letter 'Private'.

Dear Liddell Hart,
    Many thanks for your letter. First, I want to say that you have misunderstood what I said about writing merely for money: I make a very clear distinction between my real work, which is poetry and poetic criticism, and the sidelines. The sidelines have always been written with a direct money-making purpose and though I have tried to turn out a decent job of work they have no validity for me, except occasionally for some stray critical element in them. To me there is no alternative between a) poetry and b) informative prose. Written either a) for the ideal reader implicit in the poem, or b) for the actual reader who pays money at bookshops or libraries. Anything that wanders between in an ambitious and dishonest way and boasts about artistry and style makes me sick. This is not to say that I make great claims for my poetry, but at least I practise it in increasing seriousness. And I find it difficult to correspond with people who suggest that I pose. I do not pose. But I suppose if I had said anything so stupid as that I only wrote for money you would have been justified; so don't take this ill.
    About Arnie, then. He has sent me a belated letter trying to put things right and suggesting an amnesty: to which I have agreed saying that his misreading of my motives was probably due to the strain he had gone through – (I'm glad to have information of this from you. Lady Astor. That explains it. The woman thing at the

end of the letter. I suppose pique) – so everything's settled, I suppose. Thanks very much for saying that if you got a chance you would try to smooth over the perturbation. But that's not needed now, I think. What Arnie objected to was the bit at the end of my own remarks which he read as hinting that T.E. committed suicide! Even the cutting that the thing got from the *Evening Standard* surely could not have made it read like that. Anyhow I explained the somewhat metaphysical meaning that I had tried to convey; and I had written the notice in haste and emotion.

Lawrence and the Arabs was, of course, largely and confessedly a paraphrase. It was not intended as a critical book, but only as a popular account for people who would not have access to the *Seven Pillars* (*Revolt* was unintelligible in its broken sequence) in T.E.'s lifetime. It was commissioned originally by Cape as a book for boys, as a matter of fact. The typescript which I kept in safe deposit in England has arrived today. It is profusely annotated up to the last pages! But he kept up this pretence to seem not to have inspired the book. I suppose that one day these notes and accompanying letters should be published as an appendix to *Seven Pillars*, and the same with yours. There are a great many problems which could still, I suppose, be solved by getting at the secret reports of the Arab Bureau.* Others will never be solved. E.g. Aubrey Herbert and T.E. trying to arrange the Kut business. Herbert says that it was T.E. by answering the question: 'Gentlemen, after all, what stands between us?' with: 'Only a million dead Armenians', who broke up the conference; T.E. says it was Herbert. But Herbert was pro-Turk, and it was a T.E.-ish remark. Both are dead now.

About the film. I am still in the dark, but ready to be helpful now that Arnie has written a passable letter. There's probably work for us both in it, but, as I say, I'm nobody's rival in this, so whatever happens is all right by me.

Yours sincerely,   Robert Graves

PS. Three of T.E.'s best friends were 'artists' in this worst literary sense. Their books nauseate me. But 'no name, no packdrill', as the RWF used to say.

* Perhaps you have done a lot of this work: I haven't your book yet.

Postscript 3 July

This letter didn't get posted somehow. Since then I have got Arnie's quaintly worded, not to say donnish, request for *50 Angles on T.E.* And the notification in *The Times* of Siegfried Sassoon and Stirling being the chosen two scenario-writers under Arnie. I don't know Stirling except by reputation as a capable organizer, but I do know Siegfried Sassoon, better than most, and the film is doomed if Siegfried is let loose on it. As a matter of fact it is a very ironical appointment from my point of view. S.S. was . . . O hell, anyhow, unless you like the way things have turned out, I do sympathize with you for the way you seem to have been treated. To me it's all very funny otherwise. All these Councils of Nicaea and Quinquagent Gospels in the new early-Christian era: Arnie functioning well as James the brother of the Lord, and G. B. Shaw as St Joseph the pseudo-father and Pope, Lady Astor as the Magdalen: 'I would rather commit adultery than drink a glass of beer.'

In August Graves suggested to Liddell Hart that they collaborate on a book about Lawrence, using all the notes and letters he wrote to them when they were working on their biographies of him; Liddell Hart was enthusiastic about the idea and said that he thought the book would be of real historical value. He put the idea to A. W. Lawrence, who provisionally approved the project but insisted that the completed book be submitted to him and the other trustees of the Lawrence estate before the necessary permissions could be given. For the next few months Graves and Liddell Hart wrote to each other, sometimes several times a week; in the following selection of the letters I have omitted (in order to save space) several passages, mostly technical discussions of format, typing, the selling of the book.

2 December 1935

Dear Liddell Hart,
    No doubt why Jonathan[36] suggested terms to me, after asking you to suggest them, was that he knew that I am easily satisfied, and he thought that if I accepted you would have to accept too if you had not meanwhile thought out a suggestion. Does that come

under the heading of tactics or strategy? Tactics, I think.

. . . .

I shall in a day or two have got the material ready for transcribing. At the moment I am copying letters, removing private matter which does not concern his story but mine. I do hope Arnie plays ball (US slang).

You do not mention Korda. Next time you write let me know if you have heard any sequel to what I told you about his recent reapproach to me and my saying what I did.[37]

a) Tell me, is Sir A. T. Wilson alive?

You sound very busy so am I.

Good luck   Robert Graves

Later. I have been reading your T. E. Lawrence book for the first time. Good stuff in it, and clean writing. It was bad luck that you weren't allowed to make as liberal use of *Seven Pillars* as I had wangled. On the other hand some parts, such as the Deraa experience, he did not allow me to use, but allowed you. And the post-1927 stuff, which came after my *Lawrence and the Arabs*, interests me very much. It will be useful, for some of my later letters, to have your book to refer the reader to. E.g. his comments on the Beauvais disaster and the improving effect that it had on his status in the RAF.

Have just come across a forgotten passage in a letter he wrote me from the NW Frontier: identifying himself with *Belisarius*. Most interesting.

Missed the post.

Yes, I like your book a lot. You write from a very different angle, and the information T.E. gave you was from a very different angle. If I had been given 8 months instead of 2½ by the publishers to write my book in (collecting material as I went) – an impossible feat that I performed because in desperate need of cash – I could have made it a lot better. Several news-sources I could have investigated but for the time factor.

In a letter of T.E.'s in 1928 today I came upon a confession of his virginity. What would the French say to that! To be *vierge* is, as Gibbon would say, 'either above or below the character of a man' in England. In France, however . . .

. . . .

I'm glad you made that reference in your book to my half-

brother Philip: the best of my family. Poor Philip, he suddenly
lost his wife a few weeks ago. (A person to avoid is my whole
brother Charles. Gossip writer. He lives in your street, I believe.
I haven't seen him for eight or nine years.) Philip is all right.
A one-track mind that takes more traffic than most people's
4-track minds.

Lovely photographs you got.

. . . .

About the Foch story: George V in the famous interview 1918
offered T.E. the OM. T.E. refused. George V said: 'Then I
suppose it will have to go to Foch.' Nice ironical tale, but it can't
be told in George V's lifetime.

b) Is Thwaites still alive?

By December the trustees of the Lawrence estate had begun to
prevaricate about permission for the book, and A. W. Lawrence
suggested it be published as a limited edition only. Meanwhile, plans
were going ahead for an authorized biography of Lawrence, and a
collection of his letters, both books to be done by E. M. Forster.

10 December 1935

Dear Liddell Hart,

. . . .

Interested about E.M.F., who comes up in my letters from T.E.
several times. E.M.F. is just the man to write a really awful book
about T.E.: worse than T.E. could have done himself, almost,
about himself. I mean, E.M.F., whom I used to know quite well
and is a 'very decent chap', in a way, is entirely twisted in spirit.
What is that rheumatic complaint that turns hands into knobs
with the fingers emerging at a broken angle? Anyhow, E.M.F. has
that in his spirit, and his writing has it. That twistedness attracted
T.E. who thought, wrongly, he was a fellow-sufferer. (Frederic
Manning another.) Christ again, palling up with the maimed and
halt. Serves T.E. right if Forster does his *Life* as well as *Letters*.

Anyhow, so far as I am concerned, he is welcome to the job. (I
mean, I feel no proprietary right in T.E.) And another thing: if we
are generous to Arnie and E.M.F. about letters, they will have to
be generous too, about letters. Your letters and mine from T.E. are
essential to any collection they make: so though Arnie has the *veto*

as executor, we have the power of being nasty and withholding our letters. And very nasty, if we care to sell our letters in America, leaving the burden of piracy on the person we sell them to. It is always good in positions like this to realize the strength of one's reserves; it enables one to act with greater offensive assurance. (Writing as one old-soldier to another.)

. . . .   [Unsigned]

In a postscript to a letter of 12 December Graves wrote:

There is a personal favour I should like to ask you. Private Frank Richards, DCM, MM, late Second Royal Welch Fusiliers, once, in 1931, when unemployed (pit-worker at Blaina, Mon.) wrote a book about 1914–1918 called *Old Soldiers Never Die* which I think you reviewed very approvingly somewhere. I was, privately, godfather to that book, found it a publisher and put in a lot of semi-colons and full-stops and asked him a lot of questions, the answers to which he incorporated in the text. (He was in my platoon in France and a very good man.) I then urged him to write a book of even greater interest, about pre-war barrack-room life in England, India and Burmah (1900–1908). He has now done so, with great labour, and a good deal of private semi-colon-placing and question-asking work by me. To be called *Old Soldier Sahib*. It is a very fine book indeed, I think: a 'military classic' is the headline that occurs. The favour is: that Faber and Faber can send you a personal copy, and that you will read it carefully and get the reviewing of it for some decent paper, and review it on its military side. (He is the only Thomas Atkins of the old school who has ever been as good with the pen as with the musket; and I feel this as a sort of Testament of the Thomas Atkins who passed into history on October 31, 1914.) It is most worthy of serious review, or I should not ask you this.

At the top of the following letter, about Lawrence's literary friends, Graves wrote:

I assume that our letters, etc., to each other are strictly confidential. E.g. the first two pages of this are to be locked in your bosom, please. And I note that many things in your stuff are highly confidential too.

21 December 1935

Dear Liddell Hart,

Your Postscript chapters have arrived. It is all very interesting. Also Questionnaire: thanks.

What comes out more and more, for me, in your stuff, is his Irishness. As you know, I am partly Irish (Cromwellian). Remainder Scottish, German, Danish in equal proportions. And I know, feel, the Irish character in others as a half-Jew knows and feels the Jew. The Cromwellian and Plantation Irish are *Hibernicis ipsis Hibernicores*. Orpen brought it out in that portrait of T.E. very cruelly, I thought. A vein of unseriousness, which easily becomes treachery. G. B. Shaw has it. Joyce is the extreme example, and he knows the fated character of Ireland: 'The old Sow who eats her farrow.' T.E. in my opinion was at the end treacherous to you as his friend, and not very faithful to me as his friend. O'Flaherty[39] is a beast. He visited here once and was shown the door. Yeats: a spiritualist and that is inconsistent with being a poet.

Henry Williamson is all wrong; though not, so far as I know, Irish. He has that dreadfully mannered style which spells art–ambition, and is a pious crook. Nothing more disingenuous than his anonymous *Golden Falcon* which he deliberately wrote as if it were by me, in order to profit by the success of *Goodbye to All That*, could be imagined. [. . . .] The worst of it was that T.E. had supplied him with private material about me, not expecting Williamson to use it. If I had been in T.E.'s place with the case reversed (Henry Williamson writing a book as if by T.E. on information I gave him) I should have half-killed Williamson, but T.E. went on being his friend and treated it as rather a joke.

The spavined team of T.E.'s literary friends (his cultivation not only of the literature of disease but of physical and moral deformity) makes a pretty poor showing. ('Literary' in the artistic sense – I don't include you or me.) Jesus again, among the halt, lame and blind!

I am glad that you own to a deficient understanding of poetry. I do 'understand' it (I mean, as you would say to friends, 'I do understand the problems of military strategy and tactics') and it is as I told you in a recent letter the most important thing to me.

The *Claudiuses* (in your note about T.E. and me you are a little
out: but that's not your fault. Wait till you see my letters) were
undertaken, most unwillingly, to make money. I made a job of
them, because I needed about £5 or 6000 to clear me of debt: so
far they have made £8000. They have only slight relation to my
real work, which is poetry. (All my prose best-sellers are the
same.)

And about W. H. Auden. W. H. Auden is a fraud: that is to say
he is a synthetic poet, plagiarizing in a curiously wholesale way.
He gets hold of some good piece of work by someone which is not
too well known, and vulgarizes it. (Chapter and verse available.)
Homosexual and parlour communist. 'Near awe,' quotha! T.E.
wouldn't have had the face to talk W. H. Auden to me; or
D. H. Lawrence either, except as instances of his taste for the
2nd-rate.

As for D. H. Lawrence – well, there was a real mess! Male self-
defeat in an attempt to argue away the fact of woman. In the
notes to my letters I have already underlined this point. He was a
bum poet, of course, being a bum person. I can't understand
people 'admiring the work and not the man' in a poet. It's like
saying that you like Gold Flake cigarettes apart from their
suitability as smokes. (The artistic fallacy.)

– Indian ink. T.E. borrowed this from me. I used it because I
don't like blotting paper and if you use Indian ink it dries as you
write and there is no inequality of dark and light on the page. I
abandoned the practice recently because Indian ink evaporates too
quickly in the Majorcan summer. He borrowed several things from
me, including several characteristic tricks of mine in letter-writing.
If you sometimes notice a similarity and think that I am copying
T.E., you're probably wrong.

. . . .

About 'Freedom' too. 'Freedom' is the great Irish witticism, now
perpetuated in the new name of their country. It is not freedom as
the English mean it. Your 'incarnation of the spirit of freedom' is
double-edged, therefore. The fascist conversation you record is
enough to show you how equivocal his concept of freedom was.
That is how it strikes me. I note T.E.'s own comment on it: witty,
of course.

Yours ever,   Robert Graves

Please note: I am not, I assure you, laying down the law and I do not wish to draw you into any argument about this. I am merely telling you of my own feelings, for your information. If you agree, well, that is nice, but if you don't, it doesn't matter. It is only fair to tell you how I feel: it will avoid misunderstandings. And it doesn't (or shouldn't) hamper our collaboration if we keep to the main point – what T.E. told us about himself and in what circumstances.

15 January 1936

Dear L.H.

. . . .

Now, your comments and suggested cuts and queries. In 9 cases out of 10 I have accepted your suggested cuts. They were a great help. Wherever possible I have shortened the quotations from my own book. I have made two or three notes: e.g. to the 1,000,000 dead Armenians, and to his self-identification with Hippoclides, pointing out the difference between Gallio's non-caring and H.'s. (You remember H. in Herodotus?) 'Tell *Shawm*' is one spelling used by T.E. *Shawm* is one of the few Arabic words I learned in Egypt, and it only this moment occurs to me that it is also Biblical. 'Harp' is the meaning. The Bible spells it *Shawm*.

(3 people who think. T.E. stopped thinking. Had already stopped, I think, when I wrote. The other 2 were Basanta Mallik, an Indian philosopher who was 12 years at Oxford and was the Nepalese foreign minister mentioned – he thwarted Curzon by drawing up that treaty (in 1906 or something) on international law lines. (He was tutor to the King's children and happened to be an authority on international law so was made Foreign Minister for the nonce.) Then sent by the grateful King to England to learn all he could about international law and politics. Instead, he took to philosophical thinking and shortly after our invitation to Nepal resigned his political connexions as inconsistent with philosophy. His thinking, however, was Indian and in the end led to a stand-still.

The third person was Laura Riding. She continues. I have met nobody else who makes a practice of thinking; not since I wrote this in 1927. I use the word in a very special sense, which I won't try to define here conversationally except to say that it implies a complete unification of the mind, and the person along with the mind. (There may be more. I myself am only a partial thinker.) T.E. had to give this up and to fall back on good old human nature, which is the denial of thought.)

. . . .

Yours ever,   Robert

In his part of *T. E. Lawrence to His Biographers*, Liddell Hart wrote the following footnote about the 'Graves–Garnett interchange' in the *New Statesman* (see page 251):

The writer in the *New Statesman*, while reviewing my book appreciatively, had contrasted it with its predecessors to their disparagement, referring to the 'gossip-column stuff provided by such writers as Robert Graves and Lowell Thomas'. To class the former book with the latter was so obviously unfair that Robert Graves was, naturally, moved to protest . . .[40]

Graves saw the footnote in the typescript and suggested that 'the writer' should be named, but Liddell Hart replied (on 14 February): 'It seems to me a pity to put David Garnett's name. I have corrected his point, why belabour his person? It might then look as if you were wanting to get your own back.'

20 February 1936

Dear L.H.

. . . .

7.4.34. Right, then. Omit Garnett. (Personally I think that when people take advantage of their position on the editorial staff of a newspaper to tell lies about books they review they should be pilloried by name. As for getting my own back, why not? If it is my own, am I not entitled to it? I never turn the other cheek; not being either a masochist or a Christian.) Still, I seem to remember getting home quite a hard slap about his fawning presentation of 'Pocahontas, the Uncrowned Queen of America' in that letter I wrote. And he may be a friend of yours.

17.5.34. 'Sound-film' is the way to distinguish from 'silent-film', surely?

OK, boss!

The Left gains in Spain come in handy here: their logical result is that there will be a Left governor of the Balearics. And that

means that certain friends of mine, in purely local deals . . .
anyhow, I have never before stood to gain so much personally
from the result of an election. I cannot be more explicit; but I
write so much though not more, because it may have occurred to
you to wonder how the business affected me.

Yours ever,
Robert

I think you behave very decently to me: e.g. (once more) about the
title. Thanks, mister.

Liddell Hart replied:

25 February 1936

Dear Robert

Many thanks for your two letters and semi-letter of the 20th. As
so often, they make me laugh and make me like you the more.
You have got a wonderful depth of understanding combined, it
sometimes strikes me, with a readiness to a superficial
misunderstanding – a sort of compound of philosophy and
pugnacity. 'I never turn the other cheek' – is a delicious
understatement. I am sufficiently fond of the riposte myself to
appreciate your feeling, but philosophically I have come to check
the inclination except where reflection convinces me that it will be
deeply effective – or when feeling becomes too strong for my
control. I certainly have not gone so far as to believe in turning
the other cheek – but there's something in the subtler
interpretation of this as turning the other flank.

I have never met Garnett or heard from him. My doubts on this
issue were purely tactical and philosophical.

. . . .

Do explain for my private indication your habit of cutting pages
into patterns and pasting them together!

I have written straight off to Arnie letting him know the
material is ready for him to see.

I have been so rushed that I have not had time to do more than
skim through Frank Richards's new book. Perhaps because of that
it did not grip me as the first one did. It seemed rather too
'refined'. But if I can get a weekend, I will try and read it properly.

I much appreciate your comments on my comments concerning
the two-part idea. I will put it up to Jonathan. I have just had a

note from him asking that when sending the material we will attach the title we prefer and also one or two alternatives. What are we to say?

Best wishes,
Yours,   B.H.L.H.

28 February 1936

Dear L.H.

Thanks for Feb. 25. I much appreciated the 'turning the other cheek' and 'turning the other flank' quip. Yes, you are right: I am very apt to make careless superficial mistakes: my intelligence has a sort of partial-vision failing. It is only when I concentrate on a subject that I can overcome this by superimposing a number of partial-vision glimpses one on top of the other in a circular series: thus covering the field. (Is this metaphor clear?)

Why I cut pages into patterns? To save rewriting of badly over-written paragraphs, I clip off and paste on. At the top of my last letter I had written something about a local state of alarm due to the elections, but I found that I had been misinformed about details so cut it off. I write with great difficulty: almost always the first view I have of a subject is totally cock-eyed and I gradually get it right. (I have before now written a poem of 14 lines in 35 successive drafts in the course of 3 weeks.[41]) A naturally stupid gross person with a keen and hopeful sense of potential fineness: which I can only approximate by a) trial and error, b) critical observation of the errors and achievement of others.

That title again: let's not give Jonathan alternatives, he'll only take the worst. If *Two Sides to T. E. Lawrence* is all right (it is a collaborative title in a way – the *Sides* having been yours) let's fix on that. I like it very well. Unless you have any fresh ideas? I don't think the new book of Frank Richards is more refined, except in subject. (No wars.) The writing is certainly better, or more confident, perhaps.

Why is this handwriting so awful? answer: fountain pen 1 cm thick instead of my usual ordinary pen 5 mm thick, and no relief nib. Now you know.

Good luck   Robert

Apart from the Lawrence book, Graves was writing another novel, *Antigua, Penny, Puce*, translating, with Laura Riding and Karl Gay, *Almost Forgotten Germany* by Georg Schwarz, a friend and neighbour of Graves's in Deyá, and helping Riding edit *Epilogue II*. (She was also writing *A Trojan Ending*, a historical novel.)

T. E. Lawrence To His Biographers, as it was finally called after much discussion (Liddell Hart favoured *Sides and Asides of T. E. Lawrence* which Graves said sounded like a book about an actor-manager), was finished and submitted to the Lawrence trustees, who after a short delay announced that they were withholding permission from Graves and Liddell Hart to publish Lawrence's letters and sent, via the agent, a legalistic set of conditions which they would have to comply with even if they wanted to publish the book in a limited edition.

Graves was furious.

He was now even in favour of pirating the letters (see page 269), and he wrote a long letter to Tom and Julie Matthews about this and other matters.

10 May 1936

Dearest Tom and Julie,

There's perhaps been a letter gone astray from you – posts haven't been good – because nothing has come since Tom's cable about not having things ready in time for *Epilogue II*. Hope everything is all right. It is here. We are tired from working hard without interruption for some months. *Epilogue* twice a year would be enough for most people, but there have been so many other commitments. We are just passing proofs of *Epilogue II* and also of *Almost Forgotten Germany*, which was a fearful sweat to translate from the German: I don't know how we got through it. And Laura is dreadfully hard at work on *A Trojan Ending* which I like very much indeed, and when that's done there are the *Poets and Schools* booklets[42] and I suppose *Epilogue III*. I have just almost finished my light and eccentric novel, *Antigua, Penny, Puce*, whose main interest is in the complicated legal position of the stamp that is the heroine of the story: there are six possible claimants, all with very specious titles to it. Laura has still to read and approve it.

You wrote a very decent review of *Old Soldier Sahib*. (It has

gone very well in England, as it deserved.) Thank you so much.
Two things concerned with me haven't come off. The *Claudius*
film gets postponed and postponed. I don't care much, because
I've been paid; but I have got advances for a film-version and may
have to repay those – bad!

. . . .

Graves's other disappointment, he goes on to tell Tom Matthews,
is over his difficulties with the Lawrence trustees over the book on
T.E.L. which he had written with Liddell Hart. Graves became so
incensed, although quite unnecessarily, that he was now considering
pirating the letters by various devices: for example, he thought of
issuing ten copies in the USSR, and then having these pirated in the
USA. But he was not completely serious, and would never really
have carried out this plan.

In the end he did not have to do this; and the book was duly and
successfully published, with the blessing of the trustees.

No report yet of the *Moon's*[43] sales: but I don't think they are
much. A very nice book, however.

We had no winter, but then a delayed summer. After being six
weeks ahead of schedule with plants and fruit and things, we have
fallen a month behindhand. By April 20th pinks should be at their
best: there's not even a bud showing.

Looking forward so much to your coming – but it will be so
stupidly short a visit. Hundreds of new things to show you. And
probably Honor[44] will be here with her Julian-baby, also John and
Lucie. I think you'll just miss David and Sam who come here at
the end of July. David is ¼ inch under six feet already. Jenny may
come too. Since she has become independent, living alone and
earning her £5 a week in Cochran's Revue, she has become much
nicer – in her letters, I mean. She wants to move into films, is
learning tap-dancing from a nigger, and says she has all the best
understudy jobs in the show. Sam is still deaf as ever but going to
a good school where he has caught up several years in a couple of
terms.

Majorca hasn't recovered yet from the crash of the Credito
Balear bank, and talk of 'Red Riots in Spain' by the *Daily Mail*
has frightened off a lot of tourists. Deyá is suffering from there

being no demand from Barcelona for gloves, which are hand-made here by the women. But no real poverty anywhere: only anxiety.

There's been no time for *Focus*. Perhaps we'll revive it when there's a real demand from everyone. It was fun doing, but a dreadful lot of work with the Spanish printers.

Solomon[45] and the cats and the canary are very well. So are we, though Laura is over-smoking and over-working.

Gelat often speaks of you: oftener than of anyone else who has ever been here. In order to defend himself against the machinations of that awful Doctor (one of Juan March's[46] men) he has had to turn Left, and any day now will be Mayor of Deyá at the head of a council of his (and our) friends appointed directly by the Governor, who is also, of course, Left. Then Deyá will begin to develop, we foresee: the first aim is a telephone.

. . . .

Anyhow, my, our, love to both of you and all of you.

Robert

In 1935 Alan Hodge, then still an undergraduate at Oriel College, Oxford, began a correspondence with Riding; during the Christmas vacation he visited Mallorca and on Christmas Eve called at Canel-luñ, tactfully asking for Miss Riding. His visit was a success; Graves recorded in his diary at the time that he was 'decent and sensible' and: 'Said about *Claudius* had read it while ill – liked it, lot of work; I said: "written to make money" – he said "Yes he thought it read like that." I liked that – first time I have heard it.' He was invited to return in the summer, when he stayed in Ca'n Torrent where Karl Gay (then Karl Goldschmidt), who had joined Graves and Riding as their private secretary in 1934, was living; Hodge helped with *Epilogue* and worked on poems of his own.

All work was interrupted, however, and all visits cancelled when the political troubles in Spain reached a climax that summer. All over the country, though not in Mallorca, there had been scenes of violence and chaos; fascism and anarchy grew, the government lost control and on 17 July a military rising was launched from Morocco. On the next day, the day the Civil War began, Graves wrote to Julie Matthews.

18 July 1936

Dearest Julie,

Thank you for your long letter, which I shall answer not so long because you'll be here soon, I hope.

We are also having a mad time getting work done for Autumn publication and in three weeks there'll be this huge influx of children (3, perhaps Catherine[47] too, 4) for a month which will be like sand in the machinery; also Honor and James and Mary[48] will be here. Of these Honor is the only one you'll be liable to overlap with, unless Jenny stays on. Alan Hodge is going back on September 12th with my children. He is a very nice person, most remarkable for only 20, and the greatest help not only with work (getting *Epilogue III* ready and other writing jobs) but around the house and garden. When you come you'll probably live at the Posada (see *Focus*) which is a very beautiful old house with a secluded garden, and very cool and spacious. We had great fun restoring it and furnishing it appropriately without spoiling its character.

I have sent off my *Antigua, Penny, Puce* novel to the printers, and Laura is on the last few pages of *Trojan Ending* which is quite a long book and very exciting. Liddell Hart and I had trouble with the Trustees over our book about Lawrence. [. . . .] As a compromise it will probably appear in a month or two in a limited edition (trade edition postponed until 1937) which means a great disappointment in the money line. If published in a trade edition it would have been worth a whole heap of money. Honor's novel *The Heathen* is also in its last chapter (for autumn publication too with Constable–Seizin); you'll like it. We think that we have a block-agreement about Seizin books fixed with Random House; but it isn't quite sure yet. I am so glad Tom's book will appear in US at last.

You'll hardly recognize Canelluñ now – so many things developed in house and garden but Laura and I haven't changed much, except for the better. I don't think fatter: perhaps I am a little. Grey hairs, yes, lots! The Mayor will be delighted to see you again. (Brush up your Spanish!)

There is martial law in Palma today, but that's like something happening far away and anyhow it's only a reflexion of Continental trouble, not trouble originating here.

Much love to Tom and you and the children from us

Robert

When the political situation grew worse Graves and Riding were forced to leave the island. On Sunday, 2 August, Graves wrote in his diary:

At 2 o'clock Lindo Webb, ex-Consul, told us our last chance to go was this evening by a destroyer from Los Pinos, Palma. One suitcase each. We had just had lunch. Packed hurriedly and at random. Gelat came and undertook to do everything. He said '*sinverguenzas*'[49] and wept. Magdalena and Medora came. Antonia and her husband to sleep at Ca'n Torrent and look after Alice and Nicholas.[50] Gelat took keys, will keep everything for us, 'don't worry', will take Solomon for walks. Everyone weeping as we went off. Skirted Palma. Saw broken windows, no other damage. Today 60 bombs dropped. Soldiers lounging about. Growing beards already . . .

On 7 August Graves, Riding, Hodge and Karl Gay arrived in London.

To Basil Liddell Hart

8 August 1936[51]

c/o Messrs Constable & Co. Ltd
10 Orange Street
London WC2

Dear L.H.,

   Laura Riding and I have just arrived in London. We had to leave the island at a couple of hours' notice, being taken off by *Grenville,* a brand new destroyer and landed at Valencia whence home by hospital ship and third-class railway carriage. A six days' travel with all the necessary discomfort of being a refugee and without money. At the moment we are in the house of Kitty and Douglas West, 32 York Terrace, Welbeck 5365, until Wednesday. I rang you up but you were on manoeuvres. I also rang up Watt[52] who says that a letter from Savage imposes very stiff terms even for the limited edition of our book. [. . . .] After Wednesday we will probably go to the country, Great Bardfield in Essex. We intend to return to Spain the moment we can. We are glad that *The Times* (which I suppose is you) seems to favour the Government's chances. We think that this is the best hope for Spain. Best wishes and hopes for seeing you.

   Yours,

Robert

272

In September, Liddell Hart invited Graves and Riding for dinner at Gloucester Place, and thus met them for the first time. He and Graves liked each other, but he did not get on so well with Riding who quarrelled with him about his conversational 'drawing out' tactics; he later wrote to Graves that he felt that he and Riding had passed and repassed in a mist all evening. At dinner Graves and Riding offered to analyse Liddell Hart's prose style and point out its faults; a few days later they sent him a laborious and patronizing analysis (written by Riding but backed up by a blindly loyal Graves) of the opening pages of *War in Outline*, for which Liddell Hart thanked them but regretted that he found little of substance in their comments, and sent them a series of notes on their notes; he also wrote to Graves:

If you will not mind a criticism in return, the value of your notes as criticism is often impaired by what, to me, seems your chief trouble – a lack or, rather, lapse of proportion. In dealing with one point you are apt to lose sight of the others which have a bearing on it. Incidentally, I have noticed this tendency in affairs outside the literary field, and I think it may well be a cause why you give a false idea of yourself to those who are not sympathetically inclined towards you, or have a similar tendency themselves.

Graves was angered by this response and wrote, in a long letter of 9 October, proposing a separation of their works:

So communications between us are cut, I think irreparably. You have taken our analysis not as a technical exposition of why your literary style was difficult to the careful reader but as a pedantic and loose-thinking myopic attack on what is a perfectly clear and accurate passage of English prose; and have resented it so strongly as to make a counter-attack not, as might have been forgiveable, in the form of a detailed, substantiated criticism of a particular passage in L.R.'s or my own recent work as pedantic, loose-thinking or myopic, but (to deal solely with your attack on me – L.R. deals with yours on her separately) on my manner of dealing with the Lawrence Trustees . . .

The next day, Liddell Hart replied.

Dear Robert,

It is sad. We seemed to be understanding each other so well – if you were sincere in all you have said, as I have always thought you were – until our association became a 'third-party affair'.

So you have fallen out even with me – do you remember my letter of New Year's day, and also of January 10th? Why couldn't you go on reading my remarks in their exact sense, instead of reading into them what isn't there? Why suddenly imagine them as an 'attack' instead of continuing to read them as 'conversation between friends'? When I have said the same sort of things before, you have taken it in a reasonable way. Also, why be so forward in offering criticism, if your own feelings of friendship can't stand the breath of it? And you surely can't be blind to the impression you have widely made – you have never seemed so in our long correspondence – so why start imagining an attack on your 'manner in dealing with Lawrence trustees', with which I have never found fault. When I found that L.R. was twisting my casual remarks in a way that astonished me, I could not but foresee, with sadness, the possibility of it producing a distortion in your perception, and leading to the breach which you now seek.

Still, it has been a good run while it lasted. And the end is too petty to be true – to you.

As regards the book, so long as your part was the cause of difficulty in gaining approval for its publication, I naturally had to stand by you and refuse to consider dissolving the common front. But you have always been free to sever the link when you wished.

Yours,   [Only a carbon copy of this letter
                                      has survived, which is unsigned]

The breach in their friendship was not permanent, however, nor did they separate their different parts of the book. At a meeting on 8 December between Graves, Liddell Hart and the Lawrence trustees it was agreed that a limited edition of one thousand copies should be published, to be followed by a trade edition after the official *Letters* volume had been published.

To Julie Matthews

18 January 1937   c/o Constable

Dearest Julie,

We have your very nice letter of January 4th, which I am answering for the both of us. Yes, we both had flu. It lasts for three days and then one feels rotten for ten more. We are just out of that shadow. On February 5 we leave England (so as not to acquire a domicile[53]) and go to Lugano in Switzerland where old Schwarz and Emmy Strenge will be. They report: 'Sunday afternoon picture-postcard scenery; warm; one would be a snob not to like it.' On April 6th we are entitled to return. Perhaps by then Deyá will be clear of trouble: if so, we fly there like swallows. We are packing up now: lots of stuff to go to Deyá, especially the (Caledonian Market) china and glass we had to buy because we couldn't bear Woolworth's products, and will have to be crated and stored.

. . . .

Alan Hodge was going to Spain to interpret or something for the Government, but Laura said, 'don't!' She set him instead to write a novel in his six weeks' vacation, giving him a title, *Year of Damage*. He did ten pages a day and finished in the given time and the result is excellent. Alan is fine: he always delivers the goods. We hope he will come to Deyá this summer and work on the *Dictionary*[54] with us.

The *Claudius* scenario is a great joke: its permutations in and out of German, Hungarian and English as various big-shots take turns at it would make you laugh. I don't care personally. Von Sternberg[55] has it in hand now. Laura and I (anonymously) did a 'refugee' scenario for Korda. He paid us something for the job; and will pay more if he takes it.[56] (We don't care if he doesn't take it. Films are insane: if they occasionally drop gold on our hats as we pass, that's all right.)

How is Tom's narrative poem?

How is Tom's novel?

What about American Ecclesiastical Habits? Laura didn't do the lectures. Instead she had talks with a number of people about the international muddle, and women in regard to the international muddle, and about what can be done. She got quite a new line on the problem. She is therefore writing a circular letter to a number of women and what she calls 'inside' men on the subject, and when they answer will make a book out of it. She will send you and Tom a copy for you to answer, and also copies to send personally by post to the few people you know who are likely to give thoughtful answers. This sounds mysterious, but you'll soon have the letter to understand.

We are getting *Epilogue* ready before we leave. It will be a good issue, I think. Also *A Trojan Ending* is now in print. A hopeful omen was that the President of Magdalen (George Gordon) who is Merton Professor of English at Oxford and also member of the Book Society Committee got very excited by a copy we sent him and said: 'The Book Society *must* take account of this.' It would be fun if it had a popular success. (No reason why not. It is long, and scholarly, and the only book on the subject and *very* nice to read.)

. . . .

Everyone is well and Karl is a darling as usual. He is going ahead to get things mapped out for us at Lugano.

The Lawrence book is going through after all.

. . . .

Best love to you all from Laura and me and Karl.

[Unsigned]

Epilogue IV turned into *The World and Ourselves*, Riding's book on the international muddle. She wrote to four hundred people, asking for their opinion, and received about a hundred replies, sixty-five of which were published in the book with an introduction and commentary by herself. This resulted in the joining of the various 'inside people' involved into a Covenant of Literal Morality, and the forming of a code, called the *First Protocol* (published and distributed to 'endorsers') which was intended to establish the solidarity of 'inside people' and their principles of conduct. Graves and Hodge give an account of the book in *The Long Week-End*:

The conclusion was that the tragic absurdity of public events was due to a moral failure among the 'outside people' – the institutionally minded directors of affairs; but equally to a failure among independent minded and sensitive 'inside people' who should include most women and all poets – to give the outside people a lead. The remedy suggested was continued insistence by the inside people on personal integrity – an attitude to be

276

communicated from friend to friend through the close network of real friendships that made up society.[57]

All of their friends endorsed the *Protocol* at first, including Edward Marsh who in his later years was immensely proud of Graves. He was now chairman of the Contemporary Art Society, and in February was knighted by the new king, George VI, and the next day retired after forty years in the Civil Service. A special banquet was arranged at the Mayfair Hotel to celebrate the occasion and the principal guests included Churchill, Malcolm MacDonald, James Agate, William Rothenstein and several of the Georgian poets: Masefield, de la Mare, Abercrombie, Drinkwater and Squire. Graves wrote from Lugano congratulating him.

	Villa Guidi
25 February 1937	Paradiso
	Lugano

Dearest Eddie,

Congratulations on your honours: not only on the official ones but on the Tate Gallery appointment, which should prove a great benefit to the Gallery itself and also to the painters whom you will be able to put on its walls: what fun!

I haven't been invited to eat the complimentary banquet in your honour next month, but think of me eating a reflective slice of Swiss cheese in your honour and drinking 'Barbera', which is like a glorified mineral water, though pure red wine. I love it.

Thinking it all over, I have a *great deal* to be grateful for to you over a very long stretch of years, and especially during the War and on a certain occasion in 1929: and this is as good an occasion as any for sending you my most affectionate greetings.

Yours ever,   Robert

Graves and Riding returned to London in June and rented a furnished flat in Maida Vale. In July Graves began reading Gibbon, Viscount Mahon's *Life of Belisarius* (1829) and other source books for his historical novel, *Count Belisarius* which, with the help of Alan Hodge, was finished by 1 January. In June friendship was fully renewed with Liddell Hart who lent Graves several books on the subject and offered to read proofs for him.

No date [January 1938]

31 Alma Square
St John's Wood
NW8

Dear L.H.

I hope I did not give a wrong impression on the phone the other night. It was *very good indeed of you* to offer to read proofs of *Belisarius* for me from the military point of view; but I underestimated the length of the book with the result that I have had to send it to the printers, in England and USA, piece-meal as I complete each chapter in order to keep my publication-date contract. Otherwise I should have been only too glad to have your criticism (and also that of a social-history expert) but it could not be. However, I have gone straight to the original sources, including a number not translated into English; and my sympathy with your general strategical outlook makes it unlikely, I think, that you will find my reconstruction far out. Of course it is dressed up as fiction, and this makes it easier for me in a number of ways: e.g. the introduction of the stirrup, essential for the new type of heavy cavalry, can be attributed to Belisarius without a historian's 'perhaps', and I can give him a boyhood and early manhood, which otherwise he lacks.

Mahon is very good, but he misunderstood Antonina – the Christian prejudice – and in one or two passages he has missed the point of the original Greek or Latin.

I shall send you corrected proofs as soon as possible; and return Mahon with very many thanks.

Let me put in writing what I said on the phone: if the Spanish Government's strategy at Teruel[58] has been due to a study of your principles, you surely have a right to be pleased.

It would be very good if the cloud that arose last year could be dispelled. L.R. is very willing that it should be, but until things are right between you and her communication between you and me will be qualified by a sense of not-yet-right. I heard a very spiteful description of you that T.E. made to someone. As I am sure you will hear it without offence I shall tell it you when next we meet: if you laugh, you get full marks. If you put it into your book, you get the OM.

Good luck. Yours ever   Robert

At the end of June 1938 Graves and Riding, with Alan Hodge and his wife Beryl, went to live near Rennes in Brittany, where Gelat's sister Anita ran a fruit and vegetable shop with her husband Juan Vives, brother of the Deyá *médico*. They rented a château in the country and continued work: Graves and Riding prepared their separate *Collected Poems* for publication and worked together on another novel (intended for the popular market), called *The Swiss Ghost* (unpublished); most of the time, however, was spent on *The Dictionary of Exact Meanings*, with Graves and Hodge sorting out about 25,000 words for 'exact' definition by Riding.

In July Graves wrote to Karl Gay, who had remained in England (later that year he was granted Home Office permission to live and work there) where he now had a job in Harold Edwards's bookshop off the Charing Cross Road.

6 July, I think. 1938   Hotel Central

Dearest Karl,

Well, you can imagine how it was – looking for houses and no houses to be had! Yesterday I got desperate and went to work savagely, and within two hours we had got (unless anything happens to upset the plan) an 18th-century château (about 15 miles out but on the railway) called the Château de la Chevrie (i.e. 'Venison Hall') of 12 principal rooms, furnished, large and beautiful, with lake, park and game all for . . . £40 a year! (A Mrs McCormack bargain.) It is near a large village called Montauban-de-le-Bretagne.

We hope to be installed in about a fortnight. Meanwhile we have a *pied-à-terre* in the town; and so have Beryl and Alan. Living is extremely cheap and the town beautiful and the people nice.

We are dreadfully tired and have done no work at all – you know what house-hunting can be.

. . . .

Anita and Juan have been perfectly sweet. The Dr's sister has just arrived from Deyá – it is all awful there what with compulsory Mass and compulsory '*vivas*' – and recently a Government ship shelled Deyá by mistake for Sóller and a shell landed in the grotto at Canelluñ! No one hurt. They send their *memorias*.[59] The Dr's sister said that nobody will be honoured after the war who has not been in prison. All the Drs,

279

schoolmasters and intellectuals of repute have done their week or month. But now no Deyá people in prison except the old smith.

Best love to you and Marie from us all.

Robert

10 February 1939   La Chevrie

Dearest Karl,

Muchísimos abrazos y felicidades de su fiesta [*sic*].

Well, things are clearing up, aren't they? The signs are good, in a perverse way. It may take some time to clear the Pomegranates out of Spain, but they can't last long even if supported by Italy and Germany. And the Catalans have deserved their humiliation. (We are worried about Joan Junyer.[60] Perhaps he is in France, but he doesn't know our address here.)

A nice thing was that McIntyre of Little, Brown[61] got qualms about the *Dictionary* because he had showed the plan to two linguistic cranks and asked Laura to answer objections before proceeding. Laura sent him an 18-page foolscap letter by return, like a mule's kick, demolishing the cranks and giving him only till the 15th to decide about getting ahead. (I contributed two pages on the grammatical and vocabularistic errors occurring in the reports by one of the cranks: he had managed to get 14 mistakes on a single sheet!) Yesterday a penitent 34-word cable came from McIntyre admitting that the 'so-called experts' had been answered fully. 'So-called experts' was his own expression of apology. So that's all steady now.

. . . .

I work at *Dictionary* every day, and have written about seven or eight new poems since the *Collected Poems* appeared, and a children's story for the joint book, and finished my part of *Swiss Ghost*, and done a lot of minor jobs of reading, checking and so on. No new book: but keep busy and am feeling very well and happy. Laura is gradually clearing away her enormous pile of work. It is a great relief to have *Lives of Wives* and the *Greeks and Trojans* and David[62] and her *Furniture* out of the way. At the moment she is writing a very difficult poem: but always a happy thing when she can make time for that.

Did you hear that Barker is going to publish Bottrall's[63] poems?

– good, isn't it? I have stopped riding bicycles: roads too bad and too hard when one falls.

Hope you'll be able to sell the Lawrence book and buy yourself something nice with the money.

Love to Marie and Soetkin. Robert

On 20 April 1939 Graves and Riding sailed to America on the *Paris*, the same ship on which Riding had first come to Europe in 1925. (She was never to return to Europe again.) Tom Matthews had urged them many times to come to America, for the main reason that he wanted Riding to know his friend from Princeton, Schuyler Jackson: a farmer, poet (in his youth), and an endorser of the *Protocol*, for whom Matthews had an exaggerated admiration and who had recently written, assisted by Graves and Matthews, a highly laudatory review of Riding's *Collected Poems* for *Time*.

Graves and Riding went first to stay with Matthews at Princeton, where they were soon joined by Alan and Beryl Hodge, before moving to New Hope, Pennsylvania, where Jackson lived with his wife Kit and their four children.

5 May 1939   17 Hibben Road
                                                                                  Princeton, NJ
Dearest Karl

Laura has a rheumatic wrist, or of course she would be writing to you herself today which is the first that we have been able to take breath and write to our dear ones in England. The first thing she wants to say is that she is thinking very much and closely of you and that the last letter you sent to her at La Chevrie was needed as a start for the journey here. And then that as soon as her wrist is better you will hear from her. And please will you write.

The news is simple and very good. We are staying for 3 weeks or so with Julie and Tom in their own house which is large and very much like home to us. The three boys are a great success; compared with their schoolmates, who come calling with baseball bats, jazzdrums and aeroplanes, they are as porcelain to roof-tiles. Tom and Julie are very well and I cannot tell you how happy we all are here; the important thing being that Schuyler and Katherine Jackson, whom Tom and Julie have known for years and to whom before we came we felt close in a predestined sort of way, are exactly the people we knew, counted on them being, and that means an innumerability of old problems cleared up – like a game that cannot properly begin until all the players are present: now we all are. That everything is so good of course makes Tom and Julie feel like 1,000,000 dollars too. The house we are to live in is 100 yards from the Jacksons' white farmhouse with its green shutters and pines and large barns; it was a ruin and is going up very fast: 4 bedrooms, kitchen, large L-shaped living room, porch, bathroom, store-room.

Yesterday we bought a 'deluxe sedan (1936) Ford four-door pleasure car'. David will drive it.

We hope to start work very soon, as well as thinking of furnishing the house from country sales and mail order catalogues.

Will be seeing you soon – or writing soon.

Love Robert
(and to Soetkin)

Laura says: 'You know all will be done that needs to be done for all.'

PART FOUR

1939–1946

In America, work continued on the *Dictionary* and on the drawing up of the *Second Protocol*, on the 'recognition of good' (the *First Protoçol* had been on the 'judgement of evil'). However, soon after moving to Nimrod's Rise, their house on Schuyler Jackson's farm at New Hope, the partnership between Graves and Riding was dissolved. Riding underwent a profound change in thought and 'renounced' poetry, an act which she described (in the introduction to a new edition of the 1938 *Collected Poems*, published by Carcanet Press, 1980) as 'the outer manifestation of an inner experience of discovery that I could not take what was essentially an argument of hope I felt it mine to make any further within the linguistic allowances of poetry: and there was further to go.' She went to live with Jackson (whose wife Kit was removed to an asylum at this time), and married him in 1941. For the next twenty-seven years she worked with Jackson on what had originally been the *Dictionary* but which became a book (in no way a dictionary) intended to 'dissipate the confusion existing in the knowledge of word-meanings', now completed but not yet published.

In August Graves, in a state of nervous exhaustion, returned to England with Alan Hodge (he and his wife Beryl had also separated) for a holiday, intending to return to New Hope after two months to resume work on the *Dictionary*. Before he left, Riding had told him to 'make his peace' with Nancy, half in the hope that he would go back to live with her. When he arrived in England he went straight to Harlech and was joined there by his children, with whom he now became fully reacquainted.

To Karl Gay

No date	Erinfa Harlech N. Wales

Dearest Karl,

I am having a very good, very busy time with my children here – bathing, walking and finding out about what they are at.

Shall be coming up to London on the 27th I think for a day and then hope to go to Honor, John and Lucie, Ward and Dorothy.[1]

Will do my best to see you on the 27th.

With love to Marie and yourself   Robert

Graves left Harlech and for the next few months lived in a chapel rented from John Aldridge at Great Bardfield; in September Beryl, who had subsequently returned from America alone, went to live with him there.

On 3 September 1939 Britain declared war on Germany and Graves, now forty-four years old, immediately volunteered for infantry service, just as he had done in 1914, and later that month went before a medical board.

To Basil Liddell Hart

25 September 1939 (Good old battle of Loos)	The Place Great Bardfield Essex

My dear Basil

I should have answered long ago. I finally managed to get medically boarded for the Officers' Emergency Reserve, got passed Grade 2 which means that I can only be accepted for non-combatant and very dull corps – and decided that with so many people unemployed because of the war it was altogether unnecessary for me to do-my-bit in the Educational Corps or Army Pay Corps just in order to be in uniform – so am calling it off and returning to America which I am free to do because of my age and disability pension. Laura is short-handed over there and I have to work in order to support my family and various war-stranded semi-dependants.

It occurs to me suddenly that the war which is very much 'the

Next War' rather than 'The War' as it was last time is already over – I mean that we aren't fighting any Passchendaeles or Verduns this time. If this is so the War has been won largely by you: that is, your influence on military thought. It is blockade now, and more blockade, and pinning them down to the Siegfried position until they wished they had never built it, and then perhaps hysterical action from them like an invasion of Holland. (I do hope at least that we won't hear about any more bayonet charges of our gallant Kilties and such.) And then the eventual shameful dog-eat-dog collapse on the home front. I listened to Goering the other night – it was a beaten man talking.

Anyhow: may I come and see you? How do I get there and when are you free? I can get to London from here by about 10.30 if I get up early. Are you on the Baker St line? Almost any day.

I shall be in England for another three weeks I expect.

Laura sent you her best wishes and was sorry you had been ill: we also had a very thin time this summer. She sends you a poem as a gift.

In spite of the publishing stagnation I have been asked to write an historical novel on the subject of the American War of Independence. I have a good centre character: Sergeant Lamb of the 9th and 23rd – and his journal which I have been reading is pretty good stuff. It will not be really fiction, but the real stuff enlarged by other contemporary evidences of the sort of thing that happened. I hate this sort of writing; but it can be justified as making readable what is not readable at all.

I do hope you are less of a crock now.

Yours ever   Robert

In 1938 Liddell Hart had resigned from his position as personal adviser to the Minister of War because the progress being made in the reorganization and modernization of the Army (along the lines laid out by Liddell Hart) was dangerously slow compared with the imminent risk of war; he decided instead that it would be more useful to press the need for urgent military reform publicly, by his writings.

In 1939, however, he suffered a breakdown from overwork; he was convalescing with friends at Dartington in Devonshire when he wrote to Graves in September.

29 September 1939
                                              Dartington Hall
                                              Totnes
                                              Devon

My dear Robert,

I was delighted to hear from you but wish it had been earlier as I am down here now, the Elmhirsts having kindly invited me here to convalesce. Is there any chance at all of you coming this way, as I would dearly love to see you, and consult you.

I'm glad to hear of your personal decision. It is the more sensible since this war makes no sense – either as a defence of democracy or of British Civilization. It is difficult to see any purpose it can serve beyond that of establishing an authoritarian regime here, and consolidating those of Spain and Italy. That seems the logical course of events although one hopes it may be otherwise. I have had this vision so strongly since Munich and Prague that I had contemplated taking your course months ago, but felt that I must stay to finish my book as a final warning, and do what else I could, to prevent what one foresaw. The tactical and strategical part of my thesis may have had some effect, but the powers that be have been too late each time in reorganizing the moves in the grand strategical sphere. I'd like to show you some of my notes and reflections if we had a chance of meeting.

Have you actually got a permit yet, and if so did you have any difficulty? Also what about money? I'd be grateful to hear from you about these points.

I'm now able to take a decent walk without getting too tired. That is progress.

All good wishes,
Yours ever
                                              Basil

21 November 1939

My dear Basil,

Many thanks for your long letter and the invitation to Dartington. I am very glad that you are temporarily at least settled in an agreeable place. I will explain about myself. I nearly had a bad breakdown, at the same time as you did, in America and went away in August for a two months' holiday. Then the war came. Two months would not really have been enough and I am only now feeling all right. I don't remember whether you met Beryl

288

Pritchard in London; she was working with Laura and me there, and later in France and America. Anyhow, she is a good person and came over from America to me a month ago and we are sharing this chapel here, rented from friends. Laura and I (you know, I think) were colleagues and inseparables, but not what is called 'lovers', though there was/is great love between us. She now has a very close intimacy with an American (poet and also farmer – very good farmer) of whom I am very fond; his name is Schuyler Jackson – we were staying on his farm – and I am really very happy indeed that she is happy with him. And as Laura is also very fond of Beryl, it is all right all round: though confusing to people at first. Beryl and I will be going back to live with Laura and Schuyler Jackson in the spring, if there are no worse sea-warfare menaces to prevent us. This explains why, quite apart from the train-journeys, I find it difficult to come down to Devon; Beryl and I have a disinclination even to go as far as London away from this place – which is now a home, with a cat and all. I think I must wait awhile, unless something happens so that Beryl has to be away for a few days with parents or something: in which case I will let you know.

I have read about 8000 pages of American War of Independency literature, word by word not skipping and feel I will soon know the scene well enough to begin my novel. Unfortunately I still am without one of my two key books: it is Sergeant Lamb's *Memoir of His Life*, Dublin, 1812 (298 pp) (*not* his *Journal of Occurrences in the Late American War*, 1809, which I have, the other key book). This memoir book is never quoted by the usual authorities and is excessively rare and no copy in Fitzwilliam, Bodleian, British Museum or the Trade. I am writing to searchers in Dublin and have advertised in America. It does exist, but only just, apparently. Then I am sending someone to look up in (23rd) Regimental records for Captain Julian's and Sir Thomas Saumarez's journals. When you do get your books stacked and sorted I would indeed be grateful for a list of your Americana. One of the very best written histories I have come across is Winthrop Sargent's *Life of Major André* (1865 or so), (Southern States) American and done in the purest English detached style.

. . . .

I hear (from Wilfred and Nan Roberts) that 80,000 Spaniards have been rounded up in France recently and their work permits taken from them and they have been put back into the concentration camps, where the disease figures have rushed up: now black-water fever has started. There are still 196,000 men and women in the camps. The Franco newspapers show still predominant German influence, queerly enough.

Yours ever   Robert

To Karl Gay

26 January 1940

Dearest Karl,

Here is the £6: I am sure you are earning every 1d. of it, and more.

I have had a long letter from Laura in which she writes very nicely indeed and sends you her intention of writing soon. She has also sent me the *Swiss Ghost* uncompleted, which she asks me to complete and publish as my own, her play *Greeks and Trojans* which she wishes me to sell as my dramatization of her novel; and is not going on with the children's book, so sends me my *Castle-Keeper*² back. Also she wishes to deed me all the property in Majorca and to give me all the Woodbridge stuff. She ends this letter by saying that Schuyler is not writing to me at present, and that she hopes to see me in March and that she wishes Beryl and me happiness in the child.

Then she shows the letter to Schuyler and writes another to say that she doesn't want to see me in March and that there is no possibility of my helping in the *Dictionary*, which is being done in an entirely different way now, except by helping her financially from my *Sergeant Lamb* money; and that because of extraordinary expenses she cannot repay me the £450 paid to her in error last November from Random House, which Random House will now recover from my *Lamb* advance. She also will do all in her power to break the power of the *1st Protocol*, that 'infected' document, wherever it raises its head.

Schuyler then encloses a letter which is aimed at breaking all connexion between me and Laura and speaks of Beryl and me in a way for which I really could get him prosecuted for sending indecent matter by the mails (this is *not* exaggerated).

Don't let all this sadden you. Be happy in what good Laura bequeathed to us before she left us.

Always your friend, and Marie's   Robert

Graves wrote to Liddell Hart about Riding's letter and about her 'astonishing' withdrawal from the 'Covenant of Literal Morality' (of which Liddell Hart was an endorser), and told him he would soon be receiving a circular letter from Ward Hutchinson, the Covenant's secretary, about her withdrawal. Now that Graves's chief object in going to America had been removed, he decided to stay in England: 'It goes against the grain to leave one's country and friends in wartime, except for the very highest considerations – of aims transcending merely national or personal ones; and I cannot now see that to go to America in my present circumstances would be justified. How it affects you is a different matter . . .' he wrote to Liddell Hart, who replied that he understood Graves's decision not to leave, but that he himself was still vaguely considering the possibility of going. (Shortly after writing the letter he made up his mind to stay permanently in England, although he did not alter his opinions about the war.) He had received Ward Hutchinson's letter, and wrote to Graves:

It is difficult to know what to reply to Ward Hutchinson's letter without a chance to discuss it with you. Can you elucidate L.R.'s cryptic references? My own view, on reflection, was that the Covenant was a valuable step in the right direction, but that its phrasing presented an undue obstacle to some really good people – though I did not find it so myself.

Graves replied:

19 February 1940

My dear Basil
    Everything has been frozen here and I have (as it were) been waiting for a bright sky to answer your letter by: which was a very warm one and deserved an unfrozen answer. Today there is a faint dripping of snow off the trees and your letter has come as a reminder.
    . . . .

I have read several of your Beaverbrook articles, though often the *Standard* doesn't arrive because of snow and black-out, and I think it most excellent that you are able to get them published. Beaverbrook, for all his faults, is the only sensible newspaper owner and the most powerful man out of the cabinet. You must find it a bit wearisome to have to plug the same point home, in different contexts, so often but it is the only way to create a popular appreciation of them which after a time turns into a conviction as if they were the readers' own mature decision. I think it is clear that so long as you have Beaverbrook's ear and permission to write, you are doing far more good here than (say) in America. After all, your articles are read by the troops and generals concerned, as they would not be if they were first published in America; this offsets the greater freedom of frank speaking that you would have if you wrote from America. Besides, anyone who goes to America now has the odium (unjust and absurd but inescapable) of being called a rat and the credit given to his opinions is thereby reduced. Obviously too, America is not going to do or decide anything until after the Elections: election year is an *annus non*.

You mention a list of your American books but do not enclose it: however, in a postscript you mention pamphlets on Valley Forge and the Strategy of the Revolution. Thanks very much – but I can do without those. I haven't read *Gentleman Johnny Burgoyne*. Have you it? My problem at the moment is how to keep the book within bounds. The libraries refuse to stock any book beyond 9 shillings and one can't publish a long book at that price now; and I have to give a very long, leisurely book to suit the date and characters. (I always hated Tacitus.)

What can I say about Laura? She reached (for me) a point of shall we say poetic (i.e. hyper-moral) excellence that nobody has ever attained before; and then – what shall I say? Her oldest friends consider it an inexplicable abandonment of the principles that she once guarded with the fiercest intensity. The explanation is that she has made the centre of her universe no longer herself but Schuyler Jackson and herself, and thus admitted into her scope so many foreign elements that it is difficult to regard her as the same person. Her rejection of the *Protocol* is only to be understood therefore by a personal knowledge – which you can't be expected to have – of Schuyler. He has a great prejudice against the English aristocratic principle: of much the sort as made the Revolution.

I doubt whether the *First Protocol* could be made less what you say it is (and I know what you mean) without weakening it. After all, we don't want the merely well-intentioned people to join; but the active-minded. The problem now is how to provide a positive and warming statement to take the chill off the first.[3]

I hope Kathleen and the children are well and yourself.

When the weather improves Beryl and I will come down to Devon to look for a house near the sea and near my sister at Bishopsteignton. Can't move yet.

All the best   Robert

In March, Graves began writing *The Long Week-End*, a social history of Great Britain between the wars, in collaboration with Alan Hodge.

15 May 1940

Dear Alan

This is to thank you for the second lot of typescript and to reassure you that I feel capable of filling out the parts you have left a bit sketchy with a thesis and further detail. The preliminary thesis is that there were in October 1918 two Englands, the revolutionary but apathetic Fighting Forces, and The Rest. The latter included all the schemers in the Law and Order interest who side-tracked the promised social revolution; and so the rebels degenerated into mere Lefts. The Conservative party used Lloyd George as a Liberal buffer to take the preliminary shock; and then, when they felt their position secure, threw him over. The Liberal party had been knifed by Lloyd George himself. Naturally: these violent terms would not appear in the book.

Title still simmering. I think *Lull* ought to come into it. *Lull Between Wars* – A record of happenings in Great Britain between 1918 and 1939.

As for May 1939, you were right when you came back from Poland about real war being on the way: and I had underestimated the inefficiency of the Government. The whole question as to whether we win or lose the war depends on the comparative rate of wastage in Allied and German planes. If the alleged 4–1 proportion is true, and maintained, we are all right. But if not, O dear! Our fighter pilots and the French are on an average better than the Germans, it is thought: though the Germans have a few stars, just as in the last war. Apparently the great criminal is Nuffield for falling down on his contracts for Beauforts and such.

I hope Karl is keeping up his chin – and that the BM doesn't get closed down to prevent his checking up on points I raise. But I don't imagine that will happen.

Good luck, Alan, and thank you for doing the job so nicely.

Robert

. . . .

That spring Graves and Beryl, who was expecting her first baby (William), went to live in Galmpton.

Vale Farm House
Galmpton
Brixham
South Devon

14 June 1940

Dear Alan,

I am now getting into smooth water with your later stuff and see no rocks ahead. Certainly my expansion will not be nearly so full hereafter as heretofore. Your notes on business ethics have gone in, nearly whole, and the Kate Meyrick stuff will be fine for insertion in one of the chapters you already have. I have sent Karl XIII and am half-way through XIV which is a general tidy-up of the end of the Twenties. I hope you approve of what I wrote of Laura: to leave her out would have been dishonest, and one can hardly say less than I have.

As for this war: the more I hear from L.H. of the story of Army organization and the General Staff, both before and since last September, the more I understand the paradox of Nazi victory: a lunatic has no chance against an ordinary sane person but a very good chance indeed against the half-witted and suicidal.

I am not satisfied with the concatenation of argument in the chapters I have sent you – too many digressions – but it is in any case an impossible task and to make a better concatenation would be to make a less rich book.

I should very much like it if Sally⁴ could look over the chapters.
Honor comes here on Monday.
Yours   Robert

The Long Week-End was finished at the end of June and sent to
Fabers.

23 October 1940

Dear Alan

About 'pornographic'. Faber changed it himself, giving me no
time to approve: he just omitted it.

The other morning a bedraggled family bombed out of Highgate
came to our door having tried all the other houses in the village
and not having had anything to eat for 24 hours. It was raining so
I brought them in to lunch and once they were in, we couldn't
send them off again and so here they are. They are a great
acquisition: Mrs Sullivan is a railwayman's wife and a farmer's
daughter and has been a lady's maid, a char in Bush House,
worked in a dry cleaner's, etc. The daughter Lily, aged 14, has
learned to look after babies and type and run a machine. And
both are good cooks. There's a boy of 3 called Johnny, with huge
hands and a terrific punch, who's the image of the famous John L.
Sullivan the Strong Boy of Boston who Broke every Bone in Jake
Kilbrain (Vachel Lindsay). This is not surprising, as Johnny's
grand-uncle *was* John L. Sullivan (his uncle was Patsy Sullivan
too). So we are now properly looked after, and defended.

I have begun a new book, about English: it is a collection of
bad sentences by prominent politicians, lawyers, ecclesiastics,
schoolmasters, novelists, economists, etc., grouped under new
grammatical headings. (I don't think people can stomach the old
classical terms.) So far it seems that the worst writers are
schoolmasters, peers and ecclesiastics, then come economists and
scientists, then lawyers; each group has a different tendency to
error. I should be very grateful to you for any extra-special bad
sentence, with author's name and context, that you can be
bothered to send me. It is nice to find that writers I detest for their
attitude to the things they write about, such as Desmond
Macarthy, Atticus, and the Bishop of Ely, are far more

unsyntactical than the nice half-educated Morrisons and such. Now I must start with another sheet.

I should very much like, if you mean that about sending me books, to have whatever you can find by Lord Halifax, and other Governor General or Viceroy prominents; Chamberlain and other Guilty Men; schoolmasters like Lyttleton and Alington; more lawyers – Birkenhead, Hastings, and who was that Lord Chief Justice?; and I should dearly like to test I. A. Richards[5] and the Basic Englishers. Books out of the 2d. box are what I mean: because then I can use scissors to them; and pamphlets are lovely.

Deyá can't be salvaged; I shall hope that USA doesn't declare war on Spain. If it doesn't, the things there are safe. Besides, the Posada is held in Gelat's name, and he will perhaps transfer there, or to the *Fabrica*, any small valuables that might be seized; the larger stuff couldn't be moved anyhow.

Jenny's shelter programme was sabotaged by the Censorship – no mention is allowed to be made of any air raid in progress or any warden, except off duty, in a dramatic show. So it has to be just a lot of people who happen to be in a cellar, because they fancy cellars: she's doing that, instead.

Yours ever   Robert

Three of the children from Graves's first family joined the Armed Forces (Sam, the fourth and youngest of these, was unable to do so because of his deafness). Jenny, the oldest, became a WAAF war correspondent, David joined the Royal Welch Fusiliers and was killed in action in Burma in 1943, and Catherine became a WAAF radio operator until her marriage to Clifford Dalton, the nuclear scientist.

Graves and Hodge decided to work together on the 'handbook for writers of English prose', *The Reader Over Your Shoulder*, which between themselves they nicknamed *The Yardstick* or *A Short Cut to Unpopularity*. (The prose passages they took for analysis were referred to as epitomes or 'epittymes'.)

21 February 1941

Dear Alan:

. . . .

The *Yardstick* course you are setting yourself seems admirable. Note: the Elizabethan wits weren't really interested in *what* they said, only in *how* they said it. This fashion came in again in the Twenties with experimental writers of the New York–Paris–Dublin school: Classical and scientific reference, tropes and hey-nonny-nonny. A good example is the egregious (I regret to say Royal Welch Fusilier) painter–writer David Jones whose synthetic book[6] about the war won a Hawthornden Prize about 4 years ago. (Turn him up!) The Ciceronians were divided in mind: on the whole they were more interested in proving some point, but were conscious of themselves as Orators as they proved it. NB. Cicero was a barrister by profession; Seneca from whom the Elizabethans borrowed equally with Aristotle was a dramatist–schoolmaster. Bacon, I guess, was a Senecan.

The religious blokes, such as Milton, Hooker and so on, probably stem from Saint Augustine and the Fathers, as much as from Cicero. But then, so did Augustine and the Fathers themselves. Bunyan I think stemmed from the Old Testament and simple chapbooks sold by peddlers in the East Anglian market towns: with the pulpit tricks you mention. A good plain style was Caxton's prefaces: my copy of that ill-printed book (Vyvyan Richards about 1930) is in Spain: but the Museum has one. Swift was deliberately writing down to his public in *A Tale of a Tub*, and so on. He was a political journalist and conscientious about not flying too high. Defoe for the same reason: they aimed at the larger public. Sterne was the supreme example of French wit: but many of his fellow-Irishmen cultivated it too. Carlyle's Germanism to be noted. Glad you remembered Landor. Fielding is for me the high spot of educated prose. Don't forget Aphra Behn as a most important end-of-17th-century neat writer: French influence, wasn't it? She was a Creole, I think.

Anglo-Saxons: remarkable for complete disregard of graces. Not illogical, but no liveliness in varifying vocabulary or grammatic constructions.

A useful subject would be: the gradual un-grace-ing of scientific writing from the end of 17th century onwards; and then a convulsive reform by popularists of science Jeans, Eddington and Coy. Perhaps this could be inserted into our comments on those Worthies.

Yours ever   Robert

I am very pleased with John's cover for *Proceed*: shows the result of 7 years of war on Army uniform – but Lamb still walks with resolute step – and a stick does service for a spontoon. Smutchy Steel at his side has a cavalry pistol under his duffel blanket.

Proceed, Sergeant Lamb, the second Lamb novel, was published on 13 February 1941.

Hodge, Graves and Norman Cameron decided to publish their recent poems together in a volume to be called *Work in Hand*; two other poets, James Reeves and Harry Kemp, contributors to *Epilogue*, also intended to contribute but were excluded on the publisher's (Hogarth Press) insistence. At the beginning of March Graves received a new poem from Alan Hodge.

3 March 1941

Dear Alan:

Very great pleasure in the Ravenna poem.* And no comments to make but that: and thanks for the pleasure! Will substitute.

Last night I began an epittyme of Prof. A. N. Whitehead. Stap my vitals! I thought he was supposed to have the finest mind in these islands? He ranks even below the Marquess of Crewe, H. G. Wells and Viscount Samuel!

I am clearing up some of these chaps while Beryl is busy retyping the *Work in Hand* poems: when that is done, will get on with the first chapter, which is in such a mess that I need her to help me sort it out.

Have never had so many bouquets plugged at me as this week: the reviews of *Proceed*. The first volume was a slightly new taste for people and after a time they decided that they liked it: so this one was easy money. What is nice is that the intelligent reviewers are talking about Defoe and William Cobbett – Alan, don't forget Cobbett, and if you have no Cobbett handy I have a miscellany of his – thus showing the trend, which our *Yardstick* I hope will hasten, towards the plain style which you are now thinking about. I could never believe in Sir Thomas Browne: his books were only excuses, I used to think, for fine writing. The other sort of writer is Basil L.H. Did I tell you?: T. E. Lawrence once said to him: 'I think that why you write must be because you really have something to say.' A nice backhander, perfectly justified.

Jane Lye is thinking of escaping with her two children by going to S. Africa.

Ever   Robert

* Why not call it 'Ravenna'? or the angular mosaics are a literary problem to the ungeographic. O: there is one suggestion. In the last line should it be *their* history or *all* history? Really it is the town's history, not their own.

20 March 1941

Dear Alan,

Letters from all four contributors today with comments on one another: I feel like a correspondence club secretary or something.

About Schuyler: he was foreshadowed most curiously in Laura's 'John and I' back in 1924 or so. Now he is in the stage, after 'the woman's' death:

> . . . madder than before,
> With nothing but a nasty gangrened spot
> Where once had been his heart and scabrous grown.[7]

I quote from memory (book downstairs, self with a cold in bed). He always wants the last word even if he has to wake one up in the early hours of the morning to bumble it alcoholically in one's ear; the whack!

I am thrilled at your *Yardstick* progress. Have been held up again by reading some more proofs for Basil L.H. (his *Indirect Approach* reprint. Has a nasty habit of anachronistic reference – Russian steamroller getting up steam in 1762, etc.). But the whole epitome business is well under control and my introductory chapter going well, though slowly.

The mixed category heading is useful. E.g. Basil has: 'Coalition of England, Holland, Russia, Naples, Sardinia *and the Pope*,' rather than 'the Papal States' or the 'Vatican' or whatnot.

. . . .

We heard from John at Bulford Camp in the real ranks, pending his interview about a RAF job. He is Mr Aldridge to all his mates (Ginger, Bill, Lofty, Stan, etc.) and not in jest. It is just 'like one of those awful dreams of being back at school' for him; so difficult to realize that one must take the CSM seriously! But he is 'keeping his cut' all right.

Ever   Robert

Norman says: 'Alan has matured as a poet a lot.'

For a time Graves and Basil Liddell Hart were neighbours in Devon (and did not need to write to each other) until Liddell Hart moved to Westmorland in 1941. At the beginning of July he wrote to Graves telling him he was reading *Goodbye to All That* and on 10 July, when he was about halfway through the book, he wrote again, saying that it was curious 'to find how closely our respective footsteps in France coincided,' particularly between March and July 1916, when both had been wounded; he had even seen the same pair of corpses, a Welshman and a German who had bayoneted each other simultaneously in Mametz Wood, which Graves mentions in the book. The only point of fact he corrected was Graves's reference to the proportion of killed to wounded in his generation at Charterhouse; Graves had written: 'The proportions worked out at about four wounded to every one killed. Of the four, one was wounded seriously and the remaining three more or less lightly.' Liddell Hart, after consulting the official statistics, found that the ratio of killed to wounded was, in fact, considerably higher:

So far as one can gauge, the seriously and slightly wounded were about equal, so that the general proportion would run: 1 killed to 1 seriously wounded to 1 lightly wounded. It is interesting to find that this ratio seems to correspond with that which has occurred in recent 'blitzes' on our cities.

When he had finished reading the book he wrote again to Graves.

                                                    High Wray House
                                                    High Wray
14 July 1941   Near Ambleside
                                                    Westmorland

My dear Robert,
   I have now finished *Goodbye to All That* (the title reads somewhat ironically now, doesn't it?) It makes an *even* better

impression on me now than when I first read it, years ago. What a magnificently honest book!

The effect naturally gains from having come to know you, but my knowledge of you also gains from re-reading it. I wish I had been able to do so before.

A few further coincidences came in reading on beyond the point at which I wrote you last week. You followed me to Heilly – but I had been moved down to the Duchess of Westminster's before you arrived, to make room for you. There, interestingly, what your CO wrote to you (p. 278) is the same phrase as my CO reported about me – and what some of the men later put on a cigarette case which, most irregularly, they presented to me.

Afterwards, you went to a military job at Oxford where you would have gone in 1914 but for the war; and I went to a post at Cambridge, where I had been for a year before the war.

Your reflections about the war were more acute than mine at the time but very similar to what I came to later in reflection.

I like the ending of your book – the last phrase on page 441. But 'for information' will you please elucidate the reference to winning a prize at the Olympic Games, and to the statue in a London Park. (Historians desire facts and are provoked by allusiveness.)

. . . .

I agree with you as to the comedy of the new situation. Your observations are very shrewd, and I'm glad to have the chance of hearing them. I think, too, that there is a great deal in the national pathological factor.

I should love a chance of seeing your notes on G.B.S. and Fuller. This place grows more fascinating with each day spent here.

Warmest regards to all.

Yours very affectionately   Basil

Graves replied, painting on the date of the letter in characters one inch high, with a joking reference to an earlier comment of Hart's about having received 'your undated letter'.

(My dated letter of)
16 July 1941

Dear Basil:

Thank you so much for your long letters the more precious
because in mss. We are very busy here as we have no helpers.
Jenny's first nurse, Margaret Russell, a vigorous Newcastle Irish
woman comes here soon, but till then it is difficult. Tricia Carey is
away in London having a new steel jacket made, so my typing
must wait and we have nobody to dump William on. However, it
is nice to be alone with Beryl for a change – first time for nearly a
year.

Points: statue in London Park, and Olympic Games – *Goodbye
to All That* is probably full of similar examples of literary bad
manners. I got a bronze medal for a poem about Sport in the
Olympic Games 1924; the gold one went to Oliver Gogarty which
shows the sort of bad joke it was. Statue – Eric Kennington used
me for the 'Intellectual Soldier' in his group of three in the
Battersea Park 56th Division Memorial; each of the other two
soldiers was supposed to have some other characteristic. I am
anonymous, but very like what I was in 1920 when it was done.
Trees obscure the monument.

I think it was appropriate that you and I did not meet until we
did: neither of us was ready for it. It would have made for a
permanent misunderstanding.

My examination of texts is now complete up to the letter O,
except that today I have gone back to E and had a look at T. S.
Eliot. It is fantastic: he has twice as many errors or shortcomings
as anyone yet examined. I have also done preliminary work on
Shaw (a letter to the *New Statesman*) which has a record in the
Logical Weakness category. I am very dubious (to quote
B.H.L.H.'s favourite phrase) about a publisher but don't care:
have learned so much in the writing. Alan has just contributed a
most interesting chapter on Official English.

Interesting that Timoshenko is a Jew; hope that's a good sign.
Trotsky did the finest feat of military organization in the world
war (am I right?) in getting his Red Divisions up from the South
against the Whites in the North in impossibly quick time. Jew and
Russian combine well . . . So Jumbo Wilson brought it off in the

end! But only with the help of the Iraq column; and lost far too many men.

My son David expects to be posted as mortar-officer to a Service Battn. Lucky to get an independent command so soon: I hated being a platoon officer.

The blitz killed to injured ratio is higher than the ordinary military ratio chiefly because of children: children make bad surgical cases and shock kills them more easily. Trench warfare ratio higher than battle ratio: though better surgical facilities – there are more head wounds.

Thank you especially for one note on *Goodbye*: I had not hitherto been sure of those corpses in Mametz Wood: I was queer then and had since suspected it was a fanciful particularization of a general situation (like the statue by the Flemish Weitz at Brussels with the same motif but with sword for bayonet): glad to be reassured it actually occurred.

Love to all   Robert

There is a quotation in *Time*, June 16th: 'Parliamentary circles were angrily agog with suspicion that the obsolete and stubborn 1914 mentality was still in charge at GHQ, and that it had been getting a romantic gilding from the eloquence of Winston Churchill. Military historian Liddell Hart *whose theories of defensive warfare were blasted by Adolf Hitler's blitzkrieg tactics* broke his recent silence long enough to remark that the British people's hearts of oak were being betrayed by their leaders' oaken heads.' This, Basil, seems to me to be so damaging that you should write a letter of short protest and amendment and ask the *March of Time* people at Dean St, Soho, to see that it gets cabled to *Time*.

When he published his *Collected Poems* in 1938, Graves conscientiously omitted all of his war poems because 'they were too obviously written in the war-poetry boom' and, like most poems of the war, were essentially a form of higher journalism, not poetry.

In October 1941 Graves wrote an article for the *Listener* called 'Why has this War produced no War Poets?' It was reprinted in 1949 in *The Common Asphodel*, a collection of Graves's critical essays, with 'An Additional Comment: . . . Re-reading *Poems from the Forces* (1941), *More Poems from the Forces* (1943), and individual volumes of poetry published since by soldiers, sailors and airmen, I have come to the conclusion that Alun Lewis was the only poet of consequence who served and wrote in World War Two.'[8]

Lewis and Graves never met but were 'friends by correspondence'. The correspondence began in November 1941, after Graves had mentioned Lewis in a BBC programme on war poetry. At that time Lewis, a Welshman born in 1915, was a second lieutenant in the South Wales Borderers and had not yet published his poems in book form (his first book was *Raider's Dawn*, 1942).

His letters compare very interestingly with Graves's letters of the First World War, having the same essential theme: 'the difficulty of reconciling his life as a poet with his life as a soldier.'[9]

4 November 1941

c/o 7 Elm Grove
Aberdare
Glamorgan

Dear Robert Graves,

Please excuse this letter-writing – I suppose you get plagued by it – it's not in my line, but I have something I want to say.

About the poem of mine you quoted in your talk on *War Poetry* – it was called 'The Soldier'. It seemed to me you were using it to express a point of view I don't endorse: to wit, the isolation or *difference* of the poet. It was Spender's[10] fault in the first instance, for lifting the poem out of its context. It was originally only *part* of a poem, not a complete one; and as a part of a poem it's appearing in the Selection of my poems which Allen and Unwin are publishing shortly. It doesn't have the same effect in its full context, but is muted and finally harmonized in the second part, where I was watching the flash and play of finches round an old chalk-pit, which were:

> . . . As beautiful
> And as indifferent to me
> As England is, this spring morning.

By which I mean that the isolation is not that of a cultured gent timidly roughing it with a blunt gang, but the simple, cosmic loneliness that is as natural to a man today as to the old Ecclesiast.

I don't theorize or belong to schools more than I can help; apart from knowing where I stand in politics and in love I take what comes. I've never felt lonely in the Army, in the ranks anyway (I'm just going as a Subaltern to the SWB), because I've never lacked comrades: wherefore I feel it necessary to state my position to one whose poems I place second to Yeats and whose poetic influence, in setting a noble standard, I anything but undervalue. If you do read my poems or *Collected Short Stories* when they appear you'll mark them, as perhaps you mark this letter, as immature. But I hope you won't find them precious . . . I'm stuck right into this world mess and haven't much patience with the isolationists, though half my friends are COs! And I don't want to be quoted as proof that the élite of letters should be allowed to travel 'first'.

Yours sincerely,   Alun Lewis

6 *November 1941*

Dear Alun Lewis:

Thank you for writing. If you care to send me your book when it comes out I'll send you my new poems which are being published soon by Hogarth Press along with some by Norman Cameron and Alan Hodge. I am sorry about the mistake: that is the sort of thing that happens when Spenders and people take liberties with one's work.

About the 'isolation' of the poet. There was the Goethe–Byron, etc., Romantic isolation, taken into aesthetic delicacy by the late Victorians: of course there was a reaction to that, which became more and more violent until the poets became guilty of having any sensibilities at all and felt that they must learn from the simple pick and shovel man. That was silly. I hope that when you say you know where you stand in politics that does not mean *that*. To feel cosmic loneliness I think means merely that one is short of friends who also think cosmically. Since you are a poet I assume that you use the word 'cosmically' literally, the cosmos being the poetic ordering of mere mass; my conviction is that a poet who takes his function seriously and continuously rejects from his life and works everything *dis*orderly finds the friends he needs. About Yeats – You decently admit your immaturity (to be precious is to be ashamed of immaturity, so unless you have included very early work in your book I don't expect to find it precious) and please don't think me impelled by any unworthy motive when I suggest that to admire Yeats as strongly as you do may be a sign of immaturity. Test him again, by all the maturest tests you know, and see whether his glamour is really the reflection of poetic fire and not a piece of post-druidic magic, cast by a little man, over young minds.

To turn to a happier subject. You are very lucky in the SWB. I was once attached, with my command of 200 RW Fusiliers, to an SWB* battalion near Rhyl and have always thought kindly of them; and I knew their regular battalion in the 1st Division in 1915.

Let the élite of letters travel 'First'. They will be with the Generals and Black Market Bosses and why not? (Did you ever ride on a locomotive? I did once: it was grand!)[11]

Good luck   Robert Graves

If you are ever down this way . . .
* 'The 24th' have some very nice unusual battle honours – so far as I remember Rorke's Drift, Kian-Chow, and the Maori War of 1860 or so – the Maoris had a charming respect for them as enemy–friends. See also my *Sergeant Lamb of the Ninth* for their part in the American War of Independence.

Lewis replied:

15 November 1941[12]

Dear Robert Graves,

I was surprised, excited and honoured by your letter: it's as well I'm trying to write with my wife's pen: otherwise my language might become Oriental. Thank you very much for writing. I'm always beginning and beginning; no sooner do I reach a place from which I can look back, than the scene vanishes in darkness and I set out again. So your letter was a real Samaritan. I would dearly like to call on you: *ça se peut*. And I count it a privilege to send you my poems, though I am not one who can face the judgement seat with equanimity. If, however, I am able to lift my eyes, that will be a great deal. There is only one thing I want to say beforehand. If you read any of my work, please know beforehand the course from which my writing comes. *Humility*. A dangerous thing to have in one, but without it one is useless to do good. It is the source of all my long struggles, for it brings me into conflict with self-pity and pity for the world, with authority and presumption on the part of those who are not humble, with intolerance and cruelty, and with submission. Because of it I have never joined any party or school, but recently I have been able to identify myself with many men I have met in the ranks, who have their own integrity and willingness to endure. And that is why I say I know where I stand in politics and in love, and have no desire to travel first.

I am writing short stories of barracks and OCTUs and detachments and glasshouse during this leave. Typing out scribbled poems from my Woolworth notebooks. Reading Malraux and David Jones again, and T. E. Lawrence's letters. Your *Sergeant Lamb* I haven't read yet, but am waiting for W. H. Smith's to deliver it. The Army should run a monthly of its own, a sort of *Horizon*. I would like to sub-edit the Middle Eastern branch. Can you influence the IGS to consider such a venture? Though perhaps there is too much literature and not enough fighting as it is. Anyway, there is no need to be lonely, unless like Spender, one can think of nothing to write about except the last love affair, or, like Treece,[13] the Pre-Raphaelite chill. The only thing I fear is that I won't outlive this war, or rather live long enough to do something positive towards realizing for others the miracle that I know is possible.

Excuse an acolyte writing so seriously. And again, many thanks.
Yours   Alun Lewis

PS. I'm sending a sample of a new venture I am running by Welsh poets and artists from Taliesin and Aneirin in the 10th century to Dylan Thomas and others in the 20th.

15 November 1941

Dear Alun Lewis,
    Your letter came by the same post as one from Keidrych Rhys[14] who has got himself into muddy waters in that *Listener* correspondence. Spender is behaving in a very disgusting way, and really Rhys's fault is, as I have told him, the familiar Welsh fault of over-impulsive warmth: it has landed him in seeming contradictions which the Sassenach, who is comparatively free of this fault, sees as dishonesty. The important thing is not to get involved in literary politics.
    Humility is also a Welsh characteristic: and a characteristic of poets, as they learn the impossibility of poetry by experience. But I

think it is important to make the humility something that one puts between oneself and one's impossibly high standards, not between oneself and others. After all, nobody can possibly succeed in being Alun Lewis so well as yourself, and gradually you in that favourable position of being in his position can find out far better than anyone else what being him entails. It is also the best possible criterion – I mean, humility of self before standard – for judging the presumption of others. And (as you say) it therefore brings you in conflict with people who infringe on your personal life by their inability to govern their own with humility.

I think David Jones's humility has been misdirected: that long book about the RWF, for all its endearing Welshness, led him into an effect of literary ambition. I do not like synthetic work, from Virgil on through the centuries – including Milton and, in the case of D.J., I knew too many of the sources. I have never seen his paintings.

Be glad the Army has no *Horizon*. The egregious Ian Hay[15] would edit it, for a certainty.

To think one won't outlive the War is almost everyone's bogie – I had it for a time, in 1915, yet did – just as almost every mother thinks she won't survive her first confinement.

Spend a week-end here when you like – first phoning in case we have our house full – as this week-end we did with my eldest son on embarkation leave and everyone flocking – your wife too, would she like?

Thank you for the poems. I could write a great deal about them, but can't allow myself the luxury of spending time from the great amount of work I have to do today on other things. But, say, about Peter and Paul. This might mean to me any of several things but not one of them really clicks for me (am I stupid?)

a) reference to robbing Peter to pay Paul.

b) reference to the paper game in the nursery of Peter and Paul.

c) reference to the coincidence of these saints' festivals.

d) reference to Skelton's lampoon about

Gentle Paul lay down thy sweard
For Peter of Westminster hath shaven thy beard.

Tell me when you see me about this and other points.
  Signing off now.
  Good luck   Robert Graves

I prefer Taliesin to Dylan Thomas; this is a very mild way of indicating my feelings on both. Though I have only read Tn. in (literal) translation, I am also aware of his metrical marvels. D.Ts., whenever I come across his trail, is . . .

I haven't read Malraux: but guess that he made his war the excuse for a book rather than the inevitable subject.

That autumn Graves had decided to write a historical novel about Jason and the Argonauts, but postponed the idea when suddenly, at the beginning of November (while making the bed) he had an intuition about Milton, as he wrote in a letter to Alan Hodge (8 November):

I have decided not to do the *Golden Fleece* story, for I had a sudden inspiration that I know all about Milton and his wife whom he was living with when he wrote about divorce. Historically I know very little and will have to get all the relevant books together – tell me, didn't you read up Mrs Milton for Laura? Can you give me any information about books, etc.? A pity all your notes are in USA. The title is obvious: *The Tangles of Neaera's Hair*! because hair was his obsession and bound up tightly with his Samson complex. I have often been in Mrs M.'s sitting room at Forest Hill near Oxford.

He began writing *Wife to Mr Milton* (the 'obvious' title was soon abandoned) and at the same time continued working on *The Reader Over Your Shoulder*, analysing the prose of various 'prominent people', including I. A. Richards.

26 November 1941

Dear Alan:

I had never read Richards before – not word for word – what a crook he seems to be! We have a very good sort of gay Wing Commander down here, called 'Crab' Searle – last night he told me he had recently gone down for a court of inquiry into embezzlement at Cambridge. I said 'I bet the College cooks were at the bottom of it.' He said, rather surprised: 'They were! – how did you know? – feeding 170 College servants on RAF rations – yet we couldn't pin a thing on them!' When I had said that, in a poetic flash of intuition, I had been thinking of Richards, Leavis, Ogden and Coy in terms of college cooks. This seems muddled – I had, and have, a slight temperature – but it all works out if you don't tug the knots too tight.

Thank you for the *Lamb* errors. I think that when you have got the second *Lamb*, now called *Proceed, Sergeant Lamb*, you'll see that there is more than episodic interest to excuse the story – it is about the fates of war, with no dropped threads anywhere, Lamb being such a thorough fellow – until at the end Lamb and Smutchy are conversing in 1824, at a respectable tavern in Parliament Street, Dublin, about the various sticky ends of the rebel generals.

I spent all yesterday on Senator Hiram Johnson of California (an anti-Roosevelt speech). Today I don't feel capable of any work and am a-bed. The evacuees are finally going on Friday. Hardinge[16] will be here for the week-end and Jenny from martyred Bristol.

Good luck. Ever   Robert

What an admirable Coleridge 'quote': for our title page! And what an admirable letter from Sally.

In February 1942 Graves received an advance copy of Alun Lewis's first book of poems, *Raider's Dawn*.

20 February 1942

Dear Alun Lewis:

Many thanks for your poems, which came with an illiterate letter from your publisher. I do like the book, despite the disturbing sensuality which, though appropriate I suppose to the time and the place of writing, distracts the attention from the poetic argument. You will know yourself which the good ones are, though you may be attached, for other than poetic reasons, to others not so good; I don't think there is ever any doubt which are *the* poems, the necessary ones, and which are the circumstantial or extraneous ones. Your wife will know, almost certainly, if you are in doubt. But it is a very delicate matter for anyone, even your wife, to discuss this until a few years have gone by and you have written a whole lot more, and the wheat can be sorted from the tares. I could say a great deal in criticism of individual poems: e.g.

about 'The Swan's Way' which seems to me to be two poems, neither of them complete, welded together by an ingenious third stanza, like the Chimaera in the Homeric tag. But that would be ungrateful because there is a strong poetic thread going through the book, and I do wish you luck to get through this war and get on with your job as a poet without the hindrances of your present unnatural life of soldiering.

The book which I offered as barter for yours is in print but not yet published. Where may I send it when it appears?

Good luck and gratitude   Robert Graves

	D Coy
	6th SWB
1 March 1942	c/o GPO Ipswich
	Suffolk

Dear Robert Graves,

Thank you for the letter you sent me. It came before any critic opened his mouth, and said all I could ever hope for. It found me at home on a week's leave, and gave a quiet fortitude to my exaltation at being free – I wasn't thinking then in terms of days, but simply of being free – to write and live in my own natural way. Thank you most of all for not dropping me into the bag labelled 'war poets', but instead taking me as a human being with, you say, a touch of grace to compensate for all the dullness and dejected obedience that today's events impose upon me.

I value your opinion more highly than any other man's. I can't express my joy at your letter better than that.

I would have liked to know in more detail your criticism, but I think I can guess much of it. The poems are a mixture of crops, not pure Virginia I know well. But I don't know which I'd cut out without suppressing them all.

You once suggested some explanations for the Peter and Paul line in the little poem. My mother used to put bits of paper on her fingers and play a game of hiding the fingers and returning them. 'Two little sparrows sitting on a wall, One named Peter one named Paul. Fly away Peter, fly away Paul. Come back Peter, come back Paul.' That, and the bombing of St Paul's and St Peter's Westminster, are my sources. Not recondite.

I wrote like hell while I was home, and also saw Jack Yeats' paintings and Moore's and Spencer's and Ardizzone's in London.

And a lovely knockabout peasant opera of Mussorgsky's –
Sorotchinski Fair. Now I am shivering in a fireless hut again and
wishing to God this protracted blanco age would crumble for us
as it has for other more – or less – fortunate soldiers. *Que faire?*
 Yours thankfully and sincerely,   Alun Lewis

Lewis's battalion went to India towards the end of 1942 and there
he had an 'alarmingly prolific' phase of writing poetry; he wished to
make a second volume of poems and asked Graves to choose, in
collaboration with his wife Gweno, which poems to include. Graves
sent Gweno a list of suggestions and received Lewis's reply to them
in March 1944, a few days before Lewis died in the Arakan, close
to where Graves's son David had been killed. Lewis's second volume
of poems was published posthumously (*Ha! Ha! Among the Trumpets*, 1945) with an introduction by Graves.

Though he received three letters from Lewis in India, Graves only
wrote one, in May 1943, in reply, giving news of his son David,
who was also in India: he was just about to post the letter when he
learned that his son was missing, believed killed, and so did not post
it. Lewis's last letter to Graves was included in the introduction to
Ha! Ha! Among the Trumpets.

Graves and Hodge finished *The Reader Over Your Shoulder* and,
while collecting the permissions to quote the various people criticized
in it, considered writing a third book together, this time about
poetry.

31 July 1942

Dear Alan:
 Surely we have the Angell permission? With that warning
against using it to stir up sedition?
 I will ask Beryl to type out a letter to Lord Keynes.
 Yes, let's put that book about poetry on to simmer very, very
slowly. I don't know whether we'd need to quote contemporary
poems to the extent you suggest.
 Here are a couple of notes.
 1) The natural tendency when one writes really carefully to
return to the spirit of 17th-century language: the sane time when
Elizabethan–Jacobean exuberance had died down, and the

312

Augustans hadn't yet begun to over-simplify: and before
metaphors had begun to die and stink (e.g. when if you said 'I was
within an ace of winning', you knew that *ace* meant a pip of dice
in a game of 'who throws highest?').

2) The aura or halo, or whatever, that clings to the name 'poet'
in spite of the lamentable history of bad poetic behaviour. How
this shows the dim popular awareness of the supernatural power
in poetry: a poem being the magic circle in which poets by their
strange dealings with familiar things enclose a living power. The
existence of charlatan poets who try to reproduce a genuine poetic
phenomenon by literary means (gorblimy vocabulary, metrical
tricks, etc.) is an indirect indication that the real thing still exists.

Writing a poem for me is putting myself in a very odd state
indeed in which I am excessively sensitive to interruption – I can
hear, or think I can hear, people doing disturbing things behind
shut doors three houses off – and really suffer very painfully, as
though I were performing a major operation on my own skull.
Each version I write strikes me as wholly new and unfamiliar
when I go over it after a few hours' interval – I can't remember
what it is about, or even how it scans. Just as one cannot
remember a dream that takes place in a deep level of sleep, where
one's imaginative thought works on a wholly different principle
from the normal. There is a great deal of difference between a
poem which is to some extent artificial and induced – and a poem
which is wholly natural, necessary and unpreconceived; in the real
poem one has all the cords cut which tie one to ordinary thought,
and one proceeds with the frightening sense of swimming for the
first time out of one's depth and having to reach safety. Poetry is a
sort of Jack's beanstalk – I think this must be a very, very old folk
tale from somewhere or other where the Indian rope-trick and
mango-tree trick originated – there are ogres and princes when
you get to the top. Conventional poems are like the beanstalks one
sends up poles. The poles down in this village are very tall and
very metrically joined, very eighteenth-century. Modern poems are
like beans grown not from magic seed, but of the sort usually sent
up poles: but the poles aren't used and the poems all get tangled
up with one another and try to climb up any handy bit of weed in
the neighbourhood. (Hark at me!)

Well, I have written three or four poems in the last few days:

including two grotesque ones – did I mention in my last letter?
One goes:

> The Lion Faced Boy at the Fair
> And the Heir Apparent
> Were equally slow at recalling people's faces.
> Whenever they met, incognito, in the Brazilian
> Pavilion, the Row, and such-like places,
> They exchanged, it is said, their briefest nods
> Like gods of dissimilar races.

Love   Robert

Stocks of *Count Belisarius* had been lost in the 1940 Blitz and at the
beginning of 1943 Graves tried to persuade the publisher, Cassell's,
to reprint the book on the strength of recommendations from General Sir Archibald Wavell who, urged by Liddell Hart, wrote to
Cassell's saying he greatly appreciated the book; from Liddell Hart
himself, who had already acknowledged his debt to the book in the
preface to the 1941 reprint of *The Strategy of Indirect Approach*,
which contained a new chapter, inspired by a reading of *Count
Belisarius*, on Byzantine strategy, especially Belisarius's; and from
Winston Churchill who wrote to Graves saying how much he had
enjoyed and admired the book, which was one of the few he had
read during the progress of the war. It was, however, not reprinted
until 1948.

In January 1943 Graves was writing *The Golden Fleece*, which he
had resumed after finishing *Wife to Mr Milton*, and correcting the
proofs of *The Reader Over Your Shoulder* with Alan Hodge (who
was in the process of divorcing Beryl).

6 January 1943

Dear Alan:

Thanks for proofs. Could I have back the earlier set (1–192) or
has Norman[17] lost it? I will need it for queries that Cape's may
send. No, I didn't expect you to do more than you have done on
the proofs. It is an impossible book and if I had known how
impossible it would be – but I suppose I'd have worked on it just
the same. It's a necessary book I feel.

The Argonauts are now sheltering under the lee of the

Peninsula of Boz in the Sea of Marmora. I am really enjoying the book now, and have solved most of the geographical contradictions of the story. Kingsley's *The Heroes* is a funny book, but quite helpful in places: he had access to some quite good geographical material.

My blitzed *Belisarius* can't be reprinted, no paper, despite Churchill's kind consent to the reprint of his letter, and Wavell's boost for Belisarius, and the fact that at some Army Training Schools for officers the study of Belisarius's tactics is compulsory – they write to me for copies and I can't help them. It seems rather silly, with so much paper available for silly British Council cultural books about the beauties of English scenery, children, women, etc.

We all have flu or heavy colds and it never stops raining.

Sorry about your financial condition. Ours is precarious, perpetually; but there is always another book to be written for an advance to pay the income-tax of the previous one.

This divorce business is indeed silly: how much better the Mahommedan formula 'I divorce you, I divorce you, I divorce you,' spoken in front of witnesses, and the woman goes back to the father's home with her dowry and a decent sum for wear and tear. Nancy's divorce of me is held up by her private snag of refusing to be Graves – v – Graves; yet no solicitor will accept her reading of the Law that she is still Nicholson – v – Graves.

. . . .

Am just reading Xenophon for the first time: what a good book the *Anabasis* is!

Love   Robert

The Reader Over Your Shoulder (*TROYS*) was published in May.

13 July 1943

Dear Alan:

Thanks for long letter. I disagree with the critics about those historical chapters. They are short, but necessary to the argument, and it would have been awful to have to deal with E. M. Forster, Virginia Woolf and other contemporary giants and giantesses!

. . . .

I have been worried by thinking about poetry and finding that all the poems that one thinks of as most poetic in the romantic

315

style are all intricately concerned with primitive moon-worship. This sounds crazy, and I fear for my sanity; but it *is* so. The old English ballads like *Kemp Owyne*, the *Lykewake Dirge*, are all composed with a sort of neurosis-compulsion for arranging things in 3s (although the stanza is a four line one) which is the chief characteristic of the Moon Goddess – Triple Goddess – ritual; and the 17th-century *Loving Mad Tom* poem, which is generally regarded as the most 'purely poetic' of all anonymous English compositions is a perfect compendium of Ashtaroth–Cybele–Hecate worship – not a single element omitted. Of course, Apollo originally pinched Parnassus and Pegasus from the Moon Goddess. And the Muse, whom poets habitually address, was the Moon originally in her Mouse aspect. The history of English poetry has been the modifying of the original moon-poetry, which is stressed, with sun-poetry (intellectual, Apollo poetry) which is measured in regular beats and metres. Let me ramble on for a bit more: I find that Shakespeare, almost habitually, though using a five foot line only uses three interest-centres or operative words in any line; the rest is syntax or words of no particular accentuation – Chaucer seems to use four as habitually. Chaucer was very much an Apollonian: a very good poet too.

This may lead me anywhere and I am so anxious not to get dogmatic or psychological. But I find myself making the Bards into Moon-men and the minstrels into Sun-men.

Help!

Love   Robert

I have just heard from Cape that *TROYS* has sold 2000 out of 2800 copies, and wants to know by how much it should be cut down to form a concise edition, there being no paper for more copies of the full edition.

In 1943 the work of Lynette Roberts, another young Welsh poet, came to Graves's notice and impressed him. She was the wife (though she kept her maiden name) of Keidrych Rhys, with whom Graves also corresponded. A correspondence about poetry began between Graves and Roberts, who offered to look up things for him in the British Museum and to send him essential source books for the book about poetry he intended to write with Alan Hodge, and later did write, alone; the book was originally called *The Roebuck in the Thicket* but later became *The White Goddess*.

About sixty-eight letters passed between Graves and Roberts about *The White Goddess* between 1943 and 1946, when they met for the first time.

1 September 1943

Dear Mrs Rhys,

(It is stupid – I can't remember your first name – and your letter is unsigned – forgive me!)

Very many thanks for your very helpful letter and the *englynion*. I really am a very ignorant person but it happens that I was the first Englishman, so far as I know, to write a Welsh *englyn* according to the fixed ninety-odd rules. I did this when I was thirteen and the result is in my father's not very profound book *Welsh Poetry Old and New* (1913). I found the consonantal sequences too oppressive for English and modified them, slightly only, in a set of four sequent *englyns* (consecutive in thought) when I was 14!

They began, I remember:

> *To a Pot of White Heather in an Old*
> *Woman's Cottage Window*

> Thou, a poor woman's fairing – white heather
> Witherest from the ending
> Of summer's bliss to the sting
> Of winter's grey beginning . . .

This brought about my discovery of the useful trick of rhyming stressed with unstressed syllables, which I introduced into English poetry and which has since been copied by several poets; and of the use of assonance, which Wilfred Owen learned from me.

The book I have in mind is about English poetry in general and I guess that Gaelic and Brythonic influences are brought to bear in three ways: first by survival in folk memory, then by way of Brittany in the Arthurian romances and in the Irish *Gawain and the Green Knight*, then by cultural contact in Tudor times with Wales and Ireland.

I don't suppose there is any strong historical connexion between Brythonic and Greek poetry; but there was cultural contact between the two races from at least 300 BC, and there is a Greek legend that Apollo came from the British Isles to Delos.

But what is plain is that at a certain socio-religious stage in every western and southern nation, you get a Llew–Lugh–Apollo god who patronizes poetry of a *bardic* sort. You even get it in Japan, and among the Maoris! What I am interested in, as well, is the previous stage – marked in Ireland by the three Brigids. In Wales. . .?

I am very grateful to you for your offer to look things up for me in the BM, and hope that when I get really down to the job I'll find you ready to help me. I know that I can count on Keidrych and you not to let this line of study be prematurely advertised – it is too good to get into the hands of chatterers.

Yes, the Greeks went in strongly for epigrams and epitaphs. The most celebrated collection is the *Greek Anthology*. They are not so tightly laced in rules as the Welsh, or as the Japanese ones, but that is because Apollo still kept his connexion with the Muses who were pre-bardic – if you follow me.

The best thing about the *englyn* is its extraordinary memorability: this compensates for the dehydration of sense. I think yours are perfectly in the tradition.

Looking forward to Keidrych's letter.

Yours very sincerely   Robert Graves

PS. What is interesting me at the moment is the numbers 3 and 7 in Bardic poetry – you get the obsession with these numbers in the syllable-counted *englyn*, and in the tercets and triads. You get it also in the accentual poetry of English nursery rhymes and Northern ballads. Who has ever discussed this in its literary or religious aspect?

The English poetic tradition, in its highest sense, is predominantly Celtic. The Greek influence was analogical rather than direct. The Scandinavian tradition helped to relax the bardic bands.

In October Liddell Hart wrote to Graves asking: 'Can you tell me anything about Robert Nichols, whose *Anthology of War Poetry 1914–1918* I have just been reading?'

No date

?: Libel ?:

My dear Basil:

Robert ~~Nichols~~ — I never answered your query about him. He was an unbalanced undergraduate in 1914 who pelted Lloyd George with mangolds and pheasants at the Union – you remember the political context, I expect. Then he went to the war, spent 3 weeks with the Gunners in a quiet part of the line, fell off a roof, went home as shell-shocked, slept with 17 prostitutes in 3 weeks and got a bad dose. As his mother was in the looney-bin and he himself was always pretty unsettled, this did him no good; he recovered, was a terrific comet of success in poetry in 1917, went to the USA to lecture, told frightful lies about his war service and involved me in them, was always having passionate terrible love affairs – one with Nancy Cunard ended with her smacking his face in the Victory Ball at – where was it – I forget – but the smack resounded. He had written a book of poems about their love affair, you see – that was before she took to negroes . . . Then he played the genius for a bit, went to Japan, Tokyo University, as Professor, did something awful and was saved from destruction by a medical certificate and the intervention of Mrs (Banker) Lamont. Broke his heart for Daisy Kennedy the pianist, who married Bo Moserewitch [*sic*]. Went to Los Angeles to be a copy writer in Douglas Fairbanks's circus: wrote some articles in *The Times* about it – I guess 1927 or so. Married a Miss (Bacon – rich) Denny, a niece of Roger Quilter. Became a prosperous poet at Yew Tree College, Winchelsea; lost a kidney; became such a bore that wife left him recently – three or four years ago. Is now rather living on past glories. His chief gift is musical. I like him but he is too much of an embarrassment to have about. His father is (or was?) a well-known Edwardian man of letters, W. B. Nichols.

Yours ever   Robert

In November Lynette Roberts sent Graves *Celtic Researches* (1809) by the Reverend Edward Davies, 'a brilliant but hopelessly erratic Welsh scholar of the early nineteenth century' (Graves's comment on him in *The White Goddess*).

4 December 1943

Dear Lynette

Very many thanks for your letter with the notes and for all your efforts, in your obviously hard-pressed time.

The debt I owe you is greater than you realize, because that Edward Davies book you lent me, though crazy in parts, contains the key (the relations of bardic letters to months and seasons, which he himself doesn't realize; but he gives all the elements in the equation, so it is easily worked out) to Celtic religion: a key which unlocks a succession of doors in Roman and Greek religion, and (because the Jewish religion was a Semite one engrafted on a Celtic stock) also unlocks the most obstinate door of all – the story of the Nativity and Crucifixion. I am not a Christian, or a believer in religious hocus-pocus, but I can now make out a good historical case for the more improbable gospel elements and have been able to confirm my thesis, which was based wholly on Welsh–Irish–Greek–Roman–Gallic religious tradition, by a study of early Christian literature (the Apocryphal Gospels and Acts and 'Sayings of Christ') and Egyptian and Talmudic tradition, and of Josephus, etc.

The whole Christian business is badly in need of clearing up. Its formidably crystallized errors and inconsistencies get in everyone's way. Yet it can't be cleared up by persecution or ridicule: only by reason. And reason transforms it into an ethical system, based on historical and poetic fact, which one can either accept as OK or reject as unsuitable to one's temperament, but which requires no 'faith' and invites no incredulity. And until it *is* cleared up poetry is hampered by having no valid, constant set of references which all initiates of poetry can learn to use and love and refine individually. The old bards (before bardism got paralysed by technical traditionalism) had a lovely time with their Secret Doctrine, which seems to have been shared by their colleagues in a number of countries: a set of nations in fact roughly corresponding with 'Christendom'.

This letter is incomplete.

In April Graves received a copy of Liddell Hart's *Thoughts on War* and another of his books, published at the same time, called *Why Don't We Learn from History?*

1 May 1944

My dear Basil,

Very many thanks for the large book and the small one. I think that the answer to the question 'Why don't we learn from History?' is, as you say, that History is so fraudulent; and in fact all that 'we' learn is the technique of distortion. I have been studying this in some detail in the last two years, in the religious contexts of successive European faiths; and in a way I sympathize with the distorters. I mean: if there is a deeply rooted religious habit of sacrificing one's eldest son and marrying one's daughter which has to be changed for social reasons, then the religious myth in which the habit is embodied has to be changed too and given historical validity. 'So and so worshipped the Old Gods and was punished by the New Gods by being tricked into killing his son and marrying his daughter, after which he killed himself in a fit of remorse.'

Similarly, if the Scots Guards ran away at the Battle of Guildford Court House and had to be stopped from running any further by being shelled by Lord Cornwallis, it is impossible to give that event a clear niche in History while the Scots Guards are still in being and relying on regimental tradition to steady them. That your French Generals look to the future of French morale by faking orders is reprehensible from the scientific point of view, but rather grand from the human point of view. Personally, I never fake in this sense, but, as I say, I can see the point: to lie is a sacred duty to all people who wish to uphold sacred traditions.

The question then boils down to this: 'Can we afford to disband the Scots Guards?' Can we afford to uncanonize St Fulano de Tal?[18]

The Jesus question is a difficult one. The real story was historically much better than the fake one: Christ emerges from it a bigger man. But it had to be concealed for political reasons by those who had his teachings closest to their hearts; and eventually got forgotten.

Jenny is on a senior officers' court at Stannington. Sam and Catherine are here.

Crab has written a book on the technique of air-invasion: but on the secret list. He has been here and is in fine spirits.

Love to Kathleen and yourself   Robert

In a short letter of reply on 10 May Liddell Hart wrote:

Many thanks also for your letter of May 1st – which, as usual, was most stimulating to thought. I agree that one must understand the view point of those who are moved to fake history from a sense of duty to sacred traditions – and I hope that I have shown an adequate recognition of their point of view in my *Thoughts on War* – but my own conclusion has been that, on balance, the debit exceeds the profit. Some light on this practical question is thrown by opportunities of comparing the *esprit* of new corps like the Tank Corps with your example of the Scots Guards.

Also at the beginning of May Graves wrote to Lynette Roberts, whose first book, *Poems*, was soon to be published, and included in the letter an appreciation of her poems for her to pass on to her publishers, Fabers, which they used to promote the book.

No date [May 1944]

My dear Lynette,

May I keep those books a few weeks longer?

My son Sam has just gone up to N. Wales and I have given him an odd commission. I know a farmer near Mur y Castell (Tomen y Mur) who has found an ancient tile with what he thinks is the pad-mark of a wolf on it – but I am pretty certain, now I have read the relevant passage in the Mabinogion, it is a sacred paw mark of Arthur's hound Cabal. Sam is going to try to get it. What shall we do if he succeeds? There was a sacred pad-mark of Cabal's worshipped on the hill above Builth, but that was on a rock and this is on a tile. I saw it in 1939 and hope it is still extant.

. . . .

I heard from Alan today: he was praising your poetic intelligence.

Gweno wrote to ask me for a foreword to Alun's poems; I am bad at that sort of thing and did not know Alun personally but have said that I would. If you have anything that you think should be said, please let me know.

I hope you don't think my *Dog Roebuck*[19] is nonsense.
Love to K.   Robert

What gets me about the end of 'Orarium' is its exact conformity
with the most ancient poetic secrets of all, the ones that I am
exploring in *The Roebuck in the Thicket* (now a much longer
book than when you saw it). The last three lines are the end-of-
the-year calendar formula in all languages and literatures. The
man of God *has* to have sorrel red hair to be authentic.
  Quotes:

> Lynette Roberts is one of the few true poets now writing. Her best is
> the best: for example, the perfect close to 'Orarium'.
>
> Signed R.G.

(If you care to pass this on to Faber's.)

Graves wrote and rewrote *The Roebuck in the Thicket*, continually
expanding his argument, and at the same time wrote a historical
novel based on his biblical studies, called *King Jesus*.
  Alan Hodge had ceased to collaborate on the book about poetry,
though all this time Graves was testing his ideas and 'queer discoveries' on him to 'reassure me that they make sense'.

12 June 1944

Dearest Alan:
  Enclosed is an excuse for writing. The country here is
delightfully quiet again, though stocks of liquor are not yet
replenished. Today I sent off the book which began with the
Taliesin business and ended all over the place: called the *Roebuck
in the Thicket* and quite long. If Cape publish it I'll get some spare
sets of proof for sending around. It goes into some of the oddest
corners of thought, e.g. the mythical connection of Jesus with the
holly-tree – by the way, I lost that sheet of mss. and fortunately
the salvage men didn't collect our paper and I rooted it out –
which is based on the mythical identity of the holly with the holly-
oak; and of the connection of the holly-oak with the cochineal
insect; and of St Joseph's family with the cochineal trade; and of
Jesus and Mary with scarlet in Coptic tradition. I find that all such
myths are based on some honest-to-God *fact* and if university
professors of Greek and Celtic knew a little common botany and

zoology and ichthyology *and* mineralogy and conchology and anatomy they would know what everything was about in their legends. Berwyn has been of great help lately in getting me the anatomic low on why Dionysus wore buskins and Hephaestos golden foot-supports and why Jacob's sinew of the thigh was shrunken: it makes a very nice story of how the sacred king was purposely lamed at his Coronation bath by an inward dislocation of the hip which made his leg permanently flexed, so that he could never put his heel to the ground – the heel being his Achilles heel. You won't believe this until I show you the supporting evidence, but it makes a good story until you do. As you know, Jesus was lamed and I have a wonderful Hebrew and Aramaic scholar[20] here who is helping me find out how and where the laming was done. It was done on Mt Tabor, I think, with the help of a griffon-vulture as a piece of ritual furniture, a precipice, and the 'cabbages' from the centre of date-palms. What complicated minds they had! Or is it my own?

I forget whether I told you that I know about Taliesin's date. In my argument I mention the Arthurian 'Sir Kay' as one of the answers to the poem riddle: which means not earlier than 12th century AD. But I have also found by internal evidence that he had studied in Ireland – as he quotes a book which was available somewhere in Ireland at that date and nowhere else in the world unless he could read Ethiopian . . . At the last moment I found a very neat comment on my theory that there was a Romano-British bardic cult of Christ as merely one of a series of theophanies of the same chap; in Lampudius's life of Alexander Severus, Emperor (222–235), who was a good chap and had a private chapel sacred to Alexander the God (of whom he himself was a sort of son), Apollo, Abraham, Orpheus and Christ. Isn't that odd? The Spartans in BC 300 claimed to be descended from Abraham; believe it or not.

Hardinge has parachuted into France but no news yet from him.

Isn't it a bore having no St James's Library? Books are so hard to come by.

I am now going back to the Jesus book and I am afraid that when that appears my Companion of Honour which you foretold me will be no longer available, however discreet my touch.

We send our love, and to Peggy.   Robert

In July Hodge became the book critic for the *Evening Standard*.

16 July 1944

My dear Alan:

That *Evening Standard* job is enviable. Do it as well as Arnold
Bennett did and you'll have it as a stand-by for years. The reason
of Bennett's success was that he was not part of a clique and only
wrote about what really interested him; and that he had a good
working knowledge of English Literature. I agree about fiction, yet
if I were in your place I'd review Agatha's[21] new book *Towards
Zero* because for better or worse Agatha's best work is, like P. G.
Wodehouse and Noel Coward's best work, the most characteristic
pleasure-writing of this epoch and will appear one day in all
decent literary histories. As *writing* it is not distinguished, but as
story it is superb. Agatha was an only child who told herself long
stories in a small room in a big house. A lot of her early work is
crude, but she now has the technique under control and there is
none of that frightful show-off irrelevance that you get in the
Sayers:[22] Beryl and I are reading the book, chapter by chapter,
aloud and it's a great stand-by.

Yes, we know Pempie.[23] Judy Campbell is the link, and Pempie's
cousin David Birkin whom Judy (godmother to Pempie's little girl)
has, oddly enough, married. She is like something blown in glass
to look at. *Everyone* is wiser than Jenny; but Jenny is unique and
indestructible and when her unwisdom matures she'll be all right.
She is now feature editor, or something, for this Ministry of
Information magazine for the 'Liberated Areas'.

Hurry Cassell indeed about *The Golden Fleece*! The book has
been in proof since last September or so, but the printers can give
no date for publication because they are overworked, snowed
under and obliterated by vast 'priority orders of Post-War
Reconstruction Literature'. The publishing business is on the point
of expiring. I heard from a chap who had been working at Butler
and Tanner's (now switched over to a different sort of work
altogether) that the big presses were lying idle and being
constantly stripped of accessories by the workers on the other job!

. . . .

I'm so glad you like Keidrych and Lynette whom I have never
met but feel very warmly towards.

It will be lovely if you and Peggy can come. Bring Beryl's camera; and Dorothy Warner promises rum will be ready then, so bring that too. And bathing dresses. And some decent weather.

I have written the three introductory chapters of the Jesus book and had them vetted by Joshua Podro, a marvellous little Hebrew and Aramaic scholar who manages a press-cutting bureau at Paignton and has all God's words in his left-hand coat pocket, and all the comments in his overcoat and trouser pockets. Now I am well into the story and Zacharias, John the Baptist's father, has just had the frightful apparition of the *Golden Ass* in the Sanctuary as he is offering Jehovah the usual aphrodisiac incense. Next chapter, the Annunciation, new style.

Much satisfaction here that Hardinge is a prisoner, not just 'missing'.

Did you get a 'Reader's Union' *TROYS*? I have two copies. They are the only corrected edition.

Much love   Robert

In a letter of 28 October Hodge wrote: 'Now: a journalist's question: what has been your average yearly income since publishing *Goodbye to All That*? Newspapers like to have their reviewers include such odd items of information. Don't tell me if you don't want to see it in the *Standard* one day.'

No date

My dear Alan:

Between pals: my income has been £2000 a year since 1927: *Lawrence and the Arabs*. But I don't want that advertised, because what the hell has happened to it all? (and I should be besieged by demands from people who think they have a claim on me). I am broke now and am not quite sure how to keep going until I finish Jesus. He is going nicely but the job is an impossible one . . . I have got new scientific data on his lameness which clinches my argument.

. . . .

Congratulations on the pat from the Beaver's[24] paw.

Love   Robert

In October *The Golden Fleece* was published.

No date

Dearest Alan:

Christmas wishes!

Golden Fleece has sold out ten days ago – 9000 copies and I am having the best reviews of any book I've ever published. (They may even persuade some firm to publish the *Roebuck*.) Which seems rather a waste.

As I was writing out a cheque yesterday I suddenly saw the point of a joke quoted by Milton in his *Areopagitica* – Milton missed the point, of course – 'Henry VIII in merriment' named a certain notorious ribald his 'Vicar of Hell'.

Simple: John Skelton was Rector of Diss. 'Dis' = 'Hades' in Latin.

Am I very clever or is everyone else very dense? Because so far as I know nobody has yet noted the joke.

Love   Robert

Your books have been tiding Beryl over a very bad patch.

Graves and T. S. Eliot had not met or corresponded with each other since their argument about the review of *The Close Chaplet* in 1927. However, when Graves learned that Watt, his agent, had sent the manuscript of *The Roebuck in the Thicket* to Fabers, he wrote to Eliot, who was now one of the directors there.

12 January 1945

Dear Eliot

Lynette Roberts tells me that you made a generous reference to my discernment in the context of her poems. Watt, my agent, whom I have given a free hand in placing my *Roebuck in the Thicket*, tells me that he has offered it to Faber's, which means I suppose that it will go through your hands. This is gratifying, because you are one of the few people who will be able to check the Classicial and Biblical references; I don't know how expert you are in Celtic archaeology, but I can guarantee that I have used only the soundest sources.

Jonathan Cape, to whom I first offered the book, sent it back by return of post saying that he would give me the best dinner in Town if I could get it published by any of his fellow-publishers. I daresay that he is right. He does understand the market.

What I am writing to you about is this: that since I sent Watt the typescript I have been able to carry the argument further to a historical conclusion and have added two more chapters, one of which is essential to the completeness of the book, the other an embellishment. The essential chapter accounts for the heresy contained in the Taliesin conundrum with which the book begins: it turns out to be based on an Essene Ebionite formula of 1st century AD. What is stranger still, there is another mediaeval Welsh poem in the same series which contains the lost version of Adam's birth at Hebron (rather than in the Persian Gulf region) which recent Biblical critics have hopefully assumed but without textual evidence. This, and other otherwise inexplicable details in the Taliesin poems, suggests that we have here a diluted and degenerate version of the original Essene secret lore mentioned by Josephus and Pliny. (The Essenes themselves disappear from history under Domitian.)

It is possible that you have no paper at all and that you do not consider the book saleable anyhow. But if you are still considering it, and would like me to send you the two chapters I shall be pleased to send them. The other chapter is an essay on the logical connexion of nuns with fish; and you will find it throws a quite new light on both phenomena!

Yours sincerely   Robert Graves

Eliot replied (19 January) that he was extremely interested in the book and was sure that it ought to be published; he had not yet discussed it with Geoffrey Faber or the other directors, but thought that the only problem would be one of delay in publishing it, because of the paper shortage and because Fabers were already committed to bringing out a large number of books. Nevertheless, it seemed that Jonathan Cape owed Graves a lunch, and Eliot thought that he ought to be included in it.

22 January 1945[25]

My dear Eliot,
Here are the chapters and two insertions in other chapters. I am accustomed to delays in publication: it took me two years to get my *Golden Fleece* in print after it was written, though contracted for in the previous year! So don't apologize. I also enclose a

proposed wrapper for the book: Palamedes receiving the gift of mystic interpretation from Carmenta – and the Roebuck under the apple-tree, by Kenneth Gay.[26]

I have written the book like a man between two kettle-drums – the *Roebuck* is the left-hand drum and the right-hand one is a historical book for Cassell's about Jesus, whom I find, to my great surprise, to have been completely consistent in everything he did despite the apparent contradictions of the period just before the crucifixion. But I couldn't get the clue to the story except by following up the ramifications of early heretical literature, especially the extensions which go from Palestine to Syria and S. Gaul and Ireland and across to Wales; and all that material went into the *Roebuck*. I will soon have finished the Jesus book completely and when that is off my hands I'll get the *Roebuck* tightened up still more, because I have been continually making small discoveries as I get hold of the rarer books. Did you ever read Lucian's *De Syria Dea*, unobtainable in any but college libraries, but the most revealing book on Judaeo-Christian origins I have yet come across?

Well; try to persuade Geoffrey[27] that the *Roebuck* will do him good. If you can fix up something, I guarantee to get the argument still neater, when you can send it back to me for treatment. I am a bit troubled about the Byblos part, still.

Yes: what a lunch we'll have! Venison and apple sauce!

Yours very sincerely,   Robert Graves

18 March 1945

My dear Eliot.

Many thanks for your letter. I hope to finish my book about Jesus within a few weeks, and therefore to send you the revised *Roebuck* by September at latest. I'm glad you weren't put off by the eccentricity of the original form.

Now that it seems agreed in principle that you'll publish it when your own commitments allow I feel happier about it. To be frank, it was an embarrassment to have it unplaced while I was still working on another book and I sent it off on its travels prematurely.

Yours very sincerely,   Robert Graves

To Lynette Roberts

14 July 1945

My dear Lynette

I can see poor you in a great domestic flap, trudging down to the well with Angharad[28] on one hand and an old oaken bucket in the other, your mind churning over problems of vests and napkins. I have had lots of the same sort of thing in my time: with my elder family it wasn't war-time, but there was no proper way of airing clothes and the pump was always going wrong and I had no money and there were four of them.

. . . .

I am rewriting the *Roebuck in the Thicket* in a more scholarly way and keep making odd discoveries: yesterday's was that *The Tempest* begins with exactly the same *dramatis personae* as the *Mabinogi* of Taliesin:

Tegid Voel : Prospero
The damned witch Sycorax : Caridwen
Creirwy : Miranda
Afagddu : Caliban
Ariel : Gwion

How come? Same literary source, or an intuitive reconstruction of the same age-old story?

Anyhow, by the time I have got the book written the dons will have to shut up; there'll be no argument possible except on unimportant details.

Be a white angel and lend me the book you said once that you'd lend me: the book of Gallic art, by Rhys I think. I want very much to have a look at the Paris and Trèves pictures of Esus and the three cranes. I have found out who he was in Latin mythology – namely, 'Mercury who invented the alphabet by watching the flight of cranes', and I am dying to know what sort of tree the cranes are perched on. Have a look yourself first, as a botanist, and see what you think it is. Mythologically speaking, it should be a nut tree of some sort (hazel, almond, or chestnut) but the Northern Gauls were pretty strong on the ash as the tree of Gwydion (Wodin) 'the great enchanter of the Britons' so perhaps it will be that.

And if I could borrow D. W. Nash[29] again, it would be a great

330

help. If there is anything that I can do or get for you, let me know.

We are finding out about conditions in Spain, in case there's a chance of our going there before long; England is so awful in peace-time, and the only question is the political one – apart from transport.

Love from us and from Alan   Robert

21 July 1945

My dear Lynette:

What a nice letter and ever so many thanks for the books. The Thom book is a real fairy gift: untied at once two outstanding riddles in my tree-alphabet study. And your note on Cranes' breeding places was also a beautiful click-into-position of two or three legends. And T. G. Jones full of good supplementary stuff.

I have at last succeeded in disentangling from the riddling mazes of Taliesin's *Câd Goddeu* two of the five or six poems broken into pieces and muddled up in it. One is a monologue by Blodeuwedd the flowerwoman, only sixteen lines, another is a 100-line poem about the *Battle of the Trees* which for fun you'll be pleased to print in *Wales* as an original poem and see whether any big-bellied Welsh professor cottons on. They are a bunch of sad bone-heads, my God! even Gwyn Jones and Ifor Williams don't see the simple trick played on them. I shall dedicate – re-dedicate – the *Battle of the Trees* to Angharad when I can get someone to type it out.

Tell them, love and hopes to you all.   Robert

I am now going to read your *Field* articles: and will return them faithfully.

20 September 1945

My dear Lynette and Keidrych:

Sorry I can't get away for Angharad's first public appearance . . . I find that infant baptism is a heathen rite practised by the ancient Welsh and Irish, adult baptism only was practised by the early Christians; so old Druid Robert is just the chap for the job.

One of these days I'll find something for her as a christening gift.

The Bible is a most dangerous book: it should have a poison label on it. More people have gone mad from reading it without any regard for its original context or any knowledge of its history of textual amendment, than have died in the same period from pulmonary pneumonia and the plague. As literature it is of very unequal merit, and the best books are those least intelligible to Christians. But I'll do my best by Angharad, and take my responsibility seriously: I think the godfather's job in this modern world is always to be the chap to whom the godchild writes if he or she has got into a real jam and needs to be bailed out, or fished out, of a stew; and with whom he/she goes to stay, uninvited, at times of emotional crisis.

Beryl and I are taking William and Lucia[30] up to London for a few days at the end of October – my first stay there for more than a night since 1939. Perhaps it will coincide with one of your raids up to London – or can't you manage, now you have Angharad?

I have nearly finished the *Roebuck* in what I hope is the final version; but it will be twelve months, I fear, before it is published. It demonstrates the complete dependence of English poets on Irish and Welsh tradition, if they are to know what they are at.

Love to you all 3.   Robert

In September 1945 the war ended, exactly six years after it had begun. Karl Gay had served during the war first in the Pioneer Corps and then in the Royal Navy, until he was invalided out of the Navy in August 1944. Almost immediately he went to work with Graves at Galmpton, until June 1945 when he left Graves to work for Joshua Podro's Press Cutting Agency, first in Paignton and then in London; he continued to type Graves's manuscripts, however, and at the beginning of November he returned yet another draft of *The White Goddess* which, in all, went through at least five drafts. (This book, which Graves had 'thrown to the dogs' in August 1944, was still being added to in January 1946.)

8 November 1945

Dearest Karl

Thanks very much for the letter and the beautiful typing. I can't do much with it at present in the way of further disfiguration although when I was up in Wales I found a set of learned books on the subject of Taliesin and the bards generally in my father's library and will read them through to get more gen on the subject;* and Sally has a book on tree-cults in Palestine for me which may before long provide you with work. At present I am with *Jesus* again. The first 18 galleys have just turned up; printed admirably by the Edinburgh University Press. I have decided that I have put one water-jump too many at the beginning, before the story begins. Since Phanaël's introduction has to stand, I am putting my own at the end as a *Historical Commentary*. Anyhow nobody will know what it's about until they've read the book. *Time*'s review[31] is so shoddy and atomic – is the atom to be an excuse for disintegration of thought in a nihilistic bang? – that I feel I'm rather wasting my valuable conscience on these historical points.

I like Truman's saying he has no need to waste valuable atom-bombs on Europe – economic pressure suffices. That's what Jacob said in an aside when he bought Esau's birthright for a spam sandwich and a dried egg omelette.

Yes, that is the Pearson[32] – 'Mike' was an unaccountable nickname.

Devon climate makes one dreadfully sleepy on return.

When I get a spare set of galleys I'll send them to you, if I may, to cross-copy and check up on.

Love – and to Marie   Robert

*PS. I now have, and the story of Gwion and the bards gets even better, from the point of view of historical by-play.

To Lynette Roberts

No date [December 1945]

My dear Lynette

I had just sent off the *Roebuck* proofs, and now your letter comes.

The 'Orarium' business. The point is that if a poet is truly orientated in his or her work the accuracy of the universal myth is assured whatever his or her reading of the Classics or other body of myths may be.

The hero-type has red hair because of a) the red clay from which he is formed; b) the red grain at harvest; c) the scarlet colour of blood, and of the kerm-berry of the sacred oak, and sacred cinnabar and so on. 'Adam' means 'red'. David had red hair. So had Osiris, etc.

I don't think that an impressionistic use of words fits with English or Welsh. It is a counsel of despair adopted by the French since they put their language into a strait-jacket. The Americans copied it, from national recklessness. All French poetry except Rimbaud's – he was a miracle – is rhetorical. And the pre-Louis XIV stuff.

The Golden Fleece is a popular introduction, very much half-way, to the real understanding of myth and poetic thought which I have tried to convey in the enlarged *Roebuck*. This also is a necessary prologue to my book on Jesus. Jesus is simply un-understandable unless you relate the Hebrew and Greek and Syrian myths, and also understand the contemporary Palestinian setting. I think I have it fairly straight now. My point is that I can't bear muddles in poetic or religious thought. The original European myth still stands, and for heaven's sake let us get it straight, as poets. I am now straightening out the peculiarly intricate and emotional drama of Jesus's trial: his impersonation to begin with of the Foolish Shepherd in Zechariah who did all the wrong things because he got fed up, and then Judas's noble attempt to save him from the consequences of his acts.

The doctor has just been and proposes to 'induce' the new baby[33] on the 22nd: the winter solstice day.

Love

Robert

At the beginning of January, Graves sent the insertions for the fifth version of *The Roebuck in the Thicket* to Karl Gay for typing. Now that the war was over Graves was very keen to move back to Deyá.

1 January 1946
Happy New Year

Dearest Karl:
Once more I have come to the end of the book and this time, if you can type the amendments and insertions, it will be ready to send off. It is a pity we didn't keep a third copy, because one has to go to USA, and one to Faber's and I should have liked to keep

a spare: but it is my own fault. I'll send tomorrow or the next day.

What a plumpudding it is! Too much in it, and yet, why not? The whole point is the method of thought, not the results, and as many examples of the method as I can give, the better. It warms up towards the end, and I don't think that there's a dull chapter.

If you could type and paste the inserts into the copy I send, and attach the carbons, this would save the risk of getting both copies lost in transit; and I could finish the job here, and also the minor cross-copying.

We are practically over our colds, but the weather is treacherous and we hope not to spend another winter in England for a long time; however, we have found a sturdy gardener, who is a Highlander and really knows his job, to dig and plant and prune for us.

John Aldridge – did I tell you? – is back at Bardfield and has sent a very nice preliminary design for the *Jesus* wrapper.

One of these days I shall do a tidying job: collecting my various and historical studies into a book. Otherwise I haven't a thing in my pocket or head. What about your naturalization? Oughtn't you to get that started? I have been asked to sponsor R. Halkett recently.

Love   Robert

9 January 1946

Dearest Karl:

I think I see what you mean about the kick-off of the book. I think also that this will more or less do; it is the 5th version already. Excuse all the other last-minute insertions.

I had a letter from a von Ranke first cousin[34] formerly in civil aviation; he fought with the International Brigade, the German underground, the Maquis of Savoie (where he was a friend of dear Gertrude's) and finally the French Army – had a hell of a time, including concentration camp. His wife lived at Deyá once. Nice to know that they weren't all Nazis, my relations. He is now on the staff of the Paris *Esprit*.

I love that yellow-green on the wrapper – apple colour as I see it.

Yes, inquire about your naturalization, do!

Anita sent me a *Bonne Année* card from Rennes – cryingly sweet in the French style.

Lord, how it rains, but William goes off with the school pantomime treat in a bus.

Love   Robert

Graves changed the title of *The Roebuck in the Thicket* to *The White Goddess*, and sent off the new version to Eliot.

28 January 1946

Dear Tom Eliot

I hope that *The White Goddess*, the new version of *The Roebuck in the Thicket*, will meet all your former objections. Since I have got the *Jesus* book into proof (it will appear about May) I have been at leisure to work the *Roebuck* into more presentable form. The problem is clearly stated at the beginning and argued out ruthlessly to the very end: I think sufficient chapter and verse are now given, and when there is an index it will be quite readable. The typescript is clean, too!

It is a great deal longer, yet could not be cut without damage.

Looking at the original typescript, I think it was very good of you to have asked to see it again; it must have read very queerly. But I think in a sort of mythic shorthand and assume too readily that people can follow my train of thought, which is fundamentally logical.

I never thanked you for a very handsome Christmas card; and do so now.

Yours very sincerely,   Robert Graves

Best wishes to Geoffrey.

Graves had stopped corresponding with Gertrude Stein after her quarrel with Laura Riding in 1930. Soon after the war ended, however, Graves took the initiative in renewing their friendship by writing to her in France, where she had been living the whole time, even during the war years. This letter and Stein's reply have been lost; the following letter is Graves's second post-war letter to her.

28 January 1946

My dear Gertrude:

You must know what very great pleasure your letter gave me; I don't know why it is, but you have always been very close to my heart since we stayed at Belley in 1929 and I was very sorry when Laura broke with you in a fit of spleen: I think because you always mentioned the weather, and that seemed unworthy. But of course the weather is very important in the short run, and the long run consists of short runs.

I think of you often on specific occasions such as when Truman became Vice-President and I heard you saying 'not good Presidential timber' – I think Coolidge was the occasion of your remark, originally. And of course we, Beryl and I, have been very much concerned about you in this war, and I never dreamed that my cousin was in your environs. He seems a good chap: Gertrude, if I can arrange for Pavois Frère, who are publishing my *Marie Powell, Wife to Mr Milton*, to pay the advance to you, could you hand it on to Hubert? Your address is safer, I feel, than his and they would make less fuss if it were you. It would be £50 which is 2400 francs, I think, now. But say nothing to him until I know that it can be arranged. Money is so tied up these days by Defence of the Realm Acts, etc., that I don't even know if it's legal.

Our William aged 5 was very happy and excited with *The World is Round*: I think he has a good ear for rhythm and the shape of sentences.

Laura: it's a very strange but familiar story. She was possessed for a great many years by a very cruel and beautiful Muse with which she identified herself; and then she found the position intolerable, and the spirit left her and she became common clay, an average American divorcée–remarried housewife, with a repudiation of all her work. The occasion of the change was very painful and doomful, like the morning when the tenor bell in the Cathedral springs a flaw and gives out a horrid discordant noise.

. . . .

However, that is long past now, and I stand still greatly in her debt, though our life together grew more and more painful from 1930 or so onwards; and these last years – the break came in 1939 – with Beryl have been the happiest of my life and I have done my best work in them. Beryl and I aren't married, because

Nancy won't divorce me; but she has taken my name by deed-poll and we have the three children.

Money has been behaving very well lately, which is a comfort. My eldest boy was killed in Burmah, the other of the elder family is at Cambridge, and I am hoping that you'll soon meet Jenny, who will be stationed in Paris – she is *Sunday Dispatch* correspondent – with her husband Alex Clifford of the *Daily Mail*. Alex is fine, and you'll love them both.

There is going to be a bit of a startle when my new book comes out: about Jesus. You'd think that was a boring and over-explored subject – I mean 'one' not 'you' – but it turns out that nobody has ever taken the trouble to verify the quotations Jesus made from the prophets, to see what he had in mind. Believe it or not, nobody, not one. And of course it makes a completely new and real story, and he turns out to have been (despite the Gospel libels on his integrity) one of the only Jews – I don't mean Jewesses – who (to quote G. Stein) ever put down the very last cent. Yes, by God, he really did, after all; I think that's a wonderful discovery, though of course he was no more of a Christian than Isaiah or Ezekiel, or Rabbi Hillel his contemporary, or myself or you: he was pure Jew.

When we go to Spain – if – when – if – we go to Spain, we'll come *via* Paris and what a happy day that will be.

Love   Robert

Love to Alice and Basket the xth.[35]

Stein replied:

4 February 1946   5 Rue Christine
                                                                            6me Paris

My dear Robert,

I was awfully pleased to hear from you, I always had considerable tenderness for you, a very special tenderness indeed, and strangely enough part of it had to do with our first Basket and sheep, it was a very special tenderness. Yes of course I would be very pleased indeed to act as *intermédiaire* for you with Hubert, you know your 50£ would be 2400 francs, he has had a pretty tough time of it all these years, people have been very good to him but the difficulties have been very great, yes all through the occupation we pretty well watched over each other, his german melodrama did make me a little impatient at times, but he did thoroughly live up to his drama, and did xcellent and courageous work, and then beside he did know a lot, and during those dark days special knowledge was passionately xciting, and we owed him a great deal of that distraction. His worst trouble of course always is his health, sometimes indeed one thought that the return journey on bicycle would not be achieved, but somehow he always managed to get there on his old rattle trap of a bicycle, he is a good cousin, and anything I can do to help you help him you can count on.

I was much interested in the Laura story, of course it was terribly important for you to have lived her; for your Jesus book, after all, she was Jew every single bit of her, but and that was really the basis of our break, she was the materialistic jew camouflaging her materialism by intellectualism, a very very common thing in the race, I cannot say camouflaging, really the intellectualism is the reactionary violence of their materialism, in the jewish race there are really more jews like that than any other kind, I guess it is Semitic that, and it is they that make all the noise and really keep alive Anti-semitism.

I am tremendously interested in your book about Jesus. On easter day in '44, I was walking down a long hill in the country, and I heard the church bells, and of course it was the moment of the worst Jewish persecution, and the most [fervent] Easter emotion of many years, and suddenly it struck me as comical completely comical, and I met a Catholic friend on the road and I said isn't it funny, making such a fuss about Christ and Jews at the same moment and never connecting the two ideas, even the Catholic friend was for the moment impressed, but it is comical, not tragic just absurd, no one really realizing that there is a connection, not really, so you see I am interested. Will you be able to make the connection real, it is so simply there that if you can, I do hope so. Lots of love and tell your daughter to come and see us, and come yourselves, Spain seems difficult, but France not so difficult, do come the two of you, I am delighted about your little William. A new child's book is coming out in England very shortly and one in France, that I did them during the war when I needed calming and so every day I composed a child's story with a certain complication I think they are very good, and I hope William will like them, give him my love and to you and to Beryl

Always   Gtrde S. and Alice
                                                        and Basket II

No date

My dear Gertrude:

I know how busy you are and I don't want to involve you in a long correspondence, but there are things to answer in your letter.

First Hubert. Unfortunately in this crazy world, it proves that I have no right to dispose of my French earnings as I see fit: they must, by law, all come to England and stay here to be taxed and taxed and taxed. So how I am to help I don't know, unless my daughter can manage somehow. There's no lack of money or goodwill, and to think that when I was young I could travel to France or anywhere without a passport and carry bags of golden sovereigns jingling at my side if I wished!

About Laura. It was not quite so simple as you make out. She was Jew, yes, but not Jehovah-Jew; she was a sort of embodiment of the Queen of Heaven – Jehovah's former wife and mother – alias Lilith, Kadesh, Alukah, Michal, Aholibamah, Ashtaroth, Ashima, Anatha, etc., *u.s.w.* – who has been the *cherchez la femme* torment of the Jewish soul since he first divorced her during the Exile. And she was not Semite, but East European 'Asianic' and the Jews who were originally crossbred Kassites (or something) from Armenia and Semites from Harran, picked her up in Palestine when they settled there. It was *her* country, not theirs.

Anyhow, about Jesus. There are really 4 people in the story:
1) Jesus –
2) The Hebrew Messiah –
3) The Gnostic Christ, Egypto–Judaeo–Perso–Greek.
4) The European Divine Child, first found in Crete, call him Dionysus or Zagreus or Eleusis.

They don't really add up, yet are all closely connected, by the accident of Jesus having been really (not in the red-herring 'Son of David' sense) but really born as the patrilineal heir to the Herodian throne under *Roman* law, a sort of Man in the Iron Mask, and holding a *matrilineal* title to the throne of Israel.

Now what you say about intellectual, nationalist Jews does

apply very strongly to Jesus. He was a pure Nationalist intellectual, and it was he who has caused all the trouble, and the Catholics are quite right to distinguish him from the antediluvian Prince of Peace Divine Child who was celebrated at the Dionysian and Delphic mysteries ages before Jesus was born. Nevertheless Jesus was absolutely uncompromising and I do admire him, though his eschatology was plum crazy. He hadn't the least interest in us Gentiles, and was perfectly un-Christian.

Unfortunately Beryl and I with 3 small children and no help aren't at all mobile. Nothing we should like better than a hop to Paris. But . . .

We look forward greatly to the children's book, and you shall have my *King Jesus* as soon as I have a copy.

No, I don't regret a moment of the life I spent with Laura. I was learning all the time and she was a wonderful poet at her best and as good to me as I deserved, I suppose. I rather resented *Life*'s recent description of you as a 'little old woman'. Old – I can't believe – Little is libellous. You will always be 'La Grande Gertrude' when this epoch is hereafter mentioned.

Love to you all   – Robert

Gertrude Stein died later that year at the age of seventy-two.

In March 1946 T. S. Eliot wrote to Graves telling him that Fabers had definitely accepted *The White Goddess* for publication. Eliot was extremely impressed by the new version of the book, the learning and labour of which, he later wrote to Graves, was so far beyond anything of which he was capable that it was beyond his understanding.

At this time Ezra Pound was in America awaiting trial for treason because of pro-Fascist wartime broadcasts he had made to American troops from Rome. He had been pronounced insane and hospitalized, but in case he recovered his mental equilibrium sufficiently to stand trial, Eliot was organizing a plea for clemency on his behalf by eminent British poets; the plea made no reference to his guilt or innocence but simply affirmed the importance of Pound's contribution to twentieth-century English literature, and stated that his position as a poet was of the 'highest worth and dignity'.

Eliot sent Graves a copy of the plea and asked him to sign it.

5 April 1946

My dear Eliot:

I am in an unfortunate position about the Pound affair. I agree that poets should stick together in the most masonic way, and recall that Milton though he had a low opinion of Davenant did rescue him from the gallows because he was a poet: a compliment that Davenant afterwards returned. But since 1911 when I first read Pound in Harriet Monro's[36] *Poetry* magazine; and since 1922 when I met him for the first and last time at All Souls in T. E. Lawrence's rooms, I could never regard him as a poet and have consistently denied him the title.

Now if it had been you, that would have been a very different thing. I would have appealed in person to the Supreme Court, because after all though naturally I prefer some of your poems to others, you are obviously and ungainsayably a poet. *But*, you would never have gone mad dog, as Pound did from vanity, and aligned yourself with the worst of the bad wops.

I am shocked but not surprised at the treatment given him by the guards: your ex-compatriots have always been more savage and ruthless to traitors than your present ones – and that is just too bad. But the real poets have supported worse sufferings with dignity and courage.

If there were a single line or stanza of Pound's that recurred to my mind as true and beautiful, or merely as true, I should join in your plea – but to do so just because he is a 'name' would be unprincipled.

Forgive me. May I myself be judged with equal severity in the Last Day.

Yours very sincerely,   Robert Graves

I expect to return to Majorca on May 15th for good. Could I have *The White Goddess* typescript back for some last minute emendations?

Eliot replied that he was sorry not to have Graves's signature, but admitted that the plea did commit the signatories to an opinion of the value of Pound's poetry.

To Lynette Roberts

15 April 1946

My dear Lynette
    Unless something goes wrong with our visas, or the 'Spanish question' gets too questionable, we will be returning to Majorca on May 15, with a stop for the night at Rennes: by air taxi. Naturally we don't love Franco any more than anyone does, but my daughter Jenny recently visited my house and village and reported that everything was in wonderfully good order and that there was no political trouble in the neighbourhood. So, since we are getting tired of this struggle against domestic shortages and of the wet winters and the tourist-traffic in the summers, and so on, we feel we ought to go; the people in the village there are wonderfully good and I can't think of anywhere else in the world where one could leave at an hour's notice and come back after ten years to find everything waiting as if nothing had happened.
    It will be a bit lonely for Beryl and the children for a time, until they get to speak Spanish; but we hope that our friends will come and visit us when travel gets easier. It would be nice to entertain Angharad there one day.
    I return two books; both have been very useful indeed for my *Roebuck* book, now called *The White Goddess*, which is finished and accepted by Faber and Faber. I am taking the typescript with me to make a few latest additions. (*King Jesus* won't be out until July.)
    Alan comes here tomorrow for Easter and when he goes we start packing. Fortunately we don't need to take much with us except books and my daughter Catherine wants all the furniture; so the job is simple.
    May I keep Nash's *Taliesin* for a few months more?
    I hope you are in better health and spirits than when you last wrote.
    Love to you all   Robert

Graves's *Poems 1938–1945* was published in November 1945, and was very well received by many critics, as Graves wrote in a letter to Lynette Roberts, who was expecting her second child.

No date

Dear Lynette:

Thanks very much for your letter and offer of the flat; but we'll be in Brown's Hotel, Dover St, for the 7 or 8 days before we leave, so won't need it, but anyhow, it was very sweet of you.

So glad you like the Caldecott. It was got from a catalogue about 3 years ago. Every good child should have a Caldecott to cut its teeth on.

I have been rather amused by the reviews of my poems. Everyone has suddenly decided to 'recognize' me as one recognizes a new Government of some troublesome country. This is the first really cordial batch I've had since – 1916! I suppose I'm getting old and am no longer considered a rival to the younger generation. Anyhow, what the hell! Letters from friends like you who are also poets is another matter: especially if you can tell me how to improve anything there. Everyone has blind spots; that's what friends are for.

Love to Keidrych. Funny I have never met either of you, or Angharad, but as they say in Wales 'Two men will meet before two mountains.' I do hope he gets over his ulcers soon altogether.

This new child. The child itself determines on being born, I think, not the parents. Good luck to you when it comes! Yes of course one can't have 'only children'; not happily. But then the question is how to raise the second one without losing something of the unique glamour of the first born. Anyhow, it will be grateful for life and Angharad for a playmate. Very many thanks for the *Wales* and for the Pair Carridwen.

Love to you all
                                                            Robert

Gwyn Jones sent me a copy of the *Welsh Review* and some stuff about Alun Lewis. He told me he is editing a new *Mabinogion* this autumn with some other Jones – David? isn't it? – this autumn at the *Golden Cockerel*. But when I asked him whether he realized that in the story of Branwen, Bran = 'Fearn' the alder god (hence the allegory of the bridge and the riddle 'no house could contain him': houses and bridges were built on alder piles) he didn't answer, thought me crackers, I guess.

344

In May 1946 Graves met Lynette Roberts for the first time, in London just before he and his family left England. They have lived in Deyá ever since, except for a brief period in the sixties, when Graves was Professor of Poetry at Oxford.

APPENDIX A

Letter from Siegfried Sassoon

7 December 1957   Heytesbury House
                                                        Wiltshire

Mr dear Robert

I must admit that your letter was a very pleasant surprise –
though I would never have assumed that you were intolerant
about Catholics.

All I need to say now is that I experience peace beyond anything
I could have hoped for – not through my formal submission to the
RC dogma, but through the grace of faith which came to me after
prolonged perseverance in prayer (sorry if I sound sanctimonious)
and through the help I received from a very holy Catholic./

I am not at all 'bothered' by the re-issue of *Goodbye*, and hope
it will remind the present generation of what 1914–18 was for
those who endured it./ I think the reason for my being so upset in
1929 was that I was in a great state of mental fatigue and worry
with writing the *Infantry Officer*. All that you wrote about me
was entirely generous – beyond my deserts./

George[1] is progressing well at King's. He married a very nice
Scotch girl two years ago, which alarmed me at the time, but it
has worked out excellently.

Bless you, old boy.

Yours,   S.S.

APPENDIX B

Historical Reconstructions
in *I, Claudius*

Notes on the main 'twists' in the story, sent to T. S. Matthews

1 May 1934

Suggestion that the slave Clemens who pretended to be the murdered Postumus *was* really Postumus; that when Augustus visited the island in AD 13 he had substituted Clemens for Postumus, whom he intended to make his heir in spite of Livia.

Suggestion that the mysterious murder of Germanicus was an 'inside job'; and that Caligula was the accomplice of Martina and Planana. He was certainly there at the time.

Suggestion that Caligula's oriental tyranny madness was bound up with a crazy identification of himself with the coming 'Divine Ruler of the World' who was, we know from various sources, expected in the near East about this time.

Suggestion that the murder for suspicion of which Claudius divorced Urganilla was that of Apronia, related by Tacitus.

But there is no main incident in the book which does not derive from some suggestion or hint in some Classical authority, and some of the most surprising apparent inventions have historical foundation, e.g. the conversation between Hermann and Flavius, the poisoning of Augustus by Livia, Antonia's saying 'He is as stupid as my son Claudius', the letters written by Augustus about Claudius, the story of Claudius's disastrous reading of his works, the fat knight and the broken chair (Suetonius says it was a bench, not Livia's chair), the story of Cocceius Nerva's suicide, the story of the mutiny and the soldiers' sentimentality about 'Little Boot', the story of Tiberius and the fishermen, the verse which the soldiers sang at Julius Caesar's triumph:

348

Home we bring the bald whore-monger
Soldiers lock your wives away.

The story of Caligula, his sisters, and the Palace brothel (though
we don't know that Claudius was mixed up in it).

On the other hand you won't find Aristophanes's *Flood* in his
extant works, and the Sybilline oracle about the Caesars is as
apocryphal as many others that were quoted as Sibylline at the
time, and though the story of Caligula, the prominent senators and
the dancing at midnight is true we don't know that Claudius was
one of these. The account of Caligula's murder is an accurate
combination of the various accounts given, even the fact that
Cassius's leading motive was anger at being given dirty watch-
words suggestive of his being an old homosexual.

The point is that I have nowhere, so far as I know, *gone against*
history; but wherever authors have disagreed, or there has been a
gap or confusion or mystery or they were obviously lying I have
felt free to invent, in the spirit of the story, what made sense of
the story. The motto from Tacitus at the beginning refers to the
murder of Germanicus and the trial of Piso and Planana, but
covers the whole history of the imperial family. If I had written
my version of the story in the second century it would now be
taken as authentic: it would certainly be less biased than Tacitus
and held to solve a lot of outstanding historical problems.

Needless to say I'm not a Classical scholar or anything of that
sort but there is a story somewhere hidden in that confused and
rather dreary history and I have tried to dig it out. If I had been a
Classical scholar my historical conscience would not have let me
invent a thing.

(T. E. Shaw[1] in reading the proofs queried two points as
anachronistic or out of key. One was Augustus's speech about the
greatest god of all who created us, etc., which as a matter of fact
is authentic (quoted in Dio Cassius). I forget what the other was,
but it happened also to be authentic. Reviewers will have to be
careful. Another scholar queried the use of Claudius's invented
letter (⊢ for Greek *Upsilon*) in *Bibliotheca*: but I could quote a
Pompeian wall-inscription in support.)

NOTES

The abbreviation *GTAT*, followed by a date, signifies *Goodbye to All That*, first edition, Jonathan Cape Ltd, 1929, or the revised edition, Cassell Ltd, 1957.

Introduction

1. Laura Riding (born 1901). American poet, critic, editor. She was born Laura Reichenthal but changed her name by deed poll to Riding; after her marriage to Louis Gottschalk, the history professor, she became Laura Gottschalk, or Laura Riding Gottschalk; after divorcing Gottschalk she reverted to calling herself Laura Riding until her marriage to Schuyler Jackson in 1941, when she took his name. She now styles herself Laura (Riding) Jackson.

2. *The Collected Letters of Wilfred Owen*, edited by Harold Owen and John Bell, Oxford University Press, 1967. *Robert Ross, Friend of Friends*, edited by Margery Ross, Jonathan Cape Ltd, 1952.

Part One

1. Compiled by Christopher Hassall and Denis Matthews, 1953.

2. Ralph Rooper, a friend and fellow pupil of Graves's at Charterhouse.

3. This is the only occasion on which Graves included his German middle name, von Ranke, in his signature. Although he dropped the 'von' to make it less obviously German, it was a great source of trouble to him at school, at the depot and at the Front (see page 54).

4. These became the first and two final stanzas of 'It's a Queer Time', published in *Over the Brazier*, Poetry Bookshop, 1916.

5. In his early letters Graves consistently misspells Boches as 'Bosches', as did Wilfred Owen in his letters.

6. 'The Poet in the Nursery'.

7. Richard Middleton (1882–1911), poet and short-story writer, who published nothing in book form during his lifetime though contributed to several

periodicals. Best remembered for *Poems and Songs* and *The Ghost Ship and Other Stories* (1912).

8. George Harcourt Johnstone, later 3rd Baron Derwent (1899–1949), described as 'Dick' in *Goodbye to All That*.

9. *sic*. The Hon. Evelyn Mary Agar-Ellis, daughter of Viscount Clifden.

10. 'Through the Periscope', 'Limbo', 'The Adventure' and 'The First Funeral'.

11. John Masefield (1878–1967), poet and novelist; he became Poet Laureate when Robert Bridges died in 1930.

12. *GTAT*, 1957, p. 154.

13. Harold Monro (1879–1932), poet, editor of the *Poetry Review* and later founder and editor of the *Monthly Chapbook*; in 1912 he opened the Poetry Bookshop in Bloomsbury, which became a meeting place for young writers and a publishing house for many volumes of poetry, including the *Georgian Poetry* volumes. His own *Collected Poems* were published in 1933.

14. William Davies (1871–1940), Welsh poet, autobiographer and novelist.

15. Gordon Bottomley (1874–1948), poet and poetic dramatist whose then controversial verse play, *King Lear's Wife*, had place of honour in *Georgian Poetry II*.

16. Ralph Hodgson (1871–1962), poet, illustrator and printer of broadsheets and chapbooks. He was then considered to be the most promising of all the Georgian poets.

17. These lines missed out from the letter.

18. Marsh's memoir of Rupert Brooke.

19. *Letters from America*: letters by Robert Brooke originally written to the *Westminster Gazette* as articles, with a preface by Henry James.

20. 'A Psalm of Montreal', written in Canada in 1875. Butler had discovered a plaster cast of the Discobolus in the attic of the Montreal Museum of Natural History and asked a custodian, who was also in the attic (stuffing an owl), why it wasn't on view; the reply was that it was too vulgar, and then the custodian went on to talk about how his brother did all 'Mr Spurgeon's printing'. The poem, a dialogue between Butler and the custodian, ends:

'Preferrest thou the gospel of Montreal to the gospel of Hellas,
The gospel of thy connection with Mr Spurgeon's haberdashery to the gospel
  of the Discobolus?'
Yet none the less blasphemed he beauty, saying, 'The Discobolus hath no
  gospel,
But my brother-in-law is haberdasher to Mr Spurgeon.'
                        O God! O Montreal!

21. Sir Edmund Gosse (1849–1928), writer, poet and notoriously conserv-

ative, inaccurate yet nevertheless influential critic who after the war wrote a weekly article on current books for the *Sunday Times*. His books include *Father and Son* (1907) and biographical studies of Swinburne, Coventry Patmore and Sir Thomas Browne.

22. David Thomas, a fellow officer and very close friend of Sassoon and Graves; referred to as Tommy in later letters.

23. Ironic reference to one of Iago's songs in *Othello*, II.3:

Some wine, ho!
And let me the canakin clink, clink;
And let me the canakin clink;
A soldier's a man;
O, man's life's but a span;
Why, then, let a soldier drink.

A canakin is a small can or drinking vessel.

24. 'Sassons': Graves's nickname for Sassoon; see page 58.

25. Ysgol Wen, a derelict cottage on a remote hillside at Sospan Fach, which Graves bought (with his mother's money) and restored in 1915; during the 1920s and 1930s he rented it to an unemployed ex-soldier of his regiment, until 1938 when the cottage was ironically included in a slum clearance order, and the soldier made homeless.

26. Henry Festing Jones (1851–1928), Samuel Butler's close friend and biographer.

27. Claud Lovat Fraser (1890–1921), landscape painter, designer and illustrator, badly wounded early in the war and invalided out of the army. For the cover of *Over the Brazier* he used a drawing of the Menin Gate.

28. Another ironic joke: Graves was then contributing 'war letters' to the *Spectator*.

29. *Memoirs of an Infantry Officer*, Faber and Faber Ltd, 1930, p. 9.

30. Wilfred W. Gibson (1878–1962), Georgian poet. With Lascelles Abercrombie and Walter de la Mare, was one of the poets to whom Rupert Brooke willed the posthumous proceeds from his poems. *Collected Poems* (1926).

31. 'Yknarc': a word from Butler's *Erewhon*: cranky.

32. Edward Carpenter (1844–1929), unconventional Victorian thinker and writer; he was ordained in the Church of England but became an unbeliever at the age of thirty and later became a socialist. His books include *Towards Democracy* (1883), *Civilization: Its Cause and Cure* (1889) and an autobiography, *My Days and Dreams* (1916).

33. John Davidson (1857–1909), Scottish poet, best-known for his *Fleet Street Eclogues* (1893) and *The Theatrocrat* (1905), which contain a description of his 'materialistic and rebellious philosophy', and for his descriptions of slums, at a time when city landscapes were almost totally absent from English poetry.

Havelock Ellis (1859–1939), poet, novelist, physician, psychologist and literary essayist, whose famous *The Psychology of Sex* (7 vols., 1897–1928; revised 1936) was banned when first published in England.

Eugène Brieux (1858–1932), French journalist and playwright, whose plays, which are realistic and with a social purpose, were much admired by Bernard Shaw.

A.E.: pseudonym for George Russell (1867–1935), minor Irish poet and political idealist. A close friend of Yeats.

34. 'The Dragon and the Undying', *Westminster Gazette*, 20 April 1916.

35. 'A Letter Home': see page 55.

36. John St Loe Strachey (1860–1927), editor of the *Cornhill Magazine*, 1896–97, then editor and proprietor of the *Spectator* until 1925; he was an influential political and literary journalist.

37. *GTAT* (1957), p. 183.

38. *GTAT* (1957), p. 186.

39. *GTAT* (1957), p. 194.

40. 'No, you cannot kill me!' From a poem by Nietzsche, a selection of whose poems (in French translation) was one of the few books Graves had with him at the Front.

41. Mark Gertler (1891–1939), painter, close friend of D. H. Lawrence and Lytton Strachey, and a frequent guest of Lady Ottoline Morrell at Garsington Manor.

42. See Graves's poem 'Escape', *Fairies and Fusiliers*, 1917.

43. John Graves.

44. Ivor Novello (1893–1951), British composer, playwright and romantic actor in the theatre and cinema. His song 'Till the Boys Come Home' made him immensely popular in 1914. He was Marsh's closest friend at this time and Marsh arranged for him to set some of Graves's poems to music, a project which Novello began but, it seems, never completed.

45. *GTAT* (1957), p. 205.

46. *Wheels* was a 'modernist' annual anthology of poetry edited by Edith Sitwell.

47. Evan Morgan, private secretary to W. C. Bridgman, Minister of Labour. See pages 73 and 79.

48. Salvarsan, the original anti-syphilis drug.

49. Robert Hamner, a prewar friend and neighbour of Sassoon's in Kent, who served with the Royal Welch Fusiliers during the war. He is referred to throughout the letters as 'Bobby' (whereas Robert Ross is always 'Robbie' and Robert Nichols 'Bob').

50. *Goliath and David*, Graves's second book of poems, published by the Chiswick Press. See page 66.

51. Published in *Fairies and Fusiliers*, 1917.

52. Robert Bridges (1844–1930), poet, critic and playwright, who suc-

ceeded Alfred Austin as Poet Laureate in 1913. He lived on Boars Hill, near Oxford, and was one of Graves's neighbours after the war.

53. *GTAT* (1957), p. 216.

54. Garsington Manor, a farm near Oxford owned by Phillip and Lady Ottoline Morrell, which became a centre for Bloomsbury writers and intellectuals, many of whom did 'agricultural work' there as conscientious objectors after the introduction of conscription in 1916.

55. Robert Ross lived in Half Moon Street, Mayfair; the 'set' included at this time C. K. Scott-Moncrieff, the writer and translator of Proust.

56. Charles Sorley's father.

57. *Skelton's Poetical Works*, ed. Alexander Dyce, 2 vols., 1843.

58. Probably a reference to Sassoon's poem 'They', which contains the line 'Bert's gone syphilitic'; perhaps the *Spectator* had rejected it because of this. (It was first published in the *Cambridge Magazine*, 20 January 1917.)

59. 'Wingle' was a word coined by Graves's brother John and was used frequently by Graves at this time, even in his poems (see 'Finland').

60. *The Life of Algernon Charles Swinburne*, by E. Gosse, 1917; reprinted in the Bonchurch edn, vol. 19 (rev.).

61. Published in *Ardours and Endurances*, Chatto and Windus, 1917. 'Zero' was the time agreed upon by the staff when the troops should go over the parapet into the attack.

62. Julian Morrell, daughter of Lady Ottoline Morrell (later Mrs Igor Vinogradoff).

63. John Drinkwater (1882–1937), Georgian poet and minor playwright.

64. Duncan Grant (born 1885), painter; member of the Camden Town Group, 1911, and of the London Group, 1919, and part of the Bloomsbury circle.

65. *GTAT* (1957), p. 227.

66. *The Old Huntsman and Other Poems* was published by William Heinemann on 3 May 1917.

67. See Sassoon's poem 'Conscripts'.

68. 'When I'm Among a Blaze of Lights'.

69. *GTAT* (1957), p. 219.

70. *GTAT* (1957), p. 227.

71. A quotation from Sorley's 'Barbury Camp'.

72. *GTAT* (1957), p. 229.

73. Vernon Bartlett, of the Hampshire Regiment; another of his and Graves's pranks was to change all the labels around in the picture gallery at Osborne.

74. Edward Eastaway, a pseudonym used by Edward Thomas (1878–1917) when he first began to contribute poems to periodicals, as he was by then already well known as a journalist and hack writer; it was not until

after his death, in France, that he was recognized as a poet of high stature. His *Collected Poems* were published in 1917, with a foreword by Walter de la Mare.

75. W. J. Turner (1889–1946), writer, poet and music critic, whose numerous books include studies of Beethoven, Wagner, Berlioz and Mozart. He was music critic for the *New Statesman* (1916–40), drama critic of the *London Mercury* (1919–23), literary editor of the *Daily Herald* (1920–23) after Sassoon, and literary editor of the *Spectator* (1942–46). Until his death he had a respectable following as a poet and Graves subsequently revised his poor opinion of his poetry. He coedited *The Owl* with Graves in 1919.

76. Robert Bridges.

77. 'The Dead Foxhunter' described the heroic death of Captain Samson (known as 'Butty Quail') of the 2nd RWF at the Battle of Loos, September 1915.

78. *The Muse in Arms*, edited, with an introduction, by E. B. Osborn and published by John Murray, 1917.

79. Julian Grenfell (1888–1915), aristocratic soldier and poet whose poems glorified the idea of battle and sacrifice. His famous poem 'Into Battle' appeared on the day of his death in *The Times* and established a popular romantic reputation almost equal to that of Rupert Brooke's.

80. Sassoon's statement was printed as a leaflet by Francis Meynell at the Pelican Press and circulated, some of the copies being distributed from Henderson's bookshop in the Charing Cross Road, called the 'Bomb Shop' because it sold a great deal of peace propaganda. After a few weeks all remaining copies were seized by the police.

81. In *GTAT* Graves misplaces this incident, putting it in 1915.

82. *GTAT* (1957), p. 262.

83. For Graves's letter to Evan Morgan, and for a more detailed account of this episode, see *The Life of Bertrand Russell* by Ronald W. Clark, Jonathan Cape and Weidenfeld and Nicolson, 1975.

84. *GTAT* (1957), p. 233.

85. Graves believed that Bertrand Russell and Lees-Smith, the pacifist MP, had exploited Sassoon when he was in a state of nervous exhaustion; the letter Graves mentions here was to Bertrand Russell, and as far as both Graves and Russell were concerned, it marked the end of the episode:

Dear Bertrand Russell,

Sassoon has been forced to accept a medical board and is being sent to a place in the country as suffering from nerves: which is certainly the case as anyone can easily see. The evidence supplied by various friends for the medical board is most conclusive. His opinions are still unchanged but there is nothing further for you to do (with him for your cause). I blame you most strongly for your indiscretion in having allowed him to do what he has done, knowing in what state of health he was (after his damnable time at Arras). Now you can leave things until he's well enough again to think clearly about the War and how to end it.

86. On 17 July Churchill was appointed Minister of Munitions by Lloyd George.

87. *GTAT* (1957), p. 233.

88. Sassoon in fact contributed five poems to Lloyd's anthology, *Poems Written During the Great War*, George Allen and Unwin Ltd, 1918.

89. Mesopotamia.

90. Julian Dadd, a fellow-officer.

91. *The Loom of Youth*, Alec Waugh's (1898–1981) first novel, was one of the first books to deal with homosexuality in public schools. Waugh had been at Sherborne School, which regarded the book as a libel and obliterated his name from the school roll.

92. *GTAT* (1957), p. 239.

93. Frank Jones-Bateman, a friend and fellow-officer of Graves's.

94. 'Bow down in the house of Rimmon': to compromise one's convictions. Rimmon was a deity in ancient Damascus; see II *Kings* V:18.

95. A reference to the 'wild Eastern tour' they planned to make together after the war, written about in their verse letters to each other:

War's a joke for me and you
While we know such dreams are true!
    (Sassoon: 'A Letter Home')

96. This book never materialized.

97. Gilbert Frankau (1884–1952), popular novelist who also wrote poems and 'novels in verse'; best known for *Peter Jackson, Cigar Merchant* (1919).

98. Graves first met Owen (1893–1918) at Craiglockhart; see page 206.

99. Edward Shanks (1892–1953), poet, at that time assistant editor of the *London Mercury*.

100. William Nicholson's studio was at no. 11 Apple Tree Yard, St James's.

101. John Freeman (1880–1929), Georgian poet who worked as the secretary of a large insurance organization. *Collected Poems* (1928).

102. J. C. Squire (1884–1958), Georgian poet, short story writer, parodist, critic and journalist; acting editor of the *New Statesman* (1917–18), founder and editor of the influential monthly *London Mercury* (1919–34).

103. Lorraine [*sic*]. Sassoon's second name was Loraine.

104. Eric Kennington (1888–1960), portrait painter and sculptor. Kennington used Graves as a model for his statue of the Intellectual Soldier in Battersea Park; see page 302.

105. Christopher Nevinson (1889–1946).

106. Paul Nash (1889–1946).

107. Sir John Lavery (1856–1941).

108. Sir William Orpen (1878–1931).

109. Theodore Watts-Dunton (1832–1914), solicitor, critic, literary journalist and novelist (*Aylwin*, 1898); chiefly remembered as Swinburne's close friend and virtual guardian, ruling him with an iron hand and saving him from alcoholism. See Max Beerbohm's essay, 'No. 2a The Pines'.

110. *The Dark Fire*, 1918.

111. *Motley*, a collection of poems by Walter de la Mare (1873–1956) published in 1918.

112. Geoffrey Dearmer, poet and playwright. The couplet (from the poem 'Resurrection') reads:

Even the poppy on the parapet
Shall blossom as before when summer comes again.

113. 'The Leveller', *Country Sentiment* (1920).

114. *GTAT* (1957), p. 246.

115. Marsh, Ross, Roderick Meiklejohn, Robert Nichols, one of the Sitwells and Lady Ottoline Morrell ('Rottaline').

116. 'Comrade Why Do You Weep?' by Frank Prewett.

117. James Pryde (1866–1941), painter who also designed posters with his brother-in-law William Nicholson (using the pseudonyms 'J. and W. Beggarstaff') which had a profound influence on poster design.

118. Karl Liebknecht (1871–1919), son of Wilhelm Liebknecht; German Marxist revolutionary who played a leading role in the formation of the German Communist Party (KPD) and in instigating the German revolution in 1919, during which he was shot by counter-revolutionaries.

119. Aleksandr Kuprin (1870–1938), Russian story writer who did not accept the Revolution and went into exile in France, but later returned to Leningrad where he died.

120. Louis Untermeyer (1885–1980), American poet, but best known as an anthologist (principally *Modern American Poetry*, 1919 and later editions).

121. St David's Day, 1 March.

122. Graves had caught Spanish influenza in Ireland.

Part Two

1. *GTAT* (1957), pp. 254–5.

2. *GTAT* (1957), p. 255.

3. Pamela Bianco (born 1909), figure and fairy painter, whose work was shown for the first time in *The Owl*.

4. Published in *The Owl*, October 1919, reprinted (in revised form) in *The Waggoner*, Sidgwick and Jackson Ltd, 1920.

5. boyau: a branch of a trench.

6. 'The Voice of Beauty Drowned'.

7. 'Everyone Sang' by Siegfried Sassoon.

8. 'The Sprig of Lime' by Robert Nichols.

9. 'Witchcraft: New Style' by Lascelles Abercrombie.

10. Francis Brett Young (1884–1954), popular novelist.

11. *sic.* Lady Fredegond Shove (wife of G. F. Shove, a fellow of King's College Cambridge), who was well known as a poet in the twenties.

12. *The Feather Bed*, Hogarth Press, 1923.

13. *Poems Chiefly from Manuscript*, by John Clare, ed. Edmund Blunden and Alan Porter, published by Richard Cobden-Sanderson, 1920. There were two earlier selections of Clare's poems, one edited by Norman Gale (1901) the other by A. Symons (1908).

14. Alan Porter (1899–1942), prominent poet at Oxford whose collection *The Signature of Pain* (Cobden-Sanderson, 1930), was much read at the time. He was a friend of Blunden's and edited Clare's *Poems Chiefly from Manuscript* with him; he also edited *Oxford Poetry 1921* with Graves and Richard Hughes (1900–76); see page 127.

15. 'Almswomen', Blunden's much anthologized poem, was dedicated to 'Nancy and Robert'.

16. Vachel Lindsay (1879–1931), American poet who travelled a great deal as a poet-beggar, 'Preaching the Gospel of Beauty' and giving famous dramatic recitals of his own poems in public.

17. Sir Walter Raleigh (1861–1922), writer, critic; in 1904 he became the first Professor of English Literature in the University of Oxford.

18. *Travels in Arabia Deserta* by C. M. Doughty (2 vols., 1881); with new preface and introduction by T.E.L., 1921.

19. *The Penny Fiddle* was not published; in 1960, however, Graves collected together some of his poems for children in a book again called *The Penny Fiddle*, illustrated by Edward Ardizzone.

20. Lawrence recalled one of these chapters to print in the *Army Quarterly* (April 1921); Graves sold the other three in America to *The World's Work* for £200.

21. *King Cole* by John Masefield, Heinemann, 1921.

22. Margaret Russell, the children's nanny, rejoined Graves at the beginning of the Second World War to look after the children of his second marriage. See page 302.

23. *Dementia praecox* was an early name for schizophrenia; Clare is now known not to have suffered from a schizophrenic illness but to have been a manic-depressive.

24. *GTAT* (1929), p. 385.

25. Basil Blackwell, the publisher of *Oxford Poetry*.

26. 'The Dangers of Definition', also published as an appendix to *On English Poetry*.

27. *GTAT* (1929), p. 402.

28. For Sassoon's account of this quarrel see his *Diaries 1920–1922*, ed. Rupert Hart-Davis, Faber and Faber Ltd, 1981, p. 150.

29. Osbert and Sacheverall Sitwell. Sassoon had quarrelled with them because of their attacks on Graves in *Wheels*.

30. Edgell Rickword (born 1898), Left-wing poet and translator.

31. Herbert Palmer (1880–1961), poet and teacher. Both Graves and Robert Bridges urged Marsh to include Palmer in *GP*, but Marsh refused.

32. Peter Quennell (born 1905), novelist, poet and critic.

33. *The Georgian Revolt* by Robert H. Ross, University of Southern Illinois Press, 1967, p. 223.

34. *Old Homes*, by E.B., a poem privately published as a pamphlet, Clare, 1922 (republished in *English Poems*, 1926).

35. *The Shepherd and Other Poems of Peace and War* by E.B., Cobden-Sanderson, 1922, dedicated to Siegfried Sassoon; awarded the Hawthornden Prize, 1922.

36. *GTAT* (1957), p. 283.

37. John Crowe Ransom (1888–1974), Southern American poet, critic and teacher.

38. Nichols had married Norah Denny, daughter of Frederick Denny; see page 319. It seems that Graves had already revised his high opinion of Nichols and his poetry by this time.

39. i.e. a playpen.

40. Max Beerbohm.

41. Basanta Mallik, a Bengali educationist; see page 148. That Mallik's piece would have 'a shattering effect' was a characteristically optimistic prophecy by Graves: he brought the same optimism to all his enthusiasms.

42. Benedetto Croce (1866–1952), Italian literary critic and anti-Fascist 'idealist' philosopher.

43. *Comedia von der Schönen Sidea*, by Jakob Ayrer (1543–1605). The Spanish 'original' is *L'espejo de Principes y Cavalleros* by Diego Ortúñez de Calahorra (translated and printed in England in 1580).

44. The *Sea Venture* was the ship in which Sir George Somers (1554–1610) was shipwrecked in 1606 on one of the Bermuda islands.

45. *Eastward Hoe*, a comedy by George Chapman, Ben Jonson and John Marston.

46. *Bartholomew Fair*, a comedy by Ben Jonson, produced in 1614.

47. The final version of this theory, which Graves revised several times, is printed in *The Common Asphodel*, 1949.

48. A quotation from Graves's poem 'A Lover Since Childhood'.

49. *GTAT* (1929), p. 403.

50. *T. E. Lawrence to his Biographers* (1938), vol. 1, p. 24.

51. *Lord Clancarty*, never performed.

52. *Mock Beggar Hall.*

53. Henry Head, neurologist, colleague of Rivers, treated Robert Nichols for his mental breakdown.

54. Romer Wilson (1891–1930), novelist and playwright, who also wrote a biography of Emily Brontë, *All Alone* (1928).

55. In his next letter Graves disclosed the names: Turner and Sassoon.

56. Peter Quennell.

57. Graves won the Bronze Medal; see page 302.

58. *Marmion, A Tale of Flodden Field* (1808), a poem in six cantos by Sir Walter Scott (1771–1832).

59. *Contemporary Techniques of Poetry,* Hogarth Press (1925).

60. *Edward Marsh, A Biography*, by C. Hassall, p. 528.

61. *John Kemp's Wager*, a 'ballad opera' for performance by village societies (performed once only, in California). This play marks the end of the folksong period of Graves's work.

62. *GTAT* (1957), p. 285.

63. Robert Bridges.

64. Colonel John Buchan (1875–1940), the novelist and statesman.

65. Asquith, by then Earl of Oxford.

66. 'These Be Your Gods O Israel!', *The Crowning Privilege*, p. 125.

67. *The Crowning Privilege*, p. 128.

68. *The Long Week-End*, Faber and Faber Ltd, 1940, p. 115.

69. The biographical facts in this letter are inaccurate: Laura Riding was born in New York (not in the slums) and her father was Austrian, not Polish. This letter is interesting, though, because it contains all the information Graves had about Riding when he invited her to England.

70. *The Long Week-End*, p. 189.

71. 'H.D.': Initials used as pen name by Hilda Doolittle (1886–1961), American Imagist poet, novelist, memoirist and translator.

72. Eric Pinker, Graves's literary agent at that time.

73. Graves was in fact succeeded by Bonamy Dobrée.

74. Sam, Graves's fourth child.

75. Enoch Arden, the hero of Tennyson's narrative poem of that name, who returns (after being shipwrecked on a tropical island) to find his wife married to his former rival; unwilling to destroy her happiness he does not reveal his identity until his death. Sassoon had a self-confessed 'Enoch Arden complex', referring mainly to Arden's neurotic isolation and weariness of life and the morbid comfort gained from the fact that his true feelings and true 'identity' would only be known after his death. Sassoon was obsessed with his will and rewrote it several times; Graves was to have

been one of the main benefactors, but he was cut out of the will after his argument with Sassoon in 1933.

76. Phineas Fletcher (1582–1650), poet of the Spenserian school. Sassoon's gift was probably Fletcher's *Venus and Anchises, Britain's Ida and Other Poems*, edited (from ms.) by E. Seaton, Royal Society of Literature, 1926.

77. Sassoon's epigram 'Because the Duke [of York] is Duke of York', was published in the *Nation and Athenaeum*, 17 January 1925. Graves quoted it in *A Pamphlet Against Anthologies* and again in *The Crowning Privilege* (misquoting the first line).

78. Isobel.

79. Victoria Sackville-West (1892–1962), novelist, poet and travel writer, whose long pastoral poem *The Land* Heinemann had just published.

80. *Revolt in the Desert*, Lawrence's own abridgement of the *Seven Pillars of Wisdom* (not generally circulated until 1935) which was serialized in the *Daily Telegraph* in December 1926 and later published by Cape in Britain and by Doran in the USA.

81. *GTAT* (1929), p. 358.

82. *Let the Poet Choose* (1973), edited by James Gibson, p. 37.

83. Bronislaw Malinowski (1884–1942), anthropologist and author of several pioneer studies of primitive communities, one of which, *Crime and Custom in Savage Society*, Graves reviewed in the *Criterion*.

84. *Poems 1914–1926*, published June 1927.

85. Doubleday, Doran, American publishers (later just Doubleday).

86. Lawrence in fact arranged for Graves to write the book, without R.G. knowing it; all was arranged 'as the result of a conspiracy of my friends, to keep the job out of bad hands', Lawrence wrote to Dick Knowles, his Cloud's Hill neighbour, 30 June 1927 (see John E. Mack, *A Prince of Our Disorder*, Weidenfeld and Nicolson, 1976), page 367.

87. *Poems 1914–1927*, published June 1927.

88. Vyvyan Richards, a friend of Graves (through Lawrence). Owned a private press, published fine editions (including William Caxton, *Prologues and Epilogues*) and in 1928 taught Graves and Riding how to print.

89. Humbert Wolfe (1885–1940), senior civil servant, essayist, anthologist and for a time a very popular poet, also an editor for Benn, the publisher. The two 'sixpenny editions' are *John Skelton (Laureate)* and *The Less Familiar Nursery Rhymes*.

90. F. S. Flint (1885–1960), senior civil servant, prominent Imagist poet and translator.

91. In June 1927, George Bernard Shaw wrote the following postcard in answer to Graves's request for information on T.E.L.:

A great mistake. You might as well try to write a funny book about Mark Twain. T.E. has got all out of himself that is to be got. His name will rouse expectations which you will necessarily disappoint. Cape will curse his folly for proposing such a thing, and never give you another commission. Write a book (if you must) about the dullest person you know; clerical if possible. Give yourself a chance.

It later turned out that Shaw had mistaken R.G. for his brother Charles Graves, the gossip columnist (see *GTAT*, 1929).

92. E. M. Forster (1879–1970), major novelist. A close friend of Lawrence's.

Part Three

1. Riding, it seems, never wrote the book about suicide, though she did draw on her own experience of attempted suicide in *14A*, a novel she wrote in 1934 with George Ellidge. See page 234.

2. Geoffrey Phibbs.

3. Max Gate was the name of Thomas Hardy's house in Dorchester. Graves's article appeared in the *Sphere*, 28 January 1928.

4. The *Daily Mail* was the only newspaper read regularly by Graves and Riding during these years; they decided that as all newspapers were awful they might just as well read what they considered to be the worst. Graves's elder brother Charles, whom he disliked greatly, had a society gossip column on the centre page of the *Daily Mail* at this time.

5. *Memoirs of a Fox-Hunting Man* was awarded the Hawthornden Prize for 1928 and the James Tait Black Memorial Prize.

6. In his diary on 2 June 1922, Sassoon wrote that there had been up to then 'some vague sexual element lurking' in his relationship with Graves, and that in the friendship there was always a 'restless, passionate, nerve-racked quality' (*Diaries 1920–1922*, ed. Rupert Hart-Davies, Faber and Faber Ltd, 1981).

7. Richard Cobden-Sanderson, Blunden's publisher.

8. Possibly Eric Kennington, who was a close friend of Lye's and who helped Lye a lot when he first went to England, particularly in giving him part of his own studio to work in; or Eric Pinker, Graves's literary agent.

9. Joan Gelat: see page 214.

10. *Though Gently.*

11. Mrs Jessie Broadwood, a long-time British resident in Deyá.

12. Maurice Browne (1881–1955), theatre actor, producer and playwright, who had encouraged Graves to write the play; Browne at this time managed the Savoy Theatre in London, where he had put on the first production of R. C. Sherriff's *Journey's End* in January 1929.

13. Gelat's electricity was unreliable, gave too dim a light to read by and was switched off every evening at about 11 o'clock. In 1935 Graves invested money in a modern water turbine system which supplied the village with a slightly improved service.

14. Graves's eldest son.

15. From an undated, unpublished letter to T. E. Lawrence; the letter is in a private collection.

16. *The Vulgate*, later called *Epilogue*, was an anthology of criticism, poetry and essays edited by Riding and Graves; the first number did not appear until the autumn of 1935, and only three numbers were published. (*Epilogue IV* was Laura Riding's *The World and Ourselves*.)

17. *Poems 1930–1933*.

18. 7½ is a Spanish card game which was then played a lot at Canelluñ; in Mallorquín it is called *set i mitg*, which accounts for its Canelluñ nickname 'City midge'.

19. *Old Soldiers Never Die*; see page 261.

20. This refers, unfairly, to Norman Cameron.

21. The handwriting in this letter is uncharacteristically neat, with no crossings-out or insertions, which suggests it is a fair copy made after one or more drafts; when he received a letter which made him angry, it was Graves's practice to write a reply immediately, but not to post it – then the next day he would rewrite it in a cooler frame of mind.

22. Otto Kahn (1867–1934), a German banker who became a naturalized British citizen *c.* 1891, but who lived most of his life in America, where he financed Hart Crane while he wrote *The Bridge*.

23. John Aldridge and Lucie Brown.

24. Mary Ellidge.

25. Arnold Mason (1885–1963), portrait and landscape painter.

26. The book was published in America by Harrison Smith and Robert Haas, June 1934.

27. Graves's and several other peoples 'Likes' were published in the December 1935 issue of *Focus* (see note 31 below); Graves's likes were John Kelsey, the puritan preacher in the time of Charles II, Mary Tofts of Godalming who gave birth to rabbits, and Pietro Torrigiano, the Italian sculptor who broke Michelangelo's nose in a fight.

28. *The Golden Falcon*, a novel by Henry Williamson and published anonymously by Faber and Faber Ltd, which, Graves claimed with some justification, was so publicized as to suggest it was written by him. See page 262.

29. *Edward Marsh: A Biography*, by C. Hassall, p. 588.

30. Called La Posada.

31. *Focus* was a house magazine edited at Canelluñ, printed in Palma, containing news letters from friends and a record of events at Canelluñ. Contributors included Graves, Riding, Karl Gay, James Reeves, John Aldridge, Norman Cameron, Honor Wyatt and T. S. Matthews.

32. *Epilogue.*

33. *T. E. Lawrence to His Biographers*, vol. 1, p. 179.

34. The Hon. E. Eliot, Lawrence's solicitor and one of the trustees of his will.

35. David Garnett (1892–1980), novelist, had lived on and off with Phibbs's wife in the late 1920s; Graves alludes to his argument with Garnett in the Epilogue to *GTAT* (1929).

36. Jonathan Cape.

37. Early in November Alexander Korda cabled Graves, asking him to help on the scenario of the Lawrence film, and said that if R.G. couldn't go to London, then his brother, Zoltan Korda, would go to Mallorca to discuss the film. Graves replied, also by cable, that a trip to London was impossible, Z.K.'s visit inconvenient, and that he wouldn't accept the job unless Sassoon resigned and Liddell Hart was reinstated.

38. Raymond Savage, literary agent, who had at one time acted for both Graves and Liddell Hart, and who was also the literary agent for the Lawrence estate.

39. Liam O'Flaherty (born 1897), Irish novelist, born on the Aran Islands; militant Republican and Socialist, whose novels are about violence, poverty and the Irish Civil War (*The Informer*, 1925); his autobiography, *Shame the Devil*, was published in 1934, since when he has lived in America and written little.

40. *T. E. Lawrence to His Biographers*, vol. 2, p. 213n.

41. 'The Troll's Nosegay'.

42. The *Poets* and *Schools* booklets were never published.

43. Tom Matthews's novel, *The Moon's No Fool*, published by Constable and Seizin Press.

44. Honor Wyatt, writer and broadcaster, still a close friend of Graves's. Her 'Julian-baby' is Julian Glover, the actor.

45. Solomon was Graves's bulldog.

46. Juan March, the famous Mallorquín millionaire and latter-day pirate.

47. Catherine Nicholson, Graves's third child, who later married Clifford Dalton, the nuclear scientist (see page 296). Author of *Without Hardware*, Australia, 1981.

48. James Reeves and Mary Phillips, who were later married.

49. 'Scoundrels'.

50. Alice and Nicholas: the cats.

51. This letter is typed.

52. A. S. Watt (1870–1948), of A. P. Watt Ltd; A. P. Watt's son and Graves's literary agent.

53. For tax purposes.

54. *The Dictionary of Exact Meanings*; see page 297.

55. Josef von Sternberg (1894–1969), Austrian film director, who lived and worked mostly in America. The *Claudius* film broke down because of impossible tension between von Sternberg and Charles Laughton, who was having great difficulties with the part of Claudius, and, finally, because of Merle Oberon's car accident. The film was never finished, though a BBC television dramatization was made in 1976, with Derek Jacobi playing Claudius.

56. The refugee film was never produced.

57. *The Long Week-End*, p. 422.

58. Government troops had attacked the city of Teruel on 15 December 1937, pre-empting a move by Nationalist forces who, with the completion of the conquest of Northern Spain, were now moving towards Madrid and the south. On 8 January the garrison commander at Teruel surrendered to the government troops who occupied the city but who were soon besieged themselves by Franco's troops and by 20 February driven out of the city by the Nationalists. The government offensive was thus a great (and costly) failure.

59. Mallorquín for 'regards'.

60. Joan Junyer, Mallorquín painter.

61. Little, Brown, the American publishing house which contracted with Graves and Riding to publish the *Dictionary*.

62. David Reeves, brother of James Reeves, designer and maker of wood furniture; he accompanied Graves and Riding to America in 1939.

63. Ronald Bottrall (born 1906), English poet and friend of Graves; has worked for the British Council for most of his life. *Collected Poems* (1961).

Part Four

1. Ward Hutchinson, photographer, contributor to *Epilogue* and the Protocol secretary; and his wife.

2. Finally published by Peter Owen Ltd in 1980 as *An Ancient Castle*, illustrated by Elizabeth Graves.

3. Nothing further was done, however. The *Second Protocol*, drawn up with Riding's help in America, was never published, nor was any other statement.

4. Sally (Elizabeth) Chilver, Graves's niece (daughter of his brother Philip), married Richard Chilver, civil servant; Principal of Bedford College and then of Lady Margaret Hall, Oxford, until 1980 when she retired.

5. I. A. Richards (1893–1980) the Cambridge critic who, with C. K. Ogden, originated Basic English, an unsuccessful scheme for a simplification of the language for (especially non-English) learners by using a standard limited vocabulary.

6. *In Parenthesis* (1937) by David Jones (1895–1974).

7. Misquoted.

... Perceive him madder than before,
With nothing but nasty vacancy
In the dark, gangrened spot upon his brain
That she had occupied – repudication,
But nothing more: an itching, empty sore
That better had been left uncurable.

8. *The Common Asphodel*, p. 307.

9. Graves's comment on Lewis's letters in the introduction to *Ha! Ha! Among the Trumpets*.

10. Stephen Spender (born 1909), poet, critic, translator, coeditor (*Horizon*, *Encounter*) and academic.

11. In France, July 1916, on the way to the battle of the Somme!

12. This letter was published in the *Anglo-Welsh Review*, vol. 16, no. 37, Spring 1937, with two other letters from Lewis to Graves (2 May 1942 and 6 May 1943) not included here.

13. Henry Treece (1911–66), English poet, historical novelist and children's story-writer. During the war he served as an Intelligence officer in Bomber Command.

14. Keidrych Rhys (born 1915) Welsh poet, founder and coeditor, with Dylan Thomas, of the magazine *Wales*; editor of *Poems from the Forces* (1942) and *Modern Welsh Poetry* (1945).

15. Ian Hay (ps. for Major General John Hay Beith, 1876–1952), novelist, playwright, author of *The First Hundred Thousand* (1915).

16. Hardinge Pritchard, Beryl Graves's twin brother.

17. Norman Cameron.

18. Saint 'So and so'.

19. Graves's article 'Dog, Lapwing and Roebuck' was published in *Wales*, Summer 1941.

20. Joshua Podro, who owned the International Press Cutting Agency, then at Paignton. After the war Graves and Podro collaborated on *The Nazarene Gospel Restored* (1953).

21. Agatha Christie (1891–1976), detective novel writer, who was a friend and neighbour of Graves's in Devon.

22. Dorothy L. Sayers (1893–1957), detective novel writer.

23. Pempie (Penelope), at that time wife of Carol Reed (1906–76), film director; her mother is Lady Freda Dudley Ward, née Birkin. Judy Campbell, the actress and singer (mother of the actress Jane Birkin), shared a flat with Graves's daughter Jenny in London.

24. Lord Beaverbrook (1879–1964), writer, controversial public figure, millionaire newspaper proprietor (*Daily Express* and associated publications); he held various government appointments during the Second World War.

25. This letter is typed.

26. Karl Gay had been interned in July 1940 as an enemy alien, and obtained his release by joining the Pioneer Corps, for which he had to change his name (from Karl Goldschmidt) but keeping the same initials: he chose Kenneth Gay as a name and after the war called himself Karl Gay (none of his friends called him Kenneth).

27. Geoffrey Faber, Director of Faber and Faber Ltd.

28. Angharad, Lynette Roberts's daughter, Graves's godchild.

29. D. W. Nash's translation of *The Book of Taliesin* was the only translation then available.

30. Lucia, Graves's sixth child (Beryl's second); later married Ramón Farran, the Catalan jazz musician. She has translated several of Graves's books into Spanish.

31. Review of *The Golden Fleece*, published in America in September 1945.

32. The Rt Hon. Lester B. Pearson (1897–1972) became Canadian Ambassador in Washington at this time; Prime Minister of Canada, 1963. He had been one of the cadets instructed by Graves at Oxford in 1917.

33. Graves's seventh child, Juan, to whom he wrote his poem 'To Juan at the Winter Solstice'.

34. Hubert von Ranke, son of Graves's uncle mentioned in *GTAT* who, though in his sixties, served during the First World War as a lieutenant in the Bavarian Artillery and shot down the pinnacle of Rheims Cathedral (thus minimizing the damage done to the tower, which was being used by the French Army as an observation post).

35. Stein's poodle.

36. Harriet Monro (1860–1936) American poet, founder and editor of *Poetry: A Magazine of Verse*, which contained contributions from many of the young poets of the day.

Appendix A

1. George Sassoon, Sassoon's son, who by coincidence was later a contemporary of Graves's son William at Oundle School.

Appendix B

1. T. E. Shaw, the name T. E. Lawrence assumed when he joined the Air Force.

INDEX

Index

53–4, 56, 57, 58–60, 61, 62, 73–4,
75–9, 82, 90, 99, (n. 115), 99–100,
102, 105, 107–8, 114–20, 124–6,
129–32, 135–8, 140, 141–2, 146–7,
149–51, 155–7, 179, 187–90,
193–6, 239–41, 243–6, 277–8
Masefield, John, 36, 39, 49, 62, 68,
74, 75, 82, 88, 89, 98, 101, 103,
105, 107, 112, 114–15, 116, 123,
136–7, 277
Mason, Arnold, 232
Matthews, Julie, 218–19, 223–5,
233–4, 236–8, 242–3, 268–72,
275–6, 282
Matthews, T. S., 218–19, 224–5,
233–8, 242–3, 268–70, 272,
275–6, 281–2
Middleton, Richard, 34, 49
Monro, Harold, 37, 41, 46, 76, 77,
154, 156
Moore, Marianne, 166, 176
Morgan, Evan, 63, 73, 79
Morrell, Lady Ottoline, 66, 69, 99
(n. 115), 105, 133–4
Murry, Middleton, 118, 121, 126,
145

Nash, Paul, 93
Nevinson, Christopher, 93
Nichols, Robert, 61–6, 68–9, 72–6,
83, 87, 88–93, 99 (n. 115), 99, 100,
102, 104–5, 107, 112, 114, 117,
136–7, 144, 156–7, 170–71, 239,
241, 318–19
Nicholson, Ben, 86, 102, 192
Nicholson, Mabel, 86, 97, 118
Nicholson, Nancy, 12, 86, 88, 89,
90–108 *passim*, 111, 117, 119–75
passim, 179, 187–91, 203, 205–6,
228, 246, 285, 315, 337–8
Nicholson, Sir William, 86, 90, 102–4,
111–12, 118, 149, 154, 166
Novello, Ivor, 60, 93, 100

O'Flaherty, Liam, 262
Orpen, Sir William, 93, 262
Owen, Wilfred, 12, 39, 80, 86,

89–90, 94, 102, 170–71, 206–7,
317

Palmer, Herbert, 136
Phibbs, Geoffrey, 187–91, 193 (n. 2),
234, 246
Pinker, Eric, 164, 166, 247
Podro, Joshua, 324, 326, 332
Porter, Alan, 118, 127
Pound, Ezra, 341–2
Prewett, Frank, 80–81, 102 (n. 116),
105, 133, 135, 148, 167
Pryde, James, 103

Quennell, Peter, 136, 138, 141, 150,
179

Raleigh, Sir Walter, 120, 141, 143
Ranke, Hubert von, 335, 337, 338–40
Ransom, John Crowe, 12, 142–3, 162,
166, 176
Reeves, David, 281, 282
Reeves, James, 209, 245, 271, 298
Rhys, Keidrych, 307, 316, 318, 325,
331–2, 344
Richards, Frank, 12, 220, 261, 266–7
Richards, I. A., 296, 309–10
Richards, Vyvyan, 176, 297
Rickword, Edgell, 135
Riding, Laura, 11, 12, 162–79, 181–2,
187–203 *passim*, 214–19, 224–5,
229–30, 232, 234–7, 241–5, 264,
268–82, 285–7, 289–92, 294, 299,
309, 336, 337, 339–41
Rivers, Dr W. H. R., 78, 80, 82, 83,
84, 105, 111, 122–3, 126, 130, 135,
143, 147, 148, 150, 174, 206
Roberts, Eirlys, 233–4, 237
Roberts, Lynette, 316–20, 322–3, 325,
327, 330–32, 333–4, 343–4
Rooper, Ralph, 29, 49, 58, 60
Rosenberg, Isaac, 39, 75, 123, 166
Ross, Robert, 12, 66, 67, 69, 72, 76,
78, 82, 88, 91, 97, 99 (n. 115),
102–3, 105, 107, 207
Russell, Bertrand, 76, 79 (n. 85)
Russell, George ('A.E.'), 49